THE NEW NATURALIST LIBRARY

TERNS

DAVID CABOT

and

IAN NISBET

Collins

This edition published in 2013 by Collins,
an imprint of HarperCollins Publishers

HarperCollins Publishers
77–85 Fulham Palace Road
London W6 8JB
www.collins.co.uk

First published 2013

A CIP catalogue record for this book is available
from the British Library.

Set in FF Nexus

Edited and designed by
D & N Publishing
Baydon, Wiltshire

Printed in Hong Kong by Printing Express

Hardback
ISBN 978-0-00-741247-1

Paperback
ISBN 978-0-00-741248-8

Contents

Editors' Preface

I T WOULD BE A SADLY SOMBRE NATURALIST on a summer seaside visit who failed to find the terns flying and feeding close inshore both strikingly beautiful and to a degree spiritually uplifting. Few would challenge the view that amongst seabirds in general they are the most elegant and easiest on the eye. Usefully, terns have a characteristic shape and, with subtle differences between species, flight patterns that ease identification for novices.

As a family, the terns have a truly global distribution, mostly associated with tropical or subtropical waters either during the breeding season or as their winter quarters after migration. David Cabot and Ian Nisbet deal with the 'true terns' with 39 species worldwide, outlining in comparative terms their general lifestyle before focusing in detail on the five species that come each summer to breed beside British and Irish coastal seas and estuaries and, occasionally, on inland fresh waters, comparing their varied habits, habitats and migration.

Migration is an essential part of the tern way of life, much of which is spent on the wing, and some species make prodigious journeys. The Arctic tern is sometimes cited as the bird that sees more daylight than any other, breeding as it often does well to the north of the Arctic Circle. Here it enjoys a north polar summer of near-perpetual daylight, before migrating south across the Equator to the again near-perpetual daylight of the south polar summer in the Antarctic Ocean. Conservatively, an individual Arctic tern may cover in excess of 40,000 km each year, and with a life span that may exceed three decades, the potential lifetime distance travelled reaches staggering proportions. And these birds weigh little more than a garden blackbird!

Such enormous travels are inevitably accompanied by a range of natural hazards, and it is sobering to read of the threats terns face throughout their lives, at sea or on land. David Cabot in his Foreword notes that most British and Irish terns 'today are on life-support systems' under intensive management schemes and protection from an array of natural and man-made problems. A chapter is devoted to these problems in detail, the measures being taken to counteract them and the additional research and measures that in the authors' view are needed to avoid the possibility of 'several species ending up on the endangered list'.

David Cabot and Ian Nisbet are both world-respected experts on terns, and bring between them a total of more than 75 years of study and experience on both sides of the Atlantic. Their coming together in 1991 was the result of serendipity: the arrival at a colony of roseate terns on the eastern seaboard of the USA (studied by Ian Nisbet) of a roseate tern ringed as a nestling two years earlier at a similar study colony (of David Cabot's) near Dublin in Ireland. Their collective detailed knowledge and intimate familiarity with the terns radiate warmly from the text. Together, in New Naturalist 123 *Terns*, they have produced a thoroughly researched, detailed yet highly readable account of the biology and ecology of a group of well-known and well-loved seabirds, a worthy addition to any New Naturalist bookshelf.

Authors' Foreword and Acknowledgements

AMONG MY EARLY MEMORIES is the rasping '*kirrick*' of Sandwich terns as they cruised along south Devon beaches where we played and swam, but my first serious encounters with terns came some years later, lying on my belly behind the breakwater at the tip of Dawlish Warren. There I watched hordes of migrating waders, pushed up towards the sea wall by the tide, and amongst them Sandwich, common, roseate and the occasional little tern, dribbling through on autumn migration. I wrestled with the complexities of identification, and the terns intrigued me – where had they come from, where were they going? I knew a little about their legendary migrations, less about their breeding biology, and least of all about their behaviour or the many factors that ruled their lives. Little did I know then that I would later devote many years to studying the roseate tern, one of the most beautiful and intriguing of all our breeding birds.

The romance of studying terns is that apart from their inherent aesthetic attraction and biological interest, most of our terns nest in remote, wild and generally unspoilt areas, places that naturalists relish visiting. Arctic, roseate and Sandwich terns, in particular, have taken me to some stunningly beautiful places. The common tern by contrast is much less fussy about where it locates itself, and is often found nesting in noisy docklands, on roof tops, or in regimented nesting boxes on specially constructed floating platforms in flooded gravel pits or other inland waters.

I moved to Ireland in 1959, to a country with remarkably few experienced ornithologists, where even basic survey work in the more remote areas had the potential to make a major contribution. Initially I focused on establishing the locations of roseate tern colonies, and on censusing and monitoring. At that time relatively few roseate terns had been ringed, and I concentrated on ringing all available chicks. At one stage I had ringed approximately one-third of all chicks ringed in Britain and Ireland. These efforts were both fortuitous and rewarding because they coincided with the dramatic 'crash' of the roseate tern population breeding in northwestern Europe during the late 1960s and early 1970s. The unusually high recovery rate of many of these ringed birds from West Africa during the population crash helped towards a better understanding of mortality pressures exerted on the terns wintering there.

In 1965 I attended the NATO conference on pesticides at Monks Wood. I already had an interest in pesticide residues and their possible impact on seabirds, and the conference stimulated me to investigate pesticide residue levels in the eggs and food of terns, especially roseates. Norman Moore arranged analyses of eggs and fish at the laboratory of the British government chemist while Jan Koeman in the Netherlands also carried out analyses. Later Colin Walker provided additional analytical services. This was all at a time when research on pesticide residues in birds was in its early stages. It was fortunate therefore that we were able to establish baseline organochlorine levels in our terns and their food.

Later work involved measuring the productivity of roseates, using methods derived from Ian's work in the USA, at Lady's Island Lake and later at Tern Island, Wexford Harbour. Observations of food brought to chicks were made, together with notes on general tern behaviour. I also thought that it would be worth visiting the roseate tern colonies in Brittany, as the population there had also crashed but there was a paucity of data available. So Karl Partridge and I surveyed all possible roseate breeding sites in 1976 with the assistance of Yves Brien and J.-Y. Monat, supported by small grants from the French CNRS and the Irish National Science Council. The following year I made a limited follow-up survey.

The principal lesson I have learned during the two and a half years it has taken to write this New Naturalist volume with Ian is depressing. Most terns breeding in Britain and Ireland today are on life-support systems – virtually all breeding colonies are now under extensive management schemes involving protection from mammalian and avian predators, human interference, egg-collecting, recreational activities, land-use changes, and a bewildering range of issues concerning climate change, including rising sea levels and flooding of low-lying colonies. If the anti-predator and other protective measures were abandoned then the numbers of terns in Britain and Ireland would inevitably decline, with the possibility of several species ending up on the endangered list. The other big issue that emerged for me is that people involved with tern conservation have focused too much attention on the productivity of terns rather than trying to better understand all aspects of adult mortality and how to reduce it. If we were able to reduce adult mortality our tern populations would be in a much stronger position.

During my work on terns, spanning many decades, I have been extremely fortunate to receive enthusiastic support from many voluntary helpers who were most generous with their time and expertise, especially during extensive and often onerous ringing operations. Finding roseate chicks in dense vegetation in the Co. Wexford colonies, and later on Rockabill, was a challenge made easier by teams of helpers that included my late wife Penny and our three boys, and others too numerous to mention – if they were all listed it would resemble the roll call of actors and extras in *Ben Hur*. Suffice to say, I salute them all.

One of the great pleasures in writing this book with Ian has been the privilege of working with someone who has such great knowledge of tern ecology, based on more than 40 years of active research and an impressive list of publications. He was one of my early icons, unknowingly guiding me, through his writings, on how best to measure tern productivity. I was also influenced in my early tern studies by the work of Mike Cullen, Nigel Langham and Euan Dunn. Then, many years later, a remarkably serendipitous event brought Ian and myself together – the beginning of a friendship that flourished to produce this book.

David Cabot

My collaboration with David started in 1991, when I found a roseate tern with a BTO ring at the edge of a breeding colony in the USA. I used a telescope to read the ring number, and it transpired that the bird had been ringed by David as a chick at Rockabill, Co. Dublin, two years earlier. This was one of the first transatlantic ringing recoveries of any tern, and the first to suggest that a tern raised on one side of the Atlantic might breed on the other. At that time David had been studying roseate terns for 30 years, whereas I was a relative novice in my 22nd year. It has been a pleasure to work on this book with David, whose knowledge of British and Irish terns complements mine in many ways.

All my early birdwatching experience was in Britain and Ireland, and I visited several important sites for breeding terns during the 1940s and 1950s. However, most of my early knowledge of terns was derived from distant views of resting flocks, or birds migrating past headlands. I did not pay close attention to terns until 1970, soon after I moved to the USA and started a new career in environmental science. I then started a field study of terns and – although I never planned more than a year or two ahead – I continued it for more than 40 years. The study was initially focused on toxic chemicals, but gradually evolved through an interest in population dynamics and factors limiting breeding success, to studies of many aspects of ecology, demography and physiology. I started large-scale ringing of common and roseate terns in 1975 and I gradually built up large populations of known-aged birds as the birds I had ringed as chicks returned to breed and remained year after year. I forged partnerships with many academic biologists and their students who were eager to work with birds of known age, and I learned a lot of cutting-edge biology as I went along.

In later years I took part in several studies of the physiology of ageing. Gerontologists are very interested in seabirds because they live much longer than other animals of the same size, and I had many terns more than 20 years old for them to study. It was a humbling experience to hold a 29-year-old common tern in my hand and to realise that it had flown to South America and back 28 times and was breeding for probably the 27th time – and then to study its physiology and find that it was functioning nearly as well as a seven-year-old. This was when I myself had just turned 70 and was looking and feeling my age.

Through all these years I maintained my interest in tern populations in Britain and Ireland, and I kept in touch with people who were studying and conserving them. Much of my early knowledge of terns was derived from studies in Britain by Mike Cullen, Nigel Langham, Euan Dunn and Alistair Smith, among others. When in 1978 some of my common and Arctic terns suddenly started collapsing and dying before my eyes, I knew at once that this was caused by paralytic shellfish poisoning, because I had read accounts by John Coulson, Euan Dunn and Ian Armstrong of the same phenomenon in British terns. I closely followed the crash in roseate tern populations in Europe in the 1970s, which was eerily parallel to a simultaneous crash in roseate tern populations in North America. I exchanged information on roseate terns with Adrian del Nevo, Norman Ratcliffe and other biologists at the RSPB, and took part in many of the international workshops on roseate terns that were convened by the RSPB in various countries.

Although most of my experience of terns has been in North America, three of the British and Irish species – common, Arctic and roseate – are the same in both continents, and the least tern of North America is so similar to the little tern of Europe as to be effectively identical in behaviour and ecology. The only British and Irish species that I have not studied in the field is the Sandwich tern.

Except for a small book on common terns by Rob Hume, there has been no book on the natural history of British and Irish terns since George and Anne Marples published *Sea Terns or Sea Swallows* in 1934. In the 79 years since then, a vast amount of information has been gathered on the behaviour, ecology, distribution, numbers, trends and conservation of our five species of terns. We have done our best to summarise all this information, and to do justice to all the work that has been done to understand and conserve these beautiful birds. We hope that our book will be a worthy successor to that of the Marples.

Ian Nisbet

ACKNOWLEDGEMENTS

We thank the following for supplying information and ideas, for answering questions, for offering photographs that we eventually did not use, and in some cases for reading draft sections of the book and giving us comments and corrections (however, we are solely responsible for any errors or misstatements): Fred Atwood, Fiona Barclay, Mark Bolton, Vivienne Booth, Bill Bourne, Eli Bridge, Bernard Cadiou, John Coulson, Clive Craik, Dave Daly, Steve Dudley, Euan Dunn, Adrian del Nevo, Kieran Fahy, Clare Ferry, John Fox, Jeremy Hatch, Dan Hayward, Scott Hecker, Martin Heubeck, Jim Hurley, Ellen Jedrey, Ian Lawler, Joint Nature Conservation Committee (Roddy Mavor), Eleanor Mayes, Andrew Mercer, Oscar Merne, Kathy Molina, Pat Monaghan, David Monticelli, Paul Morrison, Carolyn Mostello, Killian Mullarney, Tony Murray, Blair Nikula, David Norman, Steve Oswald, James Robinson, Lucy Quinn, Karl Partridge, Martin Perrow, Wayne Petersen, Simon Perkins, Jaime Ramos, David Shealer, Jennifer & Michael Smart, Jeffrey Spendelow, Eric Stienen, Michael Szebor, Hannah Tidswell, Lauren Uttridge, Alyn Walsh and Jan van de Winden. Many of these individuals are (or have been) members of the professional staff of the Royal Society for the Protection of Birds, and both they and the Society have been unfailingly helpful in supplying information.

We thank the many people who have supplied us with photographs, and in particular those who made extra efforts to find the perfect shots to satisfy what must have seemed to them rather demanding authors. We have relied most heavily on the work of Dave Daly, Jim Fenton, John Fox, Jóhann Óli Hilmarsson and John N. Murphy.

Other photographers whose work we have used are Peter Becker, Eli Bridge, Bill Byrne, Shawn Carey, Mark Collier, Charles T. Collins, Dick Coombes, Cresswell Heritage Trust, Carsten Egevang, John Fuller, Paul Gale, Chris Gomersall, Jeremy Hatch, Scott Hecker, Dick Hoogenboom, Stanley Howe, Jørgen Kabel, Paul Kelly, Alan Ladd Gallery, W. Thomas Manders, Mitchell McConnell, Oscar Merne, Tony Mills, Paul G. Morrison, Carolyn Mostello, Killian Mullarney, Tom Murray, Tony Murray, Blair Nikula, Jack O'Connor, Michael O'Keeffe, Mike Page, Andrew Porter and Peter Cutler, RSPB, Liam Ryan, Jon Saperia, Sandy Selesky, Tom Shevlin, Eduardo del Solar, Glen Tepke, Robert Thompson, Peter Trull, Jan van de Kam, John Van de Graaff, Alyn Walsh, Karen Wilson, Shane Wolsey and Steve Young. All the photographers are individually acknowledged in the figure captions.

We are extremely grateful to Robert Gillmor, who prepared the line drawings as well as such an attractive cover design. This is the first time his artwork has been used within a New Naturalist volume, and we are very privileged to be the beneficiaries.

We thank the following publishers for permission to use various maps and diagrams: Bloomsbury for Figs 71, 86, 102 and 160 from *Seabird 2000*, and the Seabird Group for Figs 72 and 84 from *Atlantic Seabirds*; Wiley-Blackwell for Figs 95 and 123 from the *Journal of Field Ornithology*; Oxford University Press for Fig. 97 from *The Birds of the Western Palearctic*; BirdGuides for distribution maps of vagrant terns; and Munksgaard for Fig. 178.

We have been greatly supported by Myles Archibald and Julia Koppitz of HarperCollins (and we are pleased to note that with this volume Myles celebrates his fiftieth New Naturalist since taking over responsibility for the series). We are grateful to Hugh Brazier for his editorial work and for making many helpful suggestions for improvements to the text, and David Price-Goodfellow for the design and layout of the book. Finally, we both thank those around us for their forbearance, and for understanding that writing a book such as this is a most time-consuming affair.

CHAPTER 1

Terns of the World

TERNS ARE SMALL SEABIRDS that are commonly seen along coastlines and estuaries in the summer months: their graceful flight and command of the air are among the most attractive features of the coastal experience. Terns are closely related to gulls and resemble them in their grey and white plumage, but are smaller and more graceful. They feed exclusively on the wing, diving headlong into the water to catch small fish, or dipping to pick small crustaceans or insects from the surface. They even drink while on the

FIG 1. The Sandwich tern is the largest of the British and Irish terns, with fast and powerful flight. The black bill with a yellow tip is diagnostic in all plumages. The forehead is black early in the breeding season, but becomes speckled during incubation and is often white by the time birds disperse from the breeding sites in July. Lady's Island Lake, Co. Wexford. (John N. Murphy)

FIG 2. The common tern is the most widespread tern in Britain and Ireland. In the breeding season it has an orange-red bill with a black tip, and grey underparts. In flight it shows more black in the primaries (outer wing feathers) than other British and Irish terns. Plymouth, USA. (Craig Gibson)

FIG 3. The roseate tern is arguably the most beautiful of all terns, with its overall pale plumage and long white tail-streamers which flex gracefully as it flies. The underparts are creamy-white, with a pink ('roseate') tinge that is not often discernible in the field. The bill is black at the beginning of the breeding season, but becomes red at the base and is half red by August. Bird Island, USA. (Scott Hecker)

wing, gliding down repeatedly to dip their bills into the water. Unlike gulls, they do not feed on land or while swimming – in fact, they rarely settle on the water except briefly while bathing and at times in their winter quarters. Their bills are weaker and more pointed than those of gulls, so that they are incapable of tearing up prey and have to take small food items which they swallow whole. All the terns that breed in Britain and Ireland have forked tails, which – in combination with their aerial habits – was the origin of their old name 'sea-swallows'. When they come to shore, they spend their time in very open areas, roosting and resting on open beaches and sand flats, and nesting mainly on treeless islands.

Five species of tern breed regularly in Britain and Ireland (Figs 1–5). From largest to smallest, these are Sandwich tern, common tern, roseate tern, Arctic tern and little tern (see Table 1 for scientific names). Apart from size, these five species are generally similar in appearance, with grey upperparts and white or

TABLE 1. The 39 species of 'true terns'. Taxonomy and sequence are derived from Bridge *et al.* (2005), Sangster *et al.* (2005), American Ornithologists' Union (2006) and Efe *et al.* (2009). The noddies (*Anous* spp.) and the white tern (*Gygis alba*) are not treated as 'true terns', following Baker *et al.* (2007).

English name	Scientific name	English name	Scientific name
Sooty tern	*Onychoprion fuscatus*	Lesser crested tern	*Thalasseus bengalensis*
Grey-backed tern	*Onychoprion lunatus*	Crested tern	*Thalasseus bergii*
Bridled tern	*Onychoprion anaethetus*	Chinese crested tern	*Thalasseus bernsteini*
Aleutian tern	*Onychoprion aleuticus*	Sandwich tern	*Thalasseus sandvicensis*
Little tern	*Sternula albifrons*	Elegant tern	*Thalasseus elegans*
Least tern	*Sternula antillarum*	Cabot's tern (includes 'Cayenne' tern)	*Thalasseus acuflavidus* (*T. a. eurygnatha*)
Yellow-billed tern	*Sternula superciliaris*	Forster's tern	*Sterna forsteri*
Fairy tern	*Sternula nereis*	Trudeau's tern	*Sterna trudeaui*
Peruvian tern	*Sternula lorata*	Black-bellied tern	*Sterna acuticauda*
Saunders' tern	*Sternula saundersi*	Indian river tern	*Sterna aurantia*
Damara tern	*Sternula balaenarum*	White-cheeked tern	*Sterna repressa*
Large-billed tern	*Phaetusa simplex*	Kerguelen tern	*Sterna virgata*
Gull-billed tern	*Gelochelidon nilotica*	Common tern	*Sterna hirundo*
Caspian tern	*Hydroprogne caspia*	South American tern	*Sterna hirundinacea*
Inca tern	*Larosterna inca*	Antarctic tern	*Sterna vittata*
Black tern	*Chlidonias niger*	Arctic tern	*Sterna paradisaea*
White-winged tern	*Chlidonias leucopterus*	Black-naped tern	*Sterna sumatrana*
Whiskered tern	*Chlidonias hybrida*	Roseate tern	*Sterna dougallii*
Black-fronted tern	*Chlidonias albostriatus*	White-fronted tern	*Sterna striata*
Royal tern	*Thalasseus maximus*		

FIG 4. The Arctic tern is similar to the common tern, but is darker grey below and has much less black in the wing: the outer primaries appear translucent in the field. It has a shorter, dark red bill and tail-streamers that are almost as long as those of the roseate tern. The black cap extends below the eye, giving it a masked appearance. In flight it appears short-necked. Kitsissunnguit, West Greenland. (Carsten Egevang)

light grey underparts; all have some black in the wingtips and grey or white forked tails. All have black caps when breeding, but the little tern has a white forehead in summer and all species have white foreheads in winter. They are all primarily coastal, nesting on islands or beaches around all coasts of Britain and most coasts of Ireland. Small numbers of common terns also breed widely inland, nesting on small islands in lakes and gravel pits, and all five species except for the roseate tern occur sporadically inland on migration. All five are long-distance migrants, four of them wintering mainly on the west coast of Africa. Migrants of four species, from populations breeding further north and east, also occur along British coasts in spring and autumn, mainly in eastern and southern England – except for some Arctic terns that migrate through northern and western Scotland. The Arctic tern is renowned for having the longest migration of any bird, breeding as far north as the high Arctic and wintering mainly in the Antarctic, where it frequents the edge of the pack ice in the southern summer, so that it experiences more daylight in the course of the year than any other animal.

FIG 5. The little tern is much smaller than other British and Irish terns and has a white forehead in all plumages. Its bill is yellow with a black tip and the wing shows black only on the two outer primaries. Kilcoole, Co. Wicklow. (John N. Murphy)

Worldwide, terns are more varied than the five British and Irish species.[1] They are distributed mainly in the tropics and warm temperate zones; 12 species breed in cold temperate or arctic zones in the northern or southern hemispheres, but most of these migrate to spend the winter in the tropics. The majority of species are similar in plumage, grey above and white below with black caps in which the eye is concealed in the breeding season, and white foreheads in winter. However, the 'marsh' terns (three species that nest in temperate marshes) are mainly black when breeding and dark grey and white in winter. The noddies (five species) and the white tern form an aberrant group: they are all tropical, with plumages that range from all dark with a white forehead to all white. However, recent evidence suggests that these may not be true terns (see next section).

Besides the three 'marsh' terns, six species breed mainly on lakes and rivers inland, although most of these migrate to spend the non-breeding seasons along coasts or at sea. Many of the tropical species are true seabirds, feeding far from land and coming to shore primarily to breed. The sooty tern is the most abundant tropical seabird and is also one of the most aerial of all birds, spending most of the year on the wing and often feeding on flying fish: young sooty terns probably remain in the air from the time they first fly at two months old until they first attempt to breed five or more years later.[2] Although most terns nest on the ground on islands, the noddies and white tern nest in bushes or trees, the 'marsh' terns build floating nests in freshwater marshes, and the Inca tern nests on cliffs.

Most terns feed primarily on fish, but many species commonly take crustaceans, the 'marsh' terns feed mainly on insects, and several tropical species feed on squid. The gull-billed tern is an exception to many of these generalisations: it is more gull-like in proportions and flight, it has a stronger, thicker bill and it commonly feeds over land on terrestrial prey such as insects and frogs.

Like other seabirds, terns are long-lived, especially considering their small size: most do not breed until they are 3–6 years old, many survive to breed at 8–16 years old, and birds of several species have been recorded breeding at 20–25; a Caspian tern has been recorded breeding at 30, common terns at 29–30, Arctic terns at 30–34, and sooty terns at 32–36.[3]

EVOLUTIONARY PLACE AMONGST BIRDS

Terns are currently classified as comprising the family Sternidae within the order Charadriiformes, which also includes the gulls, skuas, auks, waders (shorebirds) and several smaller groups of waterbirds. Within the order, the terns are usually grouped with the gulls (family Laridae), skuas (Stercorariidae) and skimmers (Rhyncopidae). Each of these groups is relatively homogeneous in structure, appearance and ecology, and they are usually treated as distinct but closely related families, except that terns are so close to gulls that they are often treated as subfamilies of a single family Laridae.[4] However, these groupings and relationships – like many others among birds and other animals – are currently being re-evaluated using genetic methods that provide more rigorous information about relationships and rates of differentiation. A recent genetic study has indicated that skuas are more closely related to auks, despite their apparent similarity to gulls and terns, and that the noddies and white tern are less closely related to gulls and terns than these are to each other.[5] In scientific terminology, the terns as currently understood are not *monophyletic* – that is, they do not form a single branch on the evolutionary tree – and the noddies and white tern should probably not be treated as terns at all, despite their close resemblance to the other terns in everything except plumage colouration and their habit of nesting in bushes and trees. For this reason, we do not treat them as terns in this book and refer to them only briefly in the introductory chapters to point out cases where their characteristics contrast with those of the 'true terns'.

Genetic methods can also be used to estimate the times at which different groups of birds evolved and differentiated, using a combination of molecular 'clocks' and fossil records. According to the same genetic study, the order Charadriiformes can be traced back as far as the Cretaceous period about 93 million years ago; the most recent common ancestor of all the living species in the order lived at that time. The Charadriiformes differentiated into many lineages during the late Cretaceous, and the ancestral auks had already separated from the ancestral gulls and terns at the time of the mass extinction that marked the end of the Cretaceous and the beginning of the Palaeogene (Tertiary) period, 65 million years ago. The ancestral gulls and terns (and, apparently, the ancestors of the noddies and white tern) separated from each other during the Palaeocene epoch 60–65 million years ago, and the true terns differentiated into their current lineages mainly during the past 20 million years.[6]

TERN SPECIES AND THEIR ALLIES

The true terns (excluding the five noddies and the white tern) comprise about 39 species, forming a rather homogeneous group with generally similar structure, plumage and habits. On the basis of a genetic study by Bridge *et al.*,[7] the true terns are divided into seven groups, which are now recognised as comprising nine different genera (Fig. 6).

'Brown-winged' terns (*Onychoprion*) – four species, three of which are tropical (sooty tern, grey-backed tern, bridled tern) and one temperate (Aleutian tern). Three of the four species have occurred in Britain and Ireland.

'Little' terns (*Sternula*) – about seven species, breeding in mostly temperate areas on all continents except Antarctica. These species are very similar to each other and replace each other geographically, so that they have sometimes been combined into six or as few as four species. Two species have occurred in Britain and Ireland: the little tern breeds and the least tern has occurred as a vagrant.

'Atypical black-capped' terns – a mixed bag of three large species. The large-billed tern is confined to tropical South America, but the gull-billed and Caspian terns (Fig. 7) are cosmopolitan, breeding on six and five continents, respectively. The gull-billed and Caspian terns occur fairly frequently as vagrants in Britain and Ireland.

Inca tern (*Larosterna inca*) – found breeding in the tropics on the west coast of South America.

'Marsh' terns (*Chlidonias*) – four species, three of which breed in freshwater marshes: the black tern in temperate Eurasia and North America, the white-winged tern in temperate Eurasia and the whiskered tern, which is widespread

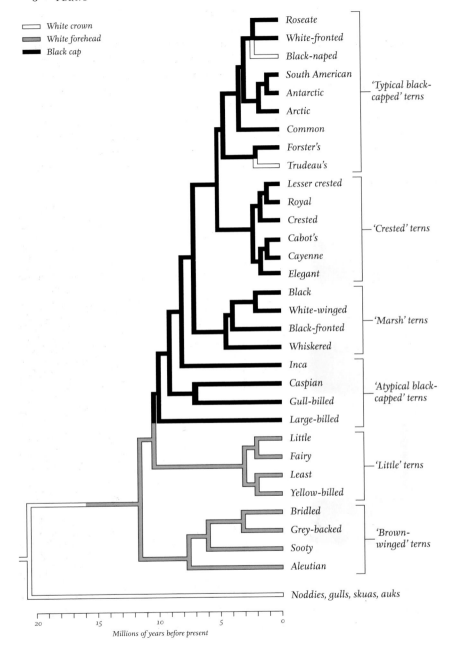

White crown
White forehead
Black cap

Roseate
White-fronted
Black-naped
South American
Antarctic
Arctic
Common
Forster's
Trudeau's
} 'Typical black-capped' terns

Lesser crested
Royal
Crested
Cabot's
Cayenne
Elegant
} 'Crested' terns

Black
White-winged
Black-fronted
Whiskered
} 'Marsh' terns

Inca
Caspian
Gull-billed
Large-billed
} 'Atypical black-capped' terns

Little
Fairy
Least
Yellow-billed
} 'Little' terns

Bridled
Grey-backed
Sooty
Aleutian
} 'Brown-winged' terns

Noddies, gulls, skuas, auks

20   15   10   5   0
Millions of years before present

OPPOSITE PAGE: **FIG 6.** Phylogenetic 'tree' showing genetic relationships among terns and the probable history of their evolutionary differentiation. Time progresses from left to right in this diagram, with the approximate scale in millions of years at the bottom. The branches of the tree indicate the sequence in which different species and groups of species separated: for example, the 'marsh' terns separated from the 'crested' and 'typical black-capped' terns before these separated from each other. The black, grey and white branches of the tree indicate the colours of the crown and forehead in breeding plumage. The oldest lineages have white foreheads and the more recent lineages have black foreheads, while two species with white crowns appear to have developed relatively recently from black-capped ancestors. (Redrawn from Bridge *et al.*, 2005). More recent genetic studies have suggested that the 'brown-winged' terns are more closely related to the 'typical black-capped' terns than to the 'little' terns (Baker *et al.*, 2007).

FIG 7. Caspian tern. This is by far the largest of all terns, with a heavy orange-red bill and extensive black on the underside of the primaries. (John N. Murphy)

from Europe and Africa to Australia. The fourth species, the black-fronted tern, breeds only on braided glacial rivers in New Zealand. The black tern formerly bred in Britain and is fairly common on migration; the white-winged and whiskered terns occur in small numbers as vagrants in both Britain and Ireland.

'Typical black-capped' terns (*Sterna*) – thirteen species, breeding on all continents and at all latitudes. The group includes one species that breeds in the Arctic and winters in the Antarctic (Arctic tern), two subantarctic species (Antarctic and Kerguelen terns), and four tropical species (black-bellied tern, white-cheeked tern and Indian river tern of south Asia, and black-naped tern which breeds on islands in the Indian and west Pacific oceans). The other six species are mainly temperate in distribution, but several also have tropical breeding populations and most winter in the tropics; the roseate tern is mainly tropical but breeds in several temperate areas. The common, roseate and Arctic terns breed in Britain and Ireland, and Forster's tern has occurred as a vagrant.

'Crested' terns (*Thalasseus*) – seven species, breeding in mostly tropical and subtropical areas in all continents, except that the Sandwich tern breeds in temperate parts of Europe and Asia. The Sandwich tern breeds in Britain and Ireland, the lesser crested tern has bred, and the elegant tern, royal tern and Cabot's tern have occurred as vagrants.

Until recently, *Onychoprion*, *Sternula* and *Thalasseus* were all included in a broader genus *Sterna*, and in some cases *Hydroprogne* and *Gelochelidon* were included in *Sterna* also. However, the division of these species into six genera, as recommended by Bridge *et al.* (Fig. 6), is now recognised as appropriate and has been widely adopted.[8]

Although terns are usually thought of as seabirds, only three of the 'brown-winged' terns (sooty, bridled and grey-backed) are truly pelagic, usually nesting on remote oceanic islands and spending their non-breeding seasons far from land. The Arctic tern is also pelagic for most of the year, except that it rests on pack ice in its winter quarters in the Antarctic (see Chapter 4). Most of the other terns are primarily coastal, frequenting relatively shallow waters inshore or on continental shelves and usually coming to land at least once each day to rest and roost. The coastal species usually breed on islands close to shore or even on mainland beaches. Ten species breed commonly or exclusively on bodies of fresh water, although most of these migrate to spend the non-breeding seasons along coasts or at sea. The large-billed tern, Indian river tern and yellow-billed tern all breed on sandbars in rivers, and in some areas little and least terns do so also.

The black-fronted tern breeds on gravel flats formed by braided glacial rivers, and the Kerguelen tern breeds on river flats or cliff tops. The common tern breeds on lakes and rivers and in marshes throughout Eurasia and most of North America, as well as on coastal islands. The Arctic tern breeds widely on freshwater ponds throughout the tundra of North America and Asia, as well as along the coast and on islands. Forster's tern and the three widespread 'marsh' terns breed in freshwater marshes (Forster's tern also in saltmarshes). All of these species except the large-billed tern and the Indian river tern migrate to spend the winter primarily along coasts or at sea; the black tern is largely pelagic in some wintering areas.[9]

The nine genera of true terns have distinctive plumage patterns and colouration, although some of the distinctions between groups and among species within groups are subtle. Most of the true terns are various shades of grey above and white below, with some black in the outer wing feathers; they have black caps in the breeding season and their bills and legs are various shades of red or yellow, often partly black. In the non-breeding season, the species become much more similar to each other: the forehead becomes white, there is a dark 'carpal bar' on the inner part of the upperwing, and the bill and legs are black. The three widespread 'marsh' terns (black, white-winged and whiskered terns) differ markedly in having the body and underparts entirely dark grey or black in the breeding season (Fig. 8), and the black-bellied tern is

FIG 8. Black tern. All the 'marsh' terns except the black-fronted tern of New Zealand have dark grey or black underparts in the breeding season. In winter the underparts become white (see illustrations in Chapter 12). They are all smaller than the common or Arctic terns, with less pointed wings, less deeply forked tails and somewhat butterfly-like flight. Zouweboezem, the Netherlands. (Mark Collier)

FIG 9. Juvenile Arctic tern at sea on autumn migration. Juvenile terns and non-breeding adults of the five British and Irish species all have white foreheads, dark 'carpal bars' on the inner part of the upperwing, white underparts, and black bill and legs. Juveniles have brown tips to the feathers on the upperparts which gradually wear off during autumn and early winter. Liscannor Bay, Co. Clare. (John N. Murphy)

mostly black below, but all these species acquire white underparts in winter. The 'brown-winged' terns have the back and upperwings dark grey, brown or black. The 'brown-winged' terns and the 'little' terns have white foreheads even in the breeding season. The gull-billed tern and Forster's tern have white heads with dark grey 'ear-patches' in winter, and Trudeau's tern has this pattern year-round, while the black-naped tern has a white forehead in all plumages. Genetic data indicate that the latter two species differentiated relatively recently within the group of 'typical black-capped' terns, suggesting that they evolved from ancestors with black caps and foreheads (Fig. 6).[10] The large-billed tern has a striking upperwing pattern with triangles of black, white and grey. The Inca tern is the most distinctive species, entirely dark grey except for a white trailing edge to the wing and a long white 'moustache' extending back from the bill and curling down at the tip. The 'crested' terns have short shaggy crests, which are usually concealed but are raised in some of the courtship and aggressive displays. Juvenile terns are generally similar to non-breeding adults, but have variable amounts of brown patterning on the back and upperwings (Fig. 9); juvenile sooty terns are distinctive in being mainly black. Most terns (excluding the 'brown-

TABLE 2. Measurements and body weights of the five British and Irish breeding terns.

	Little tern	Sandwich tern	Common tern	Roseate tern	Arctic tern
Total length (cm)	22–24	36–41	31–35	33–38	33–35
Tail length (cm)	7.5–9	12–16	13–17	16–22	15–20
Tail fork (cm)	3–5	5–8.5	6–9	9–15	8–13
Wingspan (cm)	48–55	95–105	80–95	70–80	75–85
Tarsus length (mm)	15–19	24–29	18–22	18–21	13–17
Body weight (g)	48–63	210–260	110–140	105–135	90–120

Sources: Cramp, 1985; Malling Olsen & Larsson, 1995.

winged' terns) pass through a series of plumages before acquiring full adult plumage at ages of 2–4 years.

Most of the 'true terns' are small to medium-sized, with body lengths in the range 30–40 cm, wingspans 70–80 cm and body weights 100–160 g (Table 2). The 'brown-winged' terns are generally larger, with body weights 120–220 g, and the 'crested' terns, gull-billed tern, Indian river tern, large-billed tern and Inca tern are still larger (body weights 180–400 g). The Caspian tern is by far the largest species, with body length 48–56 cm, wingspan 130–140 cm and body weight 600–750 g. The 'marsh' terns are smaller, with body weights in the range 60–70 g, and the 'little terns' are all very small, with body lengths 20–25 cm, wingspans 450–550 mm and body weights 40–55 g.

All the 'true terns' have slightly forked tails, but the 'typical black-capped' (*Sterna*) terns generally have deeper forks than the other species, with elongated outer tail feathers of varying lengths. The forked tails of terns were the basis for the former English name 'sea-swallow', the German name *Seeschwalbe*, the Portuguese name *andorinha-do-mar* and the scientific name *hirundo* (swallow) given by Linnaeus to the common tern.[11]

The roseate tern has the longest tail, with flexible tail 'streamers' up to 21 cm long, although the Arctic and white-fronted terns have tails almost as long. Many of the 'typical black-capped' terns have species-specific patterns of black, grey and white in the outer primaries. Many of them have bills and legs partly or wholly red during the breeding season; in some species the bill becomes more red and less black as the breeding cycle progresses, but in all species the bill reverts to all-black in winter. These characters vary among species and are thought to play a role in species identification and avoiding hybridisation.[12] The changes in bill colour during the breeding cycle may also serve as signals of the breeding state of the individual bird, but their functions are not fully understood. Even the physiological mechanism for the changes is uncertain, because it involves the loss of the black pigment melanin from a material (keratin) that is inert and has no biochemical connection with the body of the bird. Some of the 'crested' terns retain their full breeding plumage for only a short time at the beginning of the season and start to develop white on the forehead and crown even before eggs are laid: this also may serve as a signal of their breeding state to other birds seeking mates.

None of the tern species shows consistent differences between males and females in plumage patterns or colouration, and it is likely that the birds identify each other's sex primarily by behaviour. In many or most species, males are slightly larger than females in linear measurements, but there is considerable overlap in most cases. The length from the tip of the bill to the back of the skull usually shows the most consistent differences between males and females and is often used by researchers to identify sexes of trapped birds in the field, but it is usually necessary to measure both members of a pair to have high confidence in sex identification.

Most terns moult their body feathers twice each year, and in several species this results in a change from white underparts in winter to black ('marsh' terns and black-bellied tern) or grey (common, Arctic, Antarctic, Kerguelen, white-cheeked and black-fronted terns) in breeding plumage. In freshly moulted plumage, the roseate, black-naped, Sandwich and elegant terns have a delicate pink 'blush' on the underparts, which fades in sunlight to cream or white at the feather tips but remains pink at the base of the feathers. Terns moult their flight feathers in a pattern that is unique among birds: many of the primary and secondary feathers in the wing are replaced two or even three times per year. Each moult progresses slowly, and the second and third moults start before the first and second are complete, so that for most of the year the wings have two or even three generations of flight feathers with different degrees of wear (Fig. 10).[13] When fresh, the flight feathers have a white 'frosting' produced by a fine layer of white barbules; these gradually wear off, so that the appearance of the feathers changes from almost white when fresh to grey or black when old. The fresh feathers also reflect ultraviolet light. Birds can see in the ultraviolet, so that the feathers we see as grey or white must appear brightly coloured to them. When the birds perform their aerial courtship flights, the alternating blocks of new and old feathers in the wings probably appear to potential mates as striking coloured patterns. It has been suggested that the birds may use these patterns in selecting suitable mates, because the birds that have grown the most coloured feathers are generally those that are in better condition and hence are more desirable as mates.[14]

FIG 10. Common tern wing showing repeated moult. The innermost primary feather is denoted P1 and the outermost secondary S1. Each wave of moult starts with these feathers and progresses outwards (primaries) or inwards (secondaries). On this bird, photographed in the breeding season, the outermost four primaries were replaced early in the previous winter and are worn and faded. The longer and shorter arrows pointing to the right show the progress of a second wave of primary moult (six feathers replaced) and a third wave (two feathers replaced). The arrow pointing to the left shows the progress of a second wave of secondary moult (six feathers replaced). Bird Island, USA. (Eli Bridge)

WORLD DISTRIBUTION

Terns have a worldwide distribution: one or more species breed around all shores of all continents, except that they are absent from most of Antarctica, where the only breeding species is the Antarctic tern on a few islands off the Antarctic Peninsula. They are absent also from a few small inhospitable areas such as the west coast of Canada, tropical West Africa and the south coast of Australia. Terns are found breeding on islands throughout the world's oceans, and on fresh waters throughout six continents, except in Africa where the three inland-breeding species (little, Caspian and whiskered terns) are confined to small areas. Terns are generally absent from mountains, forested regions and deserts, but common terns breed at altitudes above 4,500 m on the Tibetan plateau and on lakes throughout the taiga (boreal forest) regions of Canada and Siberia; large-billed and yellow-billed terns nest on rivers throughout the

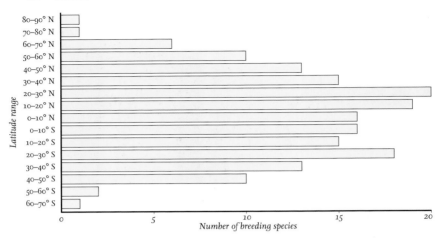

FIG 11. Distribution of breeding tern species by latitude. Each horizontal bar shows the number of breeding species in that 10° interval. Locations of peripheral or sporadic breeding are excluded. (Source: Burger & Gochfeld, 1996)

rainforests of the Amazon basin; gull-billed terns breed in the arid interior of Australia wherever and whenever suitable wetlands appear.[15]

As a group, terns are predominantly tropical and subtropical, with the largest numbers of breeding species between latitudes 40° N and 40° S (Fig. 11). However, 13 species breed regularly north of latitude 40° N and 10 species breed south of latitude 40° S. The Arctic tern has the widest latitudinal range of any bird species, breeding north to latitude 83° N in northern Greenland and wintering south to latitude 79° S in Antarctic waters: it is possible that some individual

OPPOSITE PAGE: **FIG 12.** World breeding distribution of the 'little' terns: (I) little tern; (II) least tern; (III) Saunders' tern; (IV) yellow-billed tern; (V) Peruvian tern; (VI) Damara tern; (VII) fairy tern. The little, least and fairy terns have several distinct subspecies, marked Ia – Ie, IIa – IIc and VIIa – VIId, respectively. The temperate populations of little and least terns are migratory, wintering mainly in the tropics; the migrations of the other five species are poorly known and some may be sedentary.

FOLLOWING PAGE: **FIG 13.** World breeding distribution of (I) Arctic tern, (II) Antarctic tern and (III) Kerguelen tern. The Antarctic tern has six distinct subspecies, marked IIa–IIf. The Arctic tern is migratory, wintering in the Antarctic where it overlaps with the Antarctic tern during the latter's breeding season. Although these three species are similar in appearance and replace each other geographically, genetic studies have shown that they are not each other's closest relatives (Fig. 6).

WORLD BREEDING POPULATION OF 'LITTLE' TERNS

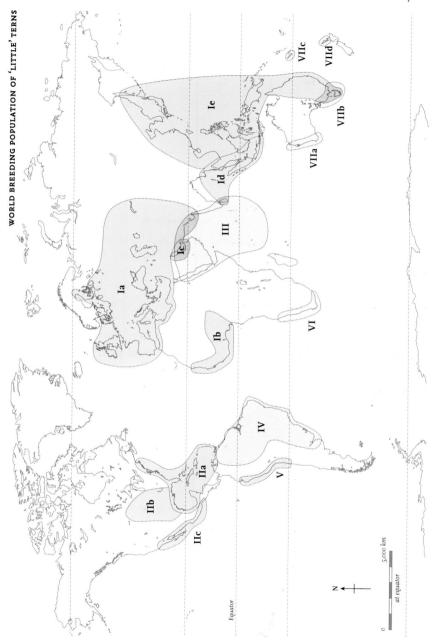

Equator

N

0   at equator   5,000 km

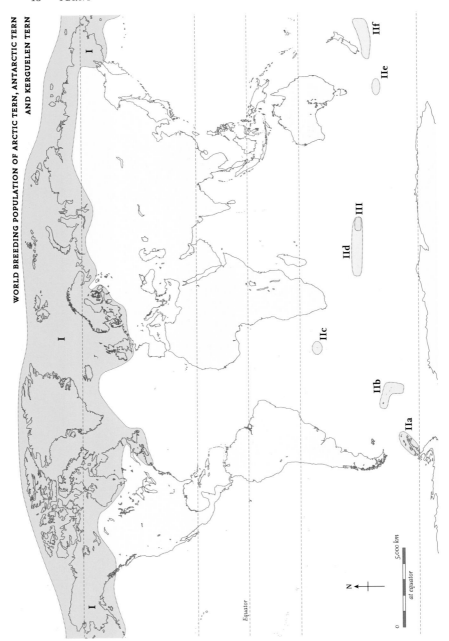

WORLD BREEDING POPULATION OF ARCTIC TERN, ANTARCTIC TERN
AND KERGUELEN TERN

WORLD BREEDING POPULATION OF COMMON TERN

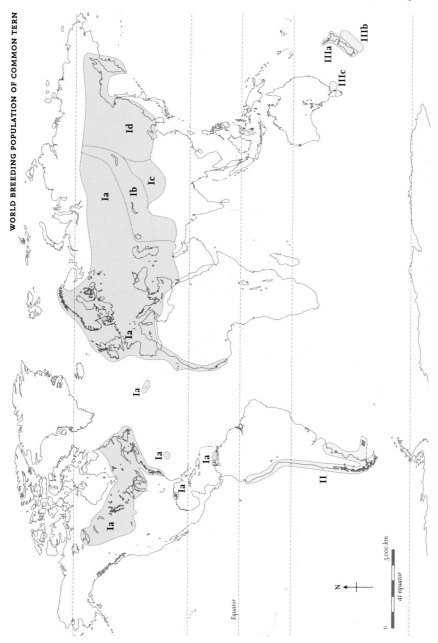

IIIa

IIIb

IIIc

Id

Ic

Ia

Ib

Ia

Ia

Ia

Ia

Ia

Ia

Ia

Ia

II

N

Equator

0

5,000 km

at equator

PREVIOUS PAGE: **FIG 14.** World breeding distribution of (I) common tern, (II) South American tern and (III) white-fronted tern. The common and white-fronted terns have differentiated into several distinct subspecies, marked Ia–Id and IIIa–IIc, respectively. The common tern is migratory, some individuals reaching the range of the South American tern during the latter's breeding season. Although these three species are similar in appearance and replace each other geographically, genetic studies have shown that they are not each other's closest relatives (Fig. 6).

OPPOSITE PAGE: **FIG 15.** World breeding distribution of the roseate tern. This species has a widely scattered distribution, mainly in tropical oceans but with several temperate populations, extending as far north as 56° N in Scotland. There are two distinct subspecies, one in the Atlantic Ocean (a) and the other in the Indian and Pacific Oceans (b). The temperate populations are migratory, wintering in the tropics.

birds reach both these latitudes. Most of the terns that breed in the temperate zones migrate south or north to spend their non-breeding seasons at tropical or subtropical latitudes, but common terns migrate across the Equator to spend the northern winter south to latitude 42° S in South America and 32° S in South Africa and Australia, and many Sandwich terns from northern Europe winter in South Africa.

Figures 12–16 show the breeding distributions of 16 of the world's 39 tern species, including the five that breed in Britain and Ireland. Terns are unusual among birds in that 11 species breed in substantial numbers in both tropical and temperate areas.[16] Some of these species, such as little, gull-billed, Caspian, whiskered, roseate, Cabot's and royal terns, are widely distributed in substantial numbers in both north and south temperate regions, as well as in tropical areas in between. In several of these species, birds breeding in temperate and tropical areas belong to the same subspecies (e.g., Cabot's terns in North and South America). The roseate tern has different subspecies in the Atlantic and Indo-Pacific oceans, but within each ocean temperate and tropical populations belong to the same subspecies. The little tern has a more complex pattern, with one subspecies (*albifrons*) largely confined to temperate areas, three subspecies confined to the tropics, and one (*sinensis*) ranging from temperate east Asia through the tropics to temperate Australia.

Among terns with primarily temperate or arctic distributions, six (Sandwich, common, Arctic, Forster's, white-winged and black terns) are confined to the northern hemisphere and seven (white-fronted, South American, Antarctic, Trudeau's, fairy, Damara and black-fronted terns) are confined to the southern hemisphere. Some of them seem to form north–south pairs with similar appearance and ecology (e.g., common and South American terns, Arctic and

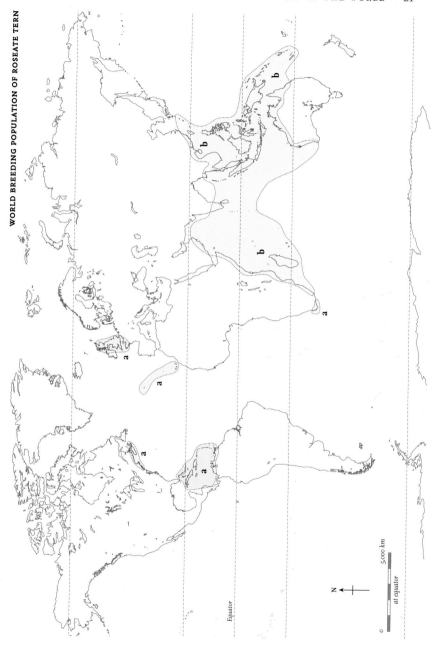

WORLD BREEDING POPULATION OF ROSEATE TERN

WORLD BREEDING POPULATION OF SANDWICH TERN, CABOT'S TERN AND CAYENNE TERN

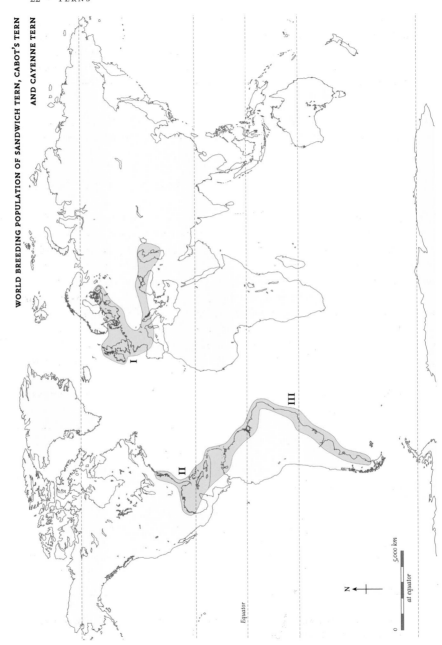

OPPOSITE PAGE: **FIG 16.** World breeding distribution of (I) Sandwich tern, (II) Cabot's tern and (III) Cayenne tern. Although the Sandwich and Cabot's terns are very similar in appearance, recent genetic studies have shown that they are not closely related. The Cabot's and Cayenne terns have sometimes been considered separate species, but they overlap and interbreed on islands in the Caribbean, and genetic studies have shown they are very closely related.

Antarctic terns, Forster's and Trudeau's terns: Figs 13 and 14),[17] but genetic data indicate that the species forming these pairs are not each others' closest relatives.[18]

SIGNIFICANCE OF BRITAIN AND IRELAND FOR TERNS

Table 3 summarises estimates of the numbers of each of our five species of tern breeding in Britain and Ireland (for more details, see Chapters 6–10) and compares them with estimates of the total numbers breeding in Europe and the world. In terms of total numbers, the most important species are the Sandwich tern, with about 30 per cent of the European and 15 per cent of the world population; the roseate tern, with about 50 per cent of the European population; and the little tern, with about 11 per cent of the European population.

Britain and Ireland have greater significance for terns than these gross numbers convey, however. These islands lie at the northwest extremity of the European continent and the continental shelf surrounding them is much wider

TABLE 3. Breeding populations of terns in Britain and Ireland compared to estimated totals in Europe and the world.

	Little tern	Sandwich tern	Common tern	Roseate tern	Arctic tern
Breeding population in Britain and Ireland (pairs)	2,200	14,000	14,000	1,300	56,000
European population (pairs)	20,000	74,000	280,000	2,600	1,200,000
Percentage in Britain and Ireland	11%	29%	5%	52%	5%
World population (pairs)	90,000	96,000	540,000	120,000	1,700,000
Percentage in Britain and Ireland	2%	15%	3%	1%	3%

Source: Mitchell *et al.*, 2004, with numbers for roseate terns updated to 2011. All estimates are rounded to two significant figures.

than that off Norway, France, Spain or Portugal. They have a very maritime climate with temperatures – especially in autumn and winter – much warmer than any other parts of the world at the same latitude. All of our terns reach the furthest limits of their ranges in Britain and Ireland: the northern and western extremities of the world range for the Sandwich tern; the western and almost the northern limit of the European range for the little tern; the northwestern fringe of the European range for the common tern; the northern limit of the world range for the roseate tern; and the southern limit of the European range for the Arctic tern. Thus, all of our five species can be studied in ecological conditions that must be marginal for them. In particular, as the climate becomes warmer, one would expect the northern and southern limits of the ranges to shift northwards.

CHAPTER 2

Food and Foraging

FEEDING TECHNIQUES AND BEHAVIOUR

MOST TERNS – INCLUDING ALL THOSE that breed in Britain and Ireland – catch prey exclusively while on the wing and hunt for food mainly over open waters. Terns feed almost entirely on live prey, except that several species have been recorded feeding on by-catch or offal from fishing operations, or freshly dead fish on the beach.

Terns use three main techniques for catching prey in open waters: *plunge-diving*, in which the bird plunges vertically into the water from a height of several metres to seize prey swimming below the surface; *diving-to-surface*, in which the bird makes a shallow dive and takes prey just below the surface without fully immersing its body; and *dipping*, in which the bird picks prey from the surface without otherwise touching the water.[1] The 'marsh' terns commonly catch insects by *hawking* in the air or by *dipping* to pick them from the surface of vegetation, and several other terns – notably common and Arctic terns – occasionally hawk for insects. Terns often try to steal fish from each other or from other birds, a technique known as *kleptoparasitism*. A few terns practise *perch-feeding*: standing on an object such as a pier, rock or boat and watching for fish swimming below – like a kingfisher.

Most terns feed only on aquatic prey, but the gull-billed tern feeds mainly on terrestrial prey such as insects, frogs, lizards and even small mammals and birds. It usually picks these items from the surface while on the wing, in the manner of other terns dipping to take prey from the water surface, but it sometimes lands on the ground and picks up insects while walking. Other terns rarely feed while swimming or walking, although common and Arctic terns have been reported walking on mudflats and picking up worms.

Plunge-diving

This feeding technique is usually practised by terns hunting for schooling fish. After locating a promising school, the tern holds itself in place above it, either by flying against the wind or by hovering in still air. When a fish is located close enough to the surface, the bird turns and plunges vertically downwards, adjusting its trajectory as it descends and folding its wings immediately before hitting the surface (Fig. 17).

It is very difficult to observe terns below the surface, so there is little precise information on how deep they dive. Some species – such as Arctic and black terns – barely immerse the entire body and re-emerge after less than a second, so that they are thought to dive only to depths of 30–60 cm. Other species – such

FIG 17. Plunge-diving. The tern hovers a few metres above the water surface, plunges vertically downwards and partly closes its wings as it enters the water. After seizing a fish 10–60 cm below the surface, it emerges, shakes water from its plumage, turns the fish in its bill with its tongue, and either swallows the fish or carries it off to feed its mate or young. (Redrawn by R. Gillmor after Glutz von Blotzheim & Bauer, 1982)

as the 'crested' terns – enter the water faster and remain submerged for up to 2 seconds, so that they are thought to dive to depths of 1 m or more. Generally, the larger species appear able to dive deeper than the smaller terns, but the little and least terns hit the water faster and often stay immersed for longer than larger species such as common terns: they are thought to be able to dive as deep as 80 cm. The roseate tern is an especially deep diver for its size, sometimes 'power-diving' by using its wings to accelerate as it descends and remaining submerged for as long as 2 seconds: it may be able to catch fish at depths below 1.2 m. The Sandwich tern has been reported as catching fish at depths below 1.5 m.[2] It is not known whether any tern species actually pursues fish under water after plunge-diving in the manner of gannets, but this is not likely: if they did so, they would probably remain submerged for longer than they actually do. More probably, they simply rely on steering accurately towards the fish as they descend through the air. The height from which terns dive is adjusted to the depth to which they have to penetrate below the surface and is typically between 1 and 6 m for most species, but ranges up to 8 m for least terns, 12 m for roseate and Sandwich terns, and 20 m for Caspian terns.[3]

Plunge-diving for fish requires great skill, and young terns require days or weeks of practice before they catch their first fish, and months or years to perfect the technique. Fish have adaptations to avoid being eaten, including cryptic colouration (most fish are dark along the back, even if they are silvery on the sides), habitually swimming at depths below those at which they are in danger from above, and taking evasive action if they see a bird diving towards them. Terns have their own cryptic colouration, most having white or light grey underparts so that they are difficult to see from below the surface, and they dive vertically towards the fish at the highest possible speeds.

Importantly, terns have to learn to adjust for parallax: light is refracted at the air–water interface, which makes fish appear always to be at shallower depths than they really are. This is an especially difficult problem when the water surface is wavy, which makes the image of the fish move around horizontally as well as vertically – as one can see by looking down at fish from a bridge or dock into rippled water. Terns must learn by trial and error to compensate for parallax and dive accurately towards a target that appears to be moving unpredictably. It has been shown that terns' success in catching fish declines with increasing wind speed, presumably because increasing waviness of the surface makes the fish increasingly hard to locate accurately. At the other extreme, terns' fishing success declines again at very low wind speeds, either because the terns have more difficulty hovering to locate the fish in still air, or because the fish can see the terns more easily when the surface is smooth.[4] Except in the most favourable

FIG 18. Sandwich tern emerging from the water after an unsuccessful plunge-dive. Terns often hit the water with their first wing-stroke as they emerge and kick with their feet: this is the action for which their webbed feet have their most important function. Typically, terns catch fish in only about one-third of their dives. Gormanstown, Co. Meath. (John Fox)

circumstances, terns' fishing success is usually quite low – typically only one fish caught for every three or four dives, with many attempts broken off even before the tern hits the water (Fig. 18).

At most times and in most places, terns are unable to catch fish because the fish are swimming deeper below the surface than the terns can dive. Terns' ability to catch fish usually depends on factors that bring the fish towards the surface. Many fishes follow vertical movements of their invertebrate prey, or zooplankton, but these prey habitually come to the surface at night when terns are usually unable to catch fish. Sandeels, one of the main prey species for terns, come to the surface to spawn, and several other fishes spawn in shallow water near the shore. These spawning events provide good opportunities for terns to catch fish, but they are usually localised and transitory. Fish larvae and juvenile fish are more likely to swim near the surface than adult fish, but these prey are often too small to be good food sources for terns. An important factor that brings larger fish close to the surface is vertical movements of the water caused by currents running over obstacles or through narrow passages. Terns regularly concentrate over tide 'races' such as that at Dungeness, Kent, where currents running around headlands generate turbulent eddies that bring fish to the surface, or at gaps in barrier beaches such as those of the north Norfolk coast, where tidal currents running in and out twice each day produce similar eddies. Other sites suitable for tern feeding are where tidal currents run over shallow rocks, reefs or sandbars, or around islands, bringing fish close to the surface at predictable times of the tidal cycle. Roseate terns in particular feed regularly over such places, and in some areas travel long distances to feed at sites where fish can be caught predictably. Roseate terns in the Azores feed in the open ocean around submerged sea-mounts where currents bring deep-water fish close to the surface.[5] Some tropical terns similarly concentrate over edges of coral reefs, where ocean swells cause regular upward and downward movements of the water, carrying schools of prey fish with them.

The most widespread factor making prey fish come towards the surface, however, is predatory fish chasing them from below. In many coastal areas, flocks of terns gather over schools of predatory fish and follow them as they feed, diving frantically in the short intervals when the prey fish are forced close to the surface by the predators pursuing them from below. Many tropical terns – and also the temperate terns that winter in the tropics – habitually follow tuna, bonito or other predatory fish that hunt in schools. The sooty tern is thought to be dependent for much of the year on tuna and the dolphins that accompany them, ranging widely over tropical oceans and aggregating wherever the tuna come near the surface to feed.[6] Terns in the temperate zones also follow and feed over marine mammals such as seals, porpoises and hump-backed whales when these are feeding, and even follow and feed over seabirds that pursue fish under water, such as cormorants, divers and auks.

Most of these factors that bring prey fish towards the surface act only in the marine environment. Very little is known about factors that make fish available to terns in freshwater environments. Terns are known to concentrate to feed in rivers where these flow over sandbars, or where fry of anadromous fish such as herrings and salmon migrate through narrow channels. However, many terns feed in lakes where there are no tidal currents and few predatory fish to drive prey towards the surface, and it is not known what makes prey fish accessible to terns in these places.

Diving-to-surface

This feeding technique is practised by plunge-diving species wherever prey fish are driven close enough to the surface for the terns to catch them without fully immersing themselves (Figs 19 and 20). Common and Arctic terns get most of their food in this way when the water is very shallow or when predatory fish or fish-eating birds are particularly active below the surface. Some tern species rarely plunge-dive at all, obtaining enough food by habitually diving-to-surface and catching fish within a few centimetres of the surface. Sooty terns, for example, virtually never dive fully into the water and are not even waterproof, rapidly becoming waterlogged if they are forced to remain swimming.[7] Bridled terns and

FIG 19. Arctic tern hovering after an unsuccessful plunge-dive. Water is still dripping from its bill. Snæfellsnes, Iceland. (Jóhann Óli Hilmarsson)

FIG 20. Common terns diving-to-surface. Fish are often concentrated in a small area close to the surface, and the terns jostle for position over the fish. In these circumstances, terns can sometimes catch fish very rapidly: all three of the terns that are clear of the water in this photograph have fish in their bills. Bremore, Co. Dublin. (John Fox)

noddies are probably waterproof, but they rarely swim and they similarly catch most or all of their prey close to the surface or even in the air.

Many small fish leap into the air to evade predators chasing them from below (to the predators, the prey fish disappear because of the internal reflection of light from the water surfacs), and terns have learned to anticipate this and to seize the fish as they 'fly'. In some tropical areas, mixed flocks of terns follow predatory fish, the noddies remaining close to the water and catching fish at the surface or in the air while roseate, black-naped and crested terns fly higher, plunge-diving through the layer of noddies.

The fish that take to the air most regularly are the flying fish of tropical oceans. Many species of terns catch flying fish, and in some tropical areas these fish form a substantial part of the diet, even of species such as Cabot's tern which usually plunge-dive for food. Although flying fish can also be caught by plunge-diving or diving-to-surface before they fly or after they return to the water, it is likely that the terns catch at least some of them in the air.

Dipping

This feeding technique is usually practised by terns feeding on very small prey swimming at the water surface, including crustaceans, aquatic insects or fry of larger fish. These prey take little or no evasive actions and the terns can catch them as fast as they can find them. Terns typically fly slowly against the wind within 1 m of the water surface, descending repeatedly with wings raised to pick up prey items one at a time, touching the water only with their bills (Fig. 21). Because the prey items are so small, this type of feeding is profitable only when they can be found at

FIG 21. Dipping. The tern flies low over the water with wings slightly raised, repeatedly dipping down to pick food items from the surface or just below it. (Redrawn by R. Gillmor after Glutz von Blotzheim & Bauer, 1982)

FIG 22. Arctic tern rising with prey after dipping. This three-spined stickleback has been caught by the tail. Arnarstapi, Snæfellsnes, Iceland. (Jóhann Óli Hilmarsson)

high densities. It is often seen when swarms of krill or other crustaceans appear at the sea surface within flying range of a breeding colony, where tidal currents run through shallow water, or along drift lines where floating weeds accumulate in the open sea. Terns dip in the same fashion when feeding on other prey at the surface, including small fish (Fig. 22) or offal discarded by fishermen, dead insects in the water or dead fish on the beach, and insects on vegetation. Gull-billed terns dip in the same way when feeding on terrestrial insects, lizards or birds. The 'marsh' terns often feed over land and have been reported following ploughs, dipping to pick prey items from the freshly turned soil. The whiskered tern sometimes hunts cooperatively and is one of the few bird species known to do so: one report described groups of up to 18 terns flying in line abreast across fields and picking up beetles, each bird apparently profiting by being able to catch insects flushed by the others.[8] Several species of tern feed on insects or crustaceans in kelp beds, and bridled terns habitually hunt for prey around the floating patches of the *Sargassum* weed from which the Sargasso Sea in the subtropical Atlantic Ocean gets its name.[9]

Hawking

This feeding technique – catching flying prey in the air – is usually practised by terns when they find swarms of insects such as ants, termites or stingless bees: the rewards are too small for terns to waste time catching dispersed insects, although 'marsh' terns sometimes take single large insects such as dragonflies. Insect swarms are usually very ephemeral and may attract large numbers of terns for only a few minutes. The terns weave backwards and forwards through the swarm in the manner of swallows or nightjars, usually flying below the prey and swooping up to take them one item at a time. Hawking is most characteristic of the 'marsh' terns, but has been reported in species as disparate as gull-billed, sooty, grey-backed, common, Arctic and little terns.

Kleptoparasitism

This technique – food-stealing, or 'piracy' – is practised by terns mainly at breeding colonies, where many food items are being brought in by other terns, carried through the colony and fed to mates or chicks. For a tern resting in the colony, it is often easier to steal a fish from another tern a few metres away than to fly many kilometres to catch a fish for itself. It certainly takes little time and energy to try, even if many attempts are necessary for each successful theft. Consequently, piracy is rife in tern colonies, and every tern bringing in a fish is at risk of having it stolen. Terns carrying fish are aware of the risk and are constantly alert and ready to take evasive action.

Among the terns of Britain and Ireland, common and roseate terns are the most habitual pirates, and their techniques are described more fully in Chapters 8 and 9. Common terns are the most prone to chase other terns in the air – including Arctic and little terns as well as their own species. Both common and roseate terns often try to steal fish as they are passed to chicks on the ground, and common tern chicks themselves often steal fish from chicks in neighbouring broods. A few roseate terns specialise in seizing fish from the bills of common terns as they fly in to their nests, circling high overhead and diving from behind when they spot an unwary victim. Away from breeding colonies, fish stealing is less frequent, in part because opportunities are limited: foraging birds are more widely spaced and few terns carry fish for more than a few seconds before swallowing them. Terns cannot pursue other terns and force them to disgorge in the manner of skuas. However, common and roseate terns sometimes try to steal fish at sea from other terns that are carrying fish towards a breeding colony. Such attempts are rarely successful, however, except in feeding flocks where several terns can join together and pursue a hapless victim.

Besides losing fish to other terns, terns are often victimised by gulls that are nesting in or near their colonies – especially black-headed gulls in Europe and laughing gulls in North America.[10] As with tern-on-tern piracy, single gulls rarely succeed in stealing fish from terns, but groups of three or more almost invariably do so.[11] At breeding sites with high levels of piracy by gulls, terns can lose so many fish that their breeding success is reduced.[12] Even at breeding sites where piracy by gulls or other terns is less frequent, the constant threat of losing fish to pirates requires terns to maintain constant vigilance and take evasive actions, and this takes a toll in lost time and energy. For example, when common tern chicks are small, both parents must be present at each feeding – one to bring the fish and deliver it to the chicks while the other stands guard and watches for thieves, flying up and attacking them if they approach too closely. This limits the rate at which chicks can be fed: one parent has to stay with the chicks, even at times when the chicks do not need brooding, so that it can defend the chicks when the other parent returns with a fish.

Terns are habitually victimised at sea by skuas, some of which depend on terns for much of their food. Even a single Arctic or pomarine skua can outmanoeuvre a tern and almost invariably succeeds in making a tern either drop its catch or vomit up its previous meal. Many Arctic tern colonies are close to colonies of skuas, and the terns are subject to continual harassment, but the terns are usually much more numerous and the skuas rarely take enough fish to reduce the terns' breeding success significantly.[13] However, as with piracy by gulls and other terns, the continual threat of losing fish to skuas takes an indirect toll on the terns because it requires constant vigilance and costly evasive actions.

Perch-feeding

This feeding technique has been described for common, Arctic, Forster's and black terns, usually individual birds that are holding feeding territories (see Chapter 8). These birds return to the same perches day after day: they stand on vantage points such as piers, bridges, rocks or boats, from which they plunge-dive when they see a fish swimming below.[14]

Finding fish

As every human fisherman knows, successful fishing requires selecting good places and times to fish, as well as selecting the right tackle and using it skilfully. Terns and other fish-eating seabirds face the same problem: fish are patchily distributed and they usually become available for easy catching in unpredictable places, at irregular intervals and only for short times. At breeding colonies, terns have months or years to learn about the distribution and behaviour of fish in the local environments, and they usually behave as though they know these intimately. Some terns go back to the same places day after day; others adjust their foraging behaviour to the tidal cycle; many have several areas where they search for fish and they select the area to visit according to their recent experience. It is easy to observe terns making these choices about when and where to fish, but it is very difficult to discern what cues they use to make decisions.

The best place to find fish is where someone else is already catching them. Terns are constantly watching what other terns are doing: when one starts to dive, others nearby respond immediately and fly towards the diving bird; others that may be out of sight of the first bird respond to the first responders, and the 'news' quickly spreads. If a good school of fish has been found, a flock gathers within minutes and remains active until the fish disperse or the factor bringing the fish to the surface (predatory fish below, or tidal currents causing turbulence) dissipates – a type of behaviour also practised by many other seabirds such as gulls and gannets. Depending on the number of terns in the neighbourhood and the persistence of the school of prey fish, such flocks may include dozens, hundreds or even thousands of terns, often of more than one species (Fig. 23). Fishermen have learned to use these flocks of terns to locate predatory fish that are actively feeding. In the Pacific Ocean, for example, tuna fishermen use flocks of sooty terns to locate feeding schools of tuna.[15]

The second-best place to fish is somewhere where you know you can catch them consistently. At some breeding colonies, roseate terns have a small number of feeding areas where they can reliably catch fish, and they visit these day after day, sometimes flying 25 km or more each way and returning with the same types of fish. During a study of roseate terns breeding on the north coast of Brittany, birds were observed flying regularly overland to feed in the Rade de Brest and then return to the breeding colony with single fish, a journey of 30 km each way.[16] Around some breeding sites, individual Caspian, common and Arctic terns defend feeding territories along the shoreline from which they exclude all other terns. These territories are usually linear strips extending up to 300 m along the shore and up to 100 m into the water. The territory owners visit them day after day, driving out intruders whenever they approach, often perch-fishing from vantage points from which they catch fish regularly.[17]

The third-best place to fish is where you caught a fish the last time. At some breeding colonies, individual terns depart in the same direction on several successive foraging trips, typically returning with the same type of fish each time. Then, apparently because this type of fish is no longer available at the favoured place, the bird switches to doing something else. Only when all three of these options are exhausted do terns start searching for a new place to fish, and even then the search is probably not random but guided by the bird's knowledge of places and times where fishing has been successful on earlier occasions.

Most studies of tern foraging have been carried out at coastal breeding colonies; much less is known about how terns locate fish at freshwater breeding sites, on migration and in winter. Most terns that breed on fresh waters spend the winter along the coast or at sea: the black tern appears to be largely pelagic in its tropical winter quarters. Tropical terns – both resident breeders and wintering terns from temperate breeding areas – habitually follow schools of tuna, which attract mixed flocks of several species of tern, sometimes numbering in the hundreds or thousands.[18] However, it is not known how terns find the tuna schools, except by cueing in on terns that have already found them. In some tropical areas such as West Africa or northern South America, wintering terns are strongly associated with human fishing, accompanying fishing boats up to

FIG 23. Arctic terns often feed in front of calving glaciers. Whenever a mass of ice falls from the face of the glacier into the water, the terns swiftly converge on the spot to catch fish or crustaceans brought to the surface by the resulting turbulence. Jökulsárlón, Iceland. (Jóhann Óli Hilmarsson)

600 km from land and frequently resting on them, feeding on small fish as the nets are hauled in or on by-catch or offal discarded during processing.[19] In the same areas, terns attend beach-seining operations and catch small fish as the nets are hauled in to the beach. The terns continue taking dead fish discarded on the beach and are often trapped there by small boys using dead fish as bait (see Chapter 11). It is not known whether all terns wintering in these areas depend on human fishing, or whether this behaviour is limited to a minority of birds that have difficulty finding enough food for themselves.

Central-place foraging

For much of the year, terns are not tied to a particular site and consume their prey as soon as they catch it. When they are breeding, however, terns have to return to their nest after every fishing trip and to carry food for their chicks (and in the case of males, for their mates prior to egg-laying). This pattern is referred to by ecologists as *central-place foraging*, and it has been much studied. Especially at large colonies where terns forage far from the colony site, birds have to spend much of their time commuting. Most terns carry fish in their bills one at a time, which severely limits the distance to which they can fly from the colony and return in time to deliver a fish large enough to justify the trip. In contrast, the more oceanic terns, such as the 'brown-winged' terns and noddies, feed their chicks by regurgitation and consequently can bring larger meals from greater distances.[20]

Although most terns catch fish no more than one at a time (Fig. 24), a few birds sometimes bring several fish together (Fig. 25). This behaviour has been reported for Sandwich, common, Arctic and roseate terns,[21] but seems to be most characteristic of roseates. Indeed, some individual roseates seem to specialise in catching multiple fish, bringing 2–4 sandeels or sprats in successive visits to feed their chicks.[22] Terns have not been observed in the act of catching multiple fish, and it is baffling how they are able to do so. Roseate terns hit the water very fast when they plunge-dive, and it is almost inconceivable that they could dive while holding one or more fish and succeed in catching another without losing those already in the bill. Roseate terns that carry multiple fish often do so with all the fish oriented in the same way across the bill (Fig. 25). It seems possible that some individuals have been able to find locations where fish are swimming in very dense schools close to the surface, and are able to catch several fish in one scoop without diving deep to do so. However the birds catch multiple fish, the individual birds that specialise in this behaviour appear to be 'geniuses' who have devised a fishing technique that almost all others have been unable to master.

FIG 24. Roseate tern with a sandeel. Terns usually carry single fish to the colony to feed their mates or chicks (Dave Daly) …

BELOW: **FIG 25.** … but occasionally they carry two, three, four, or even five. A few roseate terns specialise in catching multiple fish. It is not known whether these birds catch multiple fish simultaneously or sequentially, but either would be very difficult to achieve. Lady's Island Lake, Co. Wexford. (Tony Murray)

Successful breeding requires that terns allocate their time efficiently, so that they bring high-quality food to their chicks at the highest possible rate: they must not waste their time flying long distances with small food items, or searching for larger items in unfavourable places. Studies have suggested that terns are good 'economists', in the sense that they do allocate their time efficiently. They are willing to catch and bring back small food items from short distances, but they fly further when they know they can catch larger food items. When foraging far from the colony, they swallow the smaller and lower-quality food items that they catch and wait until they have caught a large or high-quality item before returning to the colony with it.[23] The consequence is that tern parents consume consistently smaller fish than those they feed to their chicks, and also tend to feed more on invertebrates. In one study of common terns, larger fish were brought at longer intervals than smaller fish, but the larger fish were more profitable because trip times increased less rapidly than the weight of the fish. The size of the fish brought to the chicks was limited only by the chicks' ability to swallow them, and by the fact that larger fish disproportionately attracted pirates, so that they were more often lost before they could be fed to the chicks.[24]

Terns are also efficient in the way they adjust their commuting flights to the wind. They fly high (typically 10–20 m above the water surface) when flying downwind, but very low (often 50 cm or less) when flying upwind, taking advantage of the lower wind speed close to the water surface. The consequence is that birds flying in opposite directions fly at different heights. During busy chick-feeding periods at large breeding colonies, birds fly in high with fish and fly out low without fish on the upwind side of the colony, but fly in low with fish and fly out high without fish on the downwind side.

How far terns fly to get food for their young depends on the number of birds in the colony and the distribution of the prey. Most terns of most species feed within 10 km of the colony site, but trips of 20 km each way are not unusual. Roseate terns have been recorded feeding regularly at 30 km from the colony site, Sandwich terns at 72 km and Caspian terns as far as 100 km.[25] A few common terns even defend feeding territories as far as 19 km from the colony,[26] which requires that they visit these locations regularly and spend much of their time there. A recent study in which terns were followed in a boat from breeding colonies on the north Norfolk coast tracked Sandwich terns to foraging areas up to 54 km from the breeding site, but common terns no further than 9 km away. The common terns stayed within 2 km of the coast, but some Sandwich terns flew up to 50 km offshore, with individual tracks ranging up to 72 km because the birds often did not fly straight to their foraging locations (see Figs 95 and

123, in Chapters 7 and 8).[27] Sooty terns are the most wide-ranging of all tern species, sometimes staying away from the nest for two or more days between chick feedings and probably ranging hundreds of kilometres from the breeding colony.[28]

Nocturnal feeding

Terns feed primarily during daylight hours and usually spend the night at the breeding colony or, outside the breeding season, at roosts along the shore. However, sooty terns, noddies and white terns are thought to feed at night on squid.[29] Crested, royal and common terns have been reported resting on the rigging of fishing boats and feeding on by-catch and discards under lights at night. Roseate terns in the Azores frequently feed on lantern-fish and other mid-water fish that come to the surface only at night.[30] It is difficult to observe terns at night, so nocturnal feeding may be more frequent than the few records indicate, especially in the tropics, where many of the prey species are luminescent.

Drinking and managing salt balance

Terns drink almost exclusively on the wing, gliding down with wings slightly raised and dipping the bill repeatedly into the water surface. Coastal and marine terns drink salt water and have to eliminate excess salt to maintain the sodium concentration in their body fluids at a physiologically tolerable level. Fish also regulate their sodium levels below that in sea water, but most invertebrates do not, so terns that consume a high proportion of marine invertebrates have to excrete much of the sodium that they take in. Like other seabirds, marine terns have a 'salt gland' in their nose that excretes fluid with a high sodium concentration: this fluid runs down the bill and can be seen dripping from the bill tip. Terns that breed in freshwater sites and winter at sea, such as common and black terns, must adapt twice each year to the change. Tern chicks have functioning salt glands soon after hatching, but they get water only through their food and do not drink until after fledging, so that they are sometimes stressed by dehydration, especially in hot climates.

Defecation

Like other birds, terns excrete urine and faeces together in a dense liquid stream that consists mainly of uric acid. This minimises loss of water (compared to mammals, which excrete urine containing urea and large volumes of water) and helps to maintain body water levels and salt balance, especially for species that drink salt water. Terns usually defecate while flying (Fig. 26). During incubation,

FIG 26. Common tern defecating. Terns usually defecate while flying. Plymouth, USA. (Eduardo del Solar)

however, Sandwich and other 'crested' terns defecate while on the nest, which results in a 'sunburst' of white faeces surrounding the nests, making them very conspicuous (Fig. 27). Most other terns fly off the nest to defecate many metres away, which serves to maintain camouflage. Many terns defecate while attacking predators that approach their nests, and common and Arctic terns often hit the predators with their faeces. This is often effective in deterring predators – especially human intruders into breeding colonies – but it is unlikely that the birds actually aim their faeces at the intruders (see Chapter 8).

FIG 27. Sandwich tern nests surrounded by rings or 'sunbursts' of faeces. During incubation, Sandwich terns frequently defecate while sitting on the nest, so that the nest becomes very conspicuous. Lady's Island Lake, Co. Wexford. (Dave Daly)

FORAGING HABITATS

The five tern species that breed in Britain and Ireland are primarily coastal birds, foraging mainly in shallow inshore waters within a few kilometres of the shore. Only the common tern habitually breeds inland and feeds in fresh waters during the breeding season, and the birds that do so comprise only about 12 per cent of the total breeding population (see Chapter 8). Coastal common terns feed mainly in open waters along shores or in estuaries, sometimes around rocky shores, over shallow sandbars, in coastal lagoons or even in saltmarshes. Arctic terns feed mainly at sea, sometimes 30 km or more from shore, and Sandwich terns sometimes feed as far as 50 km offshore, although they also feed in estuaries or coastal lagoons. All five species become more like seabirds on migration and in winter quarters, sometimes feeding far offshore and coming to land mainly to roost at night.

Worldwide, terns utilise much more varied habitats than those of Britain and Ireland. The 'brown-winged' terns are oceanic birds, commonly feeding far from land: the sooty tern in particular has a pelagic existence for most of the year and comes to land only to breed. The Arctic tern also spends most of the year at sea, or around pack ice in the Antarctic in the northern hemisphere winter (see Chapter 4), but it also feeds inshore on migration. The 'marsh' terns feed in marshes, usually over open waters surrounded by emergent vegetation, but the whiskered and black-fronted terns often feed over wet fields or other terrestrial habitats. The gull-billed tern feeds mainly over land, ranging from beaches to cultivated fields. The 'little' terns and the common tern often feed in rivers, and several other species feed exclusively in rivers, usually concentrating in places where shallow water runs over sandbars.

FOODS

Most terns feed primarily on fish, but many species frequently feed also on crustaceans, insects, squid or other invertebrates. The gull-billed tern commonly feeds on small reptiles, amphibians or small mammals, and the 'marsh' terns also often feed on tadpoles or other amphibians. Terns rarely feed on plant items, and the few records of them doing so may result from 'secondary' intake – consuming prey fish that themselves had recently eaten plant matter. Terns generally feed on live prey, although several species occasionally take dead fish or offal discarded by fishermen. Terns usually swallow their prey whole and alive: only the Caspian and gull-billed terns have bills that are strong enough to tear up prey, and even these species rarely do so.

The five tern species that breed in Britain and Ireland have generally similar diets. As a broad generalisation, they feed their young largely or exclusively on fish, but the adults themselves have more varied diets, often including large numbers of crustaceans or other invertebrates. One experimental study in which common tern chicks were raised in captivity suggested that they could not thrive on a diet composed entirely of crustaceans – either because crustaceans contain too much salt or because they lack some nutrient that is essential for growth.[31]

Most of the fish taken by British and Irish terns belong to three families:

Ammodytidae (sandeels). There are five species of sandeel in British and Irish marine waters. The commonest species is the lesser sandeel, a thin and elongated fish with a pointed jaw, reaching a maximum length of 25 cm (Figs 24 and 28). It is a major target species of industrial fishing, particularly in the North Sea, for animal feed, for fertiliser, and in some instances as fuel for Danish power stations. It forms a lipid-rich, high-energy food. The very similar small sandeel is the second most abundant sandeel in our waters and can reach a length of up to 20 cm. The greater sandeel can reach 32 cm in length. These three common species of sandeels are difficult to distinguish from each other, and most studies of tern diets treat them together as a single food category.

FIG 28. Common tern carrying a sandeel – and also a long string of bootlace weed, picked up while diving. Lady's Island Lake, Co. Wexford. (Dave Daly)

Sandeels are named from their habit of burrowing into sand when resting or threatened, but form large shoals that swim in open waters and often come near the surface to feed or spawn, or when pursued by predatory fish from below. Terns generally feed on '1-group' sandeels (one-year-old fish ranging in length from about 6 to 14 cm and weighing 1–10 g), whereas the industrial fisheries take older and larger fish. Hence the fisheries affect the birds indirectly, by reducing the spawning stocks which generate fish for the terns in the next year.

Clupeidae (herrings). British and Irish terns feed commonly on two species in the herring family. The European sprat (Fig. 29), common in our coastal waters, often enters estuaries as it tolerates low levels of salinity (down to levels of 4 parts per thousand, compared to 35 in the open sea). The Atlantic herring (Fig. 30) was formerly also an important food for terns, especially in the North Sea, but has been overfished and is nowadays much less frequent in tern diets. As with sandeels, commercial fisheries generally take older and larger fish than those sought by terns, so their effect on the terns is indirect.

Gadidae (cods). British and Irish terns fairly frequently feed on saithe and sporadically on whiting (Fig. 31), pollack and rocklings, of which the fivebeard

FIG 29. Common tern carrying a sprat. Sprats are the most energy-rich of the fish commonly caught by terns in Britain and Ireland. Lady's Island Lake, Co. Wexford. (Dave Daly)

FIG 30. Common tern carrying an Atlantic herring. Lady's Island Lake, Co. Wexford. (Dave Daly)

FIG 31. Common tern carrying a juvenile whiting. Fish in the cod family are difficult to identify when small enough to be caught by terns, but whiting are usually less frequent than saithe in diets of British and Irish terns. Lady's Island Lake, Co. Wexford. (Dave Daly)

rockling is the species most often identified in tern diets. All four species are taken by commercial fishermen when they are full-sized, but terns take only juvenile fish, typically when one year old. Saithe and pollack are long-lived, growing to lengths of 50–100 cm and weights of 5–10 kg, much too large for terns to catch. Whiting and rocklings are shorter-lived and smaller, growing to lengths of only 20–30 cm and weights of around 1 kg. All four are demersal (bottom-feeding) fish frequenting cold waters, but the juveniles come close inshore in shallow waters during the summer months. They are yellowish or greenish in colour, in contrast to sandeels, sprats and herrings, which are silvery. The cod family also includes Atlantic cod and several species of hake, but these are very infrequent in the diets of British and Irish terns. Our terns feed preferentially on sprats and sandeels, and usually take saithe and other species of fish only when sprats and sandeels are unavailable (see Tables 18 and 19 in Chapter 8, and Table 24 in Chapter 10).

Common terns are the only British and Irish tern that feeds extensively in fresh waters: their diets there have not been reported, but in other parts of Europe they feed on a wide variety of fish (Fig. 32). Besides fish, British and Irish terns sometimes feed on invertebrates (see Fig. 46 in Chapter 3), especially crustaceans (shrimps, prawns, crab larvae, amphipods and euphausiids) and insects (ants, beetles, moths, mayflies, midges, etc.) and sometimes marine worms. Common and Arctic terns are the two species most prone to feed on invertebrates.

Worldwide, terns feed on a much wider range of prey. Many tropical terns, and temperate terns that winter in the tropics, commonly feed on various species of anchovies and sardines, as well as an enormous variety of other fish. Other terns frequently feed on squid and sometimes on marine molluscs (pteropods). Gull-billed terns feed on a variety of terrestrial prey including lizards, frogs, insects, small birds and small mammals. The 'marsh' terns feed on a wide variety of insects, sometimes on earthworms or spiders. The only common denominator is that terns almost always take live prey that are small enough for them to swallow whole.

Energy contents of tern diets

The energy content of prey items is a critical factor influencing the choice of prey by terns, especially during the chick-rearing period when the chicks require high energy input for growth. For example, the energy requirement of a common tern chick increases to 200–250 kJ per day as it grows towards full size;[32] the parents not only have to supply this amount of energy every day to

FIG 32. Common tern carrying a freshwater fish, probably a mosquito fish. (John N. Murphy)

each chick in the brood, but have to increase their own daily intake from about 350 kJ to about 450 kJ to meet the additional demands of flying for many hours to catch and bring fish to the colony.[33] Accordingly, they have become adapted through natural selection to select high-energy foods and bring them to the chicks at the highest possible rate.

Table 4 summarises data on the relationships between length, weight and energy content of three of the most important fish species in the diets of British and Irish terns. These data were based on fish caught around the Scottish coasts in 1976–88, including samples of each species brought by guillemots and puffins to feed their chicks on the Isle of May, Fife. Within these samples, the sprat was the most energy-rich species: under normal circumstances a sprat 9 cm long contained about 45 kJ of energy and one 13 cm long (about the maximum size that a common or roseate tern can carry) about 180 kJ. In contrast, lesser sandeels of the same length contained about 15 and 50 kJ, respectively.[34]

TABLE 4. Weights and energy contents of three fish species commonly taken by British and Irish terns.

| LENGTH (cm) | Lesser sandeel | | Sprat | | Saithe/whiting | |
	WEIGHT (g)	ENERGY CONTENT (kJ)	WEIGHT (g)	ENERGY CONTENT (kJ)	WEIGHT (g)	ENERGY CONTENT (kJ)
5	0.4	2	0.6	5	1.0	4
7	1.3	6	2.2	17	2.8	10
9	2.6	15	5.8	45	5.2	20
11	4.4	30	11	100	10	40
13	7.4	50	21	180	16	60
15	13	90	36	320	24	100
17	17	130			38	160
19	24	190				
24	34	270				

The values given are representative of fish collected in June–August, but there is considerable variation in weight and energy content among individual fish and by season, location and year (see text). For reference, typical and maximum weights of fish fed to chicks by the British and Irish species are as follows: little tern, 0.8 and 4 g; Arctic tern, 2 and 12 g; roseate tern, 3 and 15 g; common tern, 2.5 and 16 g; Sandwich tern, 6 and 30 g.

Source: recalculated from tables and regression equations in Hislop et al., 1991.

Unfortunately, there was considerable variation in these relationships, both among fish of the same species collected at the same time and between samples collected at different times. The calorific value of fish (kilojoules per gram) varies with seasonal cycles of reproduction and feeding. For example, the average energy content of sandeels of a given length was twice as high in June as in April, although the seasonal changes were smaller in the other fish species. More important, the calorific value of fish depends on how well the fish themselves are nourished, and this can vary markedly from place to place and from year to year, depending on the abundance of the zooplankton on which the fish feed. In recent years populations of copepods in northern waters have declined and the condition of the fish that feed on them has declined markedly. By 2004 the calorific values of sandeels and sprats brought in by birds to the Isle of May had declined to only about one-quarter of those measured in 1976–88, and guillemots had very low breeding success.[35] At the same time (1997–2008) Arctic terns at the Isle of May suffered almost complete reproductive failure for several years (see Table 29 in Chapter 11).[36]

ECOLOGICAL NICHES

There is a well-respected ecological principle that species cannot coexist if they have the same ecological *niche* – that is, if they overlap in range and habitat and depend on the same resources. If species did overlap in this way, they would eventually compete with each other, and either one species would be eliminated or the two species would diverge so that they did not compete, either relying on different resources or exploiting the same resources in different ways. 'Resources' is a slightly vague term which usually means different types of food, but it can be expanded to include energy, nutrients, or different ways of using space and time.

At first sight, British and Irish terns seem to contradict this principle. They all feed on the same species of fish; they take fish of the same age-classes and more or less the same sizes; and they feed in the same sort of places, often in mixed flocks. Furthermore, they happily coexist in mixed colonies and four of the five species winter in the same parts of West Africa, where again they seem to feed on the same range of fish species in the same places, often in mixed flocks.

On closer examination, small but consistent differences can be found among the five species in the ways in which they exploit the fish populations around their colonies. On average, Sandwich terns take larger fish and little terns take smaller fish than the three medium-sized species. Sandwich and roseate terns feed further away from their colonies and dive deeper than common or Arctic terns, while little terns often nest apart from the other four species and feed close to their breeding sites. Sandwich and roseate terns are very similar in their diets and feeding behaviour, but they breed together at only two sites in Britain and Ireland: Lady's Island Lake and Coquet Island. At Lady's Island Lake, Sandwich terns commence breeding about one month earlier than roseate terns, so that their fledglings are dispersing away from the breeding colony at the time when roseate terns need the most fish to feed their chicks. Also, the two species have rarely been observed using the same feeding areas.[37] Arctic and common terns are also very similar in their diets and feeding behaviour, and they nest together at many sites. Although the two species sometimes feed together in mixed flocks, commons usually feed close inshore while Arctics feed more at sea. At least in the Northern Isles, Arctic terns were much more dependent on sandeels than common terns: during a protracted shortage of sandeels, Arctic terns continued to bring very small sandeels to their chicks whereas common terns were able to switch to feeding mainly on saithe.[38] Thus, when a critical resource became scarce, the two species diverged in their ways of exploiting it.

It is therefore possible to accommodate these five species of terns into the niche principle by broadening it: species can coexist even if their niches overlap for most of the time, but they diverge at times and places when critical resources become limiting for one or both species. According to this modification of the principle, even species that appear very similar in their ecological requirements will prove to be differentiated if sufficiently studied in enough places at enough times. However, cases like this provide ammunition for critics of the niche principle. These critics argue that that the principle asserts that species do not overlap in their use of critical resources at critical times, but that there is no way to define what these critical resources and times are except by studying the species until differences are found. Hence, the critics claim, the niche principle is a tautology and explains nothing. Defenders of the principle do not contest the fact that 'resources' are difficult to define, but nevertheless argue that the 'niche' is a useful way to summarise all the ecological factors that are important for each species. For example, it can be said that the 'niches' of common and Arctic terns largely overlap, but only the former includes juvenile saithe in shallow inshore waters, whereas only the latter includes sandeels in deeper offshore waters. This long-running conceptual dispute has consumed much of the time and energy of academic ecologists.

CHAPTER 3

Breeding Biology

CHARACTERISTICS OF TERN BREEDING BIOLOGY

OST TERNS NEST ON THE GROUND without building elaborate nests, typically making 'scrapes' or shallow depressions in loose sand or gravel and depositing eggs directly onto the substrate. The main exceptions are the 'marsh' terns and Trudeau's tern, which usually construct floating platforms in flooded marshes. Forster's terns often nest on mats of floating vegetation, but apparently do not construct floating platforms themselves. Forster's, common and gull-billed terns often nest in saltmarshes, where they sometimes nest on top of mats of tide-wrack elevated above the surface of the marsh.[1] At breeding sites in the tropics, roseate terns occasionally nest on low bushy vegetation, but those that do so rely on finding flattened patches of vegetation that will support their eggs without having to build a substantial nest first. The noddies and the white tern nest in trees or on cliff ledges, but these species are now thought to be only distantly related to the 'true terns' (see Chapter 1).

Most terns nest in open habitats where they have clear views around them and can fly up freely if they see danger approaching. However, roseate terns breeding in the temperate zones usually nest under cover of rocks or vegetation, sometimes deep under rocks or in burrows of rabbits or puffins; a few nest on cliffs in the Azores. Tropical roseate terns sometimes nest in rock crevices, but more frequently they nest in the open without any surrounding cover. Bridled and grey-backed terns usually nest in crevices in coral or rock piles, and Inca terns nest in crevices, burrows or small caves in cliffs. Sooty terns nest under cover of vegetation at some breeding sites, although at most sites they nest in the open among scattered vegetation.[2] A unique nesting habitat for terns is at Aride Island in the Seychelles, where both roseate and sooty terns nest on the ground in open woodland with a canopy 4–20 m high.[3]

Birds that nest on the ground are at risk from terrestrial predators such as mammals and snakes. Most terns nest on islands or other places where they are relatively safe from these predators, but this broad characterisation includes a very wide variety of sites. The pelagic terns (sooty, bridled and grey-backed terns) and some of the southern hemisphere terns (Antarctic and Kerguelen terns) usually nest on oceanic islands hundreds or thousands of kilometres from mainland areas. Many tern species nest on inshore islands or islands in lakes or rivers, while the 'marsh' terns, Trudeau's and Forster's terns nest in the interior of marshes where they are surrounded by water. Some temperate terns, such as gull-billed, common and Forster's terns, often nest in saltmarshes, where they are surrounded by water at high tides and are protected by creeks and marsh vegetation at low tides. Black-fronted terns nest on gravel among braided rivers flowing out from glaciers in New Zealand. Arctic terns are distributed throughout the tundra regions of North America and Eurasia, where they nest on islands if these are available, but otherwise often nest on barrier beaches, glacial moraines, bogs or grassy meadows. The main exception to the generalisation that terns prefer to nest on islands is the 'little' tern group. Little, least, yellow-billed and fairy terns often nest on islands in rivers or along the coast, but in many areas they seem to prefer barrier beaches, sandbars or spits attached to the mainland, even in places where islands are available nearby and are used by other tern species. Damara and Peruvian terns often nest on barren desert plains or salt pans up to 3 km from the sea, apparently avoiding ocean beaches where they are at greater risk from predators.[4]

In developed countries, many sites formerly used for nesting by terns have become unsuitable for them because of human activities, including settlement and development of beach and island sites, recreational use of beaches and islands, connection of islands to the mainland by bridges and causeways, introduction of alien predators, drainage of freshwater marshes and saltmarshes, and management of rivers and lakes to raise water levels or to eliminate seasonal floods that in natural conditions would generate new sandbars and islands. Although many important nesting sites have been lost, terns have often proved resilient and versatile, and they now breed on many man-made sites. These include artificial islands created by deposition of dredged materials, gravel pits, industrial wastes, mine tailings, new land created at seaports and airports, dykes in salt works, bridge abutments, breakwaters, navigation markers and even rooftops.[5] Little terns sometimes nest on gravel roofs of flat-topped buildings, and in the southern USA breeding least terns are nowadays largely confined to rooftop sites because their natural beach sites are all used for human recreation. Common terns readily colonise platforms and floating rafts that are constructed and set out for them, and over much of continental Europe they nest primarily on rafts because almost all natural sites in rivers and lakes have been destroyed. Common terns sometimes nest on roofs and have even been recorded nesting on a traffic roundabout and between rails in use by small locomotives.[6] Roseate terns nest on roofs at several sites in the southern USA.[7]

Colonial nesting

Terns usually nest in colonies that may include hundreds, thousands, tens of thousands or even hundreds of thousands of pairs. The sooty tern is the most abundant tropical seabird, with several colonies of more than one million pairs on remote islands in the Pacific and Indian Oceans.[8] The 'crested' tern species often nest in colonies of thousands or tens of thousands of pairs. Colony size generally reflects the total population size in the region and the number of suitable sites for breeding, but some species seem to be aggregated much more within their ranges than others. At one extreme, more than 90 per cent of the

FIG 33. Nesting colony of elegant terns. All the 'crested' terns nest at high densities, but the elegant tern is probably the most closely packed of all. California, USA. (Charles T. Collins)

total world population of the elegant tern (about 25,000 pairs) nest on one island in western Mexico. At the other extreme, the Peruvian, Damara, fairy, Indian river and Kerguelen terns nest in small, widely dispersed groups that rarely exceed 20 pairs. The black-bellied tern is thought to be primarily a solitary breeder, with nests separated by 1 km or more, although it often nests in association with other species such as the Indian river tern and Indian skimmer.[9]

The species that aggregate into the largest colonies also seem to nest more densely: nests of the 'crested' terns are often established only 30–50 cm apart, barely beyond the range at which one sitting bird can peck the next (Fig. 33). They are sometimes crowded so closely that their distribution approaches perfect hexagonal packing, the tightest packing that is mathematically possible.[10] In contrast, nests of the species that form the smallest groups are often tens or even hundreds of metres apart. The Peruvian and Damara terns nest in 'colonies' with densities sometimes as low as one pair per square kilometre.[11] The common tern is especially variable in its settlement patterns, with some colonies in Europe and North America containing hundreds or thousands of pairs at densities greater than one nest per square metre, while on Bermuda, for example, they are scattered in single pairs on small islets, often with several kilometres between adjacent nests.[12]

Breeding seasons

Most terns nest seasonally, being present at breeding colonies for 3–5 months but spending more than half the year elsewhere. In the north temperate zone, most terns breed on very similar schedules, with eggs from early May to mid-June and chicks in June and July; they leave the breeding sites from mid-July to mid-August and disperse from late July to September while the adults moult and continue to feed juveniles, before migrating south in August–October.[13] This breeding schedule is earlier than climatic summer, so that the terns have largely finished raising young by the time air temperatures reach their maxima in July, and have left the breeding sites by the time sea-surface temperatures reach their maxima in August–September. North temperate terns that winter in the tropics or south of the Equator arrive in their breeding areas in April or early May and encounter air and water temperatures much lower than any they experience during the rest of the year. In some cases they seem to arrive before fish become readily available inshore – or even, in the case of terns breeding on northern lakes, before ice has fully broken up. Nevertheless, the birds that breed earliest in the season consistently raise more young than later breeders.[14] The advantages gained by the birds that breed early have not been fully elucidated, but appear to include feeding their chicks in June and early July when the days are longest for foraging, and bringing their chicks to fledging at times when fish are most abundant and available, and when the juveniles have plenty of time to learn how to fish before migrating south. A more subtle advantage is that the earliest-nesting pairs always have the oldest and largest chicks, and these are often able to steal food from the smaller chicks in neighbouring broods.[15]

The most northerly breeding terns – common and Caspian terns on subarctic lakes and Arctic terns throughout arctic regions of North America and Eurasia – cannot start to breed until after ice breakup and consequently have a schedule a month or more later than other north temperate terns: eggs in late June and July, chicks in late July and August. These terns have a much shorter post-breeding period before they have to migrate south, and their young have to learn to fish in a short period after fledging. It is not known how they achieve this, given that fledglings of temperate terns of the same species seem to require weeks or months of practice before they become independent. In several tern species, family parties sometimes remain together during migration and the parents continue to feed the juveniles after arriving in the winter quarters: this has been reported for Sandwich, roseate and Caspian terns.[16] It is not known whether Arctic terns do the same, but if they do it would have to be at sea.

In the south temperate zone, many terns breed in spring and early summer in the same seasonal pattern as north temperate terns, except that in the southern hemisphere these seasons run from October or November to January or February. However, this spring–summer nesting pattern is less consistent in the southern hemisphere, and several tern species there nest in autumn or winter. The roseate tern breeds in June–September (winter) in South Africa. The Antarctic tern breeds in November–January (spring–summer) at some sites, but its breeding season extends into March (autumn) at Heard Island in the southern Indian Ocean and at the Antipodes and Snares Islands south of New Zealand.[17] In Western Australia, roseate and crested terns have two discrete breeding seasons, in September–November (spring) and March–April (autumn); these are thought to involve two different populations of each species that nest on the same islands at opposite seasons, probably without interchanging and perhaps even without meeting.[18]

In the tropics, tern breeding seasons are much more variable and seem to depend more on oceanographic conditions than on climatic cycles. Several species that breed at both north temperate and tropical latitudes conform to the same north temperate cycle (breeding in April–August) throughout the northern tropics and even south of the Equator in some tropical areas. One example is the roseate tern, which breeds in May–July in the Indian Ocean south at least to the Seychelles and Kenya (4° S) and even in Madagascar (19–24° S), although its breeding season in Tanzania (7° S) extends into October. Common, Cabot's and least terns breed in May–July from temperate North America south at least to Aruba and Curaçao in the southern Caribbean (11° N), and the Cabot's tern maintains this schedule south to French Guiana (5° N). A third example is the little tern, which breeds in April–August not only in Europe and Asia but also as far south as West Africa (0–9° N) and northern Australia (11–16° S). At least one southern hemisphere species shows the opposite pattern: the yellow-billed tern breeds in November–December throughout South America, extending north with the same breeding schedule to Suriname (5° N).[19]

Terns that are primarily tropical in distribution have several seasonal patterns. Some breed seasonally but at opposite seasons in the northern and southern hemispheres: for example, the bridled tern breeds in May–July in the Caribbean and West Africa, June–August in East Africa, and October–December in Australia; the black-naped tern breeds in May in India and Polynesia but in September–November in tropical Australia; the crested tern breeds in May–August in Sudan and Somalia, in October–November in Kenya and Tanzania, in December–January in tropical Australia, and in November–January in southern Australia. Other tropical terns have two breeding seasons at the same localities (for example, lesser crested terns in Western Australia, Inca terns in Peru), or breed throughout the year with one or two seasonal peaks (Caspian, lesser crested, roseate and bridled terns in northern and eastern Australia).[20] The sooty tern probably has the most complex pattern, being strongly seasonal at some sites, breeding throughout the year at others, having two breeding seasons at others, and a cycle shorter than 1 year at others. Sooty terns breeding at Ascension Island in the South Atlantic appear to breed at 9–10-month intervals (i.e., breeding five times every 4 years), and those breeding at Michaelmas Key in northeastern Australia appear to breed at 8–9-month intervals.[21] The bridled tern has been reported to have an 8–9-month cycle at the Seychelles in the tropical Indian Ocean.[22]

Mating systems

Like other seabirds, all terns are monogamous, and successful breeding requires close coordination between mates throughout the season (Fig. 34). There is some differentiation of sex roles during breeding. In most species, males establish the nest territory and take the leading role in defending it, and males feed their mates during the period of egg formation and egg-laying. In most tern species for which this has been studied, males and females spend about the same amount of time incubating the eggs, but at least in common terns, females do most of the nocturnal incubation.[23] In some species, females spend more time

FIG 34. Pair of common terns feeding a chick. When the chicks are small, both parents have to be present at each feed to ward off attempts by neighbours to steal food as it is transferred to the chick. Here the female is brooding the remaining eggs while the male offers a fish to the chick. The chick has to learn to take the fish by the head and to swallow it head-first. Gormanstown, Co. Meath. (John Fox)

than their mates tending the chicks during the first few days of life, while males bring most of the food to the chicks in the early days. Once the chicks are old enough to be left alone, males and females play similar roles in chick feeding, but recent evidence indicates that males may perform most of the care of the juveniles after fledging, at least in common terns.[24]

Terns are long-lived birds, and many breed five, ten, or even twenty times during their lifetimes. In all tern species that have been studied, birds frequently retain the same mates from year to year, and some pairs remain together for many years. A typical pattern is for terns to change mates after the first breeding attempt, especially if this is unsuccessful; they are less likely to change mates as they get older, and the mates are usually retained after the third or fourth breeding attempt. Of course, pair bonds are often broken by death, and the surviving partner then has to find a new mate: several studies have suggested that they then usually find a new mate of about the same age. However, 'divorce' – taking a new mate when the previous mate is still alive – is not infrequent even among older birds. One study of common terns suggested that this sometimes happens when one member of the pair returns to the colony later than the other in spring: the mate is willing to wait for its partner to return for about five days, but then starts looking for a replacement and keeps its new mate even if its partner then returns.[25]

Although monogamy is the norm in human societies and is therefore familiar to human observers, it is actually rare in animals other than birds. It requires a complicated set of social 'transactions' to induce each member of the pair to play its role faithfully throughout the breeding cycle, and it is difficult for either partner to prevent 'cheating' by its mate, whether 'cheating' is manifested as working less hard than it should or as sexual promiscuity. Many recent studies of birds have revealed that the outward appearance of harmonious cooperation and social fidelity actually conceals a pattern of cheating and covert sexual promiscuity.[26] In many landbird species, both males and females frequently seek 'extra-pair copulations', and broods of chicks found in the same nest often have more than one genetic father; in some cases, they may have more than one genetic mother, if females deposit eggs in each other's nests. Genetic promiscuity appears to be much less frequent in seabirds, although it has been recorded in several seabird species.[27] A few studies of terns have suggested that males avidly seek extra-pair copulations and that females sometimes accept them, but actual cases in which chicks have been shown to be sired by males other than the social partner are rare.

Some populations of terns have an unbalanced sex-ratio, with more females than males: this probably results from higher mortality rates in males, perhaps because they work harder than females at some stages in the breeding cycle or because they are exposed to causes of mortality that affect females less. In some cases, the females that cannot get male mates remain unmated, sometimes for several years; in other cases, they pair together and make nests into which both lay eggs, often resulting in clutches double the usual size. The eggs laid by females paired to other females are often fertilised by nearby males who are not part of the social group and may be breeding successfully with other females. Consequently, some of the eggs hatch and a few chicks are raised by females who would otherwise not raise any chicks at all.

Hybridisation

On rare occasions, a tern that is unable to find a mate of its own species will mate with a tern of another species and raise hybrid young. This has been recorded most frequently at the edge of a species' range, where one or a few individuals of that species occur among much larger numbers of another species. Hybridisation has been recorded most frequently between roseate and common terns (see Chapter 9),[28] but cases have also been reported involving roseate × Arctic, roseate × Forster's, Arctic × common, lesser crested × Sandwich,

Cabot's × elegant, fairy × little, and white-winged × black terns.[29] In many of these cases, hybrid young were raised and these proved to be fertile themselves, mating with one or other of the parental species and producing second- and third-generation back-crosses (see Chapter 12 for an account of interbreeding between lesser crested and Sandwich terns).

Mate selection and courtship displays

Terns are amongst the most aerial of seabirds (matched only by gadfly petrels, frigatebirds and tropicbirds), and they perform many of their courtship displays in the air. Most terns have two types of aerial display. The *low flight* (Fig. 35) is thought to be an early stage in mate selection, in which a male advertises his unmated status and his ability to bring fish to the colony, while females compete for his attention. The *high flight* (Fig. 36) seems to be a later stage in mate selection, in which a male and a female in a tentative relationship test each other's flying ability and/or commitment to the relationship.[30]

FIG 35. Common terns performing the *low flight* aerial display. A male flies low over the colony, often carrying a fish, while several other birds (usually females) pursue it, calling loudly and jostling for position close to it. In this case, two females have moved ahead of the male while others follow. Plymouth, USA. (Eduardo del Solar)

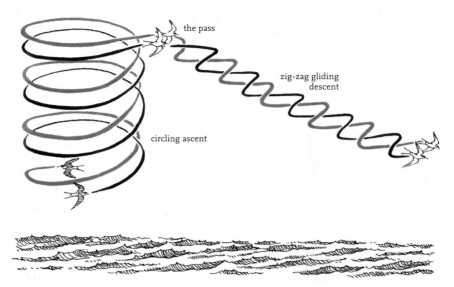

the pass

zig-zag gliding
descent

circling ascent

FIG 36. *High flight* aerial display. This display has three parts: a rapid ascent in which the two birds circle upwards; the *pass*, in which one bird passes closely above the other; and a gliding descent in which the birds sway from side to side so that their paths repeatedly cross. (Drawing by R. Gillmor)

The *high flight* is the most characteristic and stereotyped part of the courtship behaviour of terns and is performed with minor variations by all species.[31] It begins when one bird that is already in the air starts to ascend rapidly, with deep and sometimes jerky wing-beats; a second bird flying nearby starts to follow it, and sometimes others join in the pursuit. The birds fly upwards in wide circles so that their paths form intersecting helices, typically 20–50 m in diameter. At the top of the ascent, the lead bird sets its wings and starts to glide downwards. The key event in the *high flight* is the *pass*, in which the second bird (usually a female) overtakes the lead bird (usually a male) and passes just above it (Fig. 37). The two birds then glide down together, swaying from side to side so that their paths repeatedly cross.

The *pass* is the closest approach that prospective mates make to each other with their wings spread. The terns' flight feathers are reflective in the ultraviolet when freshly moulted[32] and birds can see ultraviolet light, so terns in good condition must be perceived as flashing with bright colours at this point, allowing each bird to judge the condition of the other. It is important for each bird to select a high-quality mate, and the *high flight* and the *pass* enable each

FIG 37. Pair of common terns performing the *pass*. This takes place at the top of a *high flight*, after two birds reach the highest point of their aerial ascent and start to glide down together. The lower bird in this photograph is a male in the *aerial bent* posture, with the neck extended and the head bent downwards. The upper bird is a female in the *straight* posture, with the neck extended and the head twisted away from the male so that her black cap is turned away from him. After the female passes low over the male, the two birds glide down together, swaying from side to side, with the female slightly ahead but following the direction of the male's movements, so that the male 'leads from behind'. Plymouth, USA. (Jim Fenton)

bird to select a high-quality mate, and the *high flight* and the *pass* enable each bird to assess the value of the other, simultaneously judging its availability, sexual interest, flying ability, commitment and performance in coordinated activity – much like the functions of dancing in human courtship. And the terns' aerial courtship, like dancing in humans, is not only functional but enjoyable and beautiful to watch.

FIG 38. Common tern in the *bent* posture. The displaying bird (right) bends its head forward, droops and partly spreads its wings and raises its tail. This photograph shows the extreme form of the posture: the degree to which the neck is bent and the wings are spread reflects the bird's motivation. The *bent* posture is assertive or aggressive when the black cap is directed towards the other bird, as it is here. When a bird adopts the *bent* posture in the presence of its mate, the black cap is usually directed to one side. Grand Canal Dock, Dublin. (John Fox)

FIG 39. Arctic tern in the *erect* posture. This is an appeasement display which signals lack of aggression and serves to inhibit aggression by another bird nearby. The neck and bill are stretched up and the neck is twisted so that the other bird cannot see the black cap. Seaforth, Merseyside. (Steve Young)

The courtship displays of terns on the ground are more varied. Both males and females have two main display postures: *bent*, in which the head is bent forward and the black cap is displayed (Fig. 38), and *erect*, in which the neck is stretched up and the head is twisted away from the accompanying bird, so that the black cap is concealed from it (Fig. 39).[33] The *aerial bent* and *straight* postures in the *high flight* correspond to the *bent* and *erect* postures in ground displays, modified only by the constraints of flight. *Bent* is an assertive or aggressive posture: it is directed aggressively towards intruders to present the black cap (Fig. 38), but it is directed to one side in the presence of the mate, who can see the assertiveness of the displaying bird without being threatened by the black cap. *Erect* is an appeasement posture, which functions to switch off aggression in

FIG 40. Common terns performing the *parade*. These birds are both in extreme forms of the *erect* posture, with wings widely spread; the rear bird is twisting its neck away from its mate. Plymouth, USA. (Eduardo del Solar)

FIG 41. Common tern pair in the *erect* posture, which serves to switch off any tension resulting from being too close to each other. Grand Canal Dock, Dublin. (John Fox)

the accompanying bird – conveying the message 'please let me near you,' or 'I did not mean to crowd you.' The wings are usually drooped and partly spread, and the tail is raised.

In early stages of ground courtship, the male is most often in the *bent* posture and the female in the *erect* posture. The birds are attracted to each other, but initially retain some of the defensive aggression they feel towards any other bird that approaches too closely. The prospective mates often walk around each other in circles like clockwork toys in a display called the *parade,* attracted to each other but cautious about getting too close (Fig. 40). Sometimes the male will interrupt courtship and peck the female, who either flies away or goes immediately into the *erect* posture, which often stops the male's attack.[34] The aggression that the birds retain towards each other is gradually switched off as they display to each other day by day, until they can tolerate each other's close approach and function harmoniously as a pair. Then, when one bird flies in and lands close to the other, they both adopt the *erect* posture briefly as a signal of acceptance (Fig. 41). The mates rarely touch each other, however, except when copulating, or sometimes during incubation when one bird pushes its mate off the eggs to take its place.

Courtship-feeding

All tern species practise *courtship-feeding*, in which the male feeds the female during the periods of courtship, mate selection and egg-laying. Early in the courtship period, males carry fish back to the colony and use them prominently in the aerial displays (Fig. 35): this seems to advertise their proficiency in catching fish and their availability as mates. Later in the mate selection period, males carry fish in displays with potential mates on the ground and use them to attract females into their territories. At first the males are very reluctant to part with their fish (they know that they will lose most of their attractiveness when they do so), but as pairs become established the males start to feed the females. These intermediate stages in pair formation can be very entertaining to watch, as the male tries to approach and mount the female without giving up his fish, while the female tries to get the fish without allowing the male to get too close. As soon as the pair is fully established, however, the male starts to feed the female on a regular basis with little or no accompanying display (Fig. 42).

FIG 42. Common terns courtship-feeding. The male (right) is feeding the female (left). Two fish are shown in this picture and the photographer did not record what happened: it seems likely that the male brought two fish and that the female was still holding the first when the male offered her the second. Bird Island, USA. (Craig Gibson)

This continues during a period of up to three weeks while the female is storing materials in her body to form eggs, and continues through the egg-laying period, ceasing abruptly as soon as the last egg is laid. For the last few days before the first egg is laid and during the period of egg-laying, female terns stay near the nest and catch little or no fish for themselves, relying entirely on the males. Thus, the function of courtship-feeding evolves gradually from advertising the male's proficiency, through attracting a mate, establishing and cementing a relationship, to provisioning the female and providing the nutrition required for making the eggs.[35]

Eggs and clutches

Most tropical terns lay only one egg, but temperate terns usually lay clutches of two or three eggs, while subtropical terns usually lay either one or two eggs. Within that broad generalisation, there is substantial variability. In the tropics, all the oceanic terns (sooty, bridled and grey-backed terns, plus the noddies and the white tern) lay single-egg clutches, but the terns that breed on rivers (Indian river, large-billed, black-bellied and yellow-billed) lay two, three or occasionally four eggs. Thus, clutch-size in the tropics appears to be primarily related to habitat – one egg for species that forage at sea but two to four for species that forage in fresh waters. In the north temperate zone, there is some evidence that terns nesting on fresh waters lay larger clutches than birds of the same species nesting along the coast – for example, least terns in North America, Sandwich terns in Europe – but the differences are much smaller than those in the tropics and are difficult to discern among other sources of variability.[36]

At many locations at high latitudes (north of 40° N or south of 40° S), the most frequent clutch-size is three for several species (gull-billed, Caspian, common, white-winged and black terns: Fig. 43); the 'marsh' terns not infrequently lay clutches of four eggs.[37] However, the same species often lay clutches of two eggs or even one egg at other locations at the same latitudes. For the other British and Irish terns (little, Sandwich, Arctic and roseate), the most frequent clutch-size is two, but the first three of these species often lay three eggs and all sometimes lay only one (Figs 44 and 45). Among roseate terns, average clutch-size increases with latitude, from around 1.2 eggs at sites near the Equator to about 1.8 eggs at the highest latitudes (Britain and Ireland at 52–56° N).[38] There is some evidence for similar trends in Caspian terns, little terns and perhaps other species, but again the differences are small and difficult to discern among other sources of variability, and there are several examples of differences in the opposite direction. For example, common terns at Bermuda, one of the most southerly breeding sites of the species at 32° N,

FIG 43. Clutch of three eggs laid by a common tern. The most frequent clutch-size of common terns is three eggs, but at some sites and in some years two-egg clutches are more frequent and single-egg clutches are not uncommon, especially late in the season. Bird Island, USA. (John Fuller).

FIGS 44, 45. Clutches of one and two eggs laid by Sandwich terns. In all British and Irish terns except the common tern, the most frequent clutch-size is two eggs, but many pairs lay single-egg clutches, especially late in the season. Many Sandwich, Arctic and little terns lay clutches of three eggs, but roseate terns rarely do so and most clutches of three or four roseate tern eggs result from two females laying in the same nest. Lady's Island Lake, Co. Wexford. (Dave Daly)

consistently lay clutches of three eggs (and occasionally four), whereas average clutch-sizes in the main breeding areas of the species in North America and Eurasia are usually in the range 2.0–2.9.[39] Within a species, younger birds tend to lay smaller clutches, especially during the first two or three years of breeding; average clutch-sizes usually decline towards the end of the breeding season; and in many species average clutch-sizes vary from site to site and from year to year. Some of these variations appear to be associated with variations in food availability or differences in proficiency among individual birds, but it has proved difficult to account for them all.

Seabirds generally lay large eggs relative to their body sizes, and tern eggs are somewhat larger than average even for seabirds. Among terns that lay single-egg clutches, egg weight as a percentage of body weight ranges from about 14 per cent in elegant terns to 21 per cent in grey-backed terns and 23 per cent in black noddies.[40] Among terns that regularly lay clutches of three eggs, the weight of single eggs as a percentage of body weight ranges from about 10 per cent in Caspian terns to about 17 per cent in common terns and 18 per cent in little and least terns.[41] In the last three species, the weight of three-egg clutches often exceeds 50 per cent of the weight of the female, and even as high as 60 per cent in some individual little and common terns.[42] Female terns accumulate most of the material required for producing the clutch during the 2–3 weeks prior to egg-laying, and immediately before laying the first egg they may weigh more than 1.5 times their normal weight.[43] This is one of the reasons why they rely on the males to bring all their food at this period: they are simply too heavy and unmanoeuvrable to catch fish efficiently for themselves.[44] Thus terns are 'income' breeders, in contrast to many wildfowl, which build up their body reserves prior to arrival on the breeding grounds and are 'capital' breeders.

At the time of laying, the egg must contain all the materials required for the development of the embryo and for the survival of the chick in its first few days of life. These constituents include 'macronutrients' such as fat, protein and calcium that are basic requirements for metabolism and growth, 'micronutrients' such as trace elements required for key biochemical functions, hormones that control growth of the embryo and its behaviour after hatching, and immunoglobulins that protect the chick from infection until its own immune system develops. The egg must also contain enough water to sustain the embryo throughout growth and the chick from the time of hatching until it starts to receive water through its food. The eggshell provides mechanical strength during incubation and protects the embryo from external infections, but is porous enough to support the embryo's respiration by allowing oxygen in and carbon dioxide out.[45] The shell also serves as a source of calcium for bone development. At the time of laying, tern eggs typically contain about 10 per cent fat (all located in the yolk), 15 per cent protein (divided between the yolk and the white) and 75 per cent water (mostly in the white).[46] Although they taste somewhat fishy, tern eggs provide a highly nutritious food for humans and have been harvested by coastal peoples, probably for thousands of years. Harvesting of tern eggs is now prohibited or severely regulated in most developed countries, but it continues in many developing countries and is an important conservation problem in some areas.

Parental care

In a broad sense, parental care starts soon after the adults arrive in the breeding area in spring, when males start to establish and defend nesting territories, and birds of both sexes seek and select suitable mates. Good choices made at this time may determine the bird's breeding success for the entire season. Direct parental care starts when the eggs are laid and continues through the breeding season and for weeks or months after the chicks fledge. Successful breeding requires that each member of the pair plays its role consistently and effectively, and that each coordinates its activities closely and efficiently with those of the other. Performance of these tasks improves with experience as the birds get older, including experience with the same mate in previous years: studies have shown that pairs that remain together for several years breed more successfully than newly formed pairs, even after controlling for the effects of individual age and experience.[47]

In all terns, both members of the pair incubate the eggs and feed and guard the chicks (Fig. 46), although in most species females spend more time with the

FIG 46. Pair of common terns feeding one of two chicks. The female (left) has been brooding the chicks and the male (right) has brought a small shrimp. Tern eggs typically hatch about one day apart, so the chick that hatches first is larger than the second and usually remains so throughout the period of growth. Parents usually deliver food to the chick that arrives first and begs loudest, so the oldest chick gets the lion's share of the food. Plymouth, USA. (Jon Saperia)

eggs and chicks and males do more of the provisioning. The birds start to sit on the eggs as soon as they are laid, and within a day or two after the clutch is complete the eggs are covered virtually throughout the day and night. Incubation is usually thought of as functioning to warm the eggs, but for birds that nest on the ground under the tropical or subtropical sun it is almost as important to keep the eggs cool. The embryos die within a few hours if they are heated to above about 44 °C and within a few minutes if they are heated to above about 50 °C. When stressed by heat, incubating terns stand over the eggs, shading them without sitting on them, and 'pant' (fluttering their throats to cool themselves by evaporation). When more strongly heat-stressed, they will periodically leave the nest, fly out to the water and dip their feet and bellies to cool themselves, and then return to the eggs to wet them and cool them. This helps to achieve another function of incubation: to keep the eggs moist and to prevent them from losing too much water. Eggshells are porous, which allows oxygen in and carbon dioxide out to support the embryo's respiration, but this means that they lose water continuously during the incubation period, especially if the ambient air is dry. Terns cope with this by incorporating extra water into the egg at the time of its formation, and by maintaining the humidity in the nest high enough to prevent the eggs from dehydrating; their behaviour during incubation is nicely adjusted to achieve this.[48]

In contrast to their high sensitivity to overheating, tern embryos are usually resistant to cooling. Some temperate terns respond to nocturnal predation (e.g. by owls) by deserting the colony at night, so that the eggs cool down to ambient temperature, sometimes as low as 10 °C. The embryos can survive many hours at low temperatures, but this delays their development and lengthens the incubation period, sometimes by one-third or more.[49]

Compared to most seabirds, tern embryos and chicks develop very fast: for most species, incubation periods are in the range 18–29 days and fledging periods in the range 20–42 days. Both of these periods tend to be longer in the larger species, with the smallest values in the 'little' and 'marsh' tern groups (18–23 and 20–25 days, respectively) and the longest in the 'crested' and Caspian terns (25–29 and 36–42 days, respectively). The exceptions are the pelagic terns in the tropics (sooty and bridled terns, plus the noddies and the white tern), which are more like other seabirds in having slow development, with incubation periods in the range 28–40 days and fledging periods in the range 40–60 days.[50]

Tern chicks are *semi-precocial* – that is, they can stand and walk as soon as they hatch, but they cannot regulate their body temperature at first and rely on their parents for warmth and food. When they hatch, they are brooded and guarded for several days in the same way as the eggs were, mainly by the female, while the male brings most of the food (Figs 46 and 47). The chick has to learn how to take food, and for species that feed their young on fish this requires time and practice, because fish can only be swallowed head-first (most fish have fins or spines that project backwards); the parent has to hold the fish close to the head and the chick has to learn to take it close to the parent's bill (see Fig. 34, above).[51] This is the time when the chick is most vulnerable to having its fish stolen by neighbours, and both parents attend it closely to fend off robbers. As the chick grows older, it becomes more adept at taking the fish and swallowing it quickly, and at the same time it develops the ability to regulate its body temperature. At that time – typically about one-quarter of the way through chick-rearing – the chick can be left alone for much of the daytime, and both parents can feed it (Fig. 48). In the oceanic terns that regurgitate food, it is easier for the chick to take the partially digested meal, and fish that were swallowed head-first by the adult can be swallowed tail-first by the chick.

In tern species with clutches of two or three eggs, the eggs are usually laid two or three days apart. The first egg is partly incubated before the second and third are laid, so that they hatch at shorter intervals. The first chick typically hatches 12–36 hours earlier and has been fed by the time the second hatches,

FIG 47. Common tern brooding eggs while its one-day-old chick sits outside viewing the world. Tern chicks cannot regulate their body temperature until they are about five days old: they have to be brooded to keep warm when the outside temperature is low and to keep cool when it is too hot, but they venture out when the temperature is just right. Grand Canal Dock, Dublin. (John Fox)

FIG 48. Common tern feeding shrimp to a chick about seven days old. When the chicks are older than about five days, they can be left alone for part of the day and then both parents can bring food to them. Grand Canal Dock, Dublin. (John Fox)

while the second chick hatches earlier and is fed earlier than the third. This establishes a size hierarchy that is usually maintained throughout the chick-raising period, and there is intense competition for the food items brought by the parents: the oldest chick rushes to meet the parent ahead of the others and can often steal the fish from the younger chicks even if they are able to get it first. Parents usually give the fish to the chick that reaches them first and begs for it most vigorously, so the older chicks have a strong competitive advantage over the younger ones (Fig. 46). Unless food is superabundant, so that the second and third chicks can be fed while the first is satiated, the younger chicks fall further behind and often succumb to starvation.[52] It has been suggested that asynchronous hatching has been favoured by natural selection, the size hierarchy serving as a mechanism whereby food is channelled to the largest chick in times of scarcity, so that food is not wasted on chicks that are doomed to starve anyway.[53] The degree of asynchrony – that is, the intervals between hatching of successive eggs – is determined by the birds' behaviour at the time of laying, which varies among species and among individuals. It appears that this behaviour has been nicely adjusted by natural selection, so that the degree of asynchrony in hatching is neither too great (in which case the younger chicks would be too far behind the oldest to survive even at times when food was abundant) nor too small (in which case the oldest chick would suffer competition from its younger siblings at times when there was not enough food to raise more than one).[54]

In terns that feed their chicks fish or other food items one at a time, the chicks are usually fed many times a day – typically every hour or so, depending on the type and size of food. Terns that feed their chicks by regurgitation usually make longer foraging trips, so that each parent typically feeds the chick only once per day. Except for the 'marsh' terns, most tern chicks do not have access to water and do not drink until after they fledge, so that they have to get all the water they require through their food, and to excrete excess salt through their nasal glands. In hot, dry environments tern chicks may be water-stressed: parents cannot bring water for them to ingest, but brood or shade them and occasionally cool them by wetting them in the way they sometimes cool their eggs. This is often effective in cooling the chicks when they are small, but larger chicks sometimes succumb to heat stress and dehydration because they are too large to be shaded by the parents.[55]

The extent to which tern chicks wander away from the nest site varies widely among species. In the 'little' tern group of species, nests are often located on open sand or gravel with little or no cover and are widely spaced. Chicks start to move away from the nest site within a day or two after hatching and then scatter widely, moving hundreds of even thousands of metres during the days and weeks prior to fledging and finding cover in many different places.[56] Chicks of the 'crested' terns stay near the nest for a few days, but then join together with other chicks from the same colony to form dense packs known as *crèches*, where they remain until they fledge: the chicks are fed within the crèches, where they recognise their own parents by voice as they fly in with fish. Chicks of the 'marsh' terns have to stay on their floating nests until they can fly: they swim away if threatened, returning to the nest as soon as danger has passed. Chicks of the noddies and white tern have to stay in their tree nests until they fledge, and if they fall to the ground they usually starve because their parents do not find them.

In several other species, including common, Arctic and roseate terns, chicks usually remain close to the nest site from hatching to fledging; the nesting territory serves as a rendezvous and the parents routinely return there to feed the chicks, even after the chicks can fly. Most birds of these species maintain exclusive territories around their nests throughout the chick-raising period;

chicks that wander from their parents' territory into those of neighbours are attacked on sight and pecked unmercifully, occasionally being injured, killed or even carried away and dropped. The chicks soon learn to stay at home unless they are seriously threatened by a ground predator, in which case they scatter to find cover, returning furtively when danger has passed. One function of this aggressive behaviour towards neighbouring chicks is that they learn to avoid entering the owners' territories, and so are less likely to try to steal food from the owners' chicks as they grow older and bolder. Another function appears to be to minimise the risk of adopting unrelated offspring. It takes a few days after chicks hatch before their parents learn to recognise them, and during this period the parents are in danger of accepting alien chicks that they find in or near their nests. Adoption is fairly frequent in some colonies of common and little terns, and is discussed in more detail in Chapter 8.

Post-fledging care
Tern chicks usually fly as soon as their wings will support them (Fig. 49). Most tern fledglings are completely dependent on their parents for days or weeks

FIG 49. Fledgling Sandwich tern on one of its first flights. Tern chicks start to fly when their flight feathers are only about three-quarters grown, and they struggle to keep airborne on their short, rounded wings. They have to learn how to land and often crash at the end of their first few flights. It takes about 10 more days for the wings to grow to full length. Lady's Island Lake, Co. Wexford. (John N. Murphy)

FIG 50. Common tern feeding a juvenile several weeks after fledging. Young terns need many weeks of practice before they become proficient at diving for fish. In some tern species, juveniles migrate with their parents and are still fed by them after they reach the winter quarters. Cape Cod, USA. (John Van de Graaff)

after they first fly, because it takes them a long time to practise flying and to learn how to catch prey, especially for chicks of those species that feed mainly by plunge-diving. The parents continue to feed the fledglings during this period (Fig. 50), but take them away from the breeding sites as soon as they can fly strongly, eventually bringing them out to the fishing grounds so that they can be fed there without the parents having to commute backwards and forwards.[57] In some tern species, post-fledging care continues after the birds depart on long-distance dispersal or migration, in some cases for six months or more,[58] but little is known about this because it is so difficult to keep track of family groups that move over large distances.

Flooding and predation

Most terns nest near the water in open areas with little or no vegetation. In many parts of the world, this restricts them to nesting at very low elevations where vegetation growth is limited by shifting sand, overwash in storms or salt spray. Consequently, many tern nesting areas are liable to flooding by high tides or storms during the breeding season, and eggs and chicks are often washed away. The 'marsh' terns and other terns that nest in freshwater sites or saltmarshes are similarly liable to flooding as water levels fluctuate, although the floating nests of the 'marsh' terns often survive because they rise and fall with the water level.

Terns that nest on the ground in the open are also very vulnerable to predation. Those that nest on the mainland or on islands close to the mainland often lose eggs to mammalian predators such as foxes, rats or American mink, and often lose chicks to the same mammals or to bird predators such as kestrels, owls or herons. Terns that nest on islands further offshore are more secure from predation under natural conditions, but have proved extremely vulnerable when humans have introduced alien predators such as rats and cats. Tropical terns are vulnerable to predation by snakes, lizards and land crabs as well as by mammals and birds.[59]

Re-nesting

Terns that lose eggs and chicks to predation or flooding often re-nest in the same season and are sometimes able to raise young from second clutches. The 'little' terns seem to be adapted to especially high frequencies of predation and flooding, and they routinely lay two, three or even more clutches in the same season, sometimes shifting to alternative sites after their first or second choice proves unsuitable.[60] Re-nesting is more likely to occur when eggs are lost early in the season than when chicks are lost later.[61] Laying replacement clutches requires that the female 're-cycles' to ovulate again and then to amass enough nutrients to lay down the yolk, the white and the shell; it also requires that the male switches his behaviour from feeding chicks to feeding the female. Re-laying typically takes 10–15 days from the time the first clutch is lost to the laying of the first egg in the second clutch.[62] When an entire colony loses eggs simultaneously, the re-nesting is highly synchronous, with all the second clutches appearing within a few days. Human harvesters often take advantage of this by destroying all the clutches in a colony and returning 12–15 days later to gather the new crop of eggs, which will then all be fresh (even hungry people are often squeamish about eating partially incubated eggs with visible embryos). If the birds then progress to a third wave of nesting, this may be too late in the season to raise chicks successfully. Repeatedly producing replacement clutches must also be a physiological strain on the females (and on the males too, because they do most of the foraging), but there is little information on any consequences to them such as reduced survival.

On rare occasions, common terns lay a second clutch of eggs while still feeding a chick from the first clutch. This usually happens when the first brood has been reduced to one chick but food remains abundant, and it has been suggested that laying a second clutch functions as 'insurance' in case the chick is accidentally lost or taken by a predator. If the chick survives (as usually happens), the parents then face an irreconcilable conflict between incubating the second clutch and feeding the fledgling. This is usually resolved by deserting the second clutch.[63]

ADAPTATIONS, STRATEGIES AND DIVERGENCES AMONG TERN SPECIES

Lifestyles

Terns are generally thought of as seabirds, although about one-quarter of the tern species breed primarily in freshwater environments and several live exclusively on fresh waters throughout the year. True seabirds have a distinctive 'lifestyle', related to their need to breed on land but to feed at sea, often far from their breeding sites. This requires them to spend much of their time commuting, which limits the rate at which they can bring food to their chicks. Many seabirds therefore have low reproductive rates, typically with a clutch of only one egg, a long incubation period, slow chick growth and a long fledging period. The sea is a very safe place for seabirds, which usually face predation and other hazards only when they come to land to breed. Correspondingly, many of them are long-lived, mature slowly and do not start to breed until they are 4–10 years old. All these life-history characteristics of seabirds are interrelated and can be thought of as a 'slow' lifestyle – in contrast to the 'fast' lifestyle of most small landbirds, which breed at one year old, raise many chicks in each breeding attempt, often nest two or three times in each breeding season, and die young.[64]

Within this broad generalisation, there is much variability. Seabirds can be classified along a spectrum according to their life-history characteristics and the degree to which these conform to the 'slow' lifestyle. At the extreme 'slow' end of the spectrum are the wandering, royal and Amsterdam albatrosses, which live for 50 years or more, do not breed until they are 6–12 years old, lay a single egg and take two years to complete one breeding cycle. These albatrosses fly hundreds or thousands of kilometres away from their colonies while breeding and bring back food to their chicks in large packages at long intervals, up to a week or more between feedings.[65] At the extreme 'fast' end of the seabird spectrum are the grey and red-necked phalaropes, which have lifestyles more like those of landbirds (Table 5).[66]

Among terns, the sooty, bridled and grey-backed terns have fairly 'slow' lifestyles (Table 5), and the noddies and white tern are similar. Otherwise, most terns have lifestyles towards the 'fast' end of the seabird spectrum, although there is wide variability among species.

TABLE 5. Life-histories and 'lifestyles' of terns in relation to those of other seabirds.

Life-history characteristic	Red-necked phalarope	Little tern	Sandwich tern	Sooty tern	Wandering albatross
'Lifestyle' [a]	Fastest	Very fast	Moderate	Slow	Slowest
Latitudinal: breeding range	Subarctic	Temperate/ tropical	Temperate	Tropical	Subantarctic
non-breeding	Tropical	Tropical	Tropical/ temperate	Tropical	Wide-ranging
Feeding habitat	Tundra, pelagic in winter	Inshore, freshwater	Inshore/ offshore	Pelagic	Pelagic
Feeding range (km from colony)	Less than 1	Up to 6	Up to 70	Up to 300	Up to 3,000
Body-weight (g)	29–44	48–63	210–260	160–240	8,500
Wing span (cm)	32–41	48–55	95–105	82–94	290–340
Age at first breeding (years)	1	2–4	3–4 (2–5)	6–8 (4–10)	9–13 (7–15)
Breeding frequency	Annual (females lay 2 clutches)	Annual	Annual	Every 1–2 years	2-year cycle
Clutch-size	4 (1–2 clutches per year)	1–3	1–2	1	1
Egg weight (g)	5.4–7.5	8–12	35	33-37	450–560
Clutch as % of body weight	55–70%	20–60%	12–33%	15–20%	5–7%

Life-history characteristic	Red-necked phalarope	Little tern	Sandwich tern	Sooty tern	Wandering albatross
Incubation period (days)	18–20	19–22	23–27	28–31	75–83
Incubation stints	By male only	5 minutes – 2 hours	15 minutes – 9 hours	1–2 days (up to 7)	1–5 days
Growth rate constant [b]	No data	0.43	0.16–0.28	0.07–0.13	0.026–0.038
Growth period (10–90%, days) [c]	No data	14	19–26	36–54	145–164
Fledging period (days)	16–18	17–23	28–30	56–70	250–300
Chick-feeding method	Self-feeding by chicks	Single prey in bill	Single prey in bill	Regurgitation	Regurgitation
Feeding frequency (feeds/day)	Thousands	20–120	7–15	1–4	0.3–1
Post-fledging care	Parent leaves before fledging	3 months +	6 months +	Unknown	None
Annual adult survival	70%+	88% (84–94%)	89%	>90%	97%
Oldest bird recorded (years)	6	21	23	34	48

Sources: Cramp, 1985; Schreiber and Burger, 2001; Fasola *et al.*, 2002; Rubega *et al.*, 2000; Schreiber *et al.*, 2002; Starck and Ricklefs, 1998. Survival data given for little tern are those reported by Thompson *et al.*, 1997 for least tern. Data for wandering albatross are from Croxall *et al.*, 1992; Weimerskirch, 1992.

[a] Seabird 'lifestyles' are classified on a scale from 'fast' to 'slow' based on feeding range, age at first breeding, breeding frequency, clutch-size, incubation period, chick growth rates, fledging period, adult survival and longevity. Among seabirds, the phalaropes have the 'fastest' lifestyles and the large albatrosses have the 'slowest'. Most terns fall towards the 'fast' end of this spectrum, but there is a wide range in lifestyles among tern species, from 'very fast' in little terns and other small terns to 'slow' in the sooty tern and other tropical terns. Generally, 'fast' lifestyles are more frequent among small, temperate and/or Arctic species, and 'slow' lifestyles are more frequent among larger and/or tropical species, but there are many exceptions to this generalisation.

[b] The growth rate constant is the negative exponent in the logistic growth curve and is approximately one-twentieth of the maximum growth rate in percent of asymptotic weight/day. For example, in little terns the growth rate constant of 0.43 corresponds to a maximum growth rate of about 8.6 percent of asymptotic weight per day, or about 4.3 g per day towards an asymptotic weight of 50 g.

[c] The 'growth period' is the time to grow from 10% to 90% of asymptotic weight (e.g. from 5 g to 45 g in little terns).

The most marked differentiation is in clutch-size. In general, tropical and oceanic terns lay single-egg clutches, whereas birds breeding in temperate or high-latitude zones and at freshwater sites (including in the tropics) lay clutches of two or three eggs, occasionally even four. In the roseate tern, temperate-breeding birds usually lay clutches of two eggs, whereas most tropical-breeding birds lay single-egg clutches.[67] However, there are many exceptions: for example, several species that breed in the south temperate zone (Antarctic, Kerguelen, white-fronted, fairy and Damara terns) have an average clutch-size of less than 1.5 in most locations; and in several terns whose distribution is mainly temperate (little, common, South American and Caspian terns) the scattered populations that breed in the tropics have clutch-sizes of two or three eggs, similar to those of the same species in temperate latitudes.

There is little evidence for differentiation by latitude in other life-history characteristics such as age at first breeding, incubation periods, fledging periods and longevity, after allowing for the way in which these characteristics vary with body size.[68] In fact, most of the variation in other life-history parameters is related to size: species in the 'little' tern group have the 'fastest' lifestyles, with many breeding at two years of age, clutch-sizes averaging more than two eggs, very high rates of chick feeding and rapid chick development. In contrast, the Caspian, Sandwich and other large terns have 'slower' lifestyles, with first breeding at 3–5 years of age, lower rates of chick feeding and slower chick development (Table 5).[69] The larger terns also have higher adult survival rates and greater longevity, although rigorous data on survival are scanty and even the little and least terns have been recorded living to more than 20 years of age (see Appendix 1).[70]

The factors that seem to correlate best with the position of a tern species on the 'fast–slow' spectrum are the mode of foraging and the distance it travels from the nesting site to gather food for the chicks. The pelagic tropical terns forage tens or hundreds of kilometres from the breeding site, feeding on prey that are very widely dispersed at low densities and hard to find. These terns can only feed their young once (or at most twice) each day, and consequently could not raise them if they had to bring food items one at a time. They have evolved the ability to store food in their crops and to feed their chicks by regurgitation, in the manner of other pelagic seabirds. These are the only terns that habitually feed their young on squid, which are difficult to carry in the bill. As in other pelagic seabirds, the pelagic terns' specialisation in feeding on dispersed prey at long distances from the breeding colony limits them to raising one chick at a time, and the slow rate of food delivery means that the chicks develop slowly.

All other terns feed their young with single food items which they carry in their bills, and consequently are limited to breeding in places where they can find enough food within one or two hours' flight. The 'little' terns, 'marsh' terns and other freshwater species can gather a wide variety of prey items within a few kilometres of their nesting sites, and correspondingly have the 'fastest' lifestyles, with large clutches and rapid chick development, even in the tropics. The other terns are intermediate to various degrees, with the differences between them correlated with more varied diets and shorter foraging distances in the 'typical black-capped' terns and less varied diets and longer foraging distances in the 'crested' terns (Table 5).

Colonial nesting

Almost all terns are colonial to some degree, from the sooty terns nesting in a colony of hundreds of thousands on a remote oceanic island to the Damara and Peruvian terns scattered thinly over many square kilometres in the Kalahari and Atacama deserts. The only tern species that may be exclusively solitary is the little-known black-bellied tern of south Asia: this is said to nest singly among other terns on sandbars in rivers, but further study may show that it is aggregated into groups on a scale of kilometres.[71]

Similarly, almost all terns nest on islands, although in some cases the term 'islands' means isolated patches of favourable habitat, such as flooded marshes for the 'marsh', Forster's and Trudeau's terns, mainland beaches for little and least terns, salt pans for Damara and Peruvian terns, rooftops for least and roseate terns, or cliffs for Inca terns. Colonial nesting and island nesting go together, because in most places the number of islands suitable for breeding is limited, so that the birds have no choice but to nest in groups. However, the degree of aggregation into colonies varies enormously, from the elegant tern at one extreme, with over 90 per cent of the world population in densely packed groups on one island,[72] to the common and black terns at the other, with much of their world populations scattered among many thousands of small colonies on freshwater lakes and marshes.[73] Within colonies, there is enormous variation in the degree of dispersion, from the 'crested' terns which often nest at densities higher than five nests per square metre, to the Peruvian and Damara terns with sometimes less than one nest per square kilometre. Factors responsible for these variations have been discussed extensively in the ecological literature.

Nesting on islands conveys one obvious advantage: safety from terrestrial predators such as mammals and snakes. This is most apparent for the pelagic terns, which nest in large numbers on remote oceanic islands with no native mammals or snakes. On some of these islands the terns are subject to predation by birds or crabs, but this is rarely as intense as predation by mammals and the terns are usually able to defend against it or to tolerate it. The importance of predation in limiting the terns (and other pelagic seabirds) to such islands has been demonstrated in many cases where predatory mammals such as rats or cats have been introduced by humans, usually with catastrophic results for the birds.[74] Recently, efforts have been made to remove these alien predators from many islands that formerly supported important seabird colonies, and in most cases the seabirds have responded immediately by increasing in numbers and starting to breed with high success. One local example is in western Scotland, where the accidental introduction of American mink led to the rapid decline and disappearance of virtually all colonies of terns, gulls and other seabirds from islands within 2–3 km of the mainland. In recent years, intensive control of mink by trapping during the winter has allowed terns and other seabirds to resettle on several of these islands (see Chapter 11).

In spite of clear-cut examples like this, the extent to which predation favours colonial breeding – or was responsible for its evolution in the first place – is not always clear and probably varies from species to species.[75] Although islands may initially be free of predators, the establishment of a seabird colony may actually attract predators, particularly predatory birds that have little or no difficulty in reaching islands. For terns that nest on coastal islands within a few kilometres of the mainland, on lakes or rivers, or in marshes, the most important predators are usually birds such as gulls, owls, falcons, herons or crows. There are many examples of these predators appearing on an island within a few years after a colony of terns is formed and reducing breeding success to zero.

Within colonies, predation appears to have a strong influence on the way that terns disperse over the area suitable for nesting. Across the tundra regions of Eurasia and North America, Arctic terns breed in small groups of less than 30 pairs, typically with tens of metres between adjacent nests. This is thought to be an adaptation to minimise predation by the Arctic fox, which ranges widely over the tundra and can reach islands isolated by hundreds of metres of water.[76] The terns are close enough together for each bird to see its neighbours and to respond when a neighbour sees a fox approaching, while far enough apart to make it difficult for the foxes to find each nest or to use one nest as a clue to finding the next. In the northern and western isles of Scotland, Arctic tern nests are often similarly widely spaced, perhaps as an adaptation against predation by skuas. In contrast, Arctic terns in the southernmost parts of their range (e.g. at the Farne Islands in northeast England or Machias Seal Island in southeastern Canada) commonly nest in colonies of hundreds or thousands of pairs, with nests separated by 2 m or less.[77] These colonies are on islands which were originally free of mammalian predators (although some of them are nowadays accessible to American mink). The dense packing of nests at these sites is thought to be an adaptation to minimise predation by birds such as gulls, which are deterred by the communal aerial defence that the terns mount.[78] This appears to be a general pattern: terns that are at risk primarily from terrestrial predators (such as the 'little' terns) scatter their nests widely, whereas those that are at risk primarily from aerial predators nest close together and rely on aggressive defence (common and Caspian terns) or physical crowding (Sandwich and other 'crested' terns).[79]

Dispersion of nests also depends on colony size, which is influenced primarily by food availability and mode of foraging.[80] Tern species that can forage hundreds of kilometres from the breeding site tend to have a small number of large colonies, because they can concentrate on the most favourable islands, even if these are not the closest sites to good feeding areas. These colonies on remote islands are often densely packed, because a large area of ocean can support a large number of birds. At the other extreme, terns that forage close to the breeding site, such as the 'little' and 'marsh' terns, tend to have a large number of small colonies. In larger wetlands, the 'marsh' terns usually cluster in small groups (known as 'subcolonies') 1–2 km apart rather than spreading out uniformly: this may be an 'early warning' system like that of tundra-breeding Arctic terns, because the 'marsh' terns' aerial defence against aquatic predators is not very effective.[81]

For these species, the number of pairs in each subcolony is probably limited by the availability of food within a small foraging area around it. This applies on a larger scale to the distribution of colonies, even in species with larger foraging ranges. In the eastern USA, for example, many common terns nest close to breaks in barrier beaches, where the tide flows in and out of lagoons behind the beaches and turbulent tidal currents flowing through the inlets bring prey fish to the surface. It has been shown that the number of pairs in each colony is proportional to the volume of water that runs in and out of the inlet with each tide – and hence, presumably, to the total number of fish available to the terns.[82] Under natural conditions, the distribution of little and least terns was probably governed by similar factors. However, many of the sites suitable for breeding by these species can no longer be used because of human disturbance, and their distribution is now determined at least as much by the availability of sites where they are protected. Nowadays, little and least terns are unnaturally concentrated, and sometimes form colonies of hundreds of pairs that are difficult to protect, although they still form many small colonies and shift frequently in areas where enough sites are still available (see Chapter 11).

Terns often behave as though they are attracted to nest near to others (i.e. in colonies or subcolonies), but within colonies or subcolonies as though they like to nest as far away from their neighbours as possible. Accordingly, they nest very densely at sites where there is abundant food but limited nesting space, but very sparsely at sites where there is abundant space for all the pairs in the area. Common terns, for example, settle at densities of up to four nests per square metre on some artificial sites such as rafts where nesting space is very limited, but establish their nests 1–10 m apart at sites where more space is available; the extreme case is at Bermuda, where a 'colony' of up to 30 pairs of common terns is dispersed all over the archipelago, with inter-nest distances averaging more than 1 km.[83] Even in the latter cases, nests are 'over-dispersed' – that is, the distribution of nests is more uniform than would be expected if the birds had settled at random – which implies that each pair settles as far away from its neighbours as it can, given the total space available. This wide spacing must be achieved by avoidance rather than by aggressive defence, because a pair of terns could not effectively defend an area 1 km or more in radius.

In most tern species, pairs defend exclusive territories around their nests, and this usually determines the spacing of nests within colonies. These territories are established by the males early in the courtship period, and in some species appear to be used in attracting mates.[84] They are then defended by the pair at least through the incubation period, and neighbouring pairs learn to respect the boundaries and avoid confrontations. In some species, such as common terns, the territories are defended throughout the period of chick-raising as well, and the neighbours' chicks are kept out as vigorously as are intruding adults (see *Parental care*, above). In other species the territories are no longer defended after the chicks hatch, and the chicks either scatter widely (as in little terns) or form crèches (as in 'crested' terns). Territory size varies enormously among species: the 'crested' terns defend an area scarcely larger than the pecking range around the sitting bird, while other species defend areas ranging from less than a metre to tens of metres in radius.

The factors that make a site attractive to terns – isolation, absence of predators, open terrain and proximity to food sources – usually make it attractive to more than one species. Terns commonly breed in mixed colonies with two, three or more species nesting in close proximity.[85] In Britain and Ireland, a number of sites support three species of terns, and at least five sites support four, but there is currently no site where all five species nest together, in part because little and Arctic terns have largely non-overlapping geographical ranges and in part because of differences in habitat preference (see Chapters 6 and 10). However, all five species did breed together at one time at Blakeney Point and Scolt Head, Norfolk, and on Tern Island in Wexford Harbour, Co. Wexford (see Figs 56, 68 and 69 in Chapter 5).[86] Within mixed colonies, the species are usually segregated by habitat, and it is unusual for two species to intermingle freely. For example, little terns usually nest in very open areas with little vegetation close to the high tide line, Sandwich terns nest in open areas at higher elevations, roseate terns nest in dense vegetation, and common and Arctic terns nest in partly open areas between these other species and are separated from each other by more subtle differences in microhabitat (see Fig. 69 in Chapter 5). In the North Atlantic region (northwest Europe and northeast North America) roseate terns nest exclusively within colonies of common terns and have not been recorded nesting alone, but the roseates usually nest in densely vegetated patches surrounded by common terns that occupy more open areas.[87] Wherever areas occupied by different species abut, individual pairs of each species defend nesting territories against the other species and there is no overlap. Terns in mixed-species colonies gain some of the same benefits as they do in single-species colonies, including early warning against predators and communal defence. These benefits are often enhanced by the presence of more than one species, especially for a scarce species that can benefit by nesting close to or surrounded by larger numbers of a more numerous, aggressive species.

Terns often nest in proximity to gulls and other seabirds that have similar preferences for nesting habitat, but in these cases the associations are less benign. Gulls often steal food from terns or prey on their eggs and chicks, and this can reduce the terns' breeding success, sometimes to zero if predation is heavy. Terns are generally subordinate to gulls in territorial encounters, and in the temperate zones gulls usually arrive from migration and establish their territories early in spring, so that when the terns arrive they find themselves excluded, sometimes from areas where they had nested successfully in the previous year. Many cases have been recorded where gulls have displaced terns from thriving colonies in this way, forcing the terns to move to less favourable sites. Such displacements were especially prevalent in the second half of the twentieth century, when gull populations in many developed countries were able to increase enormously by exploiting human food sources such as rubbish dumps, fishing fleets and fish processing plants. In some regions gulls displaced terns from almost all suitable sites.[88] In recent decades, the tide of gulls has been stemmed in some areas by reductions in artificial food sources and by botulism poisoning resulting from eating decaying rubbish. At least in parts of the UK and USA, some of the gulls are decreasing again and there have been several successful efforts to restore historic tern colonies by removing or displacing the remaining gulls (see Chapter 11).

Although the main benefits of nesting in colonies appear to be safety from predation, communal defence against predators that do gain access to the colony, and proximity to food sources, there are several other ways in which terns may benefit from colonial nesting, and several ways in which they may be harmed.[89] Kleptoparasitism, or food-stealing, is prevalent in most tern colonies, and sometimes a substantial fraction of the food items brought into a colony are stolen. Where the stealing is by gulls or skuas, the effect on the terns is uniformly negative. Where one tern species steals food from another – for example, roseate terns stealing from common terns – the loss to one species is a gain by the other. Similarly, where terns steal food from other terns of their own species, the loss by one individual is a gain by the other, and the process might be thought of as a 'zero-sum game'. However, in practice the net effect is strongly negative, because the pervasive risk of losing fish to other birds makes all terns take counter-measures that are often costly.

It has often been suggested that seabird colonies function as 'information centres' – that is, that individual birds may learn about sources of food by observing others that have been successful.[90] Although this idea is intuitively plausible, it has proved very difficult to establish that terns actually gain significant benefits in this way.[91] It is certainly true that terns watch each other while foraging and converge rapidly as soon as a food source is found, and when a school of fish appears close to a breeding colony, many or most terns switch quickly to feeding there, but that benefit is attributable mainly to communal foraging rather than communal nesting. Typically, terns tend to depart from a colony simultaneously or sequentially in the same direction and to return with fish in the opposite direction. This could mean that they are following each other, but it could also result from individuals' prior knowledge of good fishing areas. Generally, terns behave as though they have detailed knowledge of the opportunities for foraging around the breeding colony and can exploit the available food supplies efficiently. It has proved very hard to distinguish this 'prior knowledge' or 'spatial memory' from imitating the behaviour of other terns that may have different knowledge or memory.

A more direct consequence of nesting in a colony is that the terns compete for food in the vicinity of the colony site, either by depleting the numbers of the prey species, by occupying and defending feeding territories along the shore, or by interfering with each other when feeding in flocks. These negative effects would increase with colony size. In common terns, for example, there is evidence that chick feeding rates and chick survival decline as a colony becomes larger, and that these effects can override the positive effects of increasing age and experience of the adults.[92]

However, there is another way in which tern colonies may function as information centres. Terns that have not yet bred for the first time – for example, two-year-old common or roseate terns – commonly visit active breeding colonies late in the breeding season, and sometimes explore the nesting areas or perform courtship flights with other young birds. Although most of these birds initially visit the colony where they were raised as chicks, it has recently been discovered that they visit other breeding sites as well. The next year, many of them settle to breed for the first time in their natal colony, but a substantial minority settles at other sites. Recent evidence has indicated that they are more likely to settle at sites where breeding success had been high in the previous year than at sites where success had been low.[93] This suggests that they may have used 'information' from the site – specifically, the presence of adults feeding young and flying juveniles in the previous year – as signs that the site was favourable for breeding.[94] Such evidence of successful breeding in the previous year would be more valuable than any cues the settlers could detect early in the year of settlement.

Other costs and benefits of colonial breeding have been suggested in the literature, but appear more conjectural.[95] Breeding in close proximity to others might increase the risk of disease, but in fact few cases have been reported in which substantial numbers of terns have died from contagious diseases, and there is no evidence that such events are more frequent in larger or denser colonies. Birds that breed in colonies have more choice among potential mates than birds that breed solitarily, and this might enable high-quality birds to obtain high-quality mates. However, it would also mean that low-quality birds would be relegated to low-quality mates. Hence, it is unlikely that this would represent a net benefit of coloniality, except for species that are so scarce that birds nesting individually might not find mates at all. It was formerly suggested that birds nesting in colonies might benefit from 'social stimulation', enabling birds in groups to breed earlier and more synchronously – and consequently more successfully – than they would if they nested solitarily or in smaller groups. However, studies in seabirds other than terns have yielded little evidence for such effects.[96] More recent literature has tended to emphasise negative effects of crowding, resulting in elevated stress hormones and impairment of immune systems.

Overall, the clearest evidence for the costs and benefits of colonial breeding in terns indicates that benefits arise from from (1) isolation from predators, (2) communal defence against predators and (3) proximity to food sources; and costs from (4) competition for food and (5) kleptoparasitism. Of these, (2), (4) and (5) are direct consequences of group living and increase with the number of birds in the colony, whereas (1) and (3) are related to nesting in the most suitable places and are independent of the number of other birds that do so simultaneously. In a small colony the costs of communal living are small, but as a colony becomes larger the costs are likely to increase more rapidly than the benefits. At some point an 'optimum' colony size is reached, but there is nothing to prevent more birds from settling in the colony and increasing numbers above this optimum. Indeed, from the point of view of a young bird choosing a place to nest for the first time, a large colony is likely to be more attractive for nesting than smaller colonies nearby, so that the large colony will continue to attract recruits even after the optimum size is exceeded.[97]

Anti-predator adaptations

When terns come to land to breed, they are immediately at risk of predation from a wide variety of land-based predators. Their breeding behaviour has evolved in this context and they display a wide variety of adaptations that function to minimise the effects of predation (Table 6).

Terns fall into several groups according to the mix of anti-predator adaptations, or 'strategies', that they have adopted under the pressure of natural selection. Sooty terns and other oceanic terns nest on remote islands and appear to rely primarily on isolation, with little active response to predators. The 'crested' terns appear to rely on nesting on safe islands, nesting densely to crowd out low-intensity predators, and shifting sites in response to high-intensity predation. The 'little' terns nest in sites where predation is frequent and often heavy: they rely on good camouflage, widely spaced nests, constantly moving chicks, and shifting sites when predation is unavoidable; tundra-nesting Arctic terns behave similarly. The 'typical black-capped' terns otherwise nest on moderately safe islands and mount aggressive defences against predators that find them. Roseate terns (in the temperate zone only) rely on concealing their eggs and chicks and on nesting among aggressive common terns. None of the terns has effective defences against nocturnal predation, especially by mammals, except for the short-term response of deserting the colony at night and the long-term response of shifting to a new breeding site. More details of these anti-predator strategies are given under the individual species in Chapters 6–10.

TABLE 6. Variation in anti-predator adaptations or 'strategies' among different groups of terns. The characterisation of 'major predators' applies to each group of species worldwide: some of the predators listed in the table are not important in Britain and Ireland.

Adaptation or strategy	Oceanic terns	Crested terns	Typical black-capped terns	Marsh terns	Little terns	Roseate tern (North Atlantic)
'Lifestyle' Anti-predator adaptation	Slow	Moderate	Fast	Very fast	Very fast	Fast
Isolation on islands	Very high	High	Moderate	High (in marshes)	Low	Moderate
Camouflage of eggs and chicks	High	High	High	High	Very high	High
Concealment of eggs and chicks	Moderate	Low	Moderate	Moderate	Low	High
Aggressive defence	Low	Low	High	High	Moderate	Very low
Eggshell removal	No	No	Yes	Yes	No	No
Tendency to shift sites in response to predation	Very low	Low	Moderate	High	Very high	High
Major predators	Frigatebirds, crabs, rats, cats	Gulls, foxes	Owls, mink, gulls, falcons, foxes, rats, crows, herons	Owls, harriers, herons, bitterns, snakes	Foxes, rats, falcons, crows, cats	Owls, mink, rats, falcons

CHAPTER 4

Migration

THIS CHAPTER DESCRIBES the general characteristics of tern migrations. Detailed information on the migrations of each of the five British and Irish breeding terns is presented in Chapters 6–10.

CHARACTERISTICS OF TERN MIGRATIONS

Except at some tropical sites, all terns are seasonal breeders and are present at the breeding sites for only 3–5 months. Almost all terns that breed in the temperate zones or in the Arctic are migratory, in the sense that they make regular seasonal movements to and from non-breeding areas far away from their breeding sites.[1] However, their migration patterns fall into three contrasting groups: Arctic tern, north temperate terns and south temperate terns. Less is known about seasonal movements of tropical terns, but most disperse away from the breeding sites and at least four are known to make long-distance movements.

Arctic tern

The Arctic tern has the longest migrations of any bird species. Arctic terns breed in Arctic and subarctic regions throughout Eurasia and North America, extending north to the northernmost land in northern Greenland at 83° N latitude, and south in the North Atlantic Ocean as far south as Ireland (52° N) in the east and the northeastern USA (42° N) in the west. They migrate across the globe to spend the northern winter (southern summer) mainly in Antarctic and subantarctic waters, extending south at times as far as 79° S. It is possible that some individuals from the northernmost colonies reach the southernmost wintering areas, a span of 160 degrees in latitude or 16,000 km. These birds would experience more daylight in the course of a year than any other animal.[2]

Much has been written about the Arctic tern's epic journeys, but most of this has been speculative because until very recently there was little hard information on where the birds go or how they travel. Ringing recoveries from the main wintering area in Antarctic waters have been few and far between: most recoveries of birds ringed in the breeding areas have been along the west coasts of Europe and Africa, and at least some of these have been of birds in poor condition that may have come to shore for that reason. Arctic terns are commonly seen in small numbers at sea throughout the North and South Atlantic and in the eastern Pacific, and it is thought that most of them migrate long distances over the ocean. A steady scattering of observations and ringing recoveries far inland in Europe, Asia, Africa, North and South America suggests that some of them may migrate long distances overland as well.[3]

A recent study has thrown exciting new light on how Arctic terns migrate. Eleven Arctic terns breeding in east Greenland or Iceland were fitted with geolocators (data loggers that record locations based on times of sunrise and sunset), yielding direct information on their locations throughout the year (Fig. 51). After their short breeding season (early June to early August), the 11 birds spent the rest of the year at sea. They spent the northern winter (late November to mid-April) at latitudes of 60–70° S in the Atlantic sector of the Southern Ocean, including the Weddell Sea. Early in their autumn migration, they all spent three or four weeks during August and September in an area of high marine productivity east of Newfoundland, then crossed the Atlantic Ocean to West Africa in September. Seven of the birds then followed the West African coast southwards in October and November, four of them moving east into the Indian Ocean before travelling south and west to their wintering areas. The other four birds crossed the Atlantic Ocean again from West Africa to Brazil and then moved south off the east coast of South America in October. All 11 birds left their winter quarters in mid-April and returned to their breeding areas in about 40 days, passing through the eastern South Atlantic and the central North Atlantic. They thus took circuitous routes in both autumn and spring, involving repeated ocean crossings (Fig. 51). These routes took advantage of the prevailing winds in each sector of the Atlantic and the Southern Ocean, but meant that the total distances travelled during spring and autumn migrations were between 60,000 and 80,000 km, much longer than the distances of 40,000–50,000 km suggested by previous authors – which have themselves seemed remarkable.[4] These long journeys should be considered in the context that Arctic terns

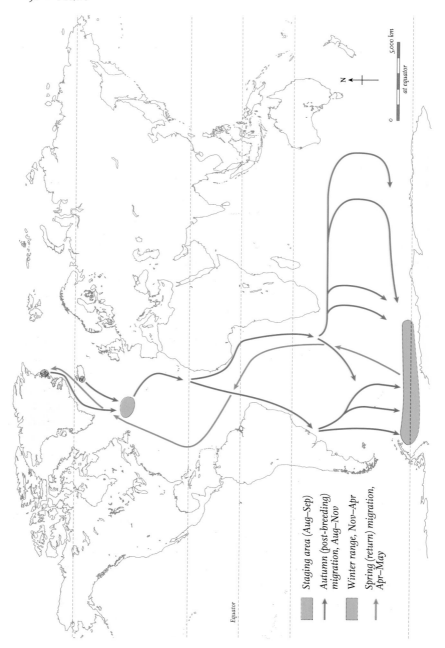

Staging area (Aug–Sep)

Autumn (post-breeding) migration, Aug–Nov

Winter range, Nov–Apr

Spring (return) migration, Apr–May

Equator

N

5,000 km

at equator

0

sometimes live for more than 30 years: such birds would fly two million kilometres on migration alone, without considering the hundreds of kilometres that they fly every day as part of their normal routine.

Although these findings relate to Arctic terns from only a small part of the species' extensive breeding area around the Arctic Ocean, they can serve as a guide to interpreting the fragmentary information available for other populations of the species. Specifically, they show that Arctic terns spend most of the year at sea, and they suggest that the sightings and ringing recoveries along the west coast of Africa represent 'fallout' from an offshore migration route rather than a concentrated migration along the coast. Most Arctic terns from the western Palearctic and from eastern North America are believed to take this route offshore from West Africa, although some birds from Greenland and probably some from North America take the alternative route off the east coast of South America. Birds from eastern Siberia and western North America migrate through the eastern Pacific Ocean, and it is thought that they have a similar circuitous route, close to the coasts of North and South America in autumn but further out to sea in spring.[5] The scattered records of Arctic terns far inland in all continents remain a mystery (see Chapter 10 for a bizarre recovery of an Arctic tern ringed in Shetland and subsequently found in the centre of the North American continent).

Juvenile Arctic terns (Fig. 52) appear to follow the same tracks as adults in autumn and may accompany them at least as far as West Africa. Although some juveniles continue to Antarctic waters, most of them do not migrate as far south as the adults, and there are winter recoveries of birds ringed in western Europe all along the western and southern coasts of Africa from Mauritania to South Africa and up the east African coast as far as Natal (see Fig. 175 in Chapter 10).[6] Juveniles from Pacific populations are thought to behave similarly, wintering mainly off the west coast of South America. In their first summers, many young Arctic terns remain in their winter quarters, but some migrate north as far as the Equator and a few continue all the way to the breeding grounds. These one-

FIG 52. Juvenile Arctic terns on autumn migration past the west coast of Ireland in September. Arctic terns appear to spend most of the year at sea far from land, except during the short breeding season in the Arctic and subarctic. Bridges of Ross, Co. Clare. (John N. Murphy)

year-old birds are rare at European colonies but are more numerous at North American colonies, where they occur sporadically in hundreds. Two-year-old birds apparently migrate like adults, but reach the breeding grounds later in spring and rarely breed.[7]

Little is known about how Arctic terns migrate. There are several accounts of terns (of several species as well as Arctic terns) departing from staging areas at dusk, ascending to high altitudes as they leave, sometimes departing overland. Two radar studies of terns have reported nocturnal movements at altitudes of 1,000–3,000 m, while another radar study reported Arctic terns migrating by day at altitudes of only 30–60 m.[8] Arctic terns are commonly seen in small numbers at low altitudes at sea, even in mid-ocean, but these birds are not necessarily migrating when they are seen.

North temperate terns

All other terns that breed in the north temperate zone are migratory, although none migrates nearly as far as the Arctic tern. Most winter in the tropics or at subtropical latitudes below 30° N or 30° S.[9] The only species that winters almost entirely in the north temperate zone is the Forster's tern of North America, which migrates short distances and winters mainly in the southern USA and northern Mexico.[10] In several other species, substantial numbers occur in winter at temperate latitudes north to 30° or 40° N (for example, in southwestern Europe, the southern USA, the Mediterranean Sea and the Black Sea, the Persian Gulf, or southern China), but their main wintering areas are further south.[11]

A few north temperate species cross the Equator and winter in numbers in the southern tropics or south temperate zone: examples are common terns in southern Africa, southern Brazil, Argentina and eastern Australia, Sandwich and white-winged terns in southern Africa, roseate terns in eastern Brazil and northeastern Australia, royal and elegant terns in Peru, and little terns in eastern Australia. However, many birds of the same species and even from the same breeding areas migrate shorter distances. For example, most North American royal terns winter north of the Equator, some even as far north as the southern part of the breeding range at 30–32° N latitude; roseate terns from Europe winter almost exclusively in West Africa north of the Equator; and many common terns from both European and North American populations winter north of the Equator, a few even in the north temperate zone.[12]

Extensive ringing has shown that European common terns perform a 'leapfrog migration': birds from western and southern Europe (from Norway to Spain) winter mainly in West Africa north of the Equator, whereas birds from northern and eastern Europe (from Finland to Ukraine) winter mainly in southern and southwestern Africa.[13] Common terns from the Azores cross the Atlantic and winter in South America (Fig. 53).[14] North American common terns are not known to perform leapfrog migrations, but are similarly differentiated from west to east: those breeding along the Atlantic coast winter on the north and east coasts of South America, from Venezuela (10° N) to northern Argentina (40° S), whereas most of those breeding in the interior winter on the Pacific coast, from southern Mexico (20° N) to Peru (20° S)[15] (Fig. 53). It is not known whether Asian populations of common terns are similarly differentiated in winter quarters.

In contrast to common terns, Sandwich terns breeding in different parts of western and northern Europe seem to show no such differentiation of wintering areas. They winter all along the west coast of Africa from Mauritania to South Africa. However, Sandwich terns from the Black and Caspian Seas winter much further north, in the southern Black Sea, eastern Mediterranean and Persian Gulf regions.[16]

Juvenile terns of these species tend to winter somewhat further north than adults, but there is much overlap. For example, European Sandwich terns are recovered mainly in southwestern Europe and West Africa during their first winter, but from West Africa to South Africa in subsequent years.[17] Recoveries

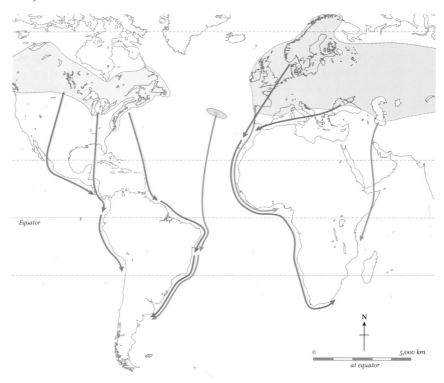

FIG 53. Migration patterns of common terns. The breeding distribution is shown in green shading (North America), orange shading (Europe and Asia), or purple shading (Azores). Birds from western Europe winter mainly in West Africa (red arrow), whereas birds from northern and eastern Europe 'leapfrog' over them and winter mainly in southern Africa (green arrows). Birds from Asia winter in East Africa (purple arrow). Birds from the Atlantic coast of North America winter in northern and eastern South America, whereas most birds from the interior winter on the Pacific coast (green arrows). Unexpectedly, common terns from the Azores winter alongside North American birds in South America (purple arrows). The arrows are schematic and oversimplify actual migration routes, especially for birds from intermediate breeding areas. (Sources: Nisbet, 2002; Becker & Ludwigs, 2004; Szczys *et al.*, 2012)

of North American common and roseate terns are mainly north of the Equator during their first winters, but mainly south of 10° S in subsequent years.[18] Likewise, few common or roseate terns from eastern Asia reach Australia in their first winters, although large numbers of adults do so.[19] In their first summers, some birds of most or all of these species migrate short distances north, but many remain within the wintering areas and very few reach the breeding areas.

Prior to autumn migration, most temperate terns disperse widely throughout their breeding ranges, sometimes moving substantial distances north and in a few cases reaching locations north of the northern limits of breeding. The elegant tern probably makes the longest of these northward movements: research shows that birds from colonies in western Mexico disperse north along the Pacific coast to California in autumn, some reaching as far north as British Columbia at 50° N, before migrating south to winter from southern Mexico to Peru and northern Chile.[20]

As is the case with Arctic terns, only fragmentary information is available on the migratory behaviour of north temperate terns. Common and roseate terns from the northeastern USA have recently been tracked using geolocators: these birds made direct crossings of the western North Atlantic Ocean to and from the eastern West Indies (Fig. 53), and roseate terns remained pelagic for several days during parts of their migrations through the Sargasso Sea.[21] It is likely that the common and roseate terns that breed in eastern Asia and winter in northeastern Australia make similar long crossings of the western Pacific Ocean.[22] Common and other terns probably cross the Gulf of Guinea from West to Southwest Africa.[23]

Terns that spend much of the year along coasts or on inland marshes are able to cross major barriers posed by mountains or deserts. For example, common terns breeding in the prairie provinces of western Canada migrate across the Rocky Mountains to and from the Pacific coast.[24] Common terns have also been recorded crossing the Alps, and all the terns that breed in central Asia must cross high mountain ranges or deserts to reach wintering grounds around the Indian Ocean. Several tern species, including gull-billed, Caspian, whiskered and white-winged terns, winter in large numbers in the Niger inundation zone in Mali and Chad, and are thought to cross the Sahara in both autumn and spring; several other species are though to cross the Sahara in spring. The same species migrate through the Rift Valley lakes in East Africa and probably have to cross deserts on their way to breeding grounds in eastern Europe or western Asia.[25] Records of evening departures and radar tracking have indicated that terns of several species migrate mainly at high altitudes at night.[26]

South temperate terns

South temperate terns generally migrate much shorter distances than north temperate terns.[27] The bridled tern is the only species known to cross the Equator: both juveniles and adults ringed at breeding sites at latitudes 30–33° S in Western Australia have been recovered in Borneo and the Philippines in the southern winter.[28] No other south temperate terns are known to cross the Equator, even as stragglers, and many remain within the south temperate zone throughout the year. Indeed, several south temperate species breed in autumn or winter (see Chapter 3), so that the local spring and summer are their non-breeding seasons. The main reason for the differences in breeding seasons and migratory patterns appears to be differences in climate: south temperate climates are much more maritime than north temperate ones, with less contrast between summer and winter, so that breeding cycles and migratory patterns are determined more by oceanographic factors than by climatic factors.

Among south temperate terns, the Kerguelen tern and several subspecies of the Antarctic tern are sedentary, remaining on or close to their isolated archipelagos throughout the year. Other subspecies of the Antarctic tern migrate relatively short distances – e.g. from South Georgia in the subantarctic Atlantic Ocean to South African waters. Among the other terns breeding in New Zealand, the black-fronted tern moves only from inland rivers to nearby coasts, the Caspian tern migrates only from the South Island to the North Island, and the white-fronted tern migrates only to southeastern Australia. Populations of crested terns that nest at temperate latitudes in Australia and South Africa remain mainly at temperate latitudes in winter, although some of them migrate short distances northwards. This contrasts with populations of crested terns that breed at temperate latitudes in China and Japan, which winter entirely in the tropics.[29] Populations of the South American tern that breed in the southern summer at temperate latitudes in Argentina apparently winter at temperate latitudes, although they migrate short distances north and would be difficult to detect if they were to migrate as far as Brazil, where the same species breeds in winter.[30] There is little or no information about migration in other south temperate species, such as the Peruvian, Damara, fairy and Trudeau's terns.

Tropical terns

Little is known about migrations of tropical terns. Most of them breed seasonally (see Chapter 3) and most are absent from the breeding sites during their non-breeding seasons. Even in species that breed around the year at some sites, or have less-than-annual cycles at others, most or all individual birds vacate their breeding sites after breeding is complete and go through other parts of the annual cycle (post-fledging chick care, moult, etc.) elsewhere. However, in most cases it is not known whether they move short or long distances, nor whether they move regularly to and from discrete non-breeding areas in the manner of true migrants.

Only two tropical-breeding terns have been shown by ringing to undertake long-distance migrations. Roseate terns that nest around the Caribbean Sea all leave their nesting sites after breeding in April to August; this even includes those that breed on islands in the southern Caribbean, less than 200 km from the wintering sites of some roseate terns from North America. Roseate terns ringed as chicks in Puerto Rico and the US Virgin Islands have been retrapped as adults alongside northern roseates in winter in eastern Brazil, more than 3,000 km to the east-southeast.[31] Sooty terns ringed as chicks in the Dry Tortugas in the Gulf of Mexico migrate across the tropical Atlantic to the Gulf of Guinea off West Africa, where many have been recovered 6,000–7,000 km to the east in their first five years of life prior to breeding for the first time. Adult birds apparently do not perform this migration and are thought to disperse only short distances into the Gulf of Mexico and Caribbean Sea. It is thought that juvenile sooty terns from all colonies in the North and South Atlantic may migrate to West African waters. Ringing has shown similar long-distance movements of juvenile sooty terns in the Pacific and Indian oceans.[32]

Several other movements of tropical terns have been documented by sightings away from breeding sites, although some of these should probably be classified as post-breeding dispersal rather than true migration. White-cheeked terns from the Red Sea, Persian Gulf and Gulf of Oman winter mainly in East Africa and the Indian subcontinent. Lesser crested terns from the same breeding area apparently have similar wintering areas, but those that breed in the southern Mediterranean winter in West Africa.[33] Sooty and bridled terns that breed around the Caribbean Sea disperse in late summer along the Gulf Stream off the east coast of the USA, north at least to 40° N latitude. Bridled terns from this breeding area probably winter mainly in the Sargasso Sea to the east, where they are closely associated with patches of floating *Sargassum* weed.[34] This may be the only regional population of terns that breeds in the tropics and winters at temperate latitudes. The tropical river terns appear to be mainly sedentary, although some are thought to move to coastal areas in winter, like the black-fronted tern of temperate New Zealand.[35] Much remains to be learned about tropical terns in their non-breeding seasons.

EVOLUTIONARY SIGNIFICANCE OF TERN MIGRATIONS

In general, bird migration has evolved because many birds can breed most successfully in one region but can survive best through the non-breeding seasons in other regions, and because the advantages they gain from migrating between these regions outweigh the risks they encounter during their travels. Migration has evolved more or less independently in each bird species, so that similarities in migration patterns among species reflect factors that act similarly in each species, whereas differences in migration patterns among species reflect factors that act differently. Study of these similarities and differences can yield important information about the ecological requirements of the various species, and about how these are matched to the various environments that they use during the course of the year.

For north temperate seabirds such as little, Sandwich and common terns, breeding at high latitudes is strongly favoured because of the high productivity of temperate seas in the summer months, combined with the long hours of daylight which allow many hours of foraging at the season when the demands of chick-rearing are greatest. These factors explain why these species generally breed ahead of climatic summer and arrive at their breeding grounds early in the spring, often before their main prey species become available (see Chapter 3). In many north temperate seas, the availability of prey species taken by terns remains high well into the autumn, and this gives the birds several months to continue parental care while their offspring learn to fish. All terns have a period of dispersal following breeding and before they start to migrate south, and they are able to move during this period into the most productive areas, often north of their breeding sites. As the northern winter approaches, however, days become shorter, temperatures decline, and the prey species move into deeper water and become unavailable. This explains why almost all north temperate terns migrate south to spend the winter in tropical or subtropical waters. Most of these terns do not breed until they are three or four years old, and another common feature of their migrations is that young birds generally stay in the winter quarters throughout the second calendar year and do not migrate north until they are two years old. This must mean that the risks they would incur by migrating in their second calendar year outweigh the advantages they might gain by moving to the breeding area, even though food is more abundant there and they could start learning how to exploit the food supplies around their future breeding sites. This trade-off is evidently different for two-year-old terns, because most of them migrate north and visit the breeding areas, even though most of them do not breed.

Within this general pattern of temperate breeding and tropical wintering, there is some diversification among the north temperate species. The diversification is greatest in the breeding season, when each species occupies its own ecological 'niche' – higher versus lower latitudes, fresh water versus salt water, inshore versus offshore, etc. The migration patterns and winter quarters of the various species are much more similar than their breeding distributions. For example, most European tern species winter in similar areas along and off the coasts of West Africa, and the differences among species are quite subtle – for example, north European common terns and most Sandwich terns migrate to southern Africa, whereas other species and populations go no further than the Gulf of Guinea. These small differences presumably reflect some minor shifts in the trade-offs between longer and shorter migrations, tropical and subtropical food supplies, etc.

The balance among all these factors is different for south temperate terns, because southern climates are more maritime and less extreme than those in the northern hemisphere. This explains why these species are less tightly bound by the seasons, often breeding in autumn or winter when local oceanographic conditions produce favourable conditions for feeding. It also explains why they are less migratory than north temperate terns, with some species more or less sedentary and many others migrating only short distances. There seems to be no information about the location or movements of one-year-old and two-year-old terns of these species.

The foregoing paragraphs provide plausible explanations of the origins and the general patterns of migration of the temperate-breeding species, but they fail to account for an important fact. The majority of tern species breed at low latitudes in the tropics or subtropics and do not migrate far, if at all (see Fig. 11 in Chapter 1). Whatever factors have favoured breeding at high latitudes and wintering at low latitudes for the temperate-breeding species must be reversed in some way for the tropical-breeding species. Presumably, they are better adapted to breeding in the less seasonal environments of the tropics than are the migratory species, and it is likely that they would out-compete any individuals of the migratory species that might remain in their winter quarters and attempt to breed there. Whatever the reasons for the differences, their consequences are well illustrated by species such as the roseate tern which have both tropical and temperate populations. A comparative analysis of tropical and temperate roseate terns showed marked differences in their ecology: tropical roseate terns have a 'slow' lifestyle (see Chapter 3) with intermittent breeding, small clutch-sizes, frequent breeding failures and very low average productivity; temperate roseate terns have a 'fast' lifestyle with annual breeding, larger clutches and consistently high productivity, and they migrate long distances to winter in the tropics.[36] Similar differences are thought to exist between tropical and temperate populations of other terns, whether the comparisons are within or between species. Because tropical terns generally have much lower productivity than temperate terns, they must have much higher survival rates, although this remains to be proved by rigorous measurements of survival. The fact that 'fast' and 'slow' lifestyles, associated with long-distance and short-distance migrations, can be found even in contiguous populations of the same species indicates that the factors determining the trade-offs between migratory and non-migratory life histories are finely balanced.

Finally, an evolutionary explanation is needed for the seemingly extraordinary migration pattern of the Arctic tern, which breeds much further north and winters much further south than any other tern. The key to understanding this adaptation seems to be the pelagic lifestyle of this species, which remains at sea throughout the year except for two or three months when breeding. This emancipates it from any connection to land, and specifically means that it does not have to stay close to land in the winter, as all other temperate terns do. All other northern hemisphere terns that migrate across the Equator have to remain north of the southernmost land – latitude 32° S in Africa, 43° S in Australia, 55° S in South America – and in fact northern hemisphere terns rarely penetrate south of 35° S in Australia or 45° S in South America. Arctic terns have no such limitations and can travel freely south into the Southern Ocean – and they were 'pre-adapted' to a polar lifestyle. It is easy to imagine a pioneering proto-Arctic tern crossing the Southern Ocean and finding itself in a wonderful environment, with pack ice to rest on, continuous daylight, abundant food at the ice edge, and no predators. Once some birds had found this paradise, natural selection would have favoured them over all other members of the species, reinforcing both their long-distance migrations and their adaptations to the polar environments. The risks they encounter in their migrations would be minor compared to the benefits they gain from their lives in continuous daylight, breeding in the Arctic and wintering in the Antarctic. The most comparable tern species that is highly pelagic is the sooty tern, and although the sooty tern is tropical and the Arctic tern is 'bipolar', they both range freely over the world's oceans at their chosen latitudes. It is probably no coincidence that these are the two longest-lived and the two most abundant of the world's terns.

CHAPTER 5

History of Terns in Britain and Ireland

D ESPITE THE IDENTIFICATION of many thousands of fossil bird bones from numerous sites ranging from the late Pleistocene to the medieval period in Britain and Ireland, very few have been identified as belonging to terns. The reason may be that far fewer coastal sites – where one would expect to find most tern bones – have been examined. Adult terns are also the most difficult to catch amongst our seabirds and therefore would be less likely to turn up in human-accumulated bone deposits from the Mesolithic and Neolithic periods. Juvenile terns are more easily caught but their bones are softer. Moreover, terns are only present in Britain and Ireland as summer migrants, for about five months each year, a relatively short period for them to be captured and killed by early humans or other predators. Other seabirds such as gulls, which are much better represented in bone deposits, would have been easier prey.

The fossil record suggests that terns were generally not present in Britain and Ireland until after the Late Glacial period (14,500 years BP [before the present day]) and even then several species are absent from the record. The earliest and most widespread fossil tern bones from these islands are of the common tern, with records dating from the Late Glacial/late Devensian period (73,000–10,000 years BP) in Herefordshire, from the Mesolithic period (c.7,000 years BP) in the Scottish Highlands, and from the Neolithic period (c.5,500 years BP) in the Inner Hebrides. There are also records from the Roman and Saxon periods.[1]

Bones of unidentified *Sterna* terns have been found in late Pleistocene/ Holocene deposits (about 15,000 years BP) from Derbyshire (Fig. 54), and Sandwich tern bones have been found at two Neolithic sites in Orkney. Other bones from the medieval period (AD 1350–1500) have been found in the City of London.

FIG 54. Cresswell Crags, set in a limestone gorge on the border between Derbyshire and Nottinghamshire. This is an artist's reconstruction of how the site would have appeared about 60,000 years before the present (BP). Bones of terns dating from about 15,000 years BP have been found here. The occurrence of terns at this inland site is unexpected, but common terns may have been nesting on rivers or lakes not far away. (Cresswell Heritage Trust)

There are records of little tern bones at single sites in Spain and in the Ukraine dating from the Middle and Lower Pleistocene periods, and Arctic tern bones have been found at two locations each in France and Italy, but there are no specific records of these two species in Britain or Ireland prior to the Late Glacial period. The absence of little and roseate terns probably reflects the relatively southern distribution of these two species, which would not have penetrated into northern areas until the climate had warmed up considerably. The absence of Arctic tern bones from Britain and Ireland is harder to explain as, of all the terns, they are the most tolerant of cold and the arctic conditions that have prevailed several times since the Late Glacial period.

Whatever the fossil record tells us about the early history of terns in Britain and Ireland, terns made their first appearance in early British literature in the West Saxon poem *The Seafarer*, written in the proximity of Bass Rock, East Lothian, sometime before AD 658. In James Fisher's translation of the poem, the critical sentence is rendered as follows: 'Storms there the stacks thrashed, there answered them the tern with icy feathers.' Fisher interpreted 'tern' ('stearn' in the original) to be the common tern, although it seems more likely from the location to have been the Arctic tern. Fisher estimated that the date of the poem related to 20–27 April, the time when the terns would be arriving on spring migration, possibly to breed on the nearby islands of Fidra, Lamb and Craigleith where they have been found in modern times.[2]

The *Seafarer* record was followed by many more reports from the sixteenth century onwards. For example, there is a reference in the *Northumberland Household Book* (1512) to 'ternes after iiij a jd' (i.e. terns were for sale at four a penny).[3] Later, the English naturalist William Turner in his *Avium praecipuarum historia* (1544) wrote 'Nostrati lingua sterna appellata' (it is called in our language 'sterna'): this probably referred to the black tern, which would almost certainly have been breeding near him in eastern England at that time.

The next documented presence of terns in Britain and Ireland dates from 1604, when terns were reported nesting in vast numbers in the estuary of the Tees: these were most likely common terns (see under common tern, p. 119).[4] The largest tern (the Sandwich) and smallest (the little) were both mentioned in 1671. The identification by naturalists of other tern species in Britain and Ireland followed in the early nineteenth century. According to James Fisher, gull-billed and roseate terns were first recorded in 1813 (in Montagu's *Supplement* to his *Ornithological Dictionary*), Arctic tern in 1819 (J. F. Naumann was the first to separate Arctic from common tern), Caspian tern in 1825 (shot at Yarmouth in October 1825), and bridled tern in 1831.[5] Other species were recorded from the beginning of the twentieth century. However, among the terns that are now vagrants – gull-billed, bridled and Caspian – it is not clear whether the nineteenth-century records indicate that they were then breeding in Britain or Ireland, although it is suspected that the gull-billed tern may have done so, as suggested by Edward Newman in 1866.[6]

So by the end of the Middle Ages at least three tern species were apparently breeding in Britain and Ireland, with the remaining two of our currently breeding species recorded in the early nineteenth century. A sixth breeding species, the black tern, nested abundantly in the marshes of eastern Britain, probably during the sixteenth century, certainly during the eighteenth century, but it then declined as its marsh habitat was drained until its demise in the middle of the nineteenth century. There was some spasmodic breeding of the black tern in the 1960s and 1970s, but it no longer breeds in Britain or Ireland (see Chapter 12).

The subsequent history of our five breeding terns from the early nineteenth century through Victorian times was largely a shameful litany of slaughter and exploitation of this elegant and graceful group of birds. Even after nearly 75 years of persecution, the five species of terns remained with us as breeding species at the end of the nineteenth century, although the fortunes of the roseate and little terns had fluctuated dramatically.

The trauma that British and Irish nesting terns had to endure during this period is best exemplified by what happened at one important tern colony: that on Mew Island, Co. Down. This was formerly one of the largest colonies in these islands and home to thousands of common, Arctic and roseate terns. Binoculars and telescopes were not available to naturalists at that time so other methods were used to 'study' them. We are indebted to William Thompson, a highly respected naturalist and member of one of the leading business families of Belfast in the nineteenth century, for his account of his visits to Mew Island. While his *Natural History of Ireland* is acclaimed for the quality of its ornithological observations, he also provided gruesome accounts of how naturalists went about their business in those days.[7]

Mew Island – a low rocky island covered by grasses and bracken – is one of the three Copeland Islands at the southern entrance of Belfast Lough (Fig. 55). Thompson first went to Mew Island on 11 June 1827 and found 'immense' numbers of breeding terns. His party landed, and after 'admiring the terns poised beautifully in the air, with their wings merely wafting' they fired their guns for some time at all birds that came within range, and having killed 11 they ceased. The tally was two roseate, one common and eight Arctic terns. They returned to the island on 13 June 1832 and shot indiscriminately – one

FIG 55. Mew Island, Copeland Islands, Co. Down. Large numbers of common, roseate and Arctic terns nested here in the early nineteenth century, but were wiped out by collectors by 1850. They had returned by 1890 and have continued to nest on the Copeland Islands to the present day. (Shane Wolsey)

roseate, three common and eight Arctic terns were 'procured'. Then on their next visit on 24 June 1833 they fired at all the terns that came close enough until 'the number required for science was obtained' – three roseate, two common and one Arctic. Fifty eggs were also collected. Moreover, Thompson reported that eggs were being collected daily and incessantly. Sometimes egg-gatherers stayed overnight to collect fresh eggs laid during the morning.

At the end of May 1833 another party had butchered not less than 50 terns, of which a dozen were roseate, all flung away as useless (for eating). Another dozen, all Arctic, were shot on 1 June. The boatman remarked that in previous years the terns were more than ten times as numerous as they were that year. In 1849 a boy took 147 eggs at the beginning of the season, while another visitor, J. R. Garrett, and his colleagues shot half a dozen terns for 'preservation' (although it seems that none of the specimens has actually been preserved). Garrett also reported that terns on Mew Island were in 'great abundance'. A year later, on 16 July 1850, Thompson was 'astonished and annoyed' to find no terns on the island. They had returned that year, but having been 'much fired at and robbed of their eggs' they all had left.

After such continuous persecution the roseate tern disappeared as a nesting species on Mew Island, and common terns virtually disappeared. And what went on at Mew Island was repeated at various other colonies, such as at Cumbrae Island in the Firth of Clyde. In 1812 Dr MacDougall and friends went there to shoot terns and gulls during the breeding season. They procured the first roseate tern known to science, but recorded little else, and the colony of 'thousands' of common terns was soon abandoned.

Sandwich terns breeding on the east and west coasts of Scotland were similarly persecuted by egg-collectors and shooters. The ornithologist Robert Gray, writing in 1871, noted that several hundred pairs breeding on the islets near Bass Rock and on islands in the Firth of Forth had deserted their colonies following egg-collecting and visits of shooters.[8] At Blakeney Point, Norfolk (Fig. 56), a local taxidermist noted that in August 1893, 'A party of gentlemen from Norwich, who generally put in an appearance the night before the 1st so as to be on the estuary by daybreak, got as usual a large bag, 156 of all sorts and ages, from full-grown Tern to birds that could scarcely rise from the ground. I was told by a gentleman who went to the Point on the 3rd and 4th that he did not see a Common Tern at all during the two days.'[9]

Despite the onslaught by Victorian and earlier naturalists, the survival of terns in Britain and Ireland during the nineteenth century was made possible by their habit of abandoning and switching breeding locations when disturbed. Terns breeding in inaccessible sites, such as Arctic terns in the northern and

FIG 56. Blakeney Point, Norfolk, viewed from the west. This is one of only three sites in Britain and Ireland where all five of our breeding species have been found nesting simultaneously. It has been protected since 1901, with a full-time warden in most years. Terns nest on the beach and dunes near the end of the barrier spit (centre) and feed along the shore, often concentrating in the mouth of the channel where tidal currents run in and out of Blakeney Harbour (foreground). (Mike Page)

western islands of Scotland, were spared some of the persecution that the more available terns had to endure.

The millinery trade was also responsible for the deaths of thousands of terns. In the latter part of the nineteenth century, hats adorned with feathers were worn by stylish women in most centres of fashon. Even whole bodies of birds were were used to embellish the hats (Fig. 57). Millions of birds were taken in Europe and in the United States at the height of the feather-trade years, between 1870 and 1920. Fine-plumed birds such as egrets and herons were especially targeted, and one auction record alone lists more than one million heron or egret skins sold in London between 1897 and 1911.[10] Terns were also extremely popular because of their long, elegant and delicate grey feathers. At one time the price of an ounce of fine feathers was five times the price of an ounce of gold.

What are thought to be the earliest bird protection laws in the world were established by the Anglo-Saxon monk St Cuthbert (634–687) who resided on the Farne Islands, Northumberland, sometime after 676. There he introduced laws to

FIG 57. A fashionable Victorian lady with a whole tern mounted on her hat. After egrets and hummingbirds, terns were among the birds most sought after for the millinery trade in the late nineteenth century. Market records indicate that hundreds of thousands of terns were killed for this purpose, both in Europe and in North America. (Unknown photographer)

protect the nesting eiders and seabirds, including terns. St Cuthbert effectively created a bird sanctuary. How effective these laws were after his death, and whether they endured until the nineteenth century, is not clear. What is certain, however, is that prior to 1869 there were very few protected areas for birds in Britain and Ireland.

Around the mid-1860s the persecution of terns and other seabirds was reaching its peak, and concern for their welfare led to the Sea Birds Preservation Act 1869. The prime mover was the Reverend Henry Frederick Barnes, who was incensed by the slaughter of seabirds at Bempton Cliffs and Flamborough Head on the Yorkshire coast. He formed the Association for the Protection of Seabirds, supported by scientists and others. Professor Alfred Newton, who was a scientific ornithologist and founder of the British Ornithologists' Union, championed the movement, gave a lecture at the British Association for the Advancement of Science in 1868 and urged for the protection of seabirds as well as birds of prey during the breeding season. The Act came into force on 24 June 1869; it was designed to reduce the effects of shooting and egg-collecting during the breeding season. The Act was ground-breaking, the first to protect wild birds in the United Kingdom, although enacted somewhat later than similar legislation in Germany and the Netherlands. Alfred Newton also started a campaign to prevent birds' feathers being used in the millinery trade, writing a letter to *The Times* on 28 June 1876 denouncing the wearing of plumage on hats. The campaign led to the formation of the Society for the Protection of Birds, which later became the Royal Society for the Protection of Birds (RSPB). The wearing of plumed headgear declined.

Alfred Newton and the Society for the Protection of Birds continued campaigning for legal protection for birds, and a series of Wild Bird Protection Acts were enacted in the UK between 1880 and 1902. However, enforcement was patchy and for a long period the most effective measures protecting terns were initiated by landowners, who sometimes employed wardens to patrol colonies. A more comprehensive Protection of Birds Act was enacted in 1954 and became a more effective tool to protect all birds, including terns. However, statutory designation of protected sites did not follow until some time later.

The collecting of wild bird eggs was considered an important part of ornithology in the nineteenth and early twentieth centuries. While initially thought of as a hobby activity 'for gentlemen inclined to natural history', it soon became 'professional', with collectors selling eggs for good prices, especially those of rare species. The eggs of roseate terns were especially high-priced after collecting had made the species rare in the late nineteenth century, but eggs of Sandwich and little terns were also much sought after. Oologists were responsible for the decline and local extermination of Sandwich and roseate terns from several colonies in Scotland and elsewhere. Although egg-collecting gradually fell out of fashion during the first few decades of the twentieth century, some oologists continued to amass large collections and to seek eggs of the rarer species to complete their coverage of British and Irish birds (Fig. 58). The leading oologist F. C. R. Jourdain was one of the authors of Witherby's *Handbook of British Birds*, and the meticulous data on the dimensions of eggs in the *Handbook* were all derived from his collection (including measurements of the first 100 eggs of each of our five breeding tern species).[11] The Protection of Birds Act 1954 finally made it impossible to collect eggs legally in the United Kingdom, but the practice of egg-collecting continued as an 'underground' or illegal activity in the UK and elsewhere. In 1962, David Bannerman commented that 'since the Bird Protection Act came into force, egg-thieving across the Irish Sea has become greatly intensified and the roseate terns have suffered accordingly.'[12] In Ireland, wild birds and their eggs were not effectively protected until after the passage of the Wildlife Act of 1976.

COMMON TERN
- *Sterna hirundo* -

SANDWICH TERN
- *Sterna sandvicensis* -

ROSEATE TERN
- *Sterna dougallii* -

SOOTY TERN
- *Sterna fuscata* -

ARCTIC TERN
- *Sterna paradisaea* -

BLACK TERN
- *Chlidonias niger* -

LITTLE TERN
- *Sterna albifrons* -

FIG 58. Eggs of British and Irish terns, plus one sooty tern egg (centre). Clockwise from top: Sandwich, roseate, black, little, Arctic and common terns. Egg-collecting was a popular pastime in the nineteenth century: large numbers of tern eggs were collected and often bought and sold. However, when they are displayed in this way with no information on the clutch, location or date, they have no scientific value. (Alan Ladd Gallery)

The remainder of this chapter summarises the history of our five breeding species from the early 1800s to approximately 1970. In 1934, George and Anne Marples published a very thorough compilation of data on the distribution, history and numbers of each species,[13] but the information available to them was fragmentary and it is difficult to discern any general patterns except for the decline of most species and the loss of breeding sites during the nineteenth century. By the end of that century at least three of our five species had reached low points, and their distributions in that period have been summarised by Holloway in his *Historical Atlas of Breeding Birds in Britain and Ireland*.[14] The Marples themselves visited many colonies between 1909 and 1933 and charted the early stages in the recovery of tern populations in several areas. However, despite the wide interest people had in terns in the ensuing decades, it was not until a survey of breeding little terns in Britain and Ireland in 1967[15] and a survey of all five species in 1969–74[16] that the first comprehensive overview of our breeding species became available. The results from that assessment and from more recent surveys on the status, distribution and trends of our five breeding species are explored in Chapters 6–10. Species which have bred in Britain or Ireland in the past, or only sporadically, are covered in Chapter 12.

LITTLE TERN

Little tern colonies were numerous and widespread around the coastlines of Britain and Ireland in the early and mid-nineteenth century (Fig. 59). The earliest breeding records appear to date from 1802, when little terns were said to be extremely common on the Lincolnshire coast, especially near Skegness. In the period from 1830 to 1850, they were said to be abundant on the coast of Northumberland near to Holy Island and were recorded at several sites in eastern and western Scotland and eastern Ireland, as well as in Suffolk and Kent.[17] By the 1870s they were nearly extinct in Lincolnshire and had declined in Northumberland, Yorkshire and Kent, but still bred in numbers in Suffolk, Essex, Dorset, north Wales and Lancashire. In 1871, Gray wrote that they were generally distributed over both the east and west coasts of Scotland, although colonies on the east coast were larger and more numerous.[18]

For the period 1875–1900, Holloway found records of nesting in 26 counties in Britain and 10 in Ireland.[19] However, most records of substantial numbers at that period were in the north and west of Britain and Ireland, including the east coast of Scotland, the Hebrides, the west coast of Ireland and a few locations around the Irish Sea. In 1895 there was a 'large colony' at Findhorn on the Moray Firth, and some 60–70 pairs at Killala Bay, Co. Mayo.

By the turn of the century, little tern populations appear to have started to recover in several parts of England. At Spurn Point in Yorkshire, protection was instituted in 1895 and numbers had built up to 100 pairs in 1900 (Fig. 60).

FIG 59. Little tern. (Engraving by John Thompson and sons from a drawing by Alexander Fussell for Yarrell's *History of British Birds*, 1843)

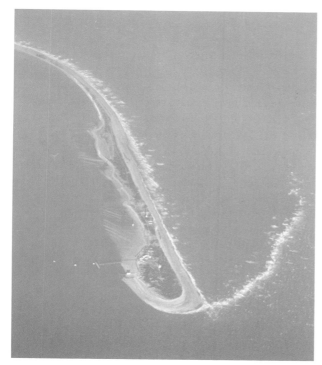

FIG 60. Spurn Point, Yorkshire. Little terns have nested at various points along this barrier spit since at least 1861 and have been protected there since 1895. (Stanley Howe)

By 1909 the little tern was nesting all along the coast of Kent, and by the 1920s and 1930s it had achieved more or less its present-day distribution, with highest numbers in eastern and southeastern England. The Marples found no records of nesting in Norfolk prior to 1919, but they thought it likely that it had bred there for many years previously. By the 1920s it was numerous all along the Norfolk coast, with more than 200 nests recorded in 1929.[20] John Parslow reviewed data for the first half of the twentieth century and concluded that little terns in Britain and Ireland had reached a peak in the 1920s and 1930s and had declined thereafter.[21] However, there is little systematic information from the 1930s until the first comprehensive surveys were conducted in 1967 and 1969–70, by which time little terns were nesting in 36 counties in Britain and 11 counties in Ireland,[22] with a total probably greater than 2,000 pairs (see Chapter 6). Little terns probably benefited from low levels of human activity on beaches during the Depression in the 1930s and the Second World War in the 1940s, but they suffered from increasing disturbance and were displaced from many nesting sites by the rapid increase in beach recreation during the 1950s and 1960s (Fig. 61).

FIG 61. Little tern with chick on a shingle beach, Kilcoole, Co. Wicklow. This is the largest and most productive colony of little terns in Ireland. Note the fence in the background, erected to keep out foxes and hedgehogs. The colony is also wardened throughout the breeding season. (Andrew Porter and Peter Cutler)

SANDWICH TERN

According to James Fisher the Sandwich tern (Fig. 62) was first mentioned in British literature in 1671, but it was not until 1784 that the first specimen was obtained at Sandwich, Kent, giving rise to its name. Dr William Boys, a former mayor of Sandwich, shot one and sent it to his fellow surgeon and friend, the ornithologist Dr John Latham, who then described and named it in 1785 in his *General Synopsis of Birds* (1781–1801).

Latham originally described it as breeding and 'pretty common' on the coast of Kent with 'vast flocks' nesting at Sandwich. In 1843, Yarrell also reported it from several localities in Kent and Essex and said that it was 'not uncommon' in Norfolk and Suffolk.[23] The first evidence of breeding away from this area was when it was discovered by the English ornithologist Prideaux John Selby nesting on the Knoxes, Farne Islands, Northumberland, prior to 1826.[24] However, Thomas Bewick had described two that were taken on the Farne Islands in 1802, by a Major Shore and Lieutenant Gibbon, 'with great trouble and risk'.[25] From then onwards until the 1940s the Farne Islands were the stronghold of the Sandwich tern in Britain.

Sandwich terns survived on the Farne Islands because of the protection afforded them there. Numbers peaked in 1892 when 2,400 nests were reported, a remarkable concentration at the end of a century noted for the pillage and plunder

FIG 62. Sandwich tern. (Engraving by John Thompson and sons from a drawing by Alexander Fussell for Yarrell's *History of British Birds*, 1843)

of terns. Following this increase in numbers there were some 1,000–1,200 nests on the Knoxes. They continued to breed in numbers on the Farnes through to 1932 with a 'temporary' desertion in 1923.[26] However, those nesting on Coquet Island, some 39 km south, were less fortunate and were exterminated by egg-collectors sometime during the 1870s, a fate similar to that suffered by those attempting to nest on small islands off Holy Island, some 15 km northwest of the Farnes.

In 1920 one or two pairs were found breeding at Blakeney Point in Norfolk, where common terns were already nesting. By 1929 Sandwich tern numbers there had risen to 1,000 pairs. From 1922 Sandwich terns were switching between the three north Norfolk colonies at Scolt Head, Blakeney Point and Salthouse Marsh. The last two of these sites were on the mainland and there was systematic protection at all three with full-time wardens. Numbers there continued to increase steadily until the north Norfolk colonies held more than a quarter of the British and Irish total in 1969 (Table 7). Sandwich terns also settled in the 1950s and 1960s at two reserves established in Suffolk by the RSPB, peaking at 800 pairs in 1962 but then decreasing again.[27]

Sandwich terns had also been nesting at Walney Island, Cumbria, from at least 1843, occupying both the north and south ends of the island. There were 40 nesting pairs in 1880 and the colony fluctuated in numbers over the years. By 1889 the colony had been broken up by several egg robberies and the terns moved to the south end of the colony where there were six pairs in 1890. Persecution by herring gulls and lesser black-backed gulls also hastened

TABLE 7. Numbers of nesting pairs of Sandwich terns in three major groups of colonies, 1920–1969. Total numbers increased steadily during this period, except for a temporary reduction in 1954–59.

Year	Firth of Forth	Farne Islands	East Anglia	Total
1920	few	1,000	1	1,000
1923	400	0	640	1,040
1932	less than 50	2,000	820	2,850
1939	500	2,000	1,000	3,500
1946	1,500	120	1,900	3,520
1954	400	960	380	1,740
1957	400	800	1,520	2,720
1959	700	1,250	1,220	3,170
1962	1,120	1,480	1,460	4,060
1964	500	1,500	2,010	4,010
1969	50	2,000	4,120	6,170

Sources: Parslow, 1967–68; Cramp et al., 1974.

the departure of the terns. Birds from Walney almost certainly spread, under pressure, to nest sometime before 1887 in the sand dunes at Ravenglass, Cumbria, some 25 km to the north. They were more successful there but again with fluctuating numbers – in 1888 there were 18 pairs, in 1889 21 pairs, in 1891 34 nests and later 71 nests.[28] By 1930 there were 12 pairs, in 1931 some 70 pairs, and the maximum colony strength was 379 pairs in 1932.[29] Upwards of 100,000 black-headed gulls were also nesting at Ravenglass at the beginning of the twentieth century, affording the Sandwich terns some security from predators. The colony flourished, as it was protected as a bird sanctuary by its owner, Lord Muncaster. Under his protection the colony thrived and the number of Sandwich tern eggs recorded there rose from 120 in 1900 to 403 in 1912.[30] One interesting technique employed to discourage egg-collectors was to label each Sandwich tern egg with the word 'Ravenglass' around its circumference and to mark both ends of the egg with an indelible pen, thus rendering the eggs unsightly and unattractive.[31] Elsewhere, Sandwich terns bred in Cornwall (1865), Anglesey (a few pairs discovered in 1914, and the next year 30–40 pairs) and the Channel Islands. On the Isle of Man there were a few isolated cases of small numbers breeding from 1854 onwards. They nested on the Isles of Scilly up to the early 1840s.

In Scotland, Sandwich terns were victimised by egg-collectors and shooters, so that some of the earliest colonies found on the Isle of May, Bass Rock and other islands in the Firth of Forth in the 1840s had disappeared by the 1850s. The Scottish ornithologist Robert Gray wrote in 1871 that 'Serious inroads have been made on its breeding haunts on both the east and west coasts, and in places where formerly their eggs could have been seen in hundreds it is now a rare occurrence to find more than ... one or two nests.'[32] They were spasmodic breeders elsewhere in Scotland during the late nineteenth and early twentieth centuries, especially along the east coast from the Borders to Orkney. In Orkney they bred spasmodically on North Ronaldsay, Sanday and at five other locations. In southwest Scotland they bred especially on the Clyde islands, on Horse and Lady Islands as well as at Troon. On the other side of Scotland the colony breeding at the protected site on Tentsmuir Point, Fife, was well known. There were 120 pairs in 1907, 110 pairs in 1933 and 500 pairs in 1939.[33] Numbers breeding in Scotland increased after 1945 with the establishment of some very large colonies such as that at the Sands of Forvie National Nature Reserve, Aberdeenshire (Fig. 63). A small colony established itself there in 1932 but did not reappear until 1954 when there were 31 pairs. Numbers increased during the 1950s and 1960s, peaking at 2,100 pairs in 1971, the largest colony ever recorded in Scotland (Table 8).

In Ireland very little was known about the Sandwich tern before 1850. It was first identified from a specimen shot in Belfast Lough on 14 August 1832 which came into the possession of William Thompson. There is also an earlier record of one being shot near Clontarf, Dublin, in October 1831. Sandwich terns possibly

TABLE 8. Numbers of Sandwich tern pairs nesting at Sands of Forvie Nature Reserve, Aberdeenshire, 1954–1971. Numbers steadily increased during this period, but with marked fluctuations from year to year.

Year	Number of pairs	Year	Number of pairs
1954	100	1963	382
1955	29	1964	565
1956	110	1965	724
1957	224	1966	743
1958	208	1967	743
1959	13	1968	1,345
1960	165	1969	740
1961	63	1970	1,281
1962	357	1971	2,100

Source: A. J. M. Smith in Cramp *et al.*, 1974.

FIG 63. Sands of Forvie Nature Reserve, Aberdeenshire, viewed from the south. Sandwich terns have nested at this site since 1954 and reached a peak of over 2,000 nesting pairs in 1971. This was the site of a major study in the early 1970s (Smith, 1975). The terns nest among the dunes on the north side of the river and forage in the estuary and at sea. (Stanley Howe)

bred there in 1834, and it is likely that they also bred in Strangford Lough in 1844. But proof of first nesting in Ireland came when John Watters visited Rockabill, a small rocky islet off the Dublin coast, on 17 July 1850. He found an egg and saw three adults. The following year the Sandwich tern was discovered breeding on Bartragh Island in the mouth of the River Moy, Co. Mayo.

One of the earliest and largest colonies known was at Cloonagh Lough, near Ballina, Co. Mayo. This was a small lough, about 10 ha, surrounded by bogland. When discovered in 1857, the terns nested on a low muddy sandbank close to a colony of black-headed gulls. Twenty-six years later the colony shifted, due to rising water levels, to the nearby Rathroen Lough. This colony was protected by the landowner, Sir Charles Knox-Gore, and the birds did well: at least 150 pairs were nesting in 1886 and the colony endured until at least 1900, underscoring the fact that during the nineteenth and early twentieth centuries tern colonies flourished wherever they were protected. There were historically more inland breeding sites in Ireland than in England, Wales or Scotland. Those breeding on two islands in Lower Lough Erne, Co. Fermanagh, in 1997, were of interest because the adults had to fly 20 km to the nearest salt water in Donegal Bay to collect sandeels to feed their chicks. On another inland site at Lough Conn, Co. Mayo, there were a few pairs in 1903 and 100 pairs in 1906, rising to 300 pairs in 1923.

Holloway's compilation indicated that Sandwich terns were found breeding in only five counties in Britain and one in Ireland in the late nineteenth century, but that these numbers had increased to 22 counties in Britain and 13 in Ireland by 1970.[34] In 1892, almost all the birds were at the Farne Islands, where 2,400 pairs were reported. They then increased and spread steadily during the twentieth century (Table 7) until about 12,000 pairs were documented in *Operation Seafarer* in 1969–70 (see Chapter 7).

COMMON TERN

The common tern (Figs 64 and 65) is today the most widely distributed of the five British and Irish breeding terns, occupying not only coastal breeding sites but also many inland freshwater locations. Nevertheless, it is only the second most numerous species after the Arctic tern. Together with the Sandwich tern it has the longest fossil history in these islands. However, historical information about colonies and identification must be treated with caution, because before the widespread use of optical equipment common terns were easily confused with roseate and Arctic terns, especially when in mixed colonies. In the past the question of identification had to be settled through the barrel of a fowling piece, and such methods yielded little useful information on relative numbers.

FIG 64. Common tern. (Engraving by John Thompson and sons from a drawing by Alexander Fussell for Yarrell's *History of British Birds*, 1843)

FIG 65. Common terns appear to have been less affected by human persecution during the nineteenth century than little, Sandwich or roseate terns, and were still widespread and fairly numerous in Britain and Ireland at the end of the century. They then increased under protection and are thought to have reached peak numbers in the 1930s. The black tip on the bill of common terns progressively decreases in extent during the breeding season: this bird, photographed in late July, shows virtually no black. Plymouth, USA. (Jim Fenton)

A further problem is that the common tern was not distinguished from the Arctic tern until J. F. Naumann described the latter as a separate species in 1819 and described it further in his *Natural History of German Birds* (1820–1844). The earliest known breeding record of any tern in these islands is of a nesting colony in the estuary of the River Tees in 1604: 'Neer unto Dobhoome (the port in the mouth of the Tease so named) … an infinite number of sea-fowle laye their egges here and there scatteringlie in such sorte that in tyme of breedinge one can hardly sette his foote so warylye that hee spoyle not many of their nestes.'[35] Another early breeding site was at Hornsea Mere, East Yorkshire, in 1693: two islands in the mere were 'so full of tern eggs and birds as can be imagined'.[36] These records are both likely to refer to common terns, because Teesmouth is now an important breeding site for common terns and Hornsea Mere is a freshwater lake south of the main breeding range of Arctic terns. Other early records of breeding terns were on Caldey Island, south Wales, and Puffin Island, north Wales, in 1662; on the Isle of Walney, Cumbria, in 1700;[37] and on islands off the coast of Co. Cork around 1750.[38] These might have been either common or Arctic terns, or both.

Thomas Bewick, writing in 1804, described the common tern as 'pretty common in the summer months on the sea-coasts, rivers and lakes of the British Isles'. This was before the separation of the Arctic tern, but he clearly described a common tern with a black tip to the bill. The reference to rivers and lakes suggests that the common tern was widespread inland at that date.

By the time the distinctions between the two species became known in the 1830s, Arctic terns appear to have been much more numerous, at least on northern coasts. The great British ornithologist and bird illustrator Prideaux John Selby wrote in 1833 that the common tern 'is of rare occurrence upon the whole extent of the eastern shores of the north of England and Scotland, where its place seems to be supplied by the Arctic and roseate species.' He noted two or three pairs on the Farne Islands.[39] He was supported by Sir William Jardine, writing in 1843, who stated that the common tern was a much more uncommon bird that the roseate or Arctic tern and agreed that it was by no means frequent on the eastern side of Britain. He observed them, sparingly, in the Firth of Forth, a few breeding on the Isle of May.[40] Both of these statements that common terns were uncommon apparently referred only to Scotland and northeastern England: they were said to be 'very common' in Norfolk in 1834.[41] Yarrell stated in 1843 that they were numerous in Sussex, Kent, Norfolk and Suffolk, but more sparingly distributed in Durham and Northumberland.[42]

The colony at Blakeney Point, Norfolk, is one of the best known in Britain. The first record of common terns nesting there was in 1815 and the site is thought to have been occupied continuously since then. We recounted earlier how it was being harassed by eggers and shooters in the 1890s, but it was acquired by Lord Calthorpe and designated as a bird sanctuary in 1901. Bob Pinchen, a former wildfowler, was appointed as the first 'watcher' with a salary of 15 shillings per week, and lived there in a houseboat each summer for about 20 years. The size and success of the tern colonies increased immediately. In 1912 the property was purchased by the National Trust, due in large part to the efforts of F. W. Oliver, a keen field ecologist and professor of botany at University College London, and following a public appeal which led to the funds being committed by Charles Rothschild.[43] Oliver built a laboratory at Blakeney Point in 1913 and William Rowan conducted the first tern study there, measuring large numbers of common tern eggs in 1913 and 1914 (see Appendix 2). By 1923, all five of our breeding species were nesting there, including more than 2,000 pairs of common terns (Table 9).[44] The nearby tern colony site at Scolt Head was also acquired by the National Trust in 1923, and both sites have been managed continuously since then.[45] Under this degree of protection, numbers of common terns at the two sites peaked at over 4,500 pairs in 1938 (Table 9), but declined again to 1,700 pairs by 1969 because predation could not be fully controlled (see Table 27 and discussion in Chapter 11).[46]

In the early nineteenth century common terns were also abundant in Kent and Sussex, and a colony at Dungeness was said to have been occupied for centuries. However, there is only scattered information from other parts of England and Wales for the entire nineteenth century. They were common in Glamorgan in the 1830s[47] and in the Isles of Scilly in the 1840s, although outnumbered there by Arctic terns and much reduced by 1864.[48] In the 1870s and 1880s they were reported to be abundant in Suffolk, and on Chesil Beach in Dorset. There were several historical breeding sites in Lancashire and Cumbria, including the famous colony at Ravenglass, but there were few actual records of nesting or estimates of numbers until the early years of the twentieth century. There were 'considerable numbers' at Foulney in 1840, and nesting was recorded at Ainsdale in 1873; both these sites were apparently occupied continuously through the nineteenth century and the colonies were flourishing in the 1930s.[49]

TABLE 9. Numbers of common tern nests at Blakeney Point and Scolt Head, Norfolk, 1921–1952. Considerable numbers were also reported nesting on Salthouse Marsh in 1927, 1931 and 1932. Total numbers at the three sites increased steadily until the late 1930s and then stabilised.

Year	Blakeney Point	Scolt Head
1921	200–300	No information
1922	Probably 2,000	627
1923	'Slight increase' on 2,000	515
1924	No figures available	1,070
1925	700	385
1926	Two colonies of several hundreds	665
1927	'Usual number'	584
1928	700	900
1929	Several hundreds	547
1930	'Usual number'	700
1931	Some thousand nests	500
1932	1,459 nests with 3,799 eggs	500–600
1933	1,543 nests counted	2,000
1934–1950	Over 2,000 pairs in 1935–40 and 1950–52	About 2,000 annually; peak 2,470 in 1938

Sources: Marples and Marples, 1934; Chestney, 1970; Cramp et al., 1974.

In Scotland the common tern was a widespread and common breeding bird on both the west and east coasts, maintaining a breeding distribution that persisted for much of the nineteenth and twentieth centuries. Both numbers and the extent of the breeding range in Scotland appeared to increase towards the end of the nineteenth century, although the picture is obscured by the movement of birds from site to site and by likely confusion with Arctic terns.[50] Common terns in Scotland seemed to have been less affected by the intensity of egg-collecting and shooting than those in other parts of Britain and Ireland. Inland breeding on freshwater lochs, riverbanks and river islands was also a historical feature.[51]

In Ireland, common terns were historically widespread throughout the country, breeding not only on the coastline and on offshore islands but also on islands in freshwater lakes. There is little information on their history, numbers or trends. We do know, however, that they were breeding on uninhabited islands off the coast of Co. Cork around 1750.[52]

One of the earliest coastal colonies noted was on the Copeland Islands, Co. Down. 'Vast numbers' were reported breeding there in 1827 and they continued to do so until at least 1849, but as described earlier they were heavily persecuted and were probably extirpated in 1850. They were again reported breeding there during the late 1890s when the Commissioners of Irish Lights directed the lighthouse keepers to prevent visitors from taking tern eggs.[53] Common terns were also reported breeding in 1830 in a saltmarsh at Killough Bay, Co. Down. William Thompson noted that they were observed there by telescope, feeding their young (if telescopes were available, one wonders why it was generally felt necessary to shoot terns in order to identify them). They were also nesting on the small islets in Strangford Lough, Co. Down, in 1850 when there were 'very many'.

Further south there was a large mixed colony with Arctic terns at Malahide, Co. Dublin, where they were breeding on the beach in 1837.[54] They bred in the 1850s, and probably sometime earlier, on the beaches in Cos. Dublin, Wicklow and Wexford, but by 1890 the Malahide colony was the only one remaining in Leinster.[55] Numbers there were considered 'incalculable' in 1908, while in 1922 the colony was estimated at 3,000–4,000 birds, of which 90 per cent were considered to be common terns.[56]

At one time there may have been more common terns nesting inland in Ireland than along the coast. Nesting on freshwater lakes was widespread, with colonies on islands in 14 major inland lakes in the late 1890s, including the Great Loughs of Connacht – Lough Corrib, Co. Galway (Fig. 66) and Loughs Carra, Conn and Mask, Co. Mayo. However, common terns were said to be less numerous than Arctic terns. Other inland nesting locations included Lough Neagh (1833) and Port Lough, Co. Donegal (1832).[57] Numbers of terns at these

FIG 66. Lough Corrib, Co. Galway, where Sandwich, common and Arctic terns were once fairly common breeders. Most of the terns disappeared during the second quarter of the twentieth century, probably because numbers of breeding gulls greatly increased, and only very small numbers of Sandwich and common terns still nest at inland sites in Ireland. Sandwich terns have never been reported breeding at freshwater sites in Britain; Arctic terns formerly nested at some freshwater sites in Scotland but apparently no longer do so. (Oscar Merne)

inland colonies declined in the 1920s and 1930s as numbers of gulls increased, and several sites were deserted by the 1940s.[58]

For the period 1875–1900, Holloway found records of common terns nesting in 37 counties in Britain and 21 counties in Ireland, making it more widespread than any of our other terns. By 1970, these numbers of counties had increased to 61 and 26, respectively.[59] However, it is not clear whether this change reflected spread into new areas or simply improved coverage. Although common terns were counted annually at many breeding sites in England and Wales during that period, there was no comprehensive survey until *Operation Seafarer* in 1969–70. Parslow considered that total numbers in England had peaked in the 1930s and declined thereafter.[60]

In summary, the common tern was the first tern species to be recorded breeding in Britain and Ireland, and appears to have been widespread and locally abundant, both along the coasts and inland, until at least the early nineteenth century. Due to heavy persecution numbers declined in some areas from the 1840s until the beginning of the twentieth century, when early protection measures led to increases at some sites. However, there were still large numbers at some sites throughout this period, especially in Scotland. Overall trends are difficult to discern, but total numbers may have peaked in the 1930s and declined thereafter. The current numbers and distribution of common terns in Britain and Ireland were more or less reached by 1969.

ROSEATE TERN

The roseate tern (Fig. 67) suffered catastrophically from persecution in the nineteenth century, in the form of egg-collecting and shooting, both for 'science' and for the millinery trade. It came close to extinction as a breeding species in Britain and Ireland in the late nineteenth century and had probably not fully recovered when it suffered another population crash in the 1970s.

There is no prehistoric evidence of the roseate tern in these islands. The species was described as new to science by the great British ornithologist George Montagu in 1813, based on one of four specimens shot on 24 May 1812 by a companion of Dr Peter MacDougall of Glasgow at a tern colony in the Firth of Clyde (hence the scientific name *Sterna dougallii*). There were 'thousands' of common terns on the islands (although these might well have been Arctic terns, as discussed above) and the ratio of roseate to common terns was thought to be about one to two hundred. Over the next few decades roseate terns were found breeding at many sites in Britain and Ireland, but their main distribution seems to have been similar to that at the present day, with largest numbers around the Irish Sea and a secondary group in northeast England and eastern Scotland.

FIG 67. Roseate tern. (Engraving by John Thompson and sons from a drawing by Alexander Fussell for Yarrell's *History of British Birds*, 1843)

In Ireland, a major colony was at Mew Island, one of the Copeland Islands, Co. Down. The fate of the terns there has been described above. First discovered in 1827, this colony with 'immense' numbers of breeding terns was destroyed by egg-collecting and shooting and was apparently deserted by 1850. Although the numbers of roseates were not specifically reported, it is worth noting that 20 roseates were among 67 terns collected, most of the rest being Arctic terns.[61]

There was another large colony on Rockabill, Co. Dublin. It was first discovered in 1837, and there were stated to be 'hundreds' of roseate terns in 1844, but this colony also was destroyed by egg-collecting and shooting. Numbers had diminished by 1847, and by 1850 they had decreased to between 70 and 80.[62] Elsewhere in Ireland the roseate tern nested off the Wexford coast but by 1865 it had become rare.

Early information for other sites around the Irish Sea is sketchy. At Foulney in Lancashire, roseates were said to be in equal numbers to common terns in 1840, but they were eliminated by egg-collectors and only one pair was found in 1865. On the Isles of Scilly, they were 'tolerably common' in 1840, when a collector 'obtained as many eggs as he required', but were harassed by egg-collectors and no longer bred in 1864 (the statement by Marples & Marples that they were abundant in 1869, citing Rodd, appears to have been erroneous).[63] They nested on the Cumbraes in the Firth of Clyde but had deserted the area by 1848. Gray discovered a large colony on an island in Kilbrannon Sound, between Arran and Kintyre in southwest Scotland, in 1853. It was still healthy in 1865 when he collected 'a basketful' of eggs for his collection, but appears to have been deserted soon afterwards.[64]

In eastern Scotland, a large colony was reported on the Isle of May in 1843, and Gray reported a colony in the Moray Firth some time before 1871. At the Farne Islands in northeastern England, Selby reported them nesting 'plentifully' from 1818 to 1833, but Hewitson said there were only a few pairs in 1831;[65] in 1843 Yarrell reported that they had greatly increased and 'now form a numerous colony, which occupies a large space of ground' on two islands: he gave a convincing description.[66] A few also nested at Coquet Island in 1830.[67]

Between 1865 and 1890 there were only scattered records of roseate terns nesting anywhere in Britain or Ireland and the species seems to have reached a very low ebb. In 1896 Seebohm wrote 'it is doubtful whether the Roseate Tern nests in any part of the British Isles at the present time',[68] and in 1900 Ussher and Warren wrote 'There is not sufficient evidence to show that the Roseate Tern breeds in Ireland at the present day.'[69] However, a few pairs may have nested at the Farne Islands throughout this period, and there is incomplete information about a colony at the Skerries, Anglesey. This colony was first described in 1907 and was then said to have been known for 'a good many years'. The lighthouse keeper shot four birds in 1892 and described it as a 'very large colony', but it is not clear that this statement referred specifically to roseate terns. Nine clutches of eggs were taken in 1896 but rats were found at the site in 1905 and the roseate terns were 'considerably reduced' by 1908, apparently moving to a new site at Llandwyn.[70] The species probably also survived through this period in France (see Appendix 2).[71]

The roseate tern population rebounded in the early years of the twentieth century and then increased very rapidly. The colony at Llandwyn, Anglesey, had 'many' roseates in 1902 and increased to 500 birds by 1910 and 300 pairs in 1918. Roseate terns colonised two other sites in Anglesey in 1916 and 1922 and recolonised the Skerries in 1925, increasing to 200–300 pairs in 1928.[72] They re-established themselves in Ireland by 1906 and several large colonies were discovered in 1913, 1917 and 1922, with 500 pairs at one site in 1923 and 1924 and 329 pairs at another in 1932. Because of the threat posed by egg-collectors (and mutual jealousy among the collectors) there was much secrecy about breeding locations, making it difficult to unravel the history of this tern in Ireland, but these sites were apparently all on the east coast. In 1941, a team of ornithologists found remarkable numbers of terns on the Copeland Islands. In all, 17,600 birds were counted, including what they considered to be a minimum of 243 pairs of roseates on Mew Island.[73] In southwest Scotland, roseate terns nested on seven islands in the Firth of Clyde from about 1942, with 90 pairs on Lady Isle in 1953, but they had been reduced to 12 pairs on one island in 1969.[74] They recolonised eastern Scotland in 1927 and subsequently bred on several islands in the Firth of Forth, including the Isle of May, with 450 pairs on Inchmickery in 1957–62

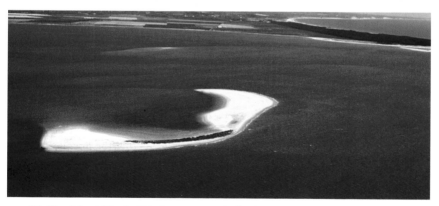

FIG 68. Tern Island, Wexford Harbour, Co. Wexford, 1975. Tern Island was one of only three sites where all five British and Irish terns have been recorded nesting together. It supported 2,000 pairs of roseate terns in 1968, the largest colony ever recorded in Britain and Ireland. (Oscar Merne)

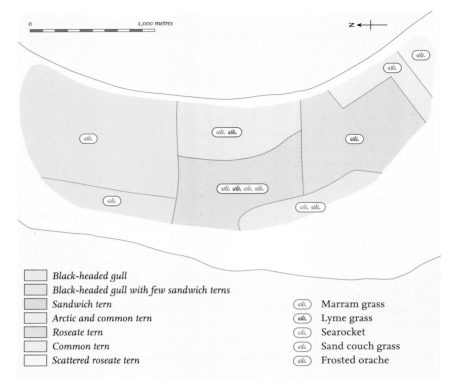

0   1,000 metres

Black-headed gull
Black-headed gull with few sandwich terns
Sandwich tern
Arctic and common tern
Roseate tern
Common tern
Scattered roseate tern

Marram grass
Lyme grass
Searocket
Sand couch grass
Frosted orache

FIG 69. Habitat partitioning by terns and black-headed gulls at Tern Island, Co. Wexford. In its heyday Tern Island was about 300 m long by 75 m wide, with a maximum elevation of 3 m. Roseate terns nested most densely under overhanging and protective lyme grass up to 1 m high, common terns favoured much shorter vegetation dominated by marram grass with patches of open sand, while Arctic terns were found in less vegetated areas, especially on pebbly sand. Sandwich terns were most dense in open areas dominated by sand couch grass, frosted orache and searocket. Black-headed gulls nested at the edge of the island with clumps of marram grass. They were mixed with Sandwich terns in an area dominated by marram and lyme grasses. The few little terns present on the island nested on open sand/shingle around the periphery. (Source: D. Cabot, unpublished data)

and 100 pairs on Fidra in 1969. In northeastern England, numbers at the Farne Islands increased to 90 pairs in 1961 and those at Coquet Island increased to 230 pairs in 1965, including birds derived from the Firth of Forth colonies (see Chapter 11). Small numbers also bred from the 1920s onwards at Walney Island, Cumbria, in north Norfolk and on the Isles of Scilly. Total numbers in Britain and

Ireland continued to increase until they exceeded 3,300 pairs in 1968, including about 2,000 pairs at Tern Island, Co. Wexford (Figs 68 and 69; see also Chapter 9).

ARCTIC TERN

The Arctic tern (Fig. 70) appears to have been the least affected of all our terns by human depredations. The reasons are unclear, but their distribution in the Northern and Western Isles and the location of many of their colonies on remote islands, often far from the coast and difficult to reach, would have made them less accessible to humans than the other terns.

In the 1830s and 1840s, Selby, Yarrell and Jardine considered that the Arctic tern was more numerous than the common and roseate terns along the coasts of northeastern England and Scotland (see above under common tern). Historically the largest Arctic tern colony on the east coast of Britain was on the Farne Islands, where it was recorded breeding as early as 1687, possibly much earlier. It was nesting there in great numbers in 1866, 1871 and 1882. Within the Farne Islands group the Wideopen and Knox islands held over 1,000 nests in 1892 with 'large numbers' in 1911, while on the Brownsman there was a large and increasing colony with 1,100 nests in 1912. There were a further 500 pairs on Longstone. Arctic terns were reputed to have outnumbered common terns by thousands. Sometime before 1920 common terns are said to have displaced the Arctic terns, but in 1932 large numbers were found breeding on the Brownsman

FIG 70. Arctic tern. (Engraving by John Thompson and sons from a drawing by Alexander Fussell for Yarrell's *History of British Birds*, 1843)

with fewer on the Lesser Farne.[75] They bred in large numbers on Coquet Island, about 39 km south, in the 1840s,[76] but ceased to breed there around 1851–62. Only small and insignificant numbers bred further south, and the great Norfolk tern colonies at Blakeney Point and Scolt Head were more or less devoid of them until a few pairs started to nest there in 1922.

Apart from a few isolated pairs, Arctic terns were generally absent from the rest of the eastern and southern English coasts, as well as from south Wales. In the Isles of Scilly, they were more numerous than common terns in the first half of the nineteenth century and were probably breeding there, although this was not clearly stated.[77] In north Wales there was one large colony on the Skerries off northwestern Anglesey, where there were several thousand pairs from 1905 to 1935, declining to zero by the 1950s.[78] Further north at the tern colony at Walney Island, Cumbria, Arctic terns were nesting in about equal numbers with common terns in 1864 when there were four nests, increasing to about 40 in 1865. They were still there in 1871 but by 1875 common terns comprised about 75 per cent of the colony. Some early ornithologists were convinced that common terns drove Arctic terns away from mixed colonies. At Ravenglass, Cumbria, there was a mixed colony of Arctic and common terns in 1865 but they had disappeared by 1892.

The Arctic tern was, historically, more at home in Scotland than anywhere else in Britain, with strongholds in the Outer Hebrides, Orkney and Shetland. It was also a common breeding bird, albeit in lower densities, on the northern and northwestern coastlines. By the time of the first comprehensive census in 1969–70, about 88 per cent of the total number of Arctic terns in Britain and Ireland were in Scotland.[79] Unfortunately, most of the detailed information on numbers, trends and productivity of Arctic terns has been obtained in the southernmost breeding areas in southern Scotland, England and Ireland, and it is not clear whether events in these peripheral breeding populations are representative of the whole.

During the latter part of the nineteenth century densities of Arctic terns were apparently highest in the Outer Hebrides (especially on Lewis, Harris and the Monachs), where many small islands and rocks were 'literally covered with terns and nests'. Large colonies were found on Haskeir in 1869 and on Ronay in 1886 and 1887. Arctic terns were first reported in Shetland in 1864 and subsequently bred there in great numbers. They were very common on the Vie Skerries in 1874 but only a few remained there by 1890. One of the largest Shetland colonies in 1874 was on the island of Hunie, off the shores of Unst. Many of the small islands and rocky islets on the west coast held colonies in the latter half of the nineteenth century.

On the Scottish east coast, there were substantial colonies in 1837 in the Firth of Forth, on the Isle of May and Bass Rock, outliers from the main distribution pattern. There was also a colony at Tentsmuir from at least 1865, with 12 pairs in

1885. The site at Findhorn has been occupied since at least 1887. There were also several Scottish inland breeding sites.[80]

There were no pronounced changes in distribution in Scotland during the nineteenth and twentieth centuries, but there is no reliable information on total numbers or trends. It is thought that numbers may have declined during the nineteenth century, but this is uncertain because identification problems with the common tern may have confused the trends.[81] The only reliable historical information is for Tentsmuir, where numbers reached a peak of 500 pairs in 1953, and the Isle of May, where 800 pairs nested in 1936; almost all birds had gone from both sites by 1969.[82]

In Ireland the naturalist William Thompson was surprised when an unknown tern 'came under his observation' – presumably meaning that had been shot – in June 1827. He did not know what it was and thought it an 'ornithological treasure'. At that time the Arctic tern was not well known, because Naumann had only described the species for the first time a few years earlier. Fortunately Selby had just published (in 1826) a paper on the birds of the Farne Islands in which he described the Arctic tern, saying that it had been 'long confounded with *Sterna hirundo*'. Thompson read Selby's paper and learned that his 'ornithological treasure' was an Arctic tern.

Although historically widely distributed around the coasts of Ireland, Arctic terns were mainly concentrated along the west and northwest coasts, especially in Cos. Donegal, Mayo, Galway and Kerry. Outside this area Co. Down also held substantial colonies on the Copeland Islands, where they were breeding in the 1840s before being persecuted by humans. There were also important historical colonies in Co. Donegal, on the islands of Inishbarnog and Inishduff, that reputedly held 'enormous colonies', but these islands were deserted by 1960.[83] The islands off the Connemara coast, especially around Slyne Head, also held significant colonies. A colony on Inishmurray, off the coast of Co. Sligo, held 500–1,000 Arctic terns in 1955 and was said to be of long standing.[84] Another significant colony was on the island of Roaninish, Gweebarra Estuary, Co. Donegal, where some 300 pairs nested during the first part of the twentieth century.[85] Most of these coastal colonies appear to have declined during the twentieth century and fewer than 1,000 pairs in total were found in Ireland during *Operation Seafarer* in 1969–70.

Inland breeding sites were a historical feature in Ireland, with Arctic tern colonies, often mixed with common terns, on islands in the Great Loughs of Carra and Mask, Co. Mayo; Lough Corrib, Co. Galway; and Lough Melvin, Co. Leitrim. Curiously William Thompson in his *Natural History of Ireland* (1851) did not mention any inland breeding colonies, despite allocating six pages to the species. He regarded the Arctic tern as a marine species. Arctic terns certainly bred on islands in those lakes at the end of the nineteenth century,[86] but by 1929 the colony on Lough Carra had gone while the others were in decline or about to disappear. They had gone from Loughs Corrib, Mask, Carra and Conn by 1960.[87]

HISTORICAL OVERVIEW: NUMBERS AND TRENDS BEFORE 1970

To summarise the scattered information that we have assembled for this chapter, there is no evidence from the fossil record that terns were present in Britain or Ireland until the warming period following the last glacial maximum about 15,000 years ago, although Arctic terns could have survived as breeders in the far southwest. Records were then scanty until the era of collecting and scientific recording started in the early nineteenth century. By then the gull-billed and Caspian terns were gone – if they had ever nested here, which is uncertain. The remaining six species were common to abundant and five of them were widely distributed in the early nineteenth century. The black tern bred abundantly at that time in the fens of eastern England, but was extirpated by the middle of the nineteenth century through loss of its habitat to drainage. The remaining five species were severely persecuted by humans throughout most of Britain and Ireland during the nineteenth century and were reduced to very low numbers by the 1880s. The roseate tern was virtually eliminated, but it apparently survived at one site in Anglesey and in very small numbers at the Farne Islands. The little tern was reduced to probably a few hundred pairs, mainly in the north and west, and the Sandwich tern to probably a few thousand pairs, mainly at the Farne Islands. The common tern, although much reduced in numbers, was still widely distributed in the period 1875–1900. Numerical estimates for that period are scanty, but some of the common tern colonies probably included hundreds or low thousands of pairs. The Arctic tern was reduced in numbers at peripheral sites in England, Wales and Ireland, but there were still more than a thousand nests on the Farne Islands in 1892, and there is no evidence that they were significantly reduced at their main breeding strongholds in the Northern and Western Isles.

Under expanding protection, all five species increased rapidly during the early part of the twentieth century and spread out to reoccupy most of their former ranges. All five species were breeding in large numbers by the 1920s and 1930s, often at sites that had been abandoned during the nineteenth century. Numbers fluctuated at many sites during ensuing decades, but there was no comprehensive census until *Operation Seafarer* in 1969–70. By that time, all five species had reached approximately the numbers and distribution that they have today.

NUMBERS AND TRENDS, 1970–2011

It was possible to make broad generalisations about breeding terns in Britain and Ireland prior to 1969, based on the monitoring of some of the larger and better-known colonies, but it was not until a survey of breeding terns in Britain and Ireland in 1969–74 that we had the first comprehensive overview.[88] This coincided with the first national survey of all seabirds, *Operation Seafarer*, which established solid baseline data on breeding terns for the period 1969–70.[89] This was succeeded by an *All-Ireland Tern Survey* in 1984.[90] Subsequently a *Seabird Colony Register* (*SCR*) was set up covering the period 1985–88.[91] There was another All-Ireland tern census in 1995.[92] The third major national seabird survey – *Seabird 2000*, covering the period 1998–2002 – provides the most complete and most reliable inventory of the seabird populations of Britain and Ireland carried out to date.[93] No comprehensive census has been conducted since 2002, but in the next five chapters we have attempted to bring the history of each species up to date from various sources. For the UK, the Joint Nature Conservation Committee (JNCC) has maintained an annual index of relative abundance of each species, based on counts at colony sites covered by the *Seabird Monitoring Programme* (see Appendix 3): this allows estimates of the total population in each year up to and including 2011. Terns are censused at some of the most important colonies in Ireland as part of the *Seabird Monitoring Programme*, but these counts have not been used to assess trends or to estimate total breeding populations.

As a group, our five breeding terns increased in numbers by 5 per cent over the period between *Operation Seafarer* (1970) and *Seabird 2000*. But they had increased by more than 35 per cent between 1970 and 1984, and then declined again almost back to the 1970 level by 2000. This represents a significant decline, particularly because it occurred in an era of enhanced conservation activity when one could have expected numbers to have generally increased (Table 10). The numbers of all breeding species, apart from the roseate tern, declined between 1984 and 2000. There has been no comprehensive census since 2000, but roseate terns have continued to increase steadily. Index counts at the major colonies of each species have suggested that numbers of the other four species have fluctuated in Britain, but have increased substantially in Ireland.

The next five chapters explore the status, distribution and trends of the five species of terns that breed in Britain and Ireland, covering the period from about 1970 until recent times. For each of our five terns we also describe breeding habitats, key features of behaviour, food and foraging, breeding biology and migrations. Each species faces its own set of conservation problems, which will be discussed in Chapter 11.

TABLE 10. Changes in numbers of the five species of breeding terns in Britain and Ireland, 1970–2000.

Species	1970	1985	2000	% change 1970–2000	% change 1985–2000
Little tern	1,917	2,857	2,153	+12	−25
Sandwich tern	12,073	16,047	14,252	+18	−11
Common tern	14,890	14,861	14,497	−3	−2
Roseate tern	2,384	550	790	−67	+44
Arctic tern	52,288	78,764	56,123	+7	−29
Total, all species	83,552	113,079	87,817	+5	−22

Source: Mitchell *et al.*, 2004.

In this and subsequent tables in Chapters 6–10, 1970 represents *Operation Seafarer* (1969–70); 1985 represents the *Seabird Colony Register* (1985–88) for the UK and the *All-Ireland Tern Survey* (1984) for Ireland; 2000 represents *Seabird 2000* (1998–2002) for the UK and the *All-Ireland Tern Survey* (1995) for Ireland.

The numbers given are estimates of 'apparently occupied nests' (AONs), more or less equivalent to breeding pairs. The AON is the unit adopted for use in seabird censuses, in which attempts are made to count all the nests in each colony, or in some cases to count attending adults and use a calibration factor to estimate the corresponding number of nests (Mitchell *et al.*, 2004). For terns, nests and adults are relatively easy to count, and the number of AONs is usually a good approximation to the number of pairs with nests on the date the census was conducted. Pairs that lose nests before the census date, or establish nests after the census date, are not included.

Here and throughout the next five chapters we cite numbers as reported in the original publications or databases. However, most of the numbers are subject to considerable uncertainty because many of the colony counts were based on estimates of adults rather than precise counts of nests, and each of the three national censuses was conducted over several years, during which many pairs may have moved from site to site. Reporting the total as '2,153' pairs carries the implication that the true total was not either 2,152 or 2,154, which would be an unwarranted claim of accuracy. It would be fairer to report this number as 'about 2,200 pairs'. We have not done this, but the qualification expressed in this note applies to all the numbers we cite.

CHAPTER 6

Little Tern

T HE LITTLE TERN IS MUCH SMALLER than our other terns and is readily identified by this character alone. It is widespread around the coasts of Britain and Ireland in the breeding season, but usually stays within a short radius around the scattered locations where it nests, so that it is less generally well known than the common or even the Sandwich tern. However, it often tries to nest on mainland beaches where it comes into conflict with human beachgoers. Because of its habitat requirements, it often nests by itself and tends to associate more with other beach-nesting birds such as ringed plovers than with other terns. Even at locations where other terns breed, it tends to nest in the most open sandy places at low elevations on the outer edges of mixed colonies, whereas the other terns nest on higher ground with more surrounding cover. After the breeding season it disperses around the coasts, but departs very early on autumn migration, so that it is rarely conspicuous among staging flocks of other terns.

STATUS, DISTRIBUTION AND TRENDS

Distribution and numbers in *Seabird 2000*

The little tern is now the second scarcest breeding tern, after the roseate tern, around our coastlines. During *Seabird 2000* some 2,153 apparently occupied nests (AONs: see Table 10 in Chapter 5) were recorded, of which 1,541 (72 per cent) were in England and the Isle of Man. Most colonies were small, on average about 30 pairs. There were only 12 colonies with 101–250 nests. In Britain most of the population, with about half the colonies, was concentrated along the coast between Lincolnshire and Hampshire, with the largest concentrations in Norfolk

OPPOSITE PAGE: **FIG 71.** Distribution of breeding little terns in Britain and Ireland in the *Seabird 2000* censuses of 1998–2002 (Britain) and 1995 (Ireland). (Source: Pickerell, 2004)

and Essex. They were absent from southwest England, and from south and west Wales, and there were scattered colonies in Scotland, mainly in the Western Isles. In Ireland the breeding population was restricted to two small colonies in northwest Donegal, one large colony each in Cos. Mayo, Kerry, Wicklow and Wexford, and one small colony in Co. Galway, although in this case there is a discrepancy between the colony size marked on the map (1–10 AONs) and in the accompanying table (45 AONs) (Fig. 71).[1]

Trends since 1970

It is thought that the little tern population breeding in Britain and Ireland had started to increase sometime around the turn of the twentieth century, with peak numbers reached in the 1930s. Thereafter numbers decreased. An incomplete census of breeding little terns in Britain and Ireland in 1967 found that they had declined to approximately 1,600 pairs.[2] Then *Operation Seafarer*, some three years later, estimated a total of 1,900 pairs, earning the little tern the dubious distinction of being the second rarest breeding seabird in these islands at that time, after the Arctic skua. Numbers then increased to about 2,850 pairs in the *SCR Census* and *All-Ireland Tern Survey* in 1984–88, but declined to about 2,150 pairs in *Seabird 2000* and the *All-Ireland Tern Survey* of 1995 (Table 11). However, a population tracking index based on year-to-year changes in numbers at well-monitored colonies suggested that total numbers had actually peaked in 1975–76, and then

TABLE 11. Numbers of breeding little terns in Britain and Ireland, 1969–2000. All numbers are estimates of breeding pairs: see footnotes to Table 10 (in Chapter 5).

Region	1970	1985	2000	% change 1970–2000	% change 1985–2000
Scotland	308	373	331	+7	−11
England	1,266	2,147	1,541	+22	−28
Wales	28	55	75	+168	+36
Great Britain, Isle of Man, Channel Islands	1,602	2,575	1,947	+22	−24
Ireland	315	282	206	−35	−27
Total Britain and Ireland	1,917	2,857	2,153	+12	−25

Source: Pickerell, 2004.

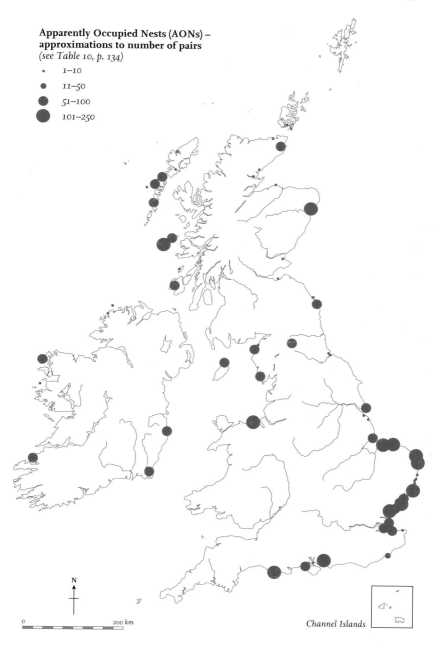

**Apparently Occupied Nests (AONs) –
approximations to number of pairs**
(see Table 10, p. 134)

- ·   1–10
- ●   11–50
- ●   51–100
- ●   101–250

N

0   200 km

Channel Islands

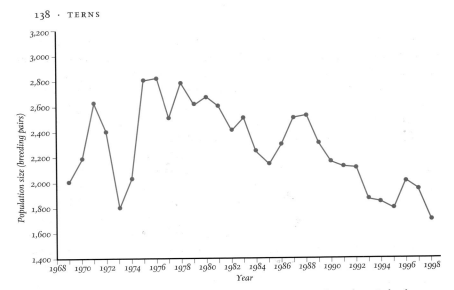

FIG 72. Estimated total numbers of little terns nesting in Britain and Northern Ireland, 1969–98, based on index counts at well-monitored colonies. (Source: Ratcliffe *et al.*, 2000)

started a long-term decline that continued until at least 1998 (Fig. 72).[3] Matching the values of that index in 1984–88 to the total numbers recorded in the censuses in those years and then projecting backwards suggests that total numbers in 1969 had actually been well over 2,000 pairs, and that the peak numbers in the mid-1970s had been well over 3,000 pairs. Based on index counts in the UK colonies, the long-term decline appears to have been reversed about 2005, and by 2011 total numbers were estimated to have been 2 per cent higher than in 2000, although still well below the peak numbers in the 1970s.[4]

The long-term decline from 1976 to 2005 has been attributed to low breeding success and consequent low recruitment of new birds to the breeding population.[5] The subsequent increase may be attributable to increased breeding success resulting from more effective management of predators at the breeding sites (see Chapter 11).

BREEDING HABITATS

The little tern is the most specific and perhaps the least flexible of our terns with regard to its breeding habitat requirements. In Britain and Ireland they nest exclusively on the coast (although in other parts of their range they commonly nest on sandbars in rivers),[6] almost always on sand or shingle beaches, sometimes on sandy spits, less frequently on inshore islands. They usually nest on barrier beaches and other sites on or attached to the mainland or on large islands; they often seem to avoid nesting on small islands, even when apparently suitable islands are located nearby and are used by other terns. Breeding sites are invariably located close to shallow sandy waters, bays, tidal inlets or estuaries, rarely more than 2 km away from areas where the terns can feed on small fish and invertebrates.

Little terns usually nest on open sand or shingle with little or no vegetation (Figs 73 and 74). Because these unvegetated sites are usually maintained open by flooding during winter storms, little terns characteristically nest at very low elevations above the high water mark, so that their nests are at risk of flooding during summer high tides, storms and tidal surges – and this can lead to the loss of entire breeding colonies. On the west coast of Ireland on North Inishkea, Co. Mayo, they often nest on machair grassland, perhaps an adaptation to avoid the high wind speeds of the western seaboard that might disrupt breeding on the island's sandy beaches (Fig. 75). The closely related least tern of North America habitually nests on gravel roofs of flat-topped buildings in areas where beach

FIG 73. Little tern at a nest on a shingle beach. Kilcoole, Co. Wicklow. (Andrew Porter and Peter Cutler)

sites are unavailable. Roof-nesting has not yet been reported for little terns in Britain or Ireland,[7] but could easily be overlooked in industrial areas near the coast that birdwatchers rarely visit.

FIG 74. Little tern at a nest on a sand beach. Little terns are equally at home on shingle and sand beaches, but even on sand beaches they prefer areas with shells or other varied substrates which enhance camouflage. Baltray, Co. Louth. (John Fox)

FIG 75. Little tern nest beside rock on machair, Inishkea, Co. Mayo. Machair is a short grass sward on sandy soils characteristic of parts of the west coast of Ireland and the Western Isles of Scotland: this is an unusual habitat for little terns. (Tony Murray)

KEY FEATURES OF BEHAVIOUR

Little terns arrive in Britain and Ireland in mid- to late April and usually continue directly to their breeding sites; they do not gather in staging flocks or spend much time at other locations. Much of their breeding behaviour is related to their habit of nesting on mainland beaches and their consequent exposure to high levels of predation. Although they start to explore potential nesting areas soon after arrival, they do not spend much time there until a few days before eggs are laid, so that much of their courtship behaviour is conducted on beaches or sand flats outside the nesting areas, as in Sandwich terns. Pair-bonds are thought to be less stable from year to year than in other terns (although information is scanty),[8] so most birds seek new mates at the beginning of each season.

In little terns, more than in other terns, many of the displays involve the male carrying a fish, and females seem to respond most strongly to long, shiny fish which the males advertise by waggling them from side to side. Aerial displays start as soon as the birds arrive. As in other terns, this includes *low flights*, in which the male flies over the resting flock carrying a fish and giving the advertising call, a rapidly-trilled *'prrrititititITT'* with the emphasis at the end, and *high flights*, in which two or three birds ascend in wide circles to high altitudes before two birds set their wings and glide down together (see Chapter 3). In little terns, *low flights* are joined by up to six birds (probably all females) which pursue the male and his fish for periods that may run up to 15 minutes. In *high flights*, the male almost invariably carries a fish (other terns usually perform *high flights* without fish) and the birds often ascend very high – up to 100 m or more – in proportion to their small size. At the top of the ascent, the female overtakes the male in the *pass* (see Chapter 3) and the two birds then descend together, weaving from side to side faster and more erratically than in other terns, often with their wings raised in a 'V'.

Ground displays also commonly feature the male carrying a fish and often end when the female takes it. When a male lands near a female, both birds go into a posture similar to the *erect* posture of other terns, with the head and bill pointing upwards and the wings partly spread, as in Sandwich terns. As in other terns, this posture functions as appeasement, switching off the aggression which each bird might otherwise display to the other in response to an over-close approach. The male then switches to the *bent* posture and starts to circle the female or walk in short arcs in front of her, gradually approaching her. If the female is receptive, she start to beg, crouching down with quivering wings (Fig. 76), and the male then often gives her the fish. Copulations are prolonged affairs in which the male slowly approaches the female from behind, waggling a

FIG 76. Early stage in courtship of little terns. The male (with head raised) is trying to approach and mount the female, who is encouraging him by crouching and shivering her wings. However, a female little tern rarely allows a male to mount her and copulate with her unless he is holding a fish. Baltray, Co. Louth. (John Fox)

fish from side to side. The female crouches, droops her wings and shivers them so that they repeatedly nudge the male's breast as he comes closer (Fig. 77). After this has continued for up to several minutes, the male jumps onto the female's back and continues waggling his fish for another period that may last several minutes (Fig. 78). Eventually, the male starts to lower his tail round the female's, who turns her head up and takes the fish at the exact moment of cloacal contact. Other terns sometimes carry and transfer fish during copulation, but only in little terns does this seem to be a requirement for successful mating. Later, in the few days before egg-laying when the female is waiting at the nest site for the male to catch fish and bring them to her, she often goes through this entire pre-copulatory display with other males, only to take the fish and shake the male off before he can complete the copulation (Fig. 79).

OPPOSITE PAGE: **FIGS 77–79.** Sequence of photographs showing an unsuccessful attempt to copulate: the birds depicted here are least terns, but little terns display in the same way. Plymouth, USA. (Jim Fenton).

FIG 77. The male approaches the female very slowly from behind, waggling his fish from side to side, while the female crouches and nudges his breast with her wing.

FIG 78. The male mounts the female and stands on her back for a minute or more, still waggling his fish from side to side.

FIG 79. The male lowers his tail to copulate and the female takes his fish, but she is already walking forward to shake him off. This is a ruse that female least and little terns often use to get a fish from a male who is not her mate without allowing him to copulate with her.

Nests are better camouflaged and more widely spaced than those of our other terns, probably another adaptation to high risks of predation. They are typically spaced 2–5 m apart, sometimes up to 30 m apart where there is plenty of space, but less than 1 m apart at some breeding locations where space is limited.[9] Little terns do not establish and defend territories prior to egg-laying, and the spacing-out is effected when the females occupy the nesting area a few days before laying. There is little overt aggression between the females at this time, so that the spacing seems to be achieved primarily by avoidance: each female settles as far as possible from all the others that are already established. The female waits at her selected spot and the male brings food to her. The eggs are laid in a bare scrape in the sand or shingle and are very hard to see, but the birds often bring small pieces of shell or seaweed during incubation and deposit them around the nest, so that the nest becomes more conspicuous by the time the chicks hatch (Fig. 80). The eggs are at risk not only from predators, but also from flooding in high tides or storms and from wind-blown sand. When sand threatens to cover the eggs, the incubating bird digs them out and brings them to the surface: little terns have been known to raise their eggs as much as 10 cm as a moving dune advances into the nesting area.

Because the nests are so widely spaced, little terns do not spend much time defending territories against intruders, although they come into conflict with neighbours when their chicks start to disperse. Both sexes incubate the eggs and feed the chicks, but the female spends about one-quarter more time at

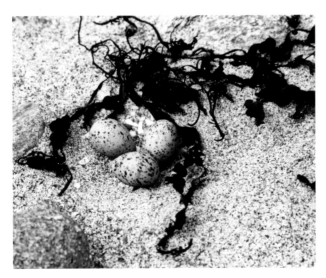

FIG 80. Little terns often decorate their nests with pieces of shell or dried seaweed, which negates the camouflage. Inishkea, Co. Mayo. (Tony Murray)

FIG 81. Little tern feeding his mate on the nest. More than in other tern species, male little terns continue to feed their mates during incubation. Kilcoole, Co. Wicklow. (Andrew Porter and Peter Cutler)

the nest during incubation and early chick care, while the male brings more food throughout the nesting cycle.[10] The male starts to feed the female early in courtship, brings most or all of her food during the egg-laying period, and continues to bring food throughout incubation (Fig. 81). He brings almost all the food to the chicks during the first few days after hatching, and about two-thirds of the total thereafter.

Little terns vigorously attack predators that enter the nesting area during the day, although because of their small size they are less intimidating than common or Arctic terns. An approaching predator (or a human intruder) triggers an *upflight*, in which some or all birds in the colony fly up and hover or circle overhead, giving alarm calls. When the predator reaches the nesting areas, individual birds start to dive on it, with buzzy '*ssschweek*' attack calls. The birds usually do not come close to or strike terrestrial predators such as foxes or dogs, but they press home their attacks on aerial predators and often peck them, diving from behind and hitting their backs. They will attack and sometimes strike birds as large as harriers, great black-backed gulls or even grey herons. The attacks often deter predatory birds that do not know there is food to be had in the colony, or make them detour around it. The attacks are ineffective against determined predators such as crows or kestrels, which can take their prey at will, but each individual tern at least has the chance to distract the predator so that it flies on and takes someone else's eggs or chicks. Little terns also attack humans who approach or enter the nesting area: they rarely strike humans but frequently defecate on them, which is often an effective deterrent to casual intruders.

If there are two eggs, they usually hatch simultaneously or within 24 hours of each other (see *Breeding biology*, p. 149). Consequently, the first chick can leave the nest soon after hatching without risk of leaving the second egg or hatchling behind. There is usually little disparity in size between the two chicks, so that they are fed more or less equally, with less of the destructive competition for food that occurs in two-chick broods of larger terns (see Chapter 3). If there is a third chick it is usually at a disadvantage relative to the first two, although it is not rare for little terns to raise all three chicks successfully (see *Breeding biology*, p. 149). The chicks are almost as well camouflaged as the eggs (Fig. 82), and they remain in the nest for the first day or two, crouching immobile if danger threatens and their parents give alarm calls. By the third day, however, they leave the nest and seek cover elsewhere. Some chicks leave their natal broods soon after hatching and get adopted by other pairs, who raise them as though they were their own (see Chapter 3).[11]

FIG 82. Little tern chicks are almost as well camouflaged as the eggs. Kilcoole, Co. Wicklow. (Andrew Porter and Peter Cutler)

FIG 83. Little tern feeding a fledgling. Little tern chicks scatter widely during the period of growth, and it is often hard to determine how many have survived until they fledge and appear on the beach outside the nesting area. Baltray, Co. Louth. (John Fox)

The chicks move frequently during their period of growth, sometimes travelling tens or hundreds of metres to areas with more vegetation or other cover. When a parent flies in with a fish and gives its advertising call, its own chicks recognise the call and run out of cover, sometimes following the parent for long distances across the sand before it feels it can land without harassment. It has been suggested that the parents deliberately make their chicks run for long distances to ensure that they do not accidentally feed the wrong chicks. The chicks grow rapidly and fly for the first time at 19–21 days, occasionally even at 17 or 18 days – again earlier than other terns and probably another adaptation to the high level of predation. The fledglings initially stay on the beach near the colony (Fig. 83), but start to accompany their parents on fishing trips within a few days after they first fly, usually returning to the colony site with their parents to roost at night if it is safe to do so. Little terns do not habitually join staging or roosting flocks of other terns, and they depart on migration soon after the chicks fledge, so they are not often seen in numbers away from the immediate vicinity of nesting sites.

FOOD AND FORAGING

Little terns in Britain and Ireland are almost exclusively coastal birds, feeding along open shores, in tidal inlets and outer parts of estuaries, in lagoons and sometimes even in creeks or ponds near the coast. When breeding, they usually forage within about 5 km of their breeding colonies – the smallest range of any of our terns – so that the habitats they use vary from site to site according to the local topography.

Foraging behaviour of little terns in Britain and Ireland has not been well studied, except in a recent radiotelemetry study. This is the only telemetry study that has been conducted of any tern in Britain or Ireland, and was an impressive technical feat given the small size of the bird. The study was part of an assessment of an offshore wind turbine installation at Scroby Sands, off Great Yarmouth in east Norfolk, within 2 km of the most important breeding colony of little terns in the UK (see case study 1 in Chapter 11). Twenty-three little terns were fitted with radio transmitters, each weighing less than one gram, attached to the back or tail feathers. Thirteen birds were tracked successfully either from the shore or by boat for up to eight days. The results showed considerable variation in foraging behaviour, but the most pronounced differences were between birds that were still attending nests and those whose nesting attempts had failed. Birds attending nests spent, on average, 56 per cent of the day foraging and only 2 per cent resting; they made between two and five foraging trips per hour, ranging up to 4.6 km from the colony site and up to 2.3 km offshore, although they usually stayed within 500 m of the shore. Birds that were not attending nests spent more time foraging and resting (about 85 per cent and 15 per cent, respectively), made longer foraging trips and ranged much more widely, travelling up to 27 km in a single trip and as far as 3.4 km offshore; two of them visited another breeding site 12 km away.[12]

Little terns get most of their food by plunge-diving. They typically fly at heights of 4–8 m while foraging – higher on average than common or Arctic terns. They hover more frequently and for longer periods than other terns, plunging vertically into the water several times per minute. They also dip or skim for invertebrates at the surface of the water and have been recorded hawking for insects in the air or picking insects from vegetation, but they appear to feed less frequently in these ways than common or Arctic terns.

Available data on diets of little terns are somewhat contradictory, with some reports indicating that they feed largely or exclusively on fish and others suggesting that at times they feed largely on crustaceans and insects. Fish are used prominently in courtship displays (see *Key features of behaviour,* above) and are usually the main or exclusive food items fed to females during courtship and to chicks. The main fish species used as prey are sandeels, pipefish, Atlantic herrings and sprats. Invertebrates recorded as prey include a wide variety of crustaceans (shrimps, prawns, mysids and isopods), insects (grasshoppers, dragonflies, flies, gnats, beetles and ants), annelid worms, flatworms, squid and pelagic molluscs (sea snails or sea slugs).[13] Even in places and at times where they feed on the same species of fish as common terns nesting nearby, little terns usually take smaller fish (typically 20–70 mm long) so that there is little competition.

In a study at the Great Yarmouth colonies mentioned above, 14 species of fish and 32 species of invertebrates were recorded as prey, but about 70 per cent of food items were small herrings or sprats.[14] In one early study of stomach contents of adult little terns in the UK, 97 per cent (by volume) consisted of crustaceans and only 2 per cent fish,[15] but in another study all stomach contents consisted of fish.[16] In the Ythan estuary (Aberdeenshire), adults were seen catching only shrimps,[17] and in a study at Gibraltar Point (Lincolnshire) more than 90 per cent of food brought to chicks consisted of crustaceans, mainly prawns. However, most other studies have reported only fish.[18] The many reports of invertebrates in the diet are puzzling in view of the fact that little terns seem to feed mainly by plunge-diving: in other species of terns, invertebrates are taken mainly by diving-to-surface or dipping, and plunge-diving is used primarily to catch fish.

One detailed study of foraging by little terns has been conducted in the winter quarters. This was around islands off Guinea-Bissau in West Africa. Little terns foraged singly (not in flocks) and fed entirely on small fish, mostly less than 60 mm long and weighing about 1 g on average. They were able to catch about nine fish during each hour of foraging, with the highest rates of capture during falling and low tides and in water of moderate clarity. Calculations of energy intake suggested that they would have been able to meet their daily food requirements in only 1–4 hours of foraging, so that 'they seem to have an easy living.'[19] Little terns have been reported feeding with other terns 600 km offshore south of Ghana.[20]

BREEDING BIOLOGY

Little terns usually lay clutches of two or three eggs, but sometimes only one egg, especially late in the season. Average clutch-sizes recorded at colonies in Britain and Ireland have usually been in the range from 1.95–2.45, with the proportion of three-egg clutches ranging from 15 per cent to 55 per cent and the proportion of single-egg clutches ranging from 10 per cent to 35 per cent, or up to 70 per cent among pairs re-laying late in the season. Reasons for the variation in clutch-size have not been studied in little terns, but probably include the age and experience of the parents and the amount of food available to them, as in other terns. The average weight of an egg is about 10 g, ranging up to 12 g, so three-egg clutches with relatively large eggs can reach or even exceed 60 per cent of the weight of the female, the highest ratio recorded in any species of tern (see Table 5 in Chapter 3). Although it is a striking feat for the female to be able to mobilise this much material within her body during the 3–4-day egg-laying interval, it is also impressive for the male, who brings most of the material that the female uses to make the eggs (see Chapter 3).

Incubation takes about 21 days: the eggs are laid one or two days apart and the first two eggs usually hatch within 24 hours of each other, although when a third egg is laid it usually hatches a day or two later. All these intervals are slightly shorter than those in larger terns, so that the eggs are at risk from predators for shorter periods.

Breeding success is highly variable because of the vagaries of weather and the high frequency of predation. Often entire colonies are wiped out overnight by flooding or predation, especially at the egg stage. When this happens, the birds sometimes re-lay at the same site nine or ten days later, but at other times they desert the area and try again somewhere else. Pairs usually remain together for re-nesting, which facilitates rapid re-cycling. Individual pairs may attempt to breed three or four times during a season, often at two or three different sites. For this reason, it is difficult to keep track of breeding success at a local or even regional level. On the other hand, when there is no tidal flooding and predators are absent or controlled, breeding success can be very high: failures due to food shortage have rarely been reported and we have found no reports of chicks dying from starvation, even in broods of three chicks. Little terns are sometimes able to breed with high success in places close to colonies of larger terns in which the birds are struggling to raise even one chick to fledging. This may be due to the fact that little terns rely on fish that are too small to be profitable for larger terns, and choose to settle in places where they can catch these small fish without having to fly very far.

Productivity has been monitored irregularly since 1969 at 110 colony sites in Britain and Ireland. Results showed wide year-to-year variations in average productivity, ranging from 0.15 to 0.85 chicks per pair between 1969 and 1998 with a long-term average of about 0.5. The annual averages over all sites increased from about 0.48 in 1969 to about 0.56 in the early 1980s, and then declined again to about 0.45 by 1998 (Fig. 84).[21] The *Seabird Monitoring Programme* (SMP) recorded productivity at 19 colonies over a 25-year period from 1986 to 2010: colony averages ranged from 0.08 to 1.11 chicks per pair with an overall average of about 0.59 (Table 12).[22] However, these broad-scale averages may underestimate true average productivities because of the little tern's habit of frequently shifting to new sites for re-laying after breeding failures (see *Key features of behaviour*, above). This means that individual pairs that fail may be recorded more than once, whereas successes can be recorded only once. Only three colonies – Crimdon Dene in Cleveland, Gronant in Flintshire and Kilcoole in Co. Wicklow – had long-term average productivities close to one chick per pair, and these high rates of success were achieved under intensive management (see Chapter 11). All sites had occasional bad years in which all birds failed completely, although six of the 19 sites had occasional very good years in which average productivity equalled or exceeded two fledglings per pair.

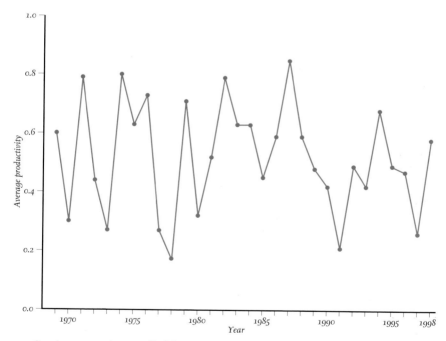

FIG 84. Average productivity (fledglings per pair) of little terns at sites in Britain and Ireland that were monitored for all or part of the period 1969–98. Data from 110 different sites are included in this chart; in 1985–87 the sample included about 65 per cent of the total number of little tern pairs in Britain and Ireland. (Redrawn from Fig. 3 in Ratcliffe *et al.*, 2000)

TABLE 12. Numbers and productivity of little terns at 19 index sites in the *Seabird Monitoring Programme*, 1986–2010.

Region	Colony site	Average number of pairs 1986–2010 (range)	Average productivity 1986–2010 (range)	Number of years
N Scotland	Dalchalm	11 (1–25)	0.64 (0.00–1.40)	14
NE Scotland	Sands of Forvie	31 (5–76)	0.38 (0.00–1.87)	23
	Lossiemouth	5 (1–12)	0.22 (0.00–2.00)	10
NE England	Long Nanny	37 (5–51)	0.48 (0.02–2.00)	25
	Gibraltar Point	32 (3–53)	0.31 (0.00–0.92)	23
	Crimdon Dene	41 (1–65)	0.91 (0.00–2.23)	15
	Easington Lagoon	37 (1–71)	0.34 (0.00–1.33)	24
	Lindisfarne	24 (1–70)	0.77 (0.00–2.00)	22
E England	Great Yarmouth	198 (9–369)	0.63 (0.00–1.82)	24
	Scolt Head Island	78 (10–169)	0.53 (0.00–2.05)	24
	Blakeney Point	113 (50–215)	0.50 (0.00–1.37)	24
	Benacre	23 (1–55)	0.52 (0.00–1.25)	23
	Hamford Water	48 (13–113)	0.52 (0.00–1.25)	16
SE England	Chichester Harbour	5 (1–20)	0.08 (0.00–1.00)	19
	Langstone Harbour	96 (29–171)	0.38 (0.00–1.56)	25
	Rye Harbour	33 (7–70)	0.38 (0.00–1.24)	22
SW England	Chesil Beach	55 (8–100)	0.25 (0.00–0.67)	23
Wales	Gronant	73 (30–115)	1.11 (0.00–1.90)	24
SE Ireland	Kilcoole	47 (18–106)	1.11 (0.00–2.32)	25
Total, 19 sites		987 [a]	0.59 [b]	

Source: Mavor *et al.*, 2008, updated to 2010 from the JNCC database.

[a] About 45 per cent of total numbers breeding in Britain and Ireland.

[b] Overall average is weighted by the average number of pairs in each colony.

MIGRATIONS

Of all our breeding terns we know least about the migrations of the little tern, because of the paucity of recoveries of ringed birds. By the end of 2009 only 17,723 little terns had been ringed in Britain and Ireland, mostly as chicks, with only 238 recoveries, a very low recovery rate of about 1.34 per cent, the second

TABLE 13. Recovery rates of the five British and Irish terns up to the end of 2009.

Species	Breeding pairs in seabird 2000	No. ringed (adults + chicks)	No. recovered	% recovered
Little tern	2,153	17,723	238	1.34
Sandwich tern	14,252	180,707	5,346	2.96
Common tern	14,497	190,292	4,947	2.35
Roseate tern	790	42,269	1,171[a]	2.77
Arctic tern	56,123	201,317	1,601	0.80

Source: Clark et al., 2010.

[a] This total does not include 8,012 resightings of 3,205 individual roseate terns recorded during the intensive mark–resighting programme conducted at the three major colony sites in Britain and Ireland between 1995 and 2007 (Ratcliffe et al., 2008a).

lowest of all our breeding terns (Table 13).[23] The recovery rate for the roseate tern is more than twice this value. Detailed analysis has been published for the first 150 recoveries reported up to the end of 1997.[24] With such a low rate of recovery it is not surprising that migration routes and even the locations of winter quarters are poorly documented.

Little terns gather in flocks near the breeding sites at the end of the breeding season. Unlike other terns, however, there is very little evidence that little terns breeding in Britain and Ireland undergo post-breeding dispersal within these islands prior to autumn migration. No little terns were either seen or heard at the massive tern roost in Dublin Bay between 21 July and 20 September 2010.[25] Instead, some or all appear to depart soon after breeding is completed. Some birds travel south remarkably fast – one bird ringed as a chick in Essex on 26 August was recovered in Portugal six days later. As with the Sandwich tern, many juveniles accompany their parents on migration. The main wintering grounds appear to be in West Africa, but there have been only three recoveries there, all in a small area between Mauritania and Guinea-Bissau, between October and February. A few little terns ringed elsewhere in western Europe have been recovered much further southeast, in Ghana and Côte d'Ivoire, but it is not known whether British and Irish birds migrate as far as this. The birds recovered and reported in Africa were deliberately taken by humans (mostly small boys), and the intensity of trapping and location of trappers will inevitably have skewed the pattern of recoveries and hence our knowledge of the wintering grounds.

As little terns do not breed until they are at least two years old it must be assumed, in the absence of any other recoveries, that most of them remain in western African coastal waters until ready for breeding. A number of birds that had been ringed as chicks in Britain and Ireland have been recovered during the breeding season in continental Europe. Those that were raised in southeast England showed a preference to move to the Netherlands, while those from further north in Britain tended to cross the North Sea to Denmark and Sweden. The extent of this non-fidelity to their natal areas is not fully known.

Large flocks of little terns have been recorded in the Netherlands during August. This concentration of birds post-breeding may represent a staging point and/or a moult migration, with the birds undergoing a complete moult while also building up body reserves for their flight to Africa. Some of these birds could be from Britain or Ireland, although there is only one recovery to date of a ringed bird to support this: a bird ringed as a chick in Britain that was recovered in the Netherlands in August. In addition, there is one record of a little tern ringed as an adult in Kent (possibly a migrant from continental Europe) and recaptured in the large post-breeding gatherings in the Lagoon of Venice, Italy. The principal origin of these birds is from colonies around the Adriatic coast, up to 133 km away, but, as indicated by the recovery of the British-ringed bird, little terns from other parts of Europe could be congregating there. During five consecutive trapping seasons at Venice 2,956 birds were caught and examined for the state of their moult cycle. Adult birds went through a complete moult, and the terns rapidly increased their body weights during the final days there before setting off on the 4,000 km flight to the West African wintering grounds.[26] Birds that breed in Britain and Ireland presumably also moult and gain weight somewhere on their way south, but nothing is known about this except for the single recoveries in the Netherlands and Portugal mentioned above.

CHAPTER 7

Sandwich Tern

S ANDWICH TERNS (FIG. 85) ARE THE LARGEST of the five tern species that breed in Britain and Ireland and can often be identified by this character alone. Their loud rasping and raucous call, *'kirrick'*, is a quintessential feature of the coastal environment wherever they are found.

FIG 85. Sandwich terns settling in their nesting area on a sandy island with cover of grass. Lady's Island Lake, Co. Wexford. (Dave Daly)

STATUS, DISTRIBUTION AND TRENDS

The distribution of breeding Sandwich terns around the coasts of Britain and Ireland is extremely patchy and almost exclusively coastal, reflecting the availability of suitable nesting habitat. Breeding colonies can change quite dramatically, with established colonies suddenly disappearing and new colonies springing up unexpectedly.

Distribution and numbers in *Seabird 2000*

During the *Seabird 2000* censuses in 1998–2000, Sandwich terns were mainly concentrated in England (63 per cent) followed by Ireland (26 per cent), Scotland (7 per cent) and Wales (3 per cent).[1] Four colonies were recorded with over 1,000 pairs: Scolt Head, Norfolk, 4,200 pairs; Farne Islands, Northumberland, 1,950 pairs; Coquet Island, Northumberland, 1,726 pairs; and Inish Island, Lady's Island Lake, Co. Wexford, 1,048 pairs. There were also two additional colonies with more than 500 pairs: islets in Strangford Lough, Co. Down, 894 pairs; and Sands of Forvie, Aberdeenshire, 524 pairs. These six colony sites supported more than 72 per cent of the breeding Sandwich terns of Britain and Ireland. The total number of colonies declined from 58 in the 1980s to 34 in 1998–2000, with 33 sites deserted and nine new ones colonised. Most of the breeding pairs were along the east coast of England and Scotland (65 per cent of the total) or around the Irish Sea (24 per cent of the total) (Fig. 86).

Trends since 1970

A total of about 12,000 pairs was recorded in 1969–70 during *Operation Seafarer*. This was considered at that time to represent a population peak, numbers having gradually increased since the 1920s and 1930s. The Sandwich tern was then the third most abundant tern in these islands. The population continued to flourish with better colony protection, and by 1985–88 the number of breeding pairs had risen to about 16,000, a 33 per cent increase in 18 years. Total numbers in Britain and Ireland then declined by 11 per cent by 2000, but were still 18 per cent higher than in 1970. The increase since 1970 was manifested in England, Wales and Ireland, but numbers in Scotland declined by more than half during this period (Table 14). The reasons for this decline are not clear.

Since 1970 key colonies representing about 80 per cent of the total population in Britain and Ireland have been censused annually, and these

FIG 86. Distribution of breeding Sandwich terns in Britain and Ireland in 1998–2002 (Britain) and 1995 (Ireland). (Source: Ratcliffe, 2004a)

**Apparently Occupied Nests (AONs) –
approximations to number of pairs**
(see Table 10, p. 134)

- 1–10
- 11–100
- 101–500
- 501–1000
- 1,001–5,000

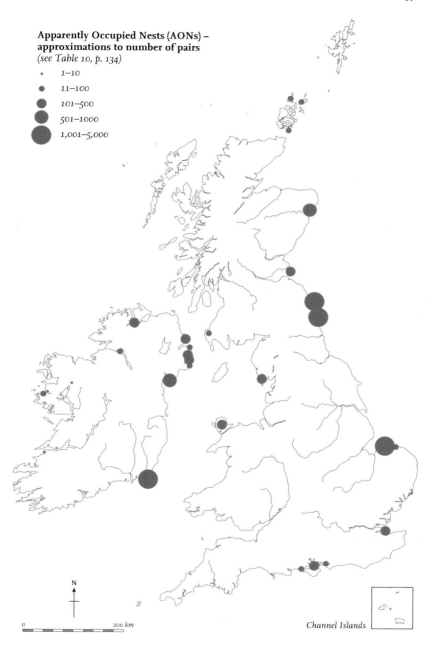

N

0   200 km

Channel Islands

TABLE 14. Numbers of breeding Sandwich terns in Britain and Ireland, 1970–2000. All numbers are estimates of breeding pairs: see footnotes to Table 10 (in Chapter 5).

Region	1970	1985	2000	% change 1970–2000	% change 1985–2000
Scotland	2,465	2,286	1,068	−57	−53
England, Isle of Man, Channel Islands	7,392	9,844	9,018	+22	+8
Wales	0	450	450	++	0
Great Britain, Isle of Man, Channel Islands	9,857	12,580	10,536	+7	−16
Ireland	2,216	3,467	3,716	+68	+7
Total Britain and Ireland	12,073	16,047	14,252	+18	−11

Source: Ratcliffe, 2004a.

counts have been used to estimate total numbers, using a statistical technique (chain indices) to allow for gaps in the data and to estimate the total population from the incomplete sample.[2] The results for the period 1970–98 demonstrate remarkably sharp declines and resurgences of the breeding population, which are thought to be caused principally by the impact of predators (Fig. 87).

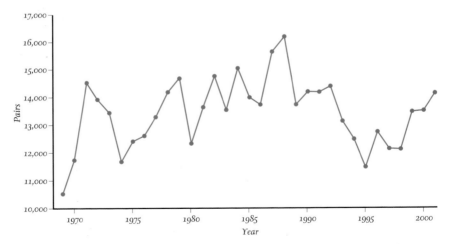

FIG 87. Year-to-year changes in total numbers of Sandwich terns nesting in Britain and Ireland, 1969–2001. Total numbers were estimated from counts in key colonies. (Source: Ratcliffe, 2004a)

Of these, the red fox causes the most damage and has been responsible for the abandonment of several colonies. There is then usually a delay of several years before a new site is colonised, during which period many adult birds apparently do not breed.[3] The fluctuations have been superimposed on a pattern of general increase during the 1970s and 1980s, a marked decline from 1988 to 1995 and a recovery from 1995 to 1998.[4] Based on index counts for the UK colonies, the fluctuations have continued since 1998, and the total number in the UK in 2011 was about 7 per cent lower than in *Seabird 2000*, i.e. close to the 1969–70 level again.[5] However, numbers at the main Irish colonies appear to have increased during that period.[6]

These numbers and trends need to be considered in a wider context, because ringing data have revealed extensive interchange of Sandwich terns among European breeding colonies, especially around the North Sea.[7] The total number of Sandwich terns breeding in western Europe is now about 50,000 pairs, mostly around the North Sea with the largest numbers in the UK, the Netherlands and Germany.[8] Numbers crashed in 1965 because of a major poisoning incident in the Netherlands (see Chapter 11), but then increased steadily until about 1990, stagnated or declined during the 1990s, and increased again in the late 1990s and early 2000s.[9] Numbers in Britain and Ireland followed the same general trends, but the increase during the 1970s and 1980s was much less marked than that in western Europe as a whole, probably indicating that there was net emigration from Britain to the Netherlands and Germany during that period. The North Sea coasts of England and Scotland probably supported more than half the west European population following the population crash in the 1960s, but this proportion has declined to only about 20 per cent at the present day as numbers in other areas have increased more rapidly.[10]

BREEDING HABITATS

The location of breeding colonies of Sandwich terns is determined both by suitable nesting sites and by the availability of feeding grounds where their principal prey, sandeels, herring and sprat, occur in abundance during the breeding season. Their colonies are widely dispersed around the coastline, often including large aggregations of more than 1,000 pairs where they nest at very high densities and are usually associated with breeding black-headed gulls or other species of terns (see under *Key features of behaviour*, below).

The largest colonies are located on the east coasts of England, Scotland and Ireland in the proximity of shallow, sheltered waters with sandy bottoms where the terns' prey are both abundant and easily captured. The more turbulent waters and windy conditions along the Atlantic coasts of Ireland and Scotland generate difficult conditions for foraging, and colonies are few and small in these regions.

Most colonies are located on low-lying coastal islands, almost always close to the shore, or on islands in brackish lagoons, estuaries and sea inlets. In the 1995 *All-Ireland Tern Survey* there were three inland colonies in Cos. Fermanagh (53 pairs) and Mayo (both less than 10 pairs),[11] but the two sites in Co. Mayo have since been deserted. However, the colony in Lower Lough Erne, Co. Fermanagh, increased to 156 pairs in 2005 and still had 68 pairs in 2008.[12] Although breeding on a freshwater lough, these birds probably feed mainly at sea in Donegal Bay, which they can reach in a 20 km overland flight. *Seabird 2000* did not record any inland colonies in Britain. In an analysis of the habitats of Sandwich terns at 26 sites in Ireland during the 1985 survey, about one-third of all colonies were on maritime turf (Fig. 88), followed by about a quarter on shingle. Other habitats occupied were rock, sand, grass and sedge, grass and rush and finally man-made habitats.[13] Nesting habitat is highly dynamic and has been described as resting 'on a knife-edge between erosion and succession'. Nesting habitat or entire breeding sites can be lost to erosion by winter storms or become overgrown with rank herbage or scrub.[14]

FIG 88. Breeding habitat of Sandwich terns on Tern Island, Wexford Harbour, Co. Wexford. Sandwich terns nested mainly on bare sand within the vegetated parts of the island. (David Cabot)

KEY FEATURES OF BEHAVIOUR

Sandwich terns are usually the first of our terns to arrive back in British and Irish waters from their wintering grounds in West and South Africa, appearing from mid-March onwards. They usually start to arrive at their breeding colonies by late March, and are exploring the future nesting areas by mid-April.

Compared to our other terns, the breeding behaviour of Sandwich terns has several distinctive features. First, their nests are very closely packed, typically only 30–50 cm apart and often with the sitting birds barely out of pecking range from their neighbours. Second, although their eggs are well camouflaged, their nests are placed out in the open and the groups of nesting birds are very conspicuous. The individual nests stand out even further because the birds defecate while on the nest, so that each nest becomes surrounded by a 'sunburst' of white faeces (see Fig. 27 in Chapter 2). Most other terns fly off the nest to defecate, which appears to be an adaptation to maintain camouflage: the conspicuously advertised nests of Sandwich terns show why this is necessary in the other species, but pose the puzzle of why it is not equally necessary for Sandwich terns. Third, the birds make only weak attempts to drive away predators, staying on the nest and cackling at predators such as gulls that approach them on the ground while they are incubating, but flying high over the nesting area or leaving it altogether when predators (or humans) that the adults perceive as threats to themselves approach closely. Fourth, they often nest in association with black-headed gulls, frequently settling in small patches or 'subcolonies' scattered within large colonies of gulls and often completely surrounded by nesting gulls (Fig. 89). At some sites in Britain and Ireland, they nest in association with common or Arctic terns rather than with gulls, but similarly tend to settle in subcolonies surrounded by the other terns.[15] Nesting is highly synchronised within each subcolony of Sandwich terns, most pairs laying within a 3–5-day period.[16] The first three of these behavioural traits are characteristic of the 'crested' terns. The fourth is not shared by any other of the 'crested' terns except for the closely related Cabot's tern in North America, which usually nests in association with royal terns, or sometimes with laughing gulls or black skimmers.[17]

The strong association between Sandwich terns and black-headed gulls initially seems paradoxical, because black-headed gulls prey on the terns' eggs and chicks, and often steal food from the adult terns as they carry fish to feed their chicks (Fig. 90). Detailed studies carried out in the Netherlands have shown, however, that the terns actually gain net benefits from the association.[18] First, the black-headed gulls protect the terns from other predators such as herring

FIG 89. Sandwich terns usually nest in association with black-headed gulls (or sometimes other terns), typically forming sub-colonies surrounded by nesting gulls. County Galway. (John N. Murphy)

FIG 90. Black-headed gulls stealing fish from a Sandwich tern. One of the gulls is standing on the back of its victim. Note that only the immediate neighbours take any action to repel the gulls. Griend, the Netherlands. (Jan van de Kam)

gulls, great black-backed gulls and short-eared owls. This works in two ways: the black-headed gulls attack the predators and either drive them away or keep them to the periphery of the breeding area, and when a determined predator nevertheless enters the colony, it usually encounters a gull egg or chick before reaching the terns.[19] Second, although the gulls steal up to 10 per cent of the fish brought in by the adult terns and make them spend much time and energy in evasive manoeuvres and additional foraging, the terns are able to temper these adverse effects by keeping their chicks moving through the gull colony, so that individual gulls do not learn to target individual pairs of terns, as they would if the chicks were not moved.[20] At sites where Sandwich terns nest among common or Arctic terns rather than black-headed gulls, they gain the benefits of this association (the aggressive defence against predators mounted by the other tern species) without the costs (stolen fish). However, the Sandwich tern's early breeding season, with egg-laying peaking in the first three weeks of May, is better synchronised with that of the black-headed gull than with those of common and Arctic terns, which nest two or three weeks later.

Sandwich terns have another behavioural trait to avoid predation. When they encounter predators such as foxes early in the breeding season, they frequently abandon the nesting attempt and move en masse to another site. Unlike most terns, they sometimes desert a site even after laying eggs. Occupation of nesting areas is often prolonged over many days or weeks, with the birds making sporadic flights over the nesting area by day and moving in at dusk as a flock to a safe patch surrounded by gulls; this behaviour perhaps serves to test whether an area where they nested successfully in previous years is still safe. However, if Sandwich terns experience heavy predation later in the breeding cycle, they will usually stay put and sometimes lose most or all of their eggs and chicks.

Aerial displays of the Sandwich tern are similar in form to those of other terns, but several features are more exaggerated. The *high flight* frequently starts with three or more birds ascending to a great height, often higher than 300 m and sometimes almost out of binocular range. The descent by the first two birds to reach the top is then very steep and fast and often seems less organised than in other terns, with wider swings from side to side and less close coordination between the two birds. *High flights* have been observed in January and February, while the birds are still in winter quarters in Africa, and are resumed as soon as the birds return in spring.

The nesting areas are usually not occupied by day until a day or two before egg-laying, so that territories are not established early and defended as in other terns. Consequently, almost all ground displays, including courtship

FIG 91. Sandwich terns copulating. Sandwich terns usually do not occupy the nesting areas until immediately before egg-laying, so most of their courtship and pair formation is conducted outside the colony, typically on adjoining sand flats. Lady's Island Lake, Co. Wexford. (Dave Daly)

and copulation, take place outside the breeding area, typically on beaches or adjoining sand flats (Fig. 91). The appeasement posture, equivalent to the *erect* posture of other terns, is highly exaggerated in Sandwich terns, with the neck stretched out, the bill pointed skyward, and the wings widely spread and drooped so that the wing tips touch the ground under the tail (Fig. 92). In the assertive posture that is equivalent to the *bent* posture of other terns, the neck is stretched up and the head tilted downward at an angle rather than bent to present the black cap to an antagonist; the wings are partially spread and the crest is raised (Fig. 93).[21] The male feeds the female frequently before egg-laying, and continues to bring food for her during the early part of incubation.

Although Sandwich tern nests are very closely packed, each pair vigorously defends the tiny patch around its nest against any intrusions by its neighbours, and the birds are constantly quarrelling over minute slivers of border territory.

FIGS 92, 93. Sandwich terns adopt more exaggerated postures than other terns while displaying.

FIG 92. *Erect* posture. (Redrawn by R. Gillmor after Glutz von Blotzheim & Bauer, 1982)

roseate tern

Sandwich tern

Arctic tern

FIG 93. *Bent* posture. (Redrawn by R. Gillmor after Cullen, 1962)

Sandwich terns share with the other 'crested' terns a distinctive type of threat display known by its Dutch name of *gakkering*. The two antagonists face each other, often only a few centimetres apart, with their shaggy crests and back feathers raised, and pump their heads up and down in unison with loud, guttural cackling calls, '*gu-gu-gu-gu-gu-gu-gu* …' (Fig. 94). In almost all cases, this contest ends in a draw, with neither bird gaining or losing a centimetre of ground, but without either having to fight for the space it already owns. Neighbouring pairs go through these contests with each other many times every day until the chicks hatch and can be moved away. The constant arguments arise in part because every time a bird flies into or out of its territory, it has to pass low over the territories owned by several other pairs and land very close to its neighbours.

FIG 94. Sandwich terns have a distinctive threat display, known by its Dutch name of *gakkering*. These two birds are sitting on their nests: note how closely the nests are packed. Griend, the Netherlands. (Jan van de Kam)

In keeping with their general failure to camouflage their nests, Sandwich terns do not remove eggshells after the chicks hatch, but leave them beside the nest site. Instead, the parents start to move the chicks away from the nest within a few days of hatching. If two chicks hatch, the parents often go off with the older chick, and the younger chick may get lost or left behind, so that it dies from starvation or is eaten by a gull.[22] The chicks from different pairs spread out over the dunes, beaches and flats adjacent to the colony. At some breeding sites, Sandwich tern chicks join together in crèches and move together in packs across the nesting area or adjoining sand flats, but this behaviour may be in response to human disturbance and is not observed at some other sites. Sandwich tern chicks do not routinely form crèches in the manner of other 'crested' terns, even including the closely related Cabot's tern.

Adult Sandwich terns start to moult the feathers on the forehead before the eggs hatch (Fig. 94), and by the time the chicks fledge the forehead is largely white and the crown speckled, as in the winter plumage. Moult of the rest of the plumage, including wing and tail feathers, starts in July and is completed by the time the birds migrate south in September and October. Juveniles in July–August are strikingly marked, with blackish ear-patches and prominent black bars or chevrons across the light grey upperparts and wing-coverts; they follow the adults with persistent begging calls. In the post-breeding period, adults and juveniles spread out and disperse very widely throughout the breeding range. Ringed juveniles have been recovered as far as 65 km from the natal colony within three days after fledging, and by August ringed juveniles from colonies in Britain and Ireland can be found all round our coasts except for western Scotland, and across the North Sea from France to Denmark.[23] The birds range widely along the coast during the daytime and roost at remote places on sandbars or beaches, sometimes in large, closely packed flocks. Parents accompany the juveniles and feed them throughout the dispersal period in July and August, and the family parties remain together during southward migration in September and October. A few juveniles are still being fed at staging areas in November–December, but not in winter quarters in January, although there is one record of a young bird persistently begging from adults in March.[24]

FOOD AND FORAGING

The large size of the Sandwich tern is reflected in every aspect of its feeding biology: it flies faster, makes longer fishing trips, dives from greater heights, dives to greater depths and catches larger fish than any of our other terns. Like the roseate tern, it is a specialist feeder on schooling fish which it catches in open waters. It is able to feed regularly in places that are too far away, or where the fish are swimming too deeply below the surface of the water, for the other terns to exploit.

Sandwich terns in Britain and Ireland feed exclusively in salt water. They prefer clear waters with sandy bottoms, so that they usually feed at sea, although they will follow the tide into sandy parts of estuaries and sometimes fish in coastal lagoons. They habitually fly 30 km or more to good feeding sites, and have been recorded as far as 70 km from their nearest breeding colony.[25] In a study in which Sandwich terns were tracked during the breeding season by following them in an inflatable boat, many birds travelled 10–20 km from the breeding site and individual birds ranged up to 54 km offshore (Fig. 95). The birds often flew higher than 20 m above the sea surface and usually followed fairly straight tracks, although they often deviated from these tracks towards porpoises or other foraging Sandwich terns. In several cases, the birds resumed their original course after one of these deviations, suggesting that they had already decided where to forage but were willing to be deflected to investigate promising situations along the way. Even when far offshore, feeding areas were usually in water less than 15 m deep.[26]

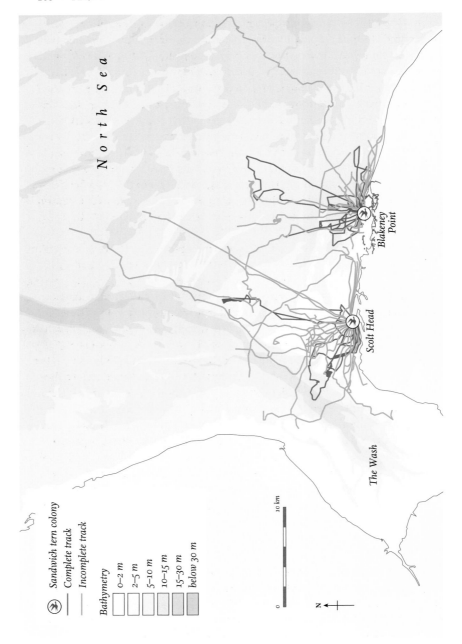

North Sea

Blakeney
Point

Scolt Head

The Wash

Sandwich tern colony
Complete track
Incomplete track

Bathymetry

0–2 m
2–5 m
5–10 m
10–15 m
15–30 m
below 30 m

N

0   10 km

Sandwich terns commonly gather to feed in flocks that may include tens or hundreds of birds, especially over predatory fish or marine mammals that are driving prey fish towards the surface. They usually fly at heights of 5–10 m above the water surface while foraging, although they will occasionally dive from as high as 20 m. Although they do not 'power dive' like roseate terns, they hit the water very fast, remaining submerged for one or two seconds and probably penetrating to depths of 1.5 m or more.[27] In a study at Coquet Island, fishing success was highest in moderate winds and when the water surface was ruffled; it was lower in light winds (probably because Sandwich terns cannot hover well) and in smooth water (possibly because the fish could see the birds).[28] In contrast, in the Ythan estuary, fishing success was highest at low wind-speeds.[29] Both studies indicated that Sandwich terns can feed successfully at wind-speeds up to 56 km per hour, although they then sought sheltered waters for fishing.

Most information on the diet of Sandwich terns is derived from observation of foods carried to the colony to feed mates or chicks. Diets recorded in this way usually consist largely of five species of fish: three sandeels, Atlantic herring and sprat (Table 15). The proportions of the different species within this mix vary from site to site, from year to year and from month to month within the breeding season. Sandwich terns generally take larger fish than other British and Irish terns, typically 60–150 mm long and weighing about 8 g on average (Fig. 96), except that smaller fish are brought to very young chicks. As in other terns, the adults usually eat the smaller fish that they catch and bring larger fish to the colony site to feed mates or chicks,[30] thereby making efficient use of the time and energy that they spend commuting.

Otherwise, there is little information on what the adults eat. The stomachs of nine adults collected in Norfolk contained 35 per cent sandeels, 31 per cent other fish, 33 per cent annelid worms and 1 per cent molluscs.[31] This is the only report of Sandwich terns taking substantial numbers of invertebrates. However, the same source reported unusually high proportions of invertebrates in the stomachs of other tern species, so it is possible that the circumstances when the birds were collected were unusual: the locations and dates were not clearly stated.

OPPOSITE PAGE: **FIG 95.** Tracks of 117 Sandwich terns after departing from breeding colonies at Scolt Head (left) in 2006 and 2007 and Blakeney Point (right) in 2007 and 2008. The tern symbols denote the breeding sites. Red lines indicate complete tracks (the bird was tracked back to the breeding colony); orange lines indicate incomplete tracks (the bird could not be followed further). (Redrawn from Fig. 6 in Perrow *et al.*, 2011)

TABLE 15. Percentages by number of food types fed to Sandwich tern chicks at five breeding sites in Britain and Ireland.

	Ythan Estuary, Aberdeenshire	*Farne Islands, Northumberland*	*Coquet Island, Northumberland*			*Cemlyn, Anglesey*	*Lady's Island Lake, Co. Wexford*
			Location and year				
Food	1973	1965	1965	1966	1969	1999	1997–98
Ammodytidae (sandeels)	50	74	11	46	c.50	82	67
Clupeidae (herring, sprat)	50	15	88	54	c.50	18	32
Gadidae (cod, whiting)		6				1	
Other fish		4				1	1
Crustacea (crustaceans)		1					
Cephalopoda (squid)		1					

Sources: Langham, 1968; Dunn, 1972; Taylor, 1979; Cramp, 1985; Newton & Crowe, 2000.

FIG 96. Sandwich terns typically catch much larger fish than other British terns. This sandeel was at least 140 mm long and probably weighed about 12 g. Corronroo, Cos. Clare/Galway border. (John N. Murphy)

In winter quarters in West Africa, Sandwich terns commonly feed over schools of tuna, but also often take fish from fishing nets as they are hauled into fishing boats or ashore onto beaches: this makes them vulnerable to trapping by humans (see Chapter 11). Common prey species include sardines and anchovies.[32] Sandwich terns were included in the detailed study of feeding terns in Guinea-Bissau mentioned in Chapter 6. As in the breeding season, they fed mainly on fish 50–150 mm long and weighing an average of 8 g. They fed singly or in small flocks, catching about eight fish per hour and thereby meeting their daily food requirements in about two hours, so that, just like the little terns, they were judged to have 'an easy living'.[33]

BREEDING BIOLOGY

The Sandwich tern is the only one of the 'crested' terns that breeds entirely within the north temperate zone, and is the only one that habitually lays two eggs. Even the closely related Cabot's tern of North and South America usually lays single-egg clutches throughout its range, from the tropics north to 38° N in the USA and south to 45° S in Argentina.[34] Average clutch-sizes reported for Sandwich terns in Britain and Ireland have ranged from 1.15 at Coquet Island in 1966 to 1.58 at Scolt Head in 1957.[35] However, the average clutch-size in France has been reported to be as high as 1.87, and in some colonies in Sweden as high as 2.07.[36] This means that the proportion of pairs that lays two eggs varies widely among sites and years: in some cases as low as 15 per cent and in others almost 100 per cent. This proportion also varies within a single year: it is usually highest (up to 80 per cent in some colonies in Britain and Ireland) early in the season and at the peak period of laying, declining almost to zero among late layers.[37] It has proved hard to explain this wide variation in the proportion of pairs laying two eggs, but variation in the availability of food near to the colony is thought to be an important factor, at least for the year-to-year changes. The age and experience of the birds are also important: birds breeding for the first time (which is usually at the age of three or four) almost invariably lay single eggs late in the season, while birds older than seven usually lay two eggs early in the season. Average clutch-size is usually higher in large colonies, which probably indicates that the older and more experienced birds move to and congregate at the sites where food availability is highest. Clutches of three eggs are very infrequent – usually less than 1 per cent except in the Swedish colonies mentioned above – and at least some of these probably result from two females laying in the same nest.

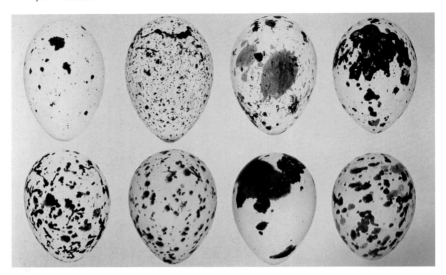

FIG 97. Sandwich tern eggs are very variable and exceptionally beautiful, so they were highly prized by egg-collectors. It has been suggested that the variability allows parents to recognise their own eggs even in crowded colonies where nests are close together in featureless terrain. (Reproduced with permission from Plate 87 in Cramp, 1985)

All terns lay well-camouflaged eggs, but those of the Sandwich tern are exceptionally finely marked and extremely variable (Fig. 97). These handsome eggs were greatly prized by egg-collectors, and in 1912 Bickerton wrote at length on their beauty, remarking that 'the ground-colour is at once fine, clear and light-toned, and therefore well adapted for setting off to fullest advantage the bold and richly-coloured markings.'[38] The average weight of an egg is about 35 g, or about 15 per cent of the weight of the female: even a clutch of two eggs rarely weighs more than one-third of the female's body weight, much less than this ratio in smaller terns that lay proportionately larger eggs and often lay clutches of three (see Table 5 in Chapter 3).

Both male and female parents incubate the eggs and feed the chicks (Fig. 98), although the male brings most of the food when the chicks are very small. The incubation period is about 25 days and the fledging period about 29 days (Table 5), so that most chicks hatch in late May or June and fledge in late June or July. The newly hatched young are very distinctive because the down sticks together in tufts, so that they look spiny, like little hedgehogs. This spiny down is a feature of all the 'crested' terns and also of roseate terns, whereas the newly hatched chicks of other terns have dense down and look fluffy.

FIG 98. Sandwich tern brooding a small chick. The adult's shaggy crest is raised in interactions with other birds. Lady's Island Lake, Co. Wexford. (Dave Daly)

As described under *Food and foraging* (see p. 167), the Sandwich tern may fly 30 km or more each way to locations where fish are abundant. Its main prey are sandeels, Atlantic herrings and sprats; other fish such as whiting, cod and pipefish are brought to the chicks at times, but the chicks often refuse to take them. At colonies in northeast England, sandeels are more frequent in the diet in April and May, when females are forming eggs and when chicks are small, whereas Atlantic herrings and sprats are more frequent in June and July as the chicks grow larger and are able to take wider food items. As a consequence of the long foraging trips, chicks are fed only 7–15 times each day (Table 5), but this is possible because the fish brought to them are relatively large – typically 80–120 mm long and weighing 5–8 g. However, the largest fish are disproportionately attractive to nearby black-headed gulls and are often stolen by them, so that fish somewhat smaller than the largest are the most economically favourable.

The eggs are usually laid three or four days apart and hatch two or three days apart, so that when the second chick hatches it is much smaller than the first. This places the second chick at a severe disadvantage in competing with the first for food, and the second chick rarely survives unless its parents bring fish in large quantities, succeed in evading thieving gulls and are skilful in keeping the chicks together as they move through the colony site. Consequently, few pairs (generally fewer than 5 per cent) succeed in raising two chicks to fledging. The question then arises: why do any Sandwich terns lay two eggs if their chances of raising two chicks are so small? Laying the second egg requires the male to spend more time foraging, is a physiological strain on the female and diverts resources from the first chick while the second is still alive. The main answer to this question seems to be that the second egg functions as 'insurance' in case the first egg fails to hatch or the first chick dies within the first few days. Where this has been studied, about 10–15 per cent of second eggs eventually gave rise to fledged chicks for one or other of these reasons. On average, pairs that laid only one egg raised fewer chicks than pairs that laid two eggs at the same place and

TABLE 16. Numbers and productivity of Sandwich terns at 12 index sites in the *Seabird Monitoring Programme*, 1986–2010.

Region	Colony site	Average number of pairs 1986–2010 (range)	Average productivity 1986–2010 (range)	Number of years
NE Scotland	Sands of Forvie	658 (4–1,126)	0.65 (0.00–1.29)	19
NE England	Coquet Island	1,387 (759–1,897)	0.57 (0.31–0.95)	17
E England	Scolt Head Island	1,688 (220–4,200)	0.76 (0.00–1.19)	22
	Blakeney Point	2,181 (100–3,500)	0.68 (0.00–1.01)	21
SE England	Rye Harbour	169 (2–750)	0.79 (0.00–1.50)	18
	Langstone Harbour	116 (2–271)	0.37 (0.00–1.07)	16
SW England	Brownsea Island	151 (25–263)	0.51 (0.01–1.40)	20
Wales	Cemlyn Lagoon	810 (349–1,563)	0.78 (0.00–1.33)	22
NW England	Hodbarrow	253 (10–420)	0.49 (0.00–1.32)	21
NW Ireland	Inch Island, Lough Swilly	249 (110–340)	1.09 (0.84–1.30)	7
	Mulroy Bay	58 (21–156)	0.38 (0.00–0.79)	13
SE Ireland	Lady's Island Lake	1,182 (47–1,945)	0.68 (0.35–1.21)	7
Total, 12 sites		8,829 [a]	0.68 [b]	

Source: Mavor *et al.*, 2008, updated to 2010 from the JNCC database.

[a] About 58 percent of total numbers breeding in Britain and Ireland.

[b] Overall average is weighted by the average number of pairs in each colony.

time.[39] Also, on some occasions when food availability and other circumstances are unusually favourable, many pairs do raise two chicks – for example, 48 per cent and 67 per cent of pairs that hatched two chicks in two years on Coquet Island in the 1960s.[40] Consequently, natural selection will have favoured birds that habitually lay two eggs over those that habitually lay one, even though the average probability of success for the second egg and chick is low. Long-term monitoring of Sandwich terns at many of their major colonies in Britain and Ireland has revealed very wide variations in breeding success from year to year (Table 16). Ten of the twelve sites have had occasional very good years, with more than one chick raised to fledging per pair. On the other hand, most of the sites have had years of total or almost total failure: only the colony at Hodbarrow in Cumbria and the small colony on Lough Swilly, Co. Donegal, have recorded consistently high productivity in all years. The average productivity over all sites and years was 0.68 chicks per pair (Table 16).

MIGRATIONS

Our knowledge of the migrations of the Sandwich tern is based mainly on the recovery of 5,346 birds from 180,707 individuals ringed up to the end of 2009,[41] mostly as chicks, in their British and Irish breeding colonies during June and July (see Table 13 in Chapter 6). Detailed analysis is based on the 4,230 recoveries reported by the end of 1997.[42]

Like other terns, Sandwich terns have a period of post-fledging dispersal commencing in late June, in which juvenile birds and their parents scatter around the coasts of Britain and Ireland, while many also cross the North Sea to Danish and Dutch coastal waters. Birds are rarely seen inland at this season, although some are thought to cross Britain overland from the east coast to the Irish Sea and vice versa.[43] By late August some juveniles have started to head south, and a few reach West Africa during September. However, about half the recoveries in September have been in Britain or Ireland and there are still a few recoveries there in October (Fig. 99). On this migration many families remain intact, with the juveniles continuing to beg for food, a behaviour that can persist well into the winter. By the end of October virtually all birds have departed from British and Irish waters and most recoveries have been in Iberia or along the west coast of Africa; the birds that continue to South Africa do not arrive there until November. Only a few enter the Mediterranean.

The wintering areas for first-winter and adult birds are mainly concentrated on the West African coast from Senegal to Ghana, where about 50 per cent of

FIG 99. Adult Sandwich tern in non-breeding plumage. Sandwich terns are lighter grey than other British and Irish terns, especially on the wings. The black bill with yellow tip remains distinctive. Galway Bay, nr New Quay, Co. Clare. (John N. Murphy)

ringing recoveries have been generated, mostly from hunting or trapping by humans. The waters off the Senegal and Ghana coasts are particularly abundant in pelagic fish, encouraged by nutrient-rich waters from the Canary and Guinea ocean currents. However, wintering birds also range from the Iberian Peninsula, Morocco and southwards to South Africa with a few birds travelling around the Cape of Good Hope to Natal; there have even been a few recoveries in November–December in Britain (Fig. 100). Other important African wintering areas are the coastal waters of Guinea-Bissau, Côte d'Ivoire, Liberia, Sierra Leone and Angola, which account for about 30 per cent of ringing recoveries due to hunting.[44] A paucity of recoveries from Nigeria, Cameroon and Gabon seems to reflect a genuine scarcity of wintering birds of all ages, associated with absence of upwellings and associated fish stocks.[45] However, recovery locations are likely to be strongly skewed by variations in the intensity of deliberate trapping of terns by boys setting baited noose traps (see Chapter 11).

Sandwich terns spend a relatively short period in their winter quarters, not reaching southern Africa until November and starting north again in February or early March. They migrate along the west coasts of Africa and southwest Europe, some reaching Britain and Ireland by late March and most adults occupying

Equator

N

0   5,000 km
at equator

FIG 100. Recovery locations of Sandwich terns ringed as chicks in Britain and Ireland. In July–August, juveniles disperse throughout the breeding area and into neighbouring countries (green shading), but a few migrate south before the end of August (red arrows) and many reach the Gulf of Guinea by late September (green arrow). In winter (November–February) Sandwich terns are much more widely distributed than other British and Irish terns, with recoveries distributed all along the coast from France to South Africa, extending into the Mediterranean Sea and Indian Ocean, and with a few even in Britain (orange band). Most birds remain in Africa throughout their first summers, migrating north in March–April when two years old and older. (Source: Noble-Rollin & Redfern, 2002)

breeding areas by the end of April. Most young birds remain in the African wintering grounds for their first summers and throughout the subsequent year, returning to the breeding colonies in Britain and Ireland for the first time generally at the age of three. However, a few one-year-old birds migrate north as far as southern Europe and some two-year-olds reach Britain and 'prospect' at breeding colonies.

A few adults that do not return to breed are found throughout the wintering range, even as far south as South Africa, during the northern summer. Birds that do return to breed usually do so to within 500 km of their natal colony. There is some interchange between British and Irish colonies and the west European breeding sites. British and Irish-ringed birds have been found breeding in Denmark, the Netherlands, Belgium and France. See under *Status, distribution and trends* (p. 159) for evidence that there was substantial net emigration from British to continental colonies during the 1970s and 1980s. Conversely, there are several instances of Continental breeding Sandwich terns moving to Britain from Belgium, the Netherlands, Denmark and Germany. Some adults have even been recovered during the breeding season from the north Mediterranean coast, the Black Sea and the Danube Delta – it is presumed that these became mixed up during the winter with birds originating from these areas and then returned with them.[46] However, most birds that breed in those areas winter in the Mediterranean and do not overlap much with birds from western Europe.[47]

A remarkable recent recovery was of a chick ringed in 2006 on the Ythan Estuary and recovered on 31 March 2011 in Iceland. This is the first British recovery of a Sandwich tern from Iceland, where the species is very rare.[48]

CHAPTER 8

Common Tern

T HE COMMON TERN IS ONE OF the most widely distributed of our seabirds, breeding in a surprising range of inland and coastal habitats. As they breed regularly at gravel pits, reservoirs, inland lakes and along river systems, as well as in dockland areas and on artificial islands and platforms, they are very much in the public eye and are thus the best known of the British and Irish terns (Fig. 101).

FIG 101. Common tern on its nest in an artificial site on a dock. Grand Canal Dock, Dublin. (John Fox)

STATUS, DISTRIBUTION AND TRENDS

Distribution and numbers in *Seabird 2000*

At the time of *Seabird 2000*, the common tern population in Britain and Ireland stood at about 14,500 pairs. These were nearly equally distributed between Scotland, Ireland and England, with relatively small numbers in Wales. In Ireland proportionately more bred at inland sites (19 per cent of the national total) than in Britain (8 per cent). Most of the coastal breeding birds were scattered around the coastlines of both Britain and Ireland in a large number of small to medium-sized colonies. They were absent only from southwest England (except that they bred in the Isles of Scilly) and most of Wales, although they were scarce in Ireland away from the east coast (Fig. 102). Only one colony exceeded 1,000 pairs (Coquet Island, Northumberland: 1,033 pairs) while the next in size (772 pairs) was in the Sound of Mull, Argyll and Bute.[1] The colony at Coquet Island has now increased to over 1,200 pairs, but has been overtaken by the colony at Rockabill, Co. Dublin, which increased to nearly 1,800 pairs by 2009.[2]

Trends since 1970

Total numbers of common terns in Britain and Ireland have remained remarkably stable over many decades, since the species recovered from persecution and other human interference during the nineteenth century. They were still widely distributed in 1875–1900, with some colonies having hundreds to low thousands of pairs. Numbers increased in some areas during the first half of the twentieth century and were thought to have reached a peak in the 1930s, declining somewhat by the 1960s (see Chapter 5). By the time of *Operation Seafarer* common terns had approximately reached the numbers and distribution of today. The total population actually decreased by only 3 per cent over the 30-year period between *Operation Seafarer* and *Seabird 2000* (Table 17). However, there were considerable fluctuations in numbers within different regions during that period. Numbers in Scotland increased to a high point of nearly 7,000 pairs in the 1980s, but then declined to less than 5,000 pairs in *Seabird 2000*. Numbers in Ireland showed the opposite pattern, with a low in 1984 and an increase back to above the 1970 level by 1995. Based on index counts at the major colony sites in the UK, the total population then increased by about 40 per cent between 2000 and 2006, but fell back to about the 2000 level by 2011.[3] Numbers have continued

OPPOSITE PAGE: **FIG 102.** Distribution of breeding common terns in Britain and Ireland in the *Seabird 2000* censuses of 1998–2002 (Britain) and 1995 (Ireland). Colonies of 'commic terns' (i.e. undistinguished Arctic and common terns) are shown in yellow. (Source: Ratcliffe, 2004c)

**Apparently Occupied Nests (AONs) –
approximations to number of pairs**
(see Table 10, p. 134)

·   1–10
●   11–50
●   51–100
●   101–500
●   501–1,100

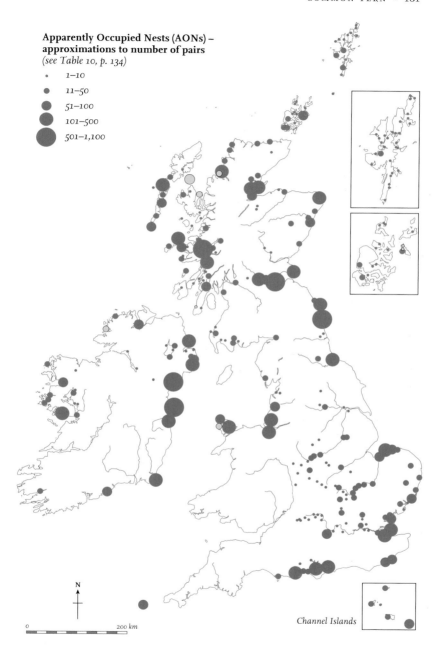

N

0   200 km

Channel Islands

TABLE 17. Numbers of breeding common terns in Britain and Ireland, 1970–2000. All numbers are estimates of breeding pairs: see footnotes to Table 10 (in Chapter 5).

Region	1970	1985	2000	% change 1970–2000	% change 1985–2000
Scotland	4,285	6,784	4,784	+12	−29
England, Isle of Man, Channel Islands	6,207	4,893	4,850	−22	−1
Wales	292	514	674	+131	+31
Great Britain, Isle of Man and Channel Islands	10,784	12,191	10,308	−4	−15
Ireland	4,106	2,670	4,189	+2	+57
Total Britain and Ireland	14,890	14,861	14,497	−3	−2

Source: Ratcliffe, 2004c.

to increase at the major Irish colonies, with a combined total of almost 3,000 pairs at Rockabill and Lady's Island Lake in 2009–10.[4] Some of the regional declines were probably due to increased levels of predation – for example, predation by American mink in western Scotland and by red foxes in southern England.[5] The increases were most pronounced at large colonies with continuous management and probably represent successful conservation (see Chapter 11).

BREEDING HABITATS

Compared to other terns, common terns are extreme generalists, occupying an extraordinarily wide range of habitats. Worldwide, they are primarily a freshwater species, breeding across the full width of Europe, Asia and most of North America. They are equally at home on forested lakes in the taiga zone and in the steppes and prairies of Siberia and Canada, ranging up to the Tibetan Plateau and down to the deltas of the Danube and the Volga. They also have large saltwater populations on the coasts of Europe, east Asia and eastern North America, where they nest on rocky or sandy islands from the Arctic Circle almost to the Equator and in temperate saltmarshes. In Britain and Ireland, they are primarily coastal, nesting on rocky islands or machair in the north and west and on sandy islands, barrier beaches and saltmarshes in the south and east. They also breed in much smaller numbers but very widely inland, where they have benefited from the proliferation of reservoirs and gravel pits during the twentieth century.

Within this wide range of habitats, common terns are very adaptable in their choice of nest sites and substrates. Their nesting habitat has been described as 'wherever they can find a place, provided that conspecific breeders have settled there before'.[6] Even this broad statement understates their adaptability, because it does not include the first pioneers that settle in unusual places.

Generally, common terns require open, well-drained ground with some vegetation cover for nesting. Their preferred nesting areas have loose substrate for making scrapes, with between 20 and 40 per cent cover, but they will nest occasionally at sites that are completely open or almost completely vegetated.[7] They prefer to nest on islands or other locations surrounded by water, but often nest at sites attached to the mainland if there is not too much risk of predation by mammals. At inland breeding sites, these conditions can be found at reservoirs, in gravel pits and on man-made sites such as artificial islands and floating rafts (see Fig. 192 in Chapter 11). In freshwater breeding areas over much of continental Europe, common terns are nowadays largely confined to rafts or other artificial sites.[8] On mainland coasts they usually nest in sandy habitats with some sparse vegetation cover (Fig. 103), while those nesting on coastal islands favour short grass swards. Some nest in man-made sites such as docklands or other industrial areas (Fig. 104), while others nest on small, elevated patches of grass or tide wrack within saltmarshes.[9]

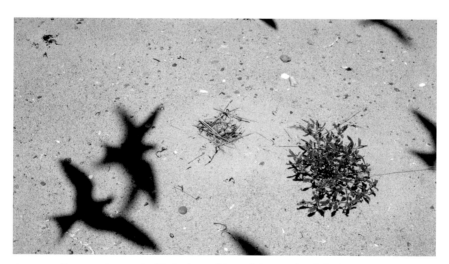

FIG 103. Common tern nest with shadows of terns flying overhead. Common terns sometimes nest on open sand with very little cover, but the chicks move to find cover wherever they can. Plymouth, USA. (Peter Trull)

FIG 104. Common tern nesting site in Dublin docks. The platform was originally built for the navigation light, but was made suitable for terns by adding a layer of gravel, a wall around the edge to prevent chicks from falling into the water, interior walls to divide the nesting area into compartments, and shelters to protect chicks from rain and predators. In recent years up to 250 pairs of common and Arctic terns have nested on managed sites in Dublin Port, with consistently high productivity. (Oscar Merne)

The larger gulls, such as the great black-backed and herring gulls, pose serious problems to the breeding success of common terns and indeed to the survival of tern colonies. At several sites gulls have been responsible for colony loss through predation of eggs and young, or simply by occupying space and displacing the terns.[10] At some of these former colonies terns have returned after the elimination of the gulls. Classic examples are the colony at Inchmickery in the Firth of Forth and Mew Island, Co. Down. Both islands held large common tern colonies that were abandoned following expansion of the gull population. Removal and control of the gulls have allowed the re-establishment of the tern colonies (see Chapter 11).

KEY FEATURES OF BEHAVIOUR

Common terns start to arrive in Britain and Ireland at the end of March, but most arrive during the last two-thirds of April and in early May. They spend the first week or so feeding at sea, but start to occupy the nesting areas gradually over the next two weeks, initially making only brief landings but coming ashore for longer periods and in increasing numbers as their urge to breed increases. Although common terns feed inshore and frequently rest on beaches, the sea is the safe place for them and the land is dangerous. They are always very jumpy as they occupy the nesting areas and frequently make mass out-flights. In these flights, known as *panics* or *dreads*, the colony suddenly falls silent, the birds all start up simultaneously and fly low and fast out to sea, typically rising after 30 seconds or so and drifting back to land to reoccupy the nesting area, calling loudly and quarrelling over space to land in. Older writers tried to interpret *panics* as group displays that had some social function, such as synchronising the birds' nesting cycles, but they are interpreted much more easily as simple alarm reactions in which each bird takes its cue from the others. *Panics* are sometimes triggered by the appearance of a falcon or other predator that poses a direct threat to the adults, but most of them have no obvious cause and seem to be false alarms.[11] *Panics* occur many times each day early in the process of settlement, but gradually become less frequent as the birds gain confidence, and by mid-season they occur only in response to real danger. Another type of group flight is the *upflight*, in which some or all birds in the colony rise up in a flock over the breeding area and swirl around, calling loudly. *Upflights* usually take place in response to intrusion by something that the adults seem to perceive as a threat to their eggs or chicks, but not to themselves – e.g. a human intruder, a gull or another large bird – and if the intruder enters the nesting area the terns start to attack it.

Although a few birds appear to be paired when they first arrive, most are seeking mates, and courtship displays start soon after they first appear at the colony site. Display postures of common terns were illustrated in Figs 35–38 and 40–41 in Chapter 3. Males bring fish to the colony and display with them, sometimes on the ground but more often in *low flights* (Fig. 35), in which the male flies low over the nesting area or over a flock loafing outside it, giving the *advertising* call (see below). *High flights* (Fig. 36) start as soon as the birds arrive and can be seen earlier in the spring, on migration or even before the birds leave winter quarters. *High flights* in common terns usually involve only two birds. They are initiated by one bird which starts to fly fast and circle, with exaggeratedly deep wing-beats; a nearby bird joins in by taking the opposite side of the circle and the two birds ascend in wide circles to a height typically of 30–50 m, but sometimes

100 m or more. The birds do not attempt to maintain position over the ground and drift steadily downwind, sometimes far away from the colony if the wind aloft is strong. At the top of the ascent the lead bird (usually the male when this can be discerned) sets his wings and glides in the *aerial bent* posture, while the female overtakes him in the *straight* posture and makes the *pass* (Fig. 37). The two birds then glide down together, each swaying from side to side so that their paths repeatedly cross; although the female usually stays slightly ahead, the male 'leads from behind' and the female tries to match any slight turns he makes.[12] The male attempts to lead the female down to a place where he can start the ground display.

Males start to establish territories soon after they occupy the nesting area. At first the territories are ill-defined, but as the number of males increases over the ensuing days and weeks the boundaries are contested and finely adjusted until each male owns and defends an area of a few square metres. Boundary disputes involve a graded series of threat displays. In the lowest-intensity threat, the male adopts the *bent* posture, presenting his black cap to a potential intruder. In the next stage, he sometimes goes into an exaggerated form of *bent* (Fig. 38), half-opening his wings and giving a '*keee-urr*' call (see below). If an intruder comes closer, the territory owner goes into the *slant* posture (Fig. 105), with the head

FIG 105. Two common terns threatening each other. The left-hand bird is in the *slant* display with the neck drawn in and the bill pointed up towards the antagonist. The right-hand bird has its wings spread in the highest state of threat before flying to attack. Bird Island, USA. (John Fuller)

and neck stretched up, often alternating with *bowing*, in which the head is bent forwards, displaying the black cap. At a higher level of confrontation, two birds may face off, each in a *crouch* position, with the body tilted forward, the tail raised and the wings partly opened. Usually these threat displays end in the retreat of one bird, reinforcing previous agreements about boundaries, but occasionally neither bird backs down and an intense fight develops (Fig. 106). Occasionally boundary disputes spill over into an aerial display known as the *upward flutter*. One bird whose airspace has been violated lunges up at the intruder, who hovers

FIG 106. Common terns fighting. Aggressive encounters between terns are usually settled by ritualised posturing, but occasionally two birds will seize each other's bills and wrestle. When one bird gives up and tries to break free, the other bird often holds on to its bill and continues twisting its neck. Here the upper bird is trying to pull away but the lower bird is hanging on. Plymouth, USA. (W. Thomas Manders)

in place and retreats upwards. The two birds then flutter upwards, sometimes as high as 20 m, the lower bird repeatedly thrusting its bill up towards the upper bird, who steadily retreats upwards but bends his bill down to parry the thrusts (Fig. 107). Unlike other aggressive encounters, the *upward flutter* is rather stereotyped and seems to have become a formalised contest over space rather than a free-for-all.[13] Once territory boundaries have been settled, most birds refrain from crossing them, so that there are few aggressive encounters

FIG 107. Two common terns performing the *upward flutter*. This is a ritualised contest over airspace in which the two birds flutter vertically upwards, the lower bird repeatedly lunging at the upper bird and the upper bird pointing its bill down defensively. Plymouth, USA. (Sandy Selesky)

between neighbours after about the middle of incubation: high-level aggression is reserved for intruding strangers, or for late-nesting pairs that try to interpose themselves between two established pairs.

When a female lands in a male's territory, whether spontaneously or at the end of a *high flight*, she goes immediately into the *erect* posture and twists her head away from the male; this usually (but not always) switches off the male's aggressive impulse to attack any bird that comes too close. When male and female land together, both go into the *erect* posture, twisting their heads away from each other (Fig. 41). They then start the ground courtship display, usually with the male in the *bent* posture (but directed sideways past the female) and the female in the *erect* posture. Each walks past the other and they start to circle in a display called the *parade* (Fig. 40). Often one bird (usually the male) breaks off and starts *scraping*, bending down with breast touching the sand and kicking a hollow, or scrape, with his feet. This signals his interest in nesting there, and if the female reciprocates, she moves in and scrapes in the same hollow. More often, she flies off and the male follows her.[14] These tentative overtures are repeated many times over a period of days, sometimes with several different females, until the male is accepted by one. The pair-bond then gradually develops over several days as the birds become more accustomed to each other and coordinate their activities.

Early in the period of settlement, males carry fish around the colony and land with them in their territories, where they give displays; this seems to advertise their proficiency in catching fish and their availability as mates. Females are strongly attracted to fish and are much more likely to land near a male with a large fish than near one with a small fish or without a fish at all. Later in the mate selection process, males carry fish in displays with potential mates on the ground and use them to attract females into their territories (Fig. 108). At first the male is reluctant to part with his fish (Fig. 109), and there

FIG 108. Early stage in courtship of common terns. The female (right) is begging for the fish; the male is attracted to her but will not come too close because she might snatch the fish and then lose interest in him. Grand Canal Dock, Dublin. (John Fox)

FIG 109. Later stage in courtship of common terns. The female (left) has seized the fish but the male is not ready to let go. Later in the courtship-feeding period, the male will bring fish regularly and will pass them over immediately. Plymouth, USA. (W. Thomas Manders)

is sometimes a lengthy standoff as the female tries to get the fish while the male tries to mount the female without giving it up (see under *Courtship-feeding* in Chapter 3). As the pair become accustomed to each other, the male starts to feed the female regularly and soon provides most of the food she needs to form eggs.

FIG 110. Common terns copulating. The male may remain on the female's back for a minute or more before lowering his tail around hers to make cloacal contact. Plymouth, USA. (J. Fenton)

Feeds are often followed by pre-copulatory displays, in which the male holds his head up and his breast feathers puffed out, and walks in short arcs around and in front of the female. If the female is unreceptive, she stays facing the male, walks away, or even pecks him to drive him off. If she is receptive, she starts low-intensity begging, crouching down, turning away from him and giving persistent '*ki-ki-ki-ki-ki...*' begging calls. The male then flutters up onto her back. If she is still unreceptive, she walks away or shakes him off, but if she is receptive, she crouches down with her wings slightly open, continuing to beg softly. The male may remain standing on her back for up to a minute before starting to wag his tail from side to side, then flaps his wings to hold his balance while he brings his tail round under the female's to make cloacal contact (Fig. 110). Unless disturbed by other birds, the male may remain mounted for several minutes and make cloacal contact up to ten times before dismounting, when both birds go into the *erect* posture and start to preen (Figs 111 and 112). Copulations sometimes occur away from the colony up to two weeks before

FIGS 111, 112. Common tern preening. Terns spend much time maintaining their plumage in immaculate condition. This is especially important for the flight feathers during the breeding season, when they spend many hours each day on the wing to bring food to their chicks.

LEFT: **FIG 111.** Like other birds, terns have a preen gland above the tail which secretes a waxy oil that helps to waterproof the plumage. This bird is rubbing its head on the preen gland to spread oil from the gland over its plumage. Grand Canal Dock, Dublin. (John Fox)
RIGHT: **FIG 112.** It refreshes the vanes of its flight feathers by running its bill along them, aligning the barbs and barbules where they have become displaced. Here it is preening the left outer tail-feather. Grand Canal Dock, Dublin. (John Fox)

egg-laying occurs, but become most frequent in the last ten days, stopping abruptly after the clutch is completed.

Common terns have a large and varied vocabulary. The basic flight call – usually the only call heard away from breeding colonies – is a sharp '*kip*'. This call is often given when flying with other terns and seems to reflect sociability but mild aggression, functioning to maintain separation from other birds while foraging, or contact with other birds flying to roost; it conveys a message something like 'I'm here, but don't come too close.' Although a simple monosyllabic call, it has a distinctive sharp, 'irritable' timbre which, once learned, is instantly recognisable and distinguishable from that of all other seabirds. At the breeding sites, the most characteristic call is the *advertising* call, used when flying in with a fish, or in other contexts to signal that the calling bird is present and occupying a space. This is a multisyllabic call of variable length, '*keee-urr..., keee-urr..., keeuri..keeuri..keeuri...*' down-slurred at first but up-slurred in the '*ri*' at the end of the later phrases. This call is variable among individuals and is learned within a few days by their chicks, who rush out of cover begging when they hear either of their own parents flying in calling, in spite of the cacophanous surrounding noise in the colony. The first syllable '*keee-urr*' is sometimes given, in combination with an exaggerated *bent* posture, by a bird asserting ownership of a space such as a breeding or feeding territory. Another distinctive call is the high-intensity alarm, a high-pitched, down-slurred '*keeee-aairrr*', often given high overhead when a human intruder approaches or enters the nesting area. Chicks instantly run to cover and freeze when they hear this or other alarm calls. Birds attacking human intruders into the nesting area come in from behind with an intimidating, machine-gun-like rattle '*ke-ke-ke-ke-ke-ke...*', ending with a harsh '*kaaaar*' as they peck the intruder's head and soar upwards.[15]

In the preceding paragraphs, we have described the sequence of events and behaviours that accompany the formation of new pairs and the development of new pair-bonds. In fact, the majority of common terns reunite with the same mate that they had in the previous year. This is especially true for the older birds that return and breed early. Most of the new pairs that are formed early in the season are composed of birds that have lost their mate of the previous year, through either death or 'divorce' (cases where both birds are still alive but take new mates). Little is known about the process whereby established pairs reunite, because they seem to do so very quickly, without much display that can be observed and recorded at the colony site. Reuniting pairs lay eggs and raise chicks as much as a week earlier than new pairs, even new pairs whose members are of comparable age and experience. This gives reunited pairs a decisive advantage, because early-breeding pairs get the best nesting sites and the best feeding territories, and have better opportunities to steal food from late-breeding pairs than vice versa.

Whether new or reunited, as soon as pairs are firmly established the males start to feed the females on a systematic basis. In the next stage, the female accompanies the male to the feeding grounds and is fed there for up to 10–15 days. This is sometimes called the *honeymoon* period, because the birds spend most of their time away from their home site, the pair stays together for most of the day, and they copulate frequently. If the male has a feeding territory, the female spends most of the day there, standing on a perch and doing little or nothing while the male catches fish and brings them to her.[16] In other circumstances, the female stands on the shore near the feeding area and waits for the male to bring fish, or accompanies the male at sea, begging persistently while he forages and alighting on the water to take a fish when he catches one. At this time, the female gains weight from the usual level of about 120 g to 180 g or more, most of which is stored in the form of yolk in up to ten ovarian follicles.[17] One reason why she stops trying to catch food for herself at this time is that she is too heavy and unmanoeuvrable to do so efficiently. The pair remains on the feeding grounds for much of the day, returning to the colony site in the evenings. There, they often have to resume territorial defence, because new pairs may have staked a claim on the territory site during the day, or established neighbours may have encroached into it.

When the female is almost ready to lay – a few hours to three days before she lays the first egg – she returns to the breeding colony and waits in the male's territory, where she spends most of the day, leaving it only to drink or bathe. The male continues to bring food to her, but he now has to fly back and forth to the feeding grounds to do so (Fig. 113). For this reason, he cannot bring food as rapidly as he could during the *honeymoon* period. At this time, the female sometimes eats fragments of mollusc shells, apparently because she needs to take in more calcium and mobilise it to form the eggshells.[18] The male continues to feed the female until she lays the last egg in the clutch, but then quickly switches to sharing incubation duties.

During the *honeymoon* period, the male stays close to the female at all times, and this is thought to be a form of *mate guarding* – watching over the female to prevent other males having access to her at the time when she is fertile and about to ovulate.[19] Once the female switches to waiting by the nest, however, the male has to spend much of his time commuting to catch fish and bring them to her, and the female is left alone for long periods. At this time, she is often courted by males other than her mate, who land next to her with fish and start performing the pre-copulatory display. Some females – perhaps because

FIG 113. Common tern scratching its head in flight. Terns are adept flyers and quite often scratch their heads while gliding along. They sometimes even turn their heads to preen the feathers on their backs or bellies while flying 'blind'. Bird Island, USA. (Tom Murray)

they are not fed enough by their own mates – actively attract males by begging vociferously when the males fly nearby carrying fish. Most other females ignore the eager suitors or rush at them and drive them off, but a few encourage the strange males by begging to them and trying to get their fish. Again, there is often a standoff between the female who only wants the fish and the male who only wants to copulate. However, in rare cases the female actually accepts copulations with the strange males, usually getting the fish before or during the copulation. The female's mate can do little to prevent this, but in fact there is little evidence that these extra-pair copulations actually result in production of a chick. By the time the female copulates with another male, she has usually laid the first egg and ovulated the second; even if the third egg is fertilised by a strange male, third eggs rarely produce chicks that survive.

Incubation is intermittent until the third egg is laid, but after that the eggs are covered for almost 24 hours each day, except during disturbances. In a three-egg clutch, the eggs are laid over a period of three or four days, but they usually hatch within one or two days; in a two-egg clutch, the eggs are usually laid about two days apart and hatch one day apart. Both parents have brood patches and both incubate more or less equally during the day, although the female does most of the incubation at night. The birds alternate incubation duties, typically changing over 10–20 times per day, although incubation bouts can be as short as one minute or as long as six hours. The incubation period is normally about 23 days for the first egg and 22 days for the second and third. However, if there is nocturnal predation by a predator (such as an owl) that threatens the adults, they desert the colony for part or all of each night and the eggs cool down to ambient temperature. The eggs are resistant to chilling, but development of the embryo is suspended when its temperature drops, so that incubation periods are extended, sometimes to as long as 29–32 days.[20]

Every time an incubating bird leaves the nest, it performs a stereotyped behaviour known as *sideways building*: it walks slowly away from the nest, picking up loose objects such as dead vegetation or fragments of shell, and tucks them backwards over its shoulder. It does this repeatedly for 15–30 seconds, sometimes continuing even after it turns and starts walking back to the nest. This behaviour seems to be necessary to switch off the bird's broodiness and allow it to fly away to feed, but it also functions to move loose material from all parts of the territory towards the nest, where it is subsequently picked up by the sitting bird and tucked into the nest. By this means, the birds convert a bare scrape into a substantial nest over the three weeks of incubation: the size of the nest is limited only by the amount of loose material in the territory at the start. Incubating birds fly off the nest to defecate: this functions to keep the nest and the territory camouflaged (unlike Sandwich terns, whose nests are ringed with faeces), although each bird defecates freely into the territories of others.

Common terns attack most birds or mammals that the terns perceive as predators when they approach the breeding area. If a peregrine falcon flies towards the colony site in hunting mode, or circles overhead 'waiting on', the terns immediately flee out to sea, and remain flying low over the water until the peregrine has left, or sometimes for up to 20 minutes longer. All other birds that threaten eggs and chicks, including harriers, kestrels, short-eared owls, herring and black-backed gulls, crows and herons, are pursued by mobs of terns which

FIG 114. Common tern attacking a great black-backed gull. Common terns vigorously attack avian predators that pose a threat to their eggs and chicks but do not pose a threat to themselves. This includes kestrels, harriers, crows, magpies and gulls. Grand Canal Dock, Dublin. (John Fox)

dive on them from behind (Fig. 114). Common terns will even chase and 'mob' a peregrine if it is not hunting, or when it has already taken a tern, although only a few terns are bold enough actually to attack a peregrine (Fig. 115). The predator usually takes evasive action and is often driven away: even though the terns rarely actually hit a flying bird, they often succeed in distracting it so that it turns away before it learns that the site is a good place to forage. However, a determined predator such as a harrier or a large gull which knows that there are eggs and chicks to be taken can usually slip in and out quickly without being harmed, and these individual predators take eggs or chicks at will.

The terns continue to harass the predator during every raid, however. It is probably worthwhile for each individual bird to do so, because it may be able

FIG 115. Common terns mobbing a peregrine that has taken a fledgling. Terns are capable of distinguishing whether a falcon is hunting or not. They often fly up and mob a peregrine that does not pose a threat to themselves, but flee low over the water to escape from a peregrine that is hunting. Lady's Island Lake, Co. Wexford. (Dave Daly)

to distract the predator from its own chicks so that it flies on to take someone else's. Predators that approach the colony on foot, such as foxes or rats, are followed by a cloud of terns who hang overhead giving alarm calls, but the terns rarely come close enough to terrestrial predators to be effective in deterring them. Common terns vigorously attack human intruders, diving from behind, pecking their heads and defecating on them. At sites that are infrequently entered by humans, the terns hang high overhead (Fig. 116), giving alarm calls, but with repeated intrusions they gradually lose their fear and approach closer until they actually peck the intruder at every dive.[21] They even learn to recognise individual humans and only peck the people they know, keeping their distance from strangers.[22] They defecate at the lowest point of each dive, frequently

FIG 116. Common terns in flight over the nesting colony. When a human intruder enters the nesting area, dozens or hundreds of terns take to the air, some hanging high overhead while others attack the intruder. These birds are holding position against the wind, so that all are heading in the same direction. Monomoy, USA. (Peter Trull)

hitting the intruders with their faeces – but they do not actually aim their faeces; rather, they defecate at the moment of closest approach, which is the moment of greatest fear.[23]

Common terns start to attack predators and human intruders shortly before eggs are laid. Both the number of birds attacking and the intensity of their attacks increases during the incubation period, peaking at the time of hatching and then declining until attacks are only desultory after the chicks fledge. The peak in aggression coincides with the hatching of the earliest chicks and wanes considerably over the following two or three weeks, even though many chicks continue to hatch throughout this period. This suggests that the most intense attacks are by the earliest breeders.

Although common terns are often successful in distracting or driving out diurnal predators, they are helpless against nocturnal predators such as owls or mink. If one of these predators finds the colony, the adult terns have no recourse but to desert their nests, flying out en masse and staying away until it is safe to return, often at first light next morning. Typically, the predator kills a few adult terns on the first two or three nights until the others learn of the danger, and it then takes as many eggs and chicks as it wants. Mink and weasels (in Britain) sometimes indulge in 'surplus killing' and kill dozens or hundreds of chicks in a single night. Tern eggs are resistant to chilling, but small chicks often succumb to hypothermia when the parents desert them on cold or wet nights, or give distress calls that advertise their location to other predators. One mink or a family of owls can destroy an entire year's crop of tern chicks, even in a colony of many hundred pairs (see Chapter 11).

As the eggs hatch, the hatched shells are removed, usually within a few minutes: the sitting bird picks them up, flies off with them and drops them 10–30 m away. This also seems to function in maintaining camouflage, because the hatched shells are white on the inside and are conspicuous against the background of sand or vegetation (see Fig. 155 in Chapter 9). During hatching and for the first few days of the chicks' lives, the female does most of the brooding while the male brings most of the fish (see Figs 46 and 47 in Chapter 3). After about four days, the female starts to make short foraging trips and to bring back food, and by about the eighth day the female brings almost as much food as the male, leaving the chicks alone for long periods during the day; they are brooded at night until they become too large for the parent to cover them (Fig. 117).

FIG 117. Common tern feeding a chick about 14 days old. By this age, common tern chicks often weigh as much as their parents, but they have to grow most of their feathers before they fledge at about 24 days old, and it takes another week or two for the wings to grow fully. Grand Canal Dock, Dublin. (John Fox)

The types of fish brought and the rates at which they are delivered vary enormously, depending on the fish that are available at different distances from the colony. Common tern chicks hatch about one day apart, and this establishes a size hierarchy that is usually maintained throughout the chick-raising period. There is intense competition for the food items brought by the parents: the oldest chick rushes to meet the parent ahead of the others and can often steal the fish from the younger chicks if they have been able to get it first. Parents usually give the fish to the chick that reaches them first and begs for it most vigorously, so the oldest chick has a strong competitive advantage over the younger ones (see Fig. 46 in Chapter 3). Unless food is superabundant, the younger chicks fall further behind and often succumb to starvation.

Except for some broods at the periphery of the nesting area, common tern chicks stay within their parents' territories until they fledge (Figs 118 and 119). They soon learn not to venture into neighbouring territories, for if they do they are viciously attacked and mercilessly pecked by the territory owners. Each pair learns to identify its own chicks and vigorously excludes all others. Nevertheless, some pairs accept alien chicks into their own broods and raise them as though they were their own. These adoptions are fairly frequent in some breeding colonies, but rare in others. It appears that it takes the parents two or three days to learn to recognise their own chicks, and during this period they cannot afford to reject a chick that looks unfamiliar, because it might be their own. This gives a 'window of opportunity' for a chick seeking adoption to slip into another

FIG 118. Common tern chick about 18 days old exercising its wings. In the week prior to fledging, common tern chicks spend much time jumping up and down and flapping their wings. This helps to develop and condition their flight muscles in preparation for their first flight. Grand Canal Dock, Dublin. (John Fox)

FIG 119. Common tern feeding a chick about 21 days old. As the chicks grow older, the parents often feed them in flight without landing. Penikese Island, USA. (Craig Gibson)

nest without being detected. Adoptions usually take place when the adoptees are less than two days old, and they are usually initiated by the chicks, which spontaneously wander away from home and approach neighbouring pairs. If rejected (as they usually are) they continue wandering and are usually rejected again, but in many cases they eventually blunder into a nest where the eggs are just starting to hatch. They are then likely to be accepted and treated as though they were the natural offspring of the adopting parents. In more cases than not, the adoptee becomes the oldest chick in its new brood and has a permanent advantage in competition for food. Adoption is a serious mistake for the adopting parents, because they spend their time and energy raising a chick that is not their genetic offspring, and they usually end up losing at least one of their own chicks that they would otherwise have raised. Likewise, it is a gain for the donor parents, who add one more of their genetic offspring to the population, and a gain for the adoptees' siblings, who are relieved of some competition.[24] It can thus be regarded as a form of parasitism, in which the donor parents 'steal' parental care from the adopting parents. Adoptions seem to be most frequent

FIG 120. This roseate tern has adopted a common tern chick. The roseates had nested inside the box (see Chapter 11) and had apparently lost their own chicks but were raising the common tern chick instead. Adoptions are fairly frequent in some common tern colonies, but it is rare for one species to adopt a chick of another species. Lady's Island Lake, Co. Wexford. (Dave Daly)

in colonies that are crowded (so that there are plenty of potential adopters close by) and are stressed by food shortage (so that many of the adopted chicks would otherwise have died from starvation).

On rare occasions, a pair of terns of one species in a mixed colony adopts and raises a chick of another species (Fig. 120). Such interspecies adoptions sometimes result when an egg is moved by a flood from one nest to the vicinity of another (terns that find an egg close to their nest treat it as their own and use their bills to roll it into the nest), but might also result from the chick itself seeking adoption in the way described in the previous paragraph.

Young common terns take their first flights when they are 22–29 days old – earlier when they are well nourished. At first they make short flights and often land in places where they are not welcome, then have to get back on foot through hostile territory. By the second day they can usually fly to the edge of the colony, and they then spend their time alternating between the beach (or other places outside the nesting area) and their home territory. The new fledglings spend much of this time unattended, and accumulate in packs on the beach. Their parents feed them either on the beach or back in the nesting territory, where some fledglings continue to return to roost at night for several weeks, if there is not too much vegetation there. By about the third day the fledglings start to venture out over the sea, practising flying and learning how to dip down and pick up objects from the surface. Their first 'prey' are usually inanimate objects such as bits of floating weed, which they carry back to the beach and try to eat, or drop and pick up repeatedly. They usually do not dip their heads into the water until about the fifth day after fledging, and do not dive fully into the water until many days later. Unless they come across a situation like a tide pool where fish are easy to catch, they do not catch their first fish until they have been on the wing for three weeks or more. By about the seventh day after fledging, however, the parents take them out to the fishing grounds where they can be fed quickly without the parents having to spend time commuting back to the colony. The fledglings fly around near their parents, begging incessantly, and land on the water momentarily to take fish from them. They continue to depend on their parents for food for many more weeks (Fig. 121), probably until they migrate

FIG 121. Common tern feeding a juvenile several weeks after fledging. Like other terns, common terns continue to feed their juveniles for two or more months, dispersing with them to staging areas that may be hundreds of kilometres from the breeding site. It is not known whether they migrate with them and continue to feed them, but other tern species are known to feed juveniles even in the wintering areas. Plymouth, USA. (John Van de Graaff)

FIG 122. Juvenile common tern in flight. Juvenile common terns have dark brown heads with whitish foreheads, dark brown 'carpal bars' on the forewing, brown bars on the back, pink legs and pink-and-black bills. Plymouth, USA. (Craig Gibson)

south and perhaps during and after their migration (Fig. 122).[25] During this period of two months or more prior to migration, the family parties disperse tens or even hundreds of kilometres away from the breeding site, concentrating in areas where the fishing is good and resting at remote places on the shore between bouts of foraging. A recent study in the USA has suggested that post-fledging care is mainly done by the male parents, and that the females migrate south in early August when the juveniles have been on the wing for only three to five weeks.[26]

Pairs that lose all their eggs or chicks to predation or flooding generally re-lay after 10–13 days – the minimum time required for females to reset their physiological cycle back to egg formation, for the males to start courtship-feeding again, and for the females to produce eggs. The proportion of pairs that re-lay is close to 100 per cent among older birds that lose eggs early in the season, declining with age, date and stage in the nesting cycle to near-zero for younger pairs that lose chicks late in the season.[27] Birds almost always retain the same mates for repeat nestings. Third attempts seem to be rare, even for experienced pairs that fail twice before mid-season. Clutch-sizes are usually smaller in re-layings and the relatively few chicks that are raised have less time after fledging to learn to fish before they have to migrate south. The probability

FIG 124. A common tern with a large fish half swallowed after successfully evading kleptoparasites. When hard pressed, terns often swallow fish they are carrying rather than drop them. If the fish is large, the tern sometimes cannot swallow it completely and arrives at the nest with the fish partially swallowed; it is then very difficult for the bird to regurgitate the fish and feed it to its chicks. Bird Island, USA. (C. Gibson)

and can usually elude a single pursuer unless it is carrying a fish large enough to hamper its flight. However, the chase is often joined by other birds: the quarry usually cannot evade a group of three or more determined pursuers and is forced either to swallow the fish or to drop it. If the fish is dropped, one of the pursuers swoops down to pick it up and the chase resumes, until eventually the fish is swallowed. Sometimes a parent arrives at the nest with a large fish partly swallowed, the tail protruding from its bill (Fig. 124). It is then very difficult for the bird to cough up the fish for its chicks, because fish are always swallowed head first and the fins or spines project backwards. When common terns bring especially large fish to the colony, they often approach very furtively, landing at the edge of the breeding area and looking around for a safe moment before flying in silently, rather than flying directly to the nest calling as they do when bringing smaller food items.[33]

A second tactic is to watch for a fish to be delivered to a nearby bird's mate or to chicks. At the moment when the bird carrying the fish stalls to drop down for a landing, it loses its ability to dodge and the thief can pounce. Another moment of vulnerability is immediately after a chick takes a fish. Small chicks are usually slow to swallow fish and often have them snatched away, while larger chicks learn to swallow fish quickly and to run into cover. Occasionally, when a chick is

FIG 125. Adult common tern attacking a small chick which has fallen into the water. This is a curious and unexplained quirk of behaviour of common terns, in which they respond aggressively to any tern that is injured or behaving abnormally. This behaviour was exploited in the nineteenth century by collectors and plume-hunters, who often shot dozens of terns hovering over a wounded bird struggling in the water. Seaforth, Merseyside. (Steve Young)

trying to swallow a large fish, a pirate swoops down, seizes the fish and flies off with the chick still attached. On rare occasions, the chick is carried away many metres before it drops off.[34] If the chick should fall into the water, it is then attacked and killed by other adults (Fig. 125).

Most adult common terns are 'part-time' pirates: they catch most of their fish for themselves, but occasionally supplement their catches when a good opportunity to steal a fish appears nearby. A few individual birds are 'professionals': they spend most of their time in the colony stealing fish and rarely go to sea to catch fish for themselves. Some of these specialists are males who steal fish to feed their mates; others are females who take time off from attending their chicks to steal food from neighbours. A recent study in Germany showed that these 'professional' pirates have higher breeding success than other 'honest' birds in the colony – disproving the adage that crime does not pay.[35]

Chicks also steal fish from each other. This starts quite early in life when the chicks within a brood compete with each other for the fish brought by their parents, and the competition is tilted in favour of the older chicks within the brood. As they grow larger (and often after their younger siblings have died), the first-hatched chicks use their experience to steal food from neighbouring broods.[36] This competition is tilted in favour of the chicks hatched earlier in the season, and this is one of the mechanisms by which pairs that nest earlier have higher breeding success than later-nesting pairs. Occasionally when food becomes short after a period when many early-hatched chicks have grown well, the large, hungry chicks band together and form 'teenage gangs' which rush in and 'mug' smaller chicks every time a fish is brought for them. The parents of the smaller chicks can do little to defend them, so that the smaller chicks are sometimes prevented from feeding altogether and die of starvation.

Common terns take an extraordinarily wide range of prey – the widest of all our five breeding terns. Besides fish of many types, they commonly feed on crustaceans (shrimps, prawns, crabs, etc.), a wide variety of insects and occasionally squid or marine worms. They frequently switch from one type of prey to another, sometimes many times during the course of each day. Despite their more varied diets, common terns seem to be food-stressed more often than little, Sandwich or roseate terns, at least during the breeding season. They frequently have low breeding success even in the absence of predation or other adverse factors, and where this has been studied the chicks grow poorly and often die of starvation. The same phenomena are often observed in Arctic terns, but more rarely in the other three species, despite the fact that they have more specialised feeding habits. Common and Arctic terns seem to be 'Jacks of all trades and masters of none'.

In the marine environment, common terns' main prey are Atlantic herrings, sprats, sandeels, saithe, whiting and cod (see Figs 28–31 in Chapter 2). Other fish such as sticklebacks, flounders or pipefish are sometimes offered to chicks, but the chicks find them difficult to swallow and they are often dropped. The variability in diets is illustrated in Tables 18 and 19, which summarise reports on the relative numbers of various prey items fed to chicks and eaten by adults, respectively. Sandeels, Atlantic herrings and sprats were the main foods in all but two of the studies. The study in Shetland in 1988 was conducted to investigate the terns' response to a collapse in sandeel stocks, and found that common terns had switched successfully to catching saithe instead.[37] The study in Norfolk in 1925–27 found that more than half the food items in the stomachs of adults were invertebrates (although invertebrates would have made up less than half of the diet by weight because they are generally smaller than the fish that the birds eat). Studies of common tern foods in other areas have also indicated that the adults have very varied diets, often including large numbers of invertebrates.[38] The other two studies of adults summarised in Table 19 were of food items brought to females during courtship-feeding, and these consisted mainly of fish. A study

TABLE 18. Percentages by number of food items brought by common terns to their chicks at five breeding colonies in Britain and Ireland.

	Location and years					
	Farne Islands, North-umberland	Coquet Island, Northumberland		Mousa, Shetland	Lady's Island Lake, Co. Wexford	Belfast Harbour, Co. Down
Food	1965–1967	1965–1967	2001	1988	1997	2006
Ammodytidae (sandeels)	44	30	82	20	55	
Clupeidae (herring, sprat)	38	70	17		38	58
Gadidae (cod, saithe)	11			80	1	
Gasterosteidae (sticklebacks)	2					
Trachinidae (weever fish)	3					
Pleuronectidae (flounders)						11
Other fishes			1		6	3
Crustacea (crabs, shrimps)	1					28
Cephalopoda (squids)	1					

Sources: Langham, 1968; Pearson, 1968; Uttley *et al.*, 1989b; Newton & Crowe, 2000; Robinson *et al.*, 2001; Chivers, 2007.

of courtship-feeding in Scotland indicated that males usually ate the shrimps and the smaller fish that they caught, but carried the larger fish to the colony to feed the females,[39] thereby making efficient use of the time and energy required to fly back and forth with each food item. In consequence, the records of fish fed during courtship-feeding, although easy to collect, may be a misleading guide to what the adults eat during most of the year.

Although adult common terns themselves consume many invertebrates, they feed their chicks mainly on fish.[40] An experimental study in which common tern chicks were raised in captivity showed that they grew best when fed herrings or other marine fish: they did not grow well when fed on sticklebacks and did not thrive on a diet of shrimps, even when the latter had a similar

TABLE 19. Percentages by number of food items eaten by adult common terns at three sites in Britain and Ireland.

Food	Location, years, type of sample		
	Norfolk 1924–1927 stomach contents	Rockabill, Co. Dublin 1998–1999 fed to mate	Belfast Harbour, Co. Down 2007 fed to mate
Ammodytidae (sandeels)	15	59	
Clupeidae (herring, sprat)		22	53
Gadidae (cod, whiting, saithe)	26	15	
Pleuronectidae (flounders)			8
Other fishes		3	11
Crustacea (crabs, shrimps)	14		28
Mollusca (molluscs)	10		
Annelida (marine worms)	15		
Insecta (insects)	15		

Sources: Collinge, 1924–27; Newton & Crowe, 2000; Chivers, 2007.

energy content to the fish diets.[41] It is not known whether the shrimp diet lacked some important nutrient, or whether the shrimps contained too much salt. In a few cases, common terns have been reported feeding large numbers of crustaceans to their chicks, but these seem to be in circumstances where more suitable foods are in short supply. However, crustaceans can be a useful supplementary food when the diet also includes nutritious fish, and may tide birds over temporary food shortages.[42]

Common tern diets are adjusted to whatever prey items are available at different times, and to the needs of the adults and chicks. Consequently, what the birds eat or bring to their chicks varies according to season, weather, tide and the number and age of the chicks in each brood. For example, at the tern colonies on the Farne Islands and the Ythan Estuary, herrings and sprats became relatively more important dietary items for the chicks as the breeding season progressed. At the Ythan Estuary sandeels and sprats were the main prey at high tide, versus shrimps and blennies at low tide.[43] At the Ribble Estuary sprats were the principal prey at high tide and whitings and saithe at low tide.[44]

There is no information available on the diets of the common terns that breed on fresh waters in Britain and Ireland. In continental Europe, freshwater common terns feed on a very wide variety of fish and insects, the main fish species being roach, bleak, perch, ruffe and smelt.[45] It has been suggested that opportunities for feeding are generally better for freshwater than for coastal common terns in Europe.[46] In Britain and Ireland, however, breeding success is not markedly higher at inland than at coastal colonies (see under *Breeding biology* and Table 20, below) and numbers breeding inland have always been small relative to those on the coast.

In winter in West Africa, common terns feed mainly on small schooling fish, including anchovies and sardines.[47]

BREEDING BIOLOGY

Common terns usually lay either two or three eggs. The proportion of birds laying three eggs varies enormously. At some colony sites almost all females lay three eggs, at least in the early part of the season; at other sites most females lay two eggs and some lay only one. Consequently, the colony average clutch-size can be greater than 2.95 or less than 2.0. First-time breeders rarely lay three eggs and often lay only one. The variations in average clutch-size among colonies and years seem to be related to the availability of food around the colony site. However, it has proved difficult to explain why some birds lay only two eggs while others at the same site and the same time lay three: these differences are not strongly related to age, laying date or other factors that have been investigated. Clutches of four or more eggs are very infrequent, usually comprising less than 1 per cent of all clutches in a colony. Although a few female common terns probably lay four eggs, many or most clutches of four, five or six eggs result from two females laying in the same nest, either a female–female pair without a male partner or a 'trio' of one male and two females. Sporadically, the proportion of these 'supernormal' clutches is unusually high (up to 5 per cent or more) at one colony for a few years. This probably results from a locally and temporarily skewed sex-ratio with an excess of females.[48]

Common tern eggs are very variable in colouration, but are usually well camouflaged, with dark brown or black spots, streaks and blotches on a buffy or brownish background (see Fig. 43 in Chapter 3). They usually weigh about 21 g, with the second egg in the clutch slightly smaller and the third (if any) distinctly smaller than the first. A clutch of three eggs typically weighs about 50 per cent of the female's body weight, and this proportion can be as high as 60 per cent for some individual females. In some sites and years, hatching success is very low or zero because of flooding or heavy predation. In the absence of these factors, however, hatching success is usually very high, typically more than 90 per cent and occasionally as high as 99 per cent for eggs laid in the first part of the season, although it usually declines among late clutches, probably because of the inexperience of the parents.

In good conditions, common tern chicks grow very rapidly: their weight increases from about 14 g at hatching to 100 g by about day 15 and to about 120 g (close to adult weight) when they fledge at around day 24. Most growth of body structures and plumage has been completed by day 24, but when the chick first flies the wing is only about 70 per cent of its full length and growth continues for at least ten days thereafter (see Fig. 49 in Chapter 3 for a fledgling Sandwich tern). However, chick growth and survival are enormously variable. Chick survival is sometimes very low because of flooding or heavy predation. Even in the absence of these factors, average chick survival can be lower than 20 per cent or higher than 80 per cent. These variations are due primarily to differences in food availability, because most chicks that die do so from starvation, and in cases where chick survival is low, the growth rates of survivors are depressed too so that they fledge late and do so at weights of 100 g or even less. Even within a single colony in a single year, chick growth and survival depend strongly on characteristics of the parents, especially age and laying date: older parents and those that lay early in the season raise more and healthier chicks.[49] Under the best conditions, even young parents laying relatively late in the season can raise two or even three chicks that grow at high rates and survive to fledging; under the worst conditions, only older parents and those laying early in the season raise even a single chick, and this may fledge at a low weight. In one comparative study, these extreme conditions were manifested at three colonies only 16–26 km apart: the differences were related to food availability, because parents at the 'best' site brought food to their chicks much more frequently than those at the other two sites.[50]

Because of the enormous variability in hatching success and chick survival, it is very difficult to arrive at a figure for the 'normal' or 'average' productivity of common terns, where productivity is defined as the average number of chicks raised to fledging per pair in a colony. Even this definition raises problems, because the number of chicks raised per pair usually declines rapidly as the season progresses, so the average that is measured depends on the length of the period over which the study is conducted. At single sites in single years, productivity can vary from zero to as high as 2.8 chicks per pair. Averaging over sites and years, average productivity is typically in the range 0.7–1.4, varying among habitats (inland fresh water vs. coastal salt water, islands vs. beaches vs. saltmarshes, etc.) and regions (southern England vs. northern England vs. Scotland vs. Ireland, etc.).[51]

Table 20 summarises measurements of productivity at 23 sites that were selected as 'index' sites for common terns in the *Seabird Monitoring Programme* over the 25-year period 1986–2010.[52] The list includes the three largest colonies in Britain and Ireland during that period, but also includes a representative selection of small colonies, freshwater sites as well as coastal sites, and locations all around Britain and Ireland. The data in Table 20 display the enormous variability in common terns' breeding success. Although 17 of the 23 sites had occasional bad years when productivity was reduced to zero or near zero, all but one had several good years in which productivity exceeded one chick raised per pair, and eight of the sites had occasional years when productivity exceeded two chicks per pair. Five of the sites had consistently high productivity over periods of 13–22 years: it is noteworthy that all of these sites were managed (see Chapter 11). Averaging over all sites and years, the average productivity was 0.87 chicks per pair.

Perhaps the largest contrast in breeding performance of common terns is that between early and late breeders. Early breeders lay larger clutches and larger eggs, hold better feeding territories, feed their chicks more food and better food and raise more chicks to fledging. An experimental study in which hatching dates were manipulated suggested that part of these differences resulted from changes in the environment (some factor such as food availability was more favourable early in the season), but that part resulted from differences in the intrinsic 'quality' of the birds that laid at different times.[53] Parental 'quality' is an elusive concept, but it encapsulates the fact that some individual parents are consistently more successful than others over multiple years and over varying conditions.[54] In common terns, birds of high quality tend to have high-quality mates, lay earlier and raise more chicks than low-quality birds. Birds that raise more chicks early in their breeding careers probably survive better, so the older breeders tend to be of higher quality, reinforcing the differences in performance. Older common terns have consistently higher breeding performance than younger birds; however, several studies have suggested that breeding performance is more closely related to laying date than to age.[55] The individuals that are older and of higher quality constitute the 'core' of the colony and generate a disproportionate number of the birds that survive to form the next generation. Although there is substantial evidence for all these differences, much remains to be learned about their implications for genetic fitness and population structure.

TABLE 20. Numbers and productivity of common terns at 23 index sites in the *Seabird Monitoring Programme*, 1986–2010.

Region	Colony site	Average number of pairs 1986–2010 (range)	Average productivity 1986–2010 (range)	Number of years
SW Scotland	Eilean an Ruisg, Loch Feochan	10 (2–26)	0.61 (0.00–3.00)	15
	Sgeir na Caillich, Loch Melfort	161 (1–442)	0.61 (0.00–2.07)	23
	Glen Eileanan, Sound of Mull	550 (117–722)	0.60 (0.00–1.53)	21
N Scotland	Avoch Fish Farm, Ross	136 (60–210)	0.98 (0.00–1.66)	11
NE Scotland	St Fergus	124 (5–288)	0.15 (0.00–0.60)	17
SE Scotland	Isle of May	110 (2–303)	0.79 (0.00–1.50)	14
NE England	Coquet Island	811 (526–1,228)	1.05 (0.57–1.76)	22
C England	Rye Meads	42 (27–52)	1.42 (0.78–2.35)	23
E England	Snettisham	76 (3–130)	0.32 (0.00–1.69)	23
	Holkham	76 (44–154)	0.36 (0.00–1.38)	19
	Blakeney Point	156 (50–260)	0.46 (0.02–1.40)	19
	Breydon Water	162 (63–202)	0.96 (0.51–1.60)	21
SE England	Pitts Deep, Hurst	203 (60–375)	0.28 (0.00–1.00)	10
	Langstone Harbour	73 (4–154)	0.41 (0.00–1.76)	21
	Rye Harbour	100 (35–341)	0.94 (0.00–2.31)	23
SW England	Brownsea Island	170 (90–246)	0.52 (0.04–1.19)	22
	Lodmoor	40 (6–60)	1.54 (0.93–2.28)	13
Wales	Shotton Pools	439 (150–762)	1.17 (0.00–2.27)	20
	Cemlyn	75 (30–120)	0.60 (0.00–2.04)	16
NW England	Seaforth	101 (3–221)	0.51 (0.00–1.09)	25
	Rockcliffe	42 (8–114)	0.06 (0.00–0.71)	18
NE Ireland	Belfast Lough	124 (12–201)	1.14 (0.24–1.80)	7
SE Ireland	Rockabill	790 (207–1,411)	1.31 (0.55–2.34)	16
Total, 23 sites		4,561 [a]	0.87 [b]	

Source: Mavor *et al.*, 2008, updated to 2010 from the JNCC database. The JNCC database has data for many more common tern breeding sites; we have selected 23 representative sites.

[a] About 31 per cent of total numbers breeding in Britain and Ireland.

[b] Overall average is weighted by the average number of pairs in each colony.

MIGRATIONS

Our knowledge of the migrations of the common tern is based in large part on the recoveries of 4,947 ringed birds from nearly 191,000 ringed in Britain and Ireland to the end of 2009.[56] Most (91 per cent) were ringed as chicks, but more than 10,000 were ringed as adults. Many of the latter were caught in mist-nets at staging sites on the east coast of England, so they probably included many migrants that had bred elsewhere. Detailed analysis has been reported for the first 2,102 recoveries obtained up to the end of 1997.[57]

As with our other terns there is a post-fledging dispersal of young birds starting in July, but these mostly remain close to their natal sites for the first two months. Many young birds travel quickly south to their West African wintering grounds, some arriving in Ghana by the end of August. The main movement south extends from August to October, and especially in October.

Very large pre-migratory flocks of common terns have been recorded on the east coast of Britain at Teesmouth, Cleveland, on the west coast at Seaforth, near Liverpool, and on the east coast of Ireland in Dublin Bay.[58] The most important of these staging sites is located on the intertidal mudflats that extend some 3 km eastwards from the shore at Sandymount Strand, south Dublin Bay (Fig. 126). Peak numbers occur there between 20 August and 20 September. In 2006, 2007 and 2010 high counts were 11,700, 9,025 and 8,020 terns, respectively, mainly commons with smaller numbers of Arctics and roseates and a sprinkling of Sandwich and black terns. Many of the birds were moulting while others had completed their moult. In 2010 the total number of breeding common terns in Dublin docks and on Rockabill, together with the Rockabill roseates and all their fledglings, would have amounted to 11,000–13,000 birds, more than enough to have accounted for the south Dublin Bay roost.[59] However, some observations have suggested that there is a continual turnover of birds at the Sandymount Strand roost, so that the overall numbers using the area could be in the order of 30,000–50,000 birds. The regular presence of black terns indicates that not all birds using the roost are of local origin. Ring-reading at Rockabill showed an influx of common terns from late July to early August originating from Norway, Finland and the staging area at Teesmouth.

Adult common terns remain in Britain and Ireland until the completion of their annual moult, which commences immediately after the breeding season. In contrast, Arctic terns almost all set off on their southward migration without moulting: their moult commences when they are in their wintering grounds. During the southward migration young common terns often travel with their parents while continuing to beg for and receive food. Both juveniles and adults

FIG 126. Terns assembling to roost at Sandymount Strand, south Dublin Bay, the largest staging area for terns in Britain and Ireland. Large numbers of terns – up to 11,700 common terns and 1,000 roseate terns, sometimes with large numbers of Sandwich and Arctic terns – gather here from late July to late September, foraging at sea during the day and coming to shore in the evening. Most of the birds moult during this period and accumulate fat as fuel for the southward migration. (Dick Coombes)

have similar timing and migration routes as well as wintering areas. Based on ringing recoveries, the birds migrate along the coasts of Iberia and West Africa. The main wintering areas for our birds are along the Gulf of Guinea between Sierra Leone and Ghana, with most recoveries in December in the area from 0° to 10° N (Fig. 127). Common terns have been recorded up to 600 km offshore, but most observations are from inshore waters. As mentioned for Sandwich terns (Chapter 7), the location and intensity of tern trapping can easily bias the importance of one country compared with another. A few probably winter off Portugal and southern Spain, and a very small number (only five of 943 recoveries) continue past the Gulf of Guinea and reach Angola or South Africa; only two of these continued past the Cape of Good Hope and were recorded in the Indian Ocean. In contrast, birds from northern Europe (Denmark, Sweden, Norway and Finland) 'leapfrog' over birds from western Europe and winter mainly in southern Africa.[60] Birds that breed in these countries probably comprise a large fraction of the staging flocks in eastern England, because many birds ringed as adults there have been recovered in northern Europe in the

FIG 127. Recovery locations of common terns ringed as chicks in Britain and Ireland. Juvenile common terns disperse in July–August throughout the breeding area and into neighbouring countries (green shading), but start to migrate south in late August. In winter (November–March), most recoveries are in coastal West Africa (orange band); most birds remain within the winter range throughout their first summers. The red arrows mark recoveries south of the main range (three in winter, three in spring/summer). In September–October recoveries are distributed throughout the entire range (green line). In May–July, two-year-old and older birds are recovered almost exclusively in Britain and Ireland. (Source: Norman, 2002)

breeding season, and five of the eleven birds recovered in Africa were reported from Namibia or South Africa.[61]

Wintering birds follow the distribution and abundance of prey fish, especially sardines and anchovies. The Atlantic upwellings off the West African and Gulf of Guinea coasts deliver shoals of sardines to spawn in the inshore waters off Ghana and Côte d'Ivoire.[62] The other important countries for our wintering common terns are Sierra Leone and Liberia.

By late February adults are beginning to move northwards, having severed their contact with the immature birds. It has been estimated that adults migrate at an average speed of 80–120 km per day as they travel northwards along the coast of northwestern Africa.[63] When they reach Britain and Ireland during April, they continue rapidly to their breeding colonies and are scarce on passage along the west coast or in the Irish Sea, so birds headed for breeding sites in northern and eastern England or Scotland are thought to fly mainly overland.[64] Adults demonstrate great site fidelity, often returning to within a few metres of the location in the colony where they bred successfully the previous year.[65]

First-winter birds generally stay on for their first summer off the West African coast, with few recoveries east of Sierra Leone and most birds recovered from Senegal to Liberia. A very small number travel back to Britain and Ireland and there are three recoveries of one-year-old birds here, but birds in first-summer plumage (Fig. 128) are rarely seen at the breeding colonies. Most two-

FIG 128. First-summer common tern (about one year old) photographed near a breeding colony. Most terns of all species remain in their winter quarters until they are two years old, but a very small number migrate north in their first summers and reach the breeding areas. The first summer plumage is similar to the winter adult, but some individuals have red legs and partly red bills. This bird is identifiable as a common tern by the extensive black on the primaries, as well as by the dark grey outer edges of the tail. Seaforth, Merseyside. (Steve Young)

year-old birds return to the British and Irish breeding areas, arriving there from late May onwards. These birds 'prospect' at breeding colonies at age two, but most nest for the first time in their third or fourth years.[66] Young breeding terns show less fidelity than adults to their natal sites, often breeding tens or hundreds of kilometres away, although most of these natal dispersal movements are to other sites within Britain and Ireland rather than to continental Europe.

Although common terns breeding in the Azores cross the Atlantic to winter in South America[67] (see Fig. 53 in Chapter 4), transatlantic crossings by common terns otherwise seem to be few and far between. No common tern ringed in Britain or Ireland has been recovered in North or South America, although one bird ringed in Finland has been recovered in Barbados. Although more than one million common terns have been ringed in North America, to date there have been just four recoveries on this side of the Atlantic. All of these were juveniles in their first autumn or winter: they were found in France (October), mid-Atlantic (November), at sea off Côte d'Ivoire (December) and in Togo (February).[68] The most remarkable recovery of a common tern ringed in these islands was an adult ringed in Northern Ireland on 17 May 1959 and found dead on 26 October 1968 some 300 km inland in Victoria, Australia.[69] However, it is thought to have been of Fennoscandian origin, passing through Ireland during spring migration.

CHAPTER 9

Roseate Tern

T HE ROSEATE TERN IS ARGUABLY the most beautiful of all terns. It is the whitest of our terns, except for the Sandwich, with a long jet-black cap, and its long white tail-streamers flutter as it flies and are raised prominently in some of its displays. The rose colour that gives it its name is usually hard to see in the field, but sometimes appears in diffuse lighting as a delicate shell-pink or peachy bloom on the underparts (Fig. 129). Unfortunately the roseate tern is rare and is not often seen away from its breeding sites, which are on protected islands off-limits to visitors. Two of the best places to see it are in Ireland. One is in Co. Wexford, near to its breeding colony on an island in Lady's Island Lake, from which the breeding birds fly to and fro across the barrier beach and feed along the southern shore east to Carnsore Point. The other is on the south side of Dublin Bay, where large numbers of roseate and other terns come in to roost every evening in August and early September. Another good place to view roseate terns is at Coquet Island, Northumberland: boats go out regularly from Amble to and around the island, allowing passengers close views of the roseates nesting there.

The roseate tern is something of a biological enigma, in three ways. First, it has an unusual geographical distribution around the world. It is primarily a tropical species, with large colonies scattered through the tropical Pacific and Indian oceans and several thousand pairs in the Caribbean (see Fig. 15 in Chapter 1). However, there are also five discrete populations in temperate seas, all of which are small.[1] Two of these temperate populations are on opposite sides of the North Atlantic Ocean, one in western Europe and the other in the northeastern USA and southeastern Canada: these are isolated from each other and from the tropical population in the Caribbean by distances of 1,500–

FIG 129. Pair of roseate terns, both ringed. Most of the roseate terns nesting in Britain and Ireland have been ringed as part of a multi-site research programme conducted since the 1980s (see Appendix 2). This photograph shows the delicate pink 'blush' on the underparts, which is usually concealed and rarely photographed. Rockabill, Co. Dublin. (Chris Gomersall)

3,000 km. The European population is itself divided into two discrete groups separated by more than 1,000 km: one in Britain, Ireland and northwest France, and the other in the Azores. North Atlantic roseate terns are morphologically somewhat distinct from the tropical populations, and some aspects of their ecology are very different. They nest in different types of habitat, feed on different species of fish and have a 'faster' lifestyle, with a larger clutch-size, more rapid chick growth and much higher breeding success (see Chapter 3) – more like the common terns with which they almost invariably nest. Roseate terns are thought to have been confined to the tropics during the last ice age and to have expanded to the north and south relatively recently.[2] They seem to have acquired some characteristics of temperate-breeding terns as they did so.

Second, roseate terns appear intermediate between the 'crested' terns and the 'typical black-capped' terns with which they are usually grouped. In many aspects of their appearance, voice and behaviour they are more like Sandwich terns than common or Arctic terns. These characteristics include several aspects of feeding behaviour (see below), as well as the disyllabic '*chi-vik*' flight call, the white underparts with a pink tinge (which is found also in Sandwich and elegant terns), the clutch-size of one or two eggs, the 'spiky' down of the newly hatched chicks, the high and fast *high flights*, the exaggerated ground display postures with wings widely spread, and the *gakkering* threat display, which is performed by all the 'crested' terns and by no other tern species. It has long been speculated that the roseate tern might actually be more closely related to the 'crested' terns than to the 'typical black-capped' terns, or form a link between them.[3] However, two recent genetic studies have decisively refuted this idea: the roseate tern is actually well separated from the 'crested' terns and falls in the middle of the 'typical black-capped' terns, being most closely related to the white-fronted tern of New Zealand.[4] It is then very difficult to explain why the roseate tern shares so many traits with the 'crested' terns.

Third, all the temperate populations of roseate terns have restricted distributions and have probably always been relatively small; several of them are now endangered. In Britain and Ireland the species seems to have always had a very restricted range, and that range has changed very little over the past two centuries, from the species' discovery through its near-extermination to its recovery (see Chapter 5). No other seabird has or had a similar distribution.[5] Despite much study in recent decades, we still have no explanation either for its restricted range or for why numbers have remained small within this range, in spite of consistently high breeding success.

STATUS, DISTRIBUTION AND TRENDS

Distribution and numbers in *Seabird 2000*

The roseate tern is the rarest and most localised of all terns breeding in Britain and Ireland, not only with the smallest population but with the fewest breeding colonies. The two largest and longest-inhabited colonies – both in Ireland, at Rockabill, Co. Dublin, and Lady's Island Lake, Co. Wexford – together held 92 per cent of the total population of 790 pairs during the *Seabird 2000* surveys. The third largest colony, at Coquet Island, Northumberland, held 4 per cent of the population. The remaining seven colonies all had small numbers, mostly less than 10 pairs each. The roseate tern population has been increasing steadily since the early 1990s and now exceeds 1,300 pairs.

The distribution is focused on the west coast of the Irish Sea, with smaller numbers in northeast England and southeast Scotland (Fig. 130). These are all marine areas traditionally associated with large numbers of sandeels and sprats,

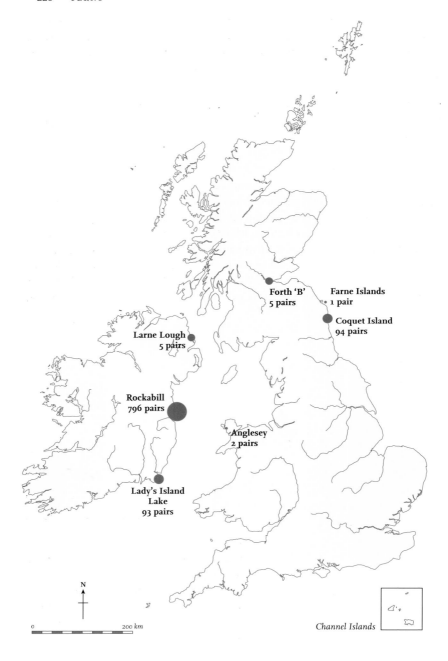

Forth 'B'
5 pairs

Farne Islands
1 pair

Coquet Island
94 pairs

Larne Lough
5 pairs

Rockabill
796 pairs

Anglesey
2 pairs

Lady's Island
Lake
93 pairs

N

0   200 km

Channel Islands

OPPOSITE PAGE: **FIG 130.** Distribution and numbers of breeding roseate terns in Britain and Ireland in 2006. Since 2006, numbers at Rockabill have increased to 1,208 pairs (2012) and those at Lady's Island Lake have increased to 126 pairs (2012), while numbers at other sites have not changed much. (Sources: Mavor *et al.*, 2008; Cadiou, 2010; unpublished data).

the principal foods for the roseate and other terns. However, sandeels and sprats are (or were) abundant in many other parts of British and Irish waters and it is hard to explain why roseate terns are so rare there.

Trends since 1970

The number of breeding pairs of roseate terns in Britain and Ireland peaked at 3,304 pairs in 1968 (Fig. 131; the *Operation Seafarer* figure of 2,384 pairs was incorrect: it did not take into account all known colonies, especially a full census of the largest colony on Tern Island). At that time the population was distributed amongst 14 colonies of which the five largest were Tern Island, Co. Wexford (c.2,000 pairs); Swan Island, Co. Antrim (250 pairs); Inchmickery, Firth of Forth (c.250 pairs); Coquet Island, Northumberland (203 pairs) and Rhosneigr, Anglesey (200 pairs). These five colonies held 88 per cent of the total population

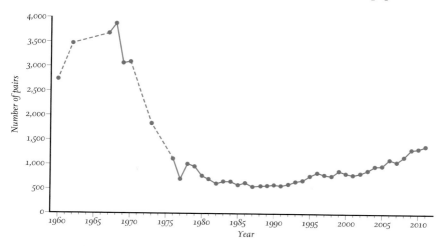

FIG 131. Numbers of pairs of roseate terns breeding in northwest Europe (Britain, Ireland and France), 1960–2011. Broken lines span intervals during which complete counts were not available. Based on logarithmic regression analysis, the total population increased by 3–4 per cent per year from 1960 to 1968, decreased by 14 per cent per year from 1968 to 1982, decreased by 1.4 per cent per year from 1982 to 1991, and finally increased by 4 per cent per year from 1991 to 2011. (Sources: Cabot, 1996; JNCC, 2009; Cadiou, 2010; unpublished data for 2009–11)

FIG 132. Rockabill, Co. Dublin. This island supports the largest colony of roseate terns in Europe, now numbering about 1,100 pairs. Roseate terns formerly nested only within the walled lighthouse garden where there is dense vegetation of tree mallow. (Liam Ryan)

FIG 133. Rockabill, Co. Dublin. Roseate terns have been drawn to nest on the rocky slopes outside the walled lighthouse garden by the provision of nest boxes. (Alyn Walsh)

in Britain and Ireland at that time. Thereafter the breeding population declined dramatically to 664 pairs in 1980 (a reduction by 80 per cent in 12 years) and then more slowly until it reached its lowest point in 1989, when only 467 pairs could be found in 11 colonies (a reduction by 86 per cent in 21 years).[6] The population breeding in northwest France also declined during this period from a high of 827 pairs in 1967 to around 100 pairs in the 1980s, a decline of 88 per cent in 13 years.[7]

Numbers in Britain and Ireland stabilised in about 1989 and have shown a gradual but steady increase since 1991, reaching 790 pairs in *Seabird 2000*, about 1,200 pairs in 2008[8] and about 1,350 pairs in 2011 (Fig. 131). Expansion at the two main Irish colonies – Rockabill, Co. Dublin (Figs 132 and 133), and Lady's Island Lake, Co. Wexford (Fig. 134), which now support about 1,100 and 155 pairs, respectively – has accounted for most of the increases in the overall population, but numbers at Coquet Island have also increased, reaching 94 pairs in 2006 and still 78 pairs in 2011.[9] Fortunately all three sites are under intensive management (see Chapter 11).

The dramatic decline in numbers from 1968 to 1989 was spread across the whole population, with many colonies reduced in size and some sites abandoned as the population declined. There was also some redistribution of birds from one colony to another. In Northern Ireland the former island colonies in Strangford Lough (peak 156 pairs in 1978) and Carlingford Lough (peak 697 pairs in 1971) were abandoned in 1988 and 1991, respectively. The colony at Swan Island, Larne Lough, Co. Antrim, held 250 pairs in 1968 but was abandoned in 1993. Coquet Island, Northumberland, held 230 pairs in 1968 but was down to 33 pairs in 2000 (and is now steadily recovering). In Scotland the roseate tern has almost disappeared. The colony on Inchmickery, Firth of Forth, held about 250 pairs in 1968 but dwindled thereafter until its abandonment in 1990. There remains one extant colony (location confidential but referred to as 'Forth B') in the Firth of Forth, with five pairs in 2006.[10] The principal colony in Wales, at Rhosneigr, Anglesey, saw breeding numbers fall from 200 pairs in 1968 to one pair in 1991 and is now extinct.[11]

FIG 134. Inish Island, Lady's Island Lake, Co, Wexford. This island supports the second largest colony of roseate terns in Britain and Ireland (now about 150 pairs), as well as important numbers of Sandwich and common and a few Arctic terns. (Alyn Walsh)

There were two breeding records in the Northern Isles during this period. Three pairs were found breeding in Orkney in 1969, one bird was seen displaying with common terns in Shetland in 1983, and one bird apparently interbred with an Arctic tern in Shetland in 1987.[12] The records in Shetland, above 60° N, are the northernmost records of the species anywhere in the world.

BREEDING HABITATS

The roseate tern selects different habitats from other terns but defends them vigorously at the margins. Its preferred breeding locations are almost exclusively small offshore islands, where it occupies areas densely covered by vegetation (Figs 135 and 136). Vegetation cover includes tree mallow at several rocky island

FIG 135. Part of the roseate tern nesting area at Inish Island at the start of the breeding season. The ground was bare except for dead vegetation from the previous year. (Dave Daly)

FIG 136. The same area in late June, when roseate terns were feeding chicks in the nest boxes. Roseate terns had selected areas where dense vegetation would grow, presumably using their knowledge of the vegetation from the previous year – with the common terns avoiding these areas based on the same knowledge. (Dave Daly)

FIG 137. Roseate terns nesting under tree mallow, Rockabill, Co. Dublin. Tree mallow is a salt-tolerant shrub native to the west coast of Europe, where it is found mainly on small islands. It grows to a height of 2–3 m and forms a miniature 'forest' with sparse ground cover, ideally suited for nesting roseate terns. (David Cabot)

sites (Fig. 137), lyme grass and marram grass on sandy islands, bracken and even gorse on islands with richer soils, together with a range of herbs and common grasses. All roseate tern breeding colonies in Britain and Ireland are within 15 km of rich feeding grounds.

The roseate tern is the least aggressive of all our terns and perhaps for this reason invariably nests in association with common or Arctic terns, which provide effective protection through their aggression towards predators. In a

FIG 138. A roseate tern nest in a typical natural site among dense vegetation. This bird laid eggs tucked into the edge of a clump of lyme grass; during incubation the grass grew and overhung the nest, providing cover for the chick to hide in. Tern Island, Co. Wexford. (David Cabot)

FIG 139. A roseate tern with its chick at a natural nest site under a rock. Roseate terns start to develop red at the base of the bill at the time the chicks hatch; the red area steadily increases until the bill is often half red during post-breeding dispersal in August, reverting to black in winter. Penikese Island, USA. (Craig Gibson)

mixed colony, roseate terns typically occupy the higher ground, with the other species nesting in more open habitats at lower elevations. Nesting on islands provides security against most mammalian predators, and nesting under cover provides protection against most avian predators. Roseate terns typically nest under clumps of vegetation (Fig. 138), sometimes deep under rocks (Fig. 139) or even in burrows made by rabbits or puffins. They take readily to artificial sites such as nesting boxes, and nowadays most of the roseate terns breeding at Rockabill and Lady's Island Lake, and many of those at Coquet Island, nest in wooden boxes (see Fig. 181 in Chapter 11). They usually select the boxes that provide the greatest concealment and sometimes squeeze into very small spaces. Roseate terns seem to prefer well-designed boxes over most natural sites, but it is uncertain whether the provision of these boxes has actually enhanced the number of terns or their productivity at these breeding colonies, as has been claimed. At least at Coquet Island, the boxes seem to provide protection against herring and lesser black-backed gulls (see Chapter 11 for fuller discussion).[13]

KEY FEATURES OF BEHAVIOUR

Roseate terns are the latest of our terns to arrive in spring, usually appearing in British and Irish waters in early May. Little is known about their behaviour in the first two or three weeks after their arrival, because they probably spend much of their time at sea and are infrequently seen except at the breeding colonies or other remote places. They usually arrive at the nesting islands a week or so later than the common terns, occupying the nesting area after the common terns are well settled into territories, and starting to lay their eggs up to eight days later than the commons.

Although roseate terns start to explore the nesting area within a week or so after arrival, they do not take up territories and do not select nest sites until a day or two before laying, so most of their early display is conducted either at sea or at the edge of the breeding islands. Their behaviour during courtship and pair formation is more like that of Sandwich terns than common terns. *High flights* commonly include three or even more birds, which fly extremely fast and commonly ascend to heights of 100–300 m. This pursuit seems to function as a flying contest, because only the first two birds to reach the top make the *pass* and descend together. They keep closer together during the descent than other terns and sway from side to side in opposite directions but in close synchrony. In the ground displays, the tail is raised high, displaying the white streamers, and the wings are characteristically half spread and drooped (Fig. 140). Most of the calls given during courtship are variants on the basic disyllabic 'chi-vik' flight call: this is lengthened into an excited series 'chivik.....chivik-chivik-chivik ...' as an advertising call during *low flights* or when flying in with a fish. In the assertive *bent* posture, as in the Sandwich tern, the neck is stretched up and the head tilted downward at a shallow angle rather than bent to present the black cap to an antagonist. In the appeasing *erect* posture, the neck is stretched far out; the head and bill are tilted up and the head is twisted sideways less than is seen in other terns.

Again like Sandwich terns, and totally unlike common or Arctic terns, roseate terns threaten each other by *gakkering* (see Fig. 94 in Chapter 7): they crouch down with body and tail elevated, raise their back feathers and pump their heads up and down in unison with loud, guttural cackling calls 'ke-KE-ke-ke ... ke-KE-ke-ke ... ke-KE-ke-ke ...', accented on every second syllable. Roseate terns even raise the feathers on the back of the head while *gakkering*, although they lack the shaggy crest that the Sandwich and other 'crested' terns use in this display. Roseate tern nests are often closely spaced, typically with more than one nest per square metre and sometimes with 50 cm or less between adjacent nests.

FIG 140. Roseate tern displaying. In most display postures, the wings are drooped and widely spread, with the wingtips crossing under the tail, which is raised high to display the long white streamers. Lady's Island Lake, Co. Wexford. (Dave Daly)

They usually nest in dense vegetation, so birds sitting on their nests may not be able to see their nearest neighbours. Sometimes a thick clump of vegetation will have two or three nests tucked underneath, approached from different angles. However, each pair vigorously defends the small area around its nest, and landing space is at a premium, so there are incessant quarrels. Typically, there is a bout of *gakkering* whenever a bird flies in and the two birds then go onto their nests and settle down quietly out of sight of each other, even though they may be only 30 cm apart. Where roseates nest in nest-boxes, it is common for one bird to be sitting on its eggs in a box while a hated neighbour stands unnoticed on top of the box a few centimetres above it.

Most copulations take place outside the nesting area, although a few continue at the nest site until the second egg is laid. Pre-copulatory displays are similar to those of common or Sandwich terns: the male puffs out his breast feathers, lifts his head high and walks in arcs ahead of the female until she crouches

FIG 141. Roseate terns copulating. While mounted on the female's back, the male utters a continuous quacking call that is not given in any other context. This is yet another way in which the roseate tern resembles the 'crested' terns and differs from the other 'typical black-capped' terns. Lady's Island Lake, Co. Wexford. (Dave Daly)

down and partly spreads her wings. The male may remain mounted for one or two minutes and make cloacal contact up to six or more times (Fig. 141). The male has a distinctive call while mounted, a low-pitched, continuous duck-like quacking 'gwa-gwa-gwa-gwa-gwa ...'. Interference with copulation by other birds is more frequent than in other terns: a nearby bird may fly at a mounted male and knock him off the female's back.

Roseate terns spend a substantial part of each day maintaining their plumage. They regularly bathe, usually choosing the same spot in shallow water near the colony. Bathing is a social activity, and there is often a closely packed flock of birds splashing in the water together (Fig. 142). The flock continually

FIG 142. Roseate terns bathing in shallow water near a breeding colony. Roseates spend more time bathing than other terns, and this is an intensely social activity: the birds pack closely together and splash vigorously for several minutes. Common terns (two birds at left) often take part in the bathing parties, although they do not pack in as tightly as the roseates. Bird Island, USA. (Jack O'Connor)

turns over as individual birds fly in, bathe vigorously for two or three minutes, and then fly to the shore where they spend 10–20 minutes meticulously preening (Fig. 143).

Roseate terns readily pursue and attack aerial predators such as gulls, herons, or even peregrine falcons. However, when a terrestrial predator or a human intruder enters the nesting area, the roseates fly off and either perch nearby and watch while the common terns attack it, or circle overhead giving alarm calls: a musical, descending 'kliu' as danger approaches, or a harsh 'aaaacch' like tearing cloth when a predator comes close. They thus appear to depend on the common terns to defend the colony for them. In combination with the concealment of their nests and chicks, this tactic is effective, because when a predator does enter the colony it usually takes only common terns' eggs or chicks. Whereas aggression by common terns wanes during the chick-raising period, aggression by roseates usually increases, peaking around the time of fledging, when some roseate terns dive on human intruders with low-pitched attack calls 'kekekekeke …'. They usually pull out before they get too close, but the boldest birds occasionally strike with their feet. It makes sense that roseates would be most

FIG 143. After bathing, roseate terns fly to the shore to preen. The preening session concludes with a thorough shake to settle all the body feathers into place. Gormanstown, Co, Meath. (John Fox)

aggressive at this stage in chick-raising, because their chicks are most vulnerable during the few days when they emerge into the open and make their first flights.

Although nesting in dense cover is effective in protecting the eggs and chicks against predators, it is occasionally disadvantageous when a nocturnal predator such as a mink enters a colony. In these circumstances, adult roseate terns are often killed in disproportionate numbers, whereas common terns escape more easily. This also occurs when a nocturnal predator such as an owl that hunts by sight enters a colony, perhaps indicating that roseate terns are more tenacious and less quick to flee than commons.[14]

Roseate tern pairs spend several days prior to egg-laying *house-hunting*: they walk together through the nesting area and take turns making scrapes in potential nest-sites, usually trying out several different places before settling on one just before laying. Most courtship-feeding probably takes place away from the nest site, but it continues at the nest until the second egg is laid. The eggs are usually laid about three days apart and the first egg is incubated more or less from the time of laying, so that they hatch about three days apart, a much longer interval than in other terns. Both sexes incubate: they change over frequently when both are present, but they take long feeding trips and incubation stints often last two to four hours. At each changeover, the departing parent performs *sideways building* in the manner of other terns (see Chapter 8).

When the eggs hatch, the parent nibbles the eggshell and deposits it just outside the nest (Sandwich terns do the same); it does not pick it up and fly away with it as common and Arctic terns do. The chicks remain in the nest for a day or two but quickly move away into dense cover, so that the first chick may be up to 30 cm away when the second chick hatches. Some roseate tern pairs lead their chicks away from the nest site, sometimes for tens of metres, but this may occur mainly where there is little cover around the nest, or in response to human disturbance. Other broods remain close to the nest site, but many move out towards the edge of the island shortly before fledging (Figs 144 and 145). At Rockabill, broods were fed at rates averaging between 1.0 and 2.2 fish per hour[15] (i.e. 0.5–1.1 fish per hour per chick in a two-chick brood), but at other sites foraging trips are longer and feeds are less frequent. Chicks are fed almost entirely on fish, larger on average than those fed to common terns (e.g. sandeels up to 140 mm long and probably weighing more than 8 g each).[16]

At some sites the vegetation grows to heights of 2 m or more during the breeding season and the parents are challenged when they have to fly in and out to feed the chicks – although they always seem able to do so, even in places where common terns would be unable to enter and consequently would desert their eggs or chicks. The parents locate their concealed chicks by voice, flying

FIG 144. As tern chicks develop towards fledging, they spend much time exercising their wings, often jumping up and down. This roseate tern chick has come out of its box to be fed, and is exercising its wings briefly before scuttling back into the box. Lady's Island Lake, Co. Wexford. (Dave Daly)

FIG 145. A roseate tern chick about 22 days old, a few days before fledging. Lady's Island Lake, Co. Wexford. (Dave Daly)

over the vegetation carrying fish and giving '*chi-vik*' calls; from close quarters, one can hear the chick respond with high-pitched '*kee-veet*' calls, and the parent then drops vertically through the vegetation, re-emerging a minute or so later without the fish.

When the chick makes its first flight, it is closely escorted by one parent, who flies around with it exchanging calls until the chick lands somewhere on the edge of the colony site. The chick rarely goes back to the nesting area and is thereafter accompanied by one or both parents. A study in the USA revealed that in cases where two chicks in a brood are raised to fledging, the first chick is fed by and accompanied by the male parent, and that they usually leave the colony together while the female stays behind to tend the second chick (which usually fledges 3–7 days later). In the more frequent case where only one chick is raised, it is attended by both parents.[17]

Roseate tern chicks are stronger on the wing when they fledge than common terns, and they seem to develop faster thereafter. They are taken to the feeding grounds by the parent(s) within three or four days and sometimes disperse tens of kilometres to good feeding areas within 5–7 days. They can sometimes catch fish for themselves within three weeks after fledging, although they remain dependent on their parent(s) throughout the post-fledging period and probably during and after autumn migration (Fig. 146). There is one record of a young bird still being fed by a parent in the winter quarters at age seven months.[18]

FIG 146. A juvenile roseate tern seeking food from its parent several weeks after fledging. Juvenile roseates are handsome birds with intricate patterns of black, grey and buff on the upperparts. Note the large area of red on the adult's bill. Gormanstown, Co, Meath. (John Fox)

After initial dispersal, roseate terns accumulate in flocks in rich feeding areas, resting and roosting in secure places nearby, usually on islands but sometimes on remote beaches. The most important staging area is in Dublin Bay, where up to 1,000 birds have been recorded in August.[19] Another staging area is in the Gulf of Morbihan in Brittany, where roseate terns are present throughout August and September.[20]

Like common terns, roseate tern adults and juveniles spend more time at sea as autumn migration approaches (Figs 147 and 148). On migration and in winter quarters, they become more like seabirds, spending much of the day at sea and

FIG 147. By mid-September, most adult roseate terns have moulted into winter plumage and their bills have reverted to all black. This bird can be identified as a roseate by its thin bill, white tail and limited extent of black in the outer primaries. Roseate terns are more vocal than commons and can usually be identified most easily by their disyllabic '*chi-vik*' calls. Chatham, USA. (Blair Nikula)

FIG 148. Roseate tern in first-winter plumage in mid-September. This plumage is similar to the winter adult, but retains some of the intricate pattern of dark chevrons on the upperparts. Plymouth, USA. (Shawn Carey)

coming to shore only in the late evening to roost at remote places. An important winter roost site is at Accra in Ghana, where large numbers of roseate and other terns arrive after dark, spend the night on partially dried salt pans and depart before first light.[21] Relatively few adult roseate terns are seen from the shore by day, but some first-winter birds forage along the shore and often feed on small fish brought in by beach seines, or are attracted to snares set along the shore with dead fish as bait (see Chapter 11).

FOOD AND FORAGING

In its feeding biology as in so much else, the roseate tern resembles the Sandwich tern more than common or Arctic terns. Like the Sandwich tern, it is specialised in its foraging, feeding mainly in open, clear water on small schooling fish. With its short wings and narrow body, it can fly faster than common or Arctic terns and dive much deeper. It is an especially deep diver for its size, sometimes 'power-diving' by using its wings to accelerate as it descends and remaining submerged for as long as two seconds: it may be able to catch fish at depths as great as 1.2 m. It is less adept at hovering than common or Arctic terns and usually flies back and forth over schools of prey fish, sometimes flying several hundred metres between dives. It typically dives from heights of 3–6 m, occasionally from up to 12 m when fish are swimming deep below the surface.[22]

Roseate terns feed exclusively at sea and in relatively clear waters; they prefer deeper water than common terns, although they often feed over shallow sandbanks where tidal currents bring prey species near the surface. Studies at Rockabill in 1998 and 1999 revealed that roseate terns foraged mainly within 10 km of the island during the chick-feeding period in June–July, occurring singly or in twos and threes over water 20–30 m deep, sometimes in association with auks that were probably driving prey towards the surface. In August and September, large numbers of roseate terns were found feeding over the Kish Bank, 30 km south of Rockabill, and roosting on the Kish lighthouse. Roseate terns from Lady's Island Lake foraged most frequently near some rocks 3 km from shore, perhaps exploiting tide rips around the rocks.[23] There is little other information on their feeding methods in Britain and Ireland. Windy conditions make it more difficult for roseates to catch fish and this results in slower chick growth. Studies at Coquet Island have revealed that wind speeds higher than 19 km per hour depressed the growth rates of chicks by 55–67 per cent over a 24-hour period.[24]

A few individual roseate terns specialise in kleptoparasitism and do most or all of their foraging at the colony without going to sea.[25] They generally steal fish from common terns: roseates usually fly faster and are more difficult to steal from. The kleptoparasites use several methods for fish-stealing, but typically they fly back and forth over the nesting area at heights of 10–20 m, looking down for a suitable quarry. This is exactly the way in which roseate terns search for fish over a sandbar or a group of predatory fish: the kleptoparasite treats the breeding colony as it would a school of fish, except that the fish are in the air rather than in the water. When it spots an unwary common tern, it dives steeply downwards, snatches the fish out of the common tern's bill from behind and flies off with it, usually to feed its own chicks. A few female roseates practise a different technique. They stand by their nests watching for fish deliveries at other nests nearby, and when they spot an opportunity they fly in low and seize the fish as it is being transferred to a chick.[26] These habitual kleptoparasites comprise only 1–2 per cent of the roseate terns in each colony, but their technique is highly profitable: a study in the USA revealed that they are consistently more successful in raising chicks than the 'honest' pairs that go to sea to catch fish for themselves.[27]

Roseate terns rely on a very restricted range of prey. In Britain and Ireland they feed mainly on sandeels and sprats, with smaller numbers of pollack and saithe; birds in northeast England formerly fed on Atlantic herring, but these have become much scarcer in recent decades.[28] Table 21 summarises results of feeding studies at four breeding sites in Britain and Ireland. Sandeels comprised 50–90 per cent of the fish brought to the colonies in most of the studies, and sprats most of the rest; however, sprats outnumbered sandeels among food items fed to chicks in most years at Rockabill. At Lady's Island Lake, immature rockling comprised 27 per cent of the chick diet in 1996, but this was exceptional. The mean length of sandeels fed to chicks at Coquet Island was 7.2 cm, but smaller sandeels were fed to smaller chicks. Food delivery rates are usually in the range one to two fish per brood per hour, so even in broods of two each chick receives eight or more fish each day.[29]

The food of roseate terns wintering in Ghana was determined in 1989 by observing foraging birds, both adults and first-winter birds, within 100 m of

TABLE 21. Percentages of food items brought to mates, chicks or fledglings by roseate terns at four breeding sites in Britain and Ireland. Ranges of yearly averages are given.

	Location, years, stage in breeding cycle				
	Tern Island, Co. Wexford	Rockabill, Co. Dublin		Coquet Island, Northumberland	Lady's Island Lake, Co. Wexford
Food type	1974–1976 Chick-rearing	1997–2002 Courtship, incubation	1996–2002 Chick-rearing	1965–1966 Chick-rearing	1996–1998 Chick-rearing, post-fledging
Ammodytidae (sandeels)	69–95	55–75	13–30	48–81	60–92
Clupeidae (sprat, herring)	5–31	10–35	32–45	19–52	8–40
Gadidae (pollack, saithe)		5–25	5–10		0–3
Unidentified			12–25		

Sources: Cabot, unpublished data; Ratcliffe et al., 2004.

open shores and in estuaries. The diet of the adults comprised 51 per cent sardines, 44 per cent anchovies and 3 per cent tilapia. For first-winter birds the figures were 42, 36 and 14 per cent, respectively. Sardines and anchovies were taken on the coastline, while tilapia were confined to lagoons and estuaries.[30]

BREEDING BIOLOGY

Roseate terns usually lay one or two eggs. In Britain and Ireland, between 40 and 85 per cent of pairs lay two eggs, so that average clutch-sizes over 12–14-year periods were 1.69 at Coquet Island, 1.76 at Rockabill and 1.64 at Lady's Island Lake.[31] The proportion of birds laying two eggs is higher early than late in the season and higher among old than young females; the variation among years at the same site (e.g., 1.53–1.84 at Rockabill) probably reflects variation in food availability at the time of laying. Clutches of 3–5 eggs are rare (1.25–2 per cent at Rockabill) and probably result from two or more females laying in the same nest (see below). Eggs usually weigh 19–24 g, so the weight of a two-egg clutch rarely exceeds 40 per cent of the female's normal weight of around 115 g.

Once it is dry, the newly hatched chick (Fig. 149) has a 'spiky' appearance – like a little hedgehog – because the down sticks together in tufts (see Figs 156 and 240); this is yet another way in which roseate terns resemble Sandwich terns

FIG 149. Roseate tern chick emerging from its shell. Tern chicks hatch with 1–2 g of material from the egg yolk still in their bodies: this is gradually absorbed and helps to support their early growth and survival, although most of them are fed within a few hours after hatching. Lady's Island Lake, Co. Wexford. (Dave Daly)

or other 'crested' terns rather than common or Arctic terns. This may function in some way as waterproofing, because after rainstorms roseate tern chicks can be found completely dry underneath dense wet vegetation – unlike common tern chicks, which get wet and cold in the same circumstances. The chicks come in two basic colours, dark grey and sandy-brown, although they are not as strongly dimorphic as Arctic tern chicks. The legs are dull pinkish-purple at hatching but quickly change to black, again like the Sandwich tern but unlike common or Arctic terns.

The chicks grow rapidly: typically from about 15 g at hatching to 80 g by day 11 and 100 g just before fledging on days 19–25; the second chick in the brood grows more slowly and fledges at an average weight of only 96 g, less than 85 per cent of the adults' weight.[32] In the absence of predation, chick survival is usually very high: typically over 95 per cent from hatching to fledging for first-hatched chicks, lower and more variable for second-hatched chicks but often 40 per cent or more. Averaged over 17–21-year periods, productivity was about 1.03 fledglings per pair at Coquet Island, 1.35 at Rockabill and 1.03 at Lady's Island Lake, with yearly averages ranging up to 1.32, 1.52 and 1.70, respectively.[33] Because Rockabill was by far the largest colony at that period, the regional average productivity for Britain and Ireland was close to 1.31: this is much higher than that of common terns at the same sites, despite the larger clutch-sizes of the latter (Table 22).

TABLE 22. Numbers and productivity of roseate terns at five index sites in the *Seabird Monitoring Programme*, 1991–2006.

Region	Colony site	Average number of pairs 1989–2010 (range)	Average productivity 1991–2006 (range)	Number of years
E Scotland	Forth 'B'	9 (1–23)	1.21 (1.00–1.60)	6
NE England	Coquet Island	46 (19–94)	1.03 (0.73–1.32)	17
NE Ireland	Larne Lough	7 (0–19)	0.53 (0.37–0.83)	6
SE Ireland	Rockabill	566 (320–820)	1.39 (0.87–1.52)	18
	Lady's Island Lake	85 (48–125)	1.03 (0.00–1.70)	21
Total, 5 sites		713 [a]	1.31 [b]	

Sources: Casey *et al.*, 1995; Mavor *et al.*, 2003, 2005, 2008; Nisbet & Ratcliffe, 2008; Rockabill and Lady's Island Lake annual reports.

[a] About 97 per cent of total numbers breeding in Britain and Ireland.

[b] Overall average is weighted by the average number of pairs in each colony.

This nicely demonstrates the effectiveness of the roseate tern's strategy of nesting at a few secure sites with dependable food supplies and relying on common terns for protection of its eggs and chicks. Productivity was high at the major colonies even during the population crash in the 1970s: productivity at Tern Island and Lady's Island Lake, Co. Wexford, in 1975–78 averaged 1.19 fledglings per pair.[34] As in common terns, breeding success is much higher for pairs that lay earlier in the season, and much higher for older than for younger pairs: for example, at Rockabill the probability of raising two chicks to fledging increased from 20 per cent for three-year-old birds to 62 per cent for birds 9–13 years old and 100 per cent for birds older than 13.[35]

FEMALE–FEMALE PAIRS, TRIOS AND HYBRIDISATION

Roseate tern populations often have an unbalanced sex-ratio, with more females than males, so that some adult females are unable to get male mates. This is manifested early in the season by females competing among themselves to display with males. For example, *high flights* in roseate terns often include from three to eight or more birds, whereas in other terns these aerial displays usually involve only two, or at most three birds. When a male displays with a fish within the colony, he is often joined by several females.

Although some females remain unmated throughout the season, others form pairs with each other, lay eggs in the same nest and incubate them together in the same way as a male–female pair. These nests often stand out because they contain 'supernormal' clutches of three or four eggs instead of the usual one or two. However, many females in female–female pairs only lay one egg each, so that the joint clutch contains only two eggs and cannot be distinguished from that of a male–female pair without catching the birds and sexing them genetically. At a site in the USA where a detailed study was carried out, about 11 per cent of all nests were attended by two females, and more than half of these had 'normal' clutches of two eggs.[36] In Britain and Ireland, 'supernormal' clutches are less frequent than in the USA (1.25–2 per cent of all clutches at Rockabill[37]), suggesting that about 4 per cent of the nests there are attended by female–female pairs (see Appendix 2). Although these nests are not attended by males, about half the eggs laid in them are fertile, presumably sired by neighbouring males who are doubtless willing to oblige. Consequently about half the eggs hatch, and some females are able to raise young even though they could not obtain male mates.

In rare cases, a female unable to get a male mate attaches herself to a male–female pair to form a 'trio', both females laying eggs in the same nest and all

FIG 150. Three female roseate terns attending the same nest. Females unable to get male mates often pair together and lay eggs in the same nest, sometimes raising young if one or both of them copulate with males from neighbouring pairs. This 'trio' hatched two chicks and raised one to fledging. Two of the birds were marked with coloured spots to facilitate behavioural studies. Bird Island, USA. (Bill Byrne)

FIG 151. Male common tern feeding a female roseate tern. On rare occasions, a female roseate tern that is unable to acquire a mate of its own species will mate with a male common tern. This pair raised one hybrid chick to fledging (see Fig. 152). Seaforth, Merseyside. (Steve Young)

three birds contributing to incubation and chick-raising. However, most 'trios' that have been studied actually consisted of three females which laid three, four or five eggs (Fig. 150), and there are even cases of four females attending the same nest.[38]

Even more rarely, a female roseate tern unable to get a male mate pairs with a male common tern (Fig. 151) and raises hybrid young (Fig. 152). The hybrids are viable and often survive to breed, mating with either of the parental species and raising backcross young; there are even records of two hybrids paired together (Figs 153–156). Hybrids between common and roseate terns seem to be more frequent than those between other pairs of tern species, perhaps a consequence of the unbalanced sex-ratio which leaves many female roseates unable to obtain a male mate of their own species. Even in these circumstances, hybridisation is rare; common terns usually display and mate only with other common terns, and it is not known why male common terns occasionally accept female roseates as mates. Interbreeding or backcrossing pairs have been recorded in England, Wales and Ireland, as well as in several other European countries where roseates are rare and in North America. There is also one record of a roseate tern interbreeding with an Arctic tern in Shetland.[39]

FIG 152. Hybrid juvenile tern, the offspring of the interbreeding pair of common and roseate terns shown in Fig. 151. Hybrid and backcross juveniles are intermediate between those of the parental species in many characteristics, including bill and leg colour and the patterns on the feathers of the head, back, wings and tail. Seaforth, Merseyside. (Steve Young)

FIG 153. Hybrid common × roseate tern, trapped on a nest in the USA. Hybrid and backcross adults are intermediate between the parental species in many characteristics, most notably the colour of the bill (see Fig. 154), the tail (grey without a dark outer edge and with tail-streamers intermediate in length) and the patterning of black, white and grey on the primary wing feathers. Monomoy, USA. (Ian Nisbet)

FIG 154. Head of the common × roseate hybrid shown in Fig. 153. The bill is nearly half red (at a date when roseates' bills are all black and commons' are three-quarters red), with the red and black intergrading rather than sharply demarcated as in the parental species. Monomoy, USA. (Ian Nisbet)

FIG 155. Common tern removing an eggshell from the nest shortly after hatching. This behaviour serves to maintain camouflage: the inside of the hatched eggshell is white and would make the nest conspicuous to a predator flying overhead if it were left there. This photograph is of an interbreeding pair with a male common tern and a female roseate. Common terns remove hatched eggshells, whereas roseate terns do not. Monomoy, USA. (Karen Wilson)

FIG 156. Downy chicks of roseate (left), hybrid (centre) and common (right) terns. These hybrid chicks were the offspring of two hybrids mated together. The structure of the down on the hybrid chicks was intermediate between the spiky down of roseates and the fluffy down of commons. The hybrid chicks also had dull purple legs, intermediate between roseates (black) and commons (pink). The hybrid chicks shown in this photograph were darker than those of either parental species, but most hybrid chicks are similar or intermediate. Monomoy, USA. (Ian Nisbet)

MIGRATIONS

Much of our knowledge of the migrations of roseate terns from Britain and Ireland is derived from 1,171 recoveries from 42,269 birds ringed up to the end of 2009, mainly as chicks.[40] Detailed analysis has been reported for the first 873 recoveries recorded by the end of 1997.[41]

The roseate tern has the second highest recovery rate – 2.77 per cent – of all our five species of terns, exceeded only by the Sandwich tern (see Table 13 in Chapter 6). This probably reflects the susceptibility of both species to trapping and capture on the wintering grounds. Besides recoveries away from breeding colonies, large numbers of roseate terns have been identified in recent decades by reading ring numbers with telescopes at breeding colonies (see Appendix 1).[42] Among recoveries of ringed roseate terns for which the cause of death was known, some 75 per cent were deliberately taken by humans, a rate shared with the Sandwich tern and considerably higher than that for little terns (45 per cent) and Arctic terns (23 per cent).[43] As recounted in Chapters 6 and 7, however, the trapping of terns along the West African coast from Senegal to Ghana seriously skews recovery patterns, so that our knowledge of the wintering grounds may just reflect the distribution of the trapping. Furthermore, 94 per cent of the winter recoveries of roseate terns have been of immature birds,[44] so we could be overlooking other wintering areas used by adults. Wintering in neighbouring countries may be under-represented because of low ring reporting rates. For example, large flocks of roseate terns have been observed at Lagos harbour, Nigeria, from where there have been virtually no ringing recoveries.[45]

During the post-breeding dispersal of juveniles in July and August the birds remain closer to their natal colonies than our other terns. Both adults and juveniles from Irish Sea colonies, and some from elsewhere, gather in large flocks in Dublin Bay where they probably undergo a moult and build up reserves for their migratory flight to West Africa. Roseates generally comprise less than 5 per cent of the terns roosting at Sandymount Strand (see Fig. 126, Chapter 8), but on 14 September 2010 there were at least 645.[46] Another roosting site is at Maiden Rock, Dalkey, about 1 km south of Sandymount Strand, where upwards of 1,000 were counted from late July to late September in the 1980s. Based on observations of colour-rings, these were derived primarily from Rockabill, but also from breeding sites in Co. Wexford, Northern Ireland and Wales.[47]

There are no ringing recoveries to suggest any staging grounds on the way south to West Africa, although some birds from Britain and Ireland may join staging flocks in the Gulf of Morbihan, as mentioned earlier. During September and October birds move quickly southwards along the coasts of western Iberia and West Africa to the wintering grounds in the Gulf of Guinea.

During the period November–May virtually all recoveries have been north of the Equator, extending to 10° N, with most recoveries from Ghana, Togo and Côte d'Ivoire (Fig. 157). In Ghana they mix with the roseate terns breeding in the

FIG 157. Recovery locations of roseate terns ringed as chicks in Britain and Ireland. This species has a much more restricted distribution in winter (November–February) than other British and Irish terns (blue band, with two outlying recoveries marked by blue arrows). Most recoveries in the breeding and post-breeding seasons (orange shading) have been close to the breeding area (green shading). Recoveries in September–October and April–May are distributed all along the coast from the breeding area to the easternmost limit of the winter range in Nigeria (green arrow). (Source: Ratcliffe & Merne, 2002)

FIG 158. First-summer roseate tern inside the nesting area at Lady's Island Lake, Co. Wexford. Roseate terns rarely migrate north to the breeding area in their first summers, but a few do so and visit breeding colonies. Terns in first-summer plumage resemble adults in winter plumage, and the species look rather similar to each other. This bird can be identified as a roseate by its slender bill and white outer tail feathers. Lady's Island Lake, Co. Wexford. (Dave Daly)

Azores. Most first-summer birds remain in West Africa, a very small minority moving northward to their breeding grounds (Fig. 158). Only 23 first-summer birds have been re-sighted at Rockabill over nine years.[48] More second-year birds return to the colonies, but most do not breed until they are three years old. Many chicks disperse from their natal colonies to settle at other breeding sites in Britain and Ireland, and each year a small fraction of adults also change breeding sites (see Appendix 1).[49]

There have been more records of transatlantic movements by roseate terns than of other tern species.[50] A roseate chick ringed on Rockabill, Co. Dublin, in 1991 was seen two years later in the breeding season on Bird Island, Massachusetts, USA (Fig. 159). A second bird ringed at Lady's Island Lake, Co. Wexford, as a chick on 13 July 1996 was observed at Bird Island on three

FIG 159. Bird Island, Massachusetts, USA. This is one of two sites in the USA where roseate terns ringed in Ireland have been identified associating with breeding roseate terns from the North American population. (Jeremy Hatch)

occasions in July 2001. A third bird, ringed at Rockabill as a chick on 1 July 2009, was seen on 28 July 2011 at a breeding colony on the Isles of Shoals, New Hampshire, USA. Another Rockabill bird was caught in winter at a site in eastern Brazil where many North American birds winter. Transatlantic movements in the opposite direction include a North American bird trapped on a nest on Flores in the Azores in May 2000, a bird ringed in winter in Brazil trapped on a nest on Terceira in the Azores in June 2000, and two unconfirmed sight-records of birds ringed in North America at Rockabill in 1999. Except for the bird at Flores, there was no evidence that any of these birds was actually breeding on the 'wrong' side of the Atlantic. Because at least 70 per cent of the roseate terns in both the northwest European and North American populations are now ringed, and at least 80 per cent of the breeding birds in both populations have their rings read every year,[51] it is very likely that any birds that actually switched from one population to breed in the other in the last 15 years would have been detected.

However, the theory of population genetics indicates that only one migrant per generation is sufficient to maintain genetic continuity between two populations. It is possible that the continued records of roseate terns from one side of the North Atlantic at least 'prospecting' on the other reflect actual exchange of breeders at this very low rate.

CHAPTER 10

Arctic Tern

A LTHOUGH THE ARCTIC TERN is the most numerous tern breeding in Britain and Ireland, it is one of the least familiar. Its main breeding range is in the Northern and Western Isles, it spends most of the year at sea, and it does not often join staging flocks of other terns in late summer. Many birdwatchers in Britain and Ireland know it mainly from fleeting visits on migration. It is superficially similar in appearance to the common tern, and beginners often have much difficulty in distinguishing it using the characters described in field guides. However, it actually differs from the common tern in many subtle ways, and once these have been learned it is very easy to distinguish (see Fig. 4 in Chapter 1).[1]

STATUS, DISTRIBUTION AND TRENDS

Distribution and numbers in *Seabird 2000*

Some 56,000 pairs of Arctic terns were recorded breeding in Britain and Ireland in the censuses of *Seabird 2000*.[2] As their name implies they are most characteristic of the Arctic and are the most northerly of the northern hemisphere terns. In Europe Arctic terns are distributed mainly along the Atlantic coast and on offshore islands. Their main distribution centre is in Iceland, where some 60 per cent of the European total breed.[3] Within Britain and Ireland most (85 per cent) breed in Scotland, with Shetland and Orkney hosting most of the Scottish population. Ireland and England each hold 6 per cent of the population, and Wales only 3 per cent (Fig. 160). The distribution of Arctic terns within Britain and Ireland, with a strong concentration in the northwest,

**Apparently Occupied Nests (AONs) –
approximations to number of pairs**
(see Table 10, p. 134)

- 1–10
- 11–100
- 101–500
- 501–1,000
- 1,001–5,000
- 5,001–10,000

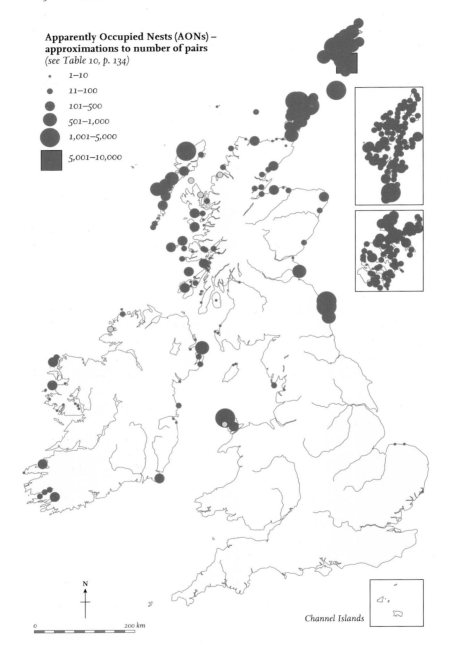

N

0   200 km

Channel Islands

OPPOSITE PAGE: **FIG 160.** Abundance and distribution of breeding Arctic terns as revealed by the *Seabird 2000* censuses in 1998–2002 (Britain) and 1995 (Ireland). Colonies of 'commic terns' (i.e. undistinguished Arctic and common terns) are shown in yellow. (Source: Ratcliffe, 2004b)

has remained more or less constant for the past 30 years[4] and probably for much longer (see Chapter 5).

Within Scotland, *Seabird 2000* recorded large colonies in Shetland at Dalsetter, with 4,444 pairs, Papa Stour with 2,007 pairs, and Fair Isle with 1,254 pairs. The largest colony in England was on the Farne Islands, Northumberland, where there were 3,965 pairs. Within Ireland, Arctic terns were concentrated on the western seaboard, particularly in Galway and Mayo, while there were also significant colonies in Co. Down and Co. Wexford. Arctic terns do not nest in southern or eastern England south of the Farne Islands, except for a few scattered pairs in Norfolk, Suffolk and Essex. They do not nest in Wales south of Anglesey, although they nest further south in Ireland (Fig. 160) and they formerly nested in the Isles of Scilly.[5]

Trends since 1970

The Arctic tern population suffered a significant population decline, exceeded only by that of the roseate tern, during the period from 1984 to 2000. The total number breeding in Britain and Ireland was estimated at nearly 80,000 pairs in the 1984–88 surveys, but fell by almost one-third to about 56,000 pairs in 1998–2002 (Table 23). The greatest declines occurred in Orkney and Shetland, where the

TABLE 23. Numbers of breeding Arctic terns in Britain and Ireland 1970–2000. All numbers are estimates of breeding pairs: see footnotes to Table 10 (in Chapter 5).

Region	1970	1985	2000	% change 1970–2000	% change 1985–2000
Scotland	46,385	71,178	47,306	+2	−34
England, Isle of Man, Channel Islands	4,498	4,566	3,610	−20	−21
Wales	436	732	1,705	+291	+133
Great Britain, Isle of Man, Channel Islands	51,319	76,476	52,621	+3	−31
Ireland	969	2,288	3,502	+261	+53
Total Britain and Ireland	52,288	78,764	56,123	+7	−29

Source: Ratcliffe, 2004b.

number of pairs fell from an estimated 64,863 pairs to 38,192 pairs, a loss of 41 per cent, based on complete surveys in 1980 and 2000. The estimated total in *Operation Seafarer* in 1969–70 had been much smaller, but it seems likely that numbers were underestimated then, especially in Shetland, where only 7,295 pairs were recorded in 1969–70, compared to 30,352 in 1984–88. However, this conclusion has been disputed and the issue is impossible to resolve at this late date.[6]

Elsewhere in Britain and Ireland the decline from 1984–88 to 1998–2002 was not so great, and some regions actually reported increases: in Ireland, for example, numbers rose by 53 per cent, and in Wales by 133 per cent.[7] However, the population base in both these countries had been small compared with those in the Northern Isles. Since 2000, the total population in the UK has increased slightly based on counts in index colonies, whereas numbers in index colonies in Ireland have continued to increase steadily.[8] There has been no sign of decline or abandonment of the southernmost breeding colonies, as might be expected under current patterns of global warming; indeed, some of the most southerly colonies have shown the largest increases in recent decades.

BREEDING HABITATS

The preferred breeding location for Arctic terns is on offshore marine islands, amongst rocks and shingle with some maritime turf. They also nest on sandy substrates, often in mixed colonies with common terns; where the two species breed together, Arctic terns tend to occupy more open areas, with sparser vegetation or shorter sward (Fig. 161). During the 1984 *All-Ireland Tern Survey* the habitat frequency distribution of 106 Arctic tern colonies was 31 per cent in rocky habitats, 30 per cent on maritime turf and 13 per cent on shingle, while only 6 per cent were on sandy substrates (Figs 162–164). Only two small colonies were on freshwater lakes: at Lough Corrib in Co. Galway and Lough Conn in Co. Mayo.[9] Arctic terns seldom nest in association with black-headed gulls: their pugnacity is in most cases adequate to deter predators such as the larger gulls, hooded crows and various mammals.

KEY FEATURES OF BEHAVIOUR

In their main range on the tundra of Arctic Eurasia and North America, Arctic terns do not arrive until late May and do not start to breed until mid- or late June. However, at the southern limits of their breeding range in western Europe,

FIG 161. Arctic tern in nesting habitat. Sand Island, east Greenland. (Carsten Egevang)

FIG 162. Arctic tern nesting habitat on a shingle beach backed by machair. Inishdegil Mor, Co. Mayo. (David Cabot)

FIG 163. Arctic tern nesting habitat on Tern Island, Wexford Harbour, Co. Wexford. Arctic terns nested on shelly sand surrounding the vegetated area shown in Fig. 69. (Oscar Merne)

FIG 164. Arctic terns nest on open sand beaches at the southern limits of their range, and they have to cope with drifting sand in high winds. They frequently dig their eggs out from drifted sand and can raise their eggs several centimetres when necessary. This bird is 'panting' (fluttering its throat to cool itself by evaporation). Plymouth, USA. (Jim Fenton)

including Britain and Ireland, they migrate and breed a month earlier, arriving in late April and starting to breed in mid- to late May.[10] Although pelagic for most of their migrations, many Arctic terns appear to cross Britain and Ireland overland on spring migration and are sporadically seen in large numbers at inland reservoirs and lakes.[11] Yarrell described an unusual fallout of exhausted Arctic terns in southwest England following a gale on 8 May 1842, when hundreds were killed in Bridgwater, Somerset, and dozens were collected at inland locations and brought to taxidermists in Evesham, Worcester, Tewkesbury, Hereford, Devizes and Trowbridge.[12]

In most respects, the behaviour of Arctic terns is closely similar to that of common terns (see Chapter 8). Perhaps the largest difference is in their calls at the breeding sites. Generally, Arctic terns have higher-pitched calls than common terns. The advertising call of the Arctic tern is completely different from that of the common: a four-syllable '*kitt-i-weee-wit*' or '*kittikeeyer*', with the accent on the third syllable, commonly given in displays such as the *low flight* or when flying in with a fish to feed a mate or chicks.[13] When Arctic terns attack a human intruder, they usually approach silently from behind, peck the intruder's head and give a loud '*kyaaar*' as they swoop upwards: the uncertainty about when the strike will come makes their attacks even more disconcerting than those of common terns, which give a loud warning as they approach.

Most other differences between the behaviour of Arctic and common terns are related to the fact that Arctics are lighter on the wing, so that they are more aerial and more manoeuvrable than commons. In *low flights*, Arctic terns often perform *V-flying*, in which they hold both wings elevated in a 'V' and either glide or make shallow wing-beats with the wings elevated even at the lowest point of the downstroke (Fig. 165); common terns are too heavy to fly easily with the wings elevated so high. Arctics are more prone to fly both in courtship displays (a male and female in a tentative relationship will often repeatedly touch down, display

FIG 165. Arctic tern *V-flying*. Arctic terns are lighter on the wing than other terns and commonly raise their wings in a 'V' while displaying, sometimes gliding in this position or flapping without lowering their wings to the horizontal. Suðurnes, Seltjarnarnes, Iceland. (Jóhann Óli Hilmarsson)

briefly and take off again) and in aggressive displays (they perform *upward flutters* more frequently than common terns).[14] Biologists who trap terns for study soon learn that Arctics like to land on their nests and take off vertically. Whereas common terns will usually land beside the nest and walk into a trap with an entrance door on one side, Arctic terns can often be caught only in a trap with a hole cut in the top above the nest, large enough for the bird to drop through with wings half-closed but too small for it to fly out with wings spread. Arctic terns' ground displays (Fig. 166), aggressive interactions (Fig. 167), courtship and copulation (Fig. 168) are all very similar to those of common terns. In *high flights*, the roles of males and females are said to alternate: the male takes the role of pursuer and swoops past the female at the end of the ascent, and she then makes the *pass*, followed by alternating passes and glides with roles reversed.[15] However, this purported difference between Arctic and other terns has not been confirmed with recorded observations on marked birds of known sex – and it would be very

FIG 166. Arctic terns displaying. The male (right) is in an extreme assertive or aggressive posture, with its wings raised and spread. The female (left) is in the *erect* posture with its head turned away from the male. Jökulsárlón, Iceland. (Jóhann Óli Hilmarsson)

FIG 167. Arctic terns fighting. The right-hand bird has seized the bill of the left-hand bird and will not let go. Note the translucent primaries and the flexible outer tail feathers. Flatey, Iceland. (Jóhann Óli Hilmarsson)

difficult to do this because terns usually cannot be caught and marked until they have eggs.

Arctic terns vigorously attack avian predators such as gulls and skuas (Fig. 169). They usually attack mammalian predators more vigorously than common terns do, and are probably more effective in deterring them from entering the nesting areas.[16] This is important in the Arctic tern's main range on the tundra, where Arctic foxes are major predators and the wide spacing of the terns' nests is probably an adaptation to reduce the risk of fox predation. However, it has limited value in Britain and Ireland, where the most important predator is the American mink, against which the terns have no defences because mink hunt by scent at night.

Except when breeding or on spring migration, Arctic terns spend most of the year at sea, although they probably rest on pack ice in winter quarters, especially when they are almost flightless during their wing-moult (see Chapter 4). It is not known whether they remain in the air 24 hours a day at other times, or whether they rest on the water periodically; nor is it known how they cope with stormy weather in the North Atlantic or the Southern Ocean.

FIG 168. Arctic terns copulating. This photograph illustrates well the characters distinguishing Arctic from common terns in breeding plumage: dark red bill and legs, very short legs, long tail-streamers, and very little black in the wings. Another subtle character is that Arctics have jet black caps that extend down through the eye, giving them a 'masked' look: common terns have brownish-black caps that reach the upper side of the eye and their eyelids are white. Lady's Island Lake, Co. Wexford. (Dave Daly)

FIG 169. Arctic tern pecking an Arctic skua. In most of their range, including the Northern Isles of Scotland, Arctic terns have to coexist with nesting skuas. The skuas persistently harass them to steal fish, but the terns do their best to prevent the skuas from entering their nesting areas. Jökulsárlón, Iceland. (Jóhann Óli Hilmarsson)

Arctic tern fledglings usually leave their breeding sites with their parents within a week or so after they fledge in July–August. Adults and juveniles are infrequently seen among staging flocks of other terns in August–September, but birds ringed in Britain and Ireland have been recovered in those months over a wide area from Scandinavia through western Europe and West Africa south as far as Angola.[17] It seems likely that they go to sea even before the juveniles have learned to fish and have become independent, adopting the pelagic lifestyle that they follow for most of the year, and that they start to migrate south very early in the autumn.

FOOD AND FORAGING

Britain and Ireland are among the few areas where Arctic and common terns breed alongside each other. The Arctic terns that breed in southwest Ireland and around the Irish Sea are (except for a few in Belgium) the southernmost birds of the species that breed anywhere in Europe. Arctic and common terns pose a challenge to the ecological principle that closely related species can only coexist if they differ in some important characteristic that prevents them from competing for limiting resources (see Chapter 2). These two species often breed on the same islands, and where they co-occur they consume the same prey species, in similar sizes, and catch them by the same methods; they often form mixed feeding flocks. Both species are clearly limited by the availability of food, because they usually have much lower breeding success than can be achieved when food is abundant, and many of their chicks that die in these circumstances do so from starvation. It is therefore a puzzle how Arctic and common terns can continue to coexist without one species out-competing the other for limited resources. Their feeding biology is generally very similar and the differences are quite subtle: Arctic terns tend to feed further offshore and take slightly smaller fish than common terns. These differences reflect the Arctic tern's subarctic and Arctic distribution in the breeding season and its pelagic lifestyle during the rest of the year. However, the differences seem to be minor where the two species overlap at temperate latitudes such as those of Britain and Ireland.

In Britain and Ireland, Arctic terns feed almost exclusively over salt waters, although in their main range in the Arctic they also breed on tundra far from the ocean and feed there mainly in freshwater ponds. They often feed over the open sea, but sometimes forage along the edges of sandy or rocky shores, tidal flats or shoals. At sea, they sometimes feed singly but often gather in flocks over predatory fish, marine mammals, cormorants or other diving birds which drive prey fish to the surface. They also tend to concentrate over tide rips or along drift lines. In a study in which terns were tracked from a colony at the Skerries, Anglesey, by following them in an inflatable boat, seven Arctic terns were successfully tracked for part of their foraging trips. One bird was followed for 57 km and was last seen 29 km out to sea; the others followed erratic tracks that took them up to 15 km from the colony site and 18 km from the mainland. Most of the birds that were tracked foraged mainly over waters 10–20 m deep.[18] Although the sample size was too small for firm generalisations, these Arctic terns foraged further offshore and over deeper water than common terns tracked from a colony in Norfolk in the same study. Similar differences have been reported consistently in other comparative studies of the two species.[19]

Like common terns, Arctic terns use all the feeding methods described in Chapter 2 – *plunge-diving, diving-to-surface, dipping, hawking, kleptoparasitism* and *perch-feeding* – switching from one to another as opportunities arise. When feeding at sea, they typically fly less than 5 m above the water and make shallow dives, rarely penetrating more than 50 cm below the surface. They often dip to pick up crustaceans or insects from the water surface. Occasionally when a swarm of amphipods or euphausiids appears close to a breeding colony, all the breeding terns switch to feeding on them for an hour or two. They frequently catch insects such as ants or midges, flying through the swarms and taking one insect at a time, and there is one report of them picking caterpillars off vegetation. They apparently do not steal fish from each other or from other terns as regularly as roseate or common terns do, but they often steal fish from puffins or black guillemots, or pick up fish dropped by puffins that are chased by skuas. At many breeding sites in the Northern Isles, Arctic terns nest near to Arctic or great skuas, and they often have fish stolen by the skuas as they try to bring them in to feed their chicks. Territorial feeding by Arctic terns has been reported from other countries, but not from Britain or Ireland.

The Arctic tern's diet is almost as varied as the common's. A large fraction of the diet consists of fish, of which sandeels are the most important species, and Atlantic herrings and sprats often make up most of the remainder. However, Arctic terns have been recorded taking many other fish species, plus a wide variety of crustaceans (especially amphipods and euphausiids), insects (especially ants and midges), annelid worms, squid and pelagic molluscs (sea snails or sea slugs). As in other terns, invertebrates seem to be more important among the food items the adults eat themselves than in those they feed to their chicks. Although there seem to be no records of the diets of adults in Britain or Ireland, high proportions of invertebrates have been reported in samples from adult Arctic terns in several other European countries.[20]

Arctic terns feed their young mainly on fish. Even at times when they bring large numbers of crustaceans or insects to the chicks, fish still comprise most of the diet by weight, because the invertebrate items are usually very small. Table 24 summarises proportions of different food types among foods fed to chicks at five sites in Britain and Ireland. Sandeels were the predominant food items in the diet in all five samples, and Atlantic herrings or sprats made up most of the rest in four of them. Fish brought to Arctic tern chicks were of fairly uniform size, averaging about 75 mm long and weighing about 2 g, although smaller fish were brought to small chicks in their first week of life.[21] Fish brought to chicks by Arctic terns are generally somewhat smaller than those brought by common or roseate terns at the same sites.

The study at Mousa in Shetland in 1988 that is summarised in Table 24 was part of a series of studies investigating reproductive failures among Arctic terns in the Northern Isles during the 1980s. Simplifying a complex series of events, sandeel stocks in coastal waters of the Northern Isles increased during the 1970s and early 1980s, when there was a corresponding increase in the population of Arctic terns.[22] Sandeel stocks then seriously declined between 1983 and 1990, due probably to oceanographic changes that affected larval transport and led to reduced

TABLE 24. Percentages by number of food items brought by Arctic terns to their chicks at five breeding sites in Britain and Ireland.

	Location and years				
	Farne Islands, Northumberland	Coquet Island, Northumberland	Mousa, Shetland	The Skerries, Anglesey	Ynys Feurig, Anglesey
Food type	1965–1967	1965–1967	1988	1997–1999	1997–1999
Ammodytidae (sandeels)	65	61	71	95	78
Clupeidae (herring, sprat)	22	39		3	13
Gadidae (saithe)			19		
Other fishes	8			2	
Crustacea (crabs, shrimps)	2				
Cephalopoda (squid)	2				
Insecta (insects)	1				

Sources: Langham, 1968; Pearson, 1968; Uttley *et al.*, 1989b; Newton & Crowe, 2000.

recruitment of young fish to the population and rapid decline in numbers of older fish. The Arctic tern populations experienced dramatic and complete breeding failures during the period 1984–90. The numbers of breeding pairs declined markedly at several sites (probably indicating that many birds did not breed at all); the body weights of adults were abnormally low; many clutches were abandoned during incubation, and most of the chicks that hatched died of starvation.[23] The study at Mousa in 1988 compared the responses of common and Arctic terns breeding at the same site to the shortage of sandeels. Whereas common terns switched successfully to catching saithe instead of sandeels and fed their chicks adequately (see Table 18 in Chapter 8), Arctic terns brought only small numbers of saithe (Table 24). Instead, they continued to bring sandeels that were much smaller than usual, and most of their chicks failed to grow and died or disappeared within a week after hatching.[24] In 1991 the sandeel stocks recovered and the productivity of the Arctic terns returned more or less to normal for a few years.[25] However, productivity has again been very low at colonies in the Northern Isles and eastern Scotland since 1994 (see Table 29 in Chapter 11). In contrast to colonies further south in England, Wales and Ireland, Arctic terns in the Northern Isles apparently did not have enough herrings and sprats to serve as alternative foods, and they were unable to raise young adequately with the reduced stocks of sandeels (see Table 25, below). Although Arctic terns are generalist feeders in most of their range, those in the Northern Isles (the bulk of the British and Irish population) were de facto specialists on sandeels and paid the price when their main food became scarce.

BREEDING BIOLOGY

The breeding behaviour and biology of Arctic terns are very similar to those of common terns, and only the more pronounced differences are summarised here.

Arctic terns lay substantially smaller clutches than common terns. The most frequent clutch-size is two eggs, but single-egg and three-egg clutches are frequent at some sites. In Britain and Ireland, average clutch-sizes are usually in the range 1.5–2.0, with three-egg clutches accounting for up to 15 per cent of the total and single-egg clutches up to 50 per cent or more. At Coquet Island in the 1960s, average clutch-sizes were close to 2.0 in late May, declining to 1.7 or less during June. At three Irish Sea sites in the 1990s, average clutch-sizes were in the range 1.66–2.02 with an overall mean of 1.95. At the Farne Islands in the 1960s, mean clutch-sizes were highest (1.86) among birds aged 6–8 years and lower (1.47–1.56) among older and younger birds; clutches were smaller (1.56 and 1.29–1.49, respectively) in a year when food supply was reduced because of a 'red tide'.[26]

Arctic tern eggs are variable in colour, but usually fall into one of two categories, either buff (Fig. 170) or grey (Fig. 171). Downy chicks of Arctic terns also come in two colours, silvery-grey and warm buff, respectively more on the blue side of grey and on the orange side of buff than most common tern chicks. It is not known whether grey chicks hatch from grey eggs and buff chicks from buff eggs. Arctic tern chicks also have blackish foreheads, and chicks of the two species can be distinguished with at least 90 per cent accuracy by these characteristics (Fig. 172). The relative frequency of the two colour morphs varies from place to place, in a way that does not seem to form a coherent pattern. It has been suggested that grey chicks are more frequent at sites where Arctic terns nest on greyish rocks and buff chicks more frequent on brown soils,[27] but this is certainly not a universal association.

FIGS 170, 171. Arctic tern eggs come in two colours, buff and grey, with few intermediates.

FIG 170. Buff eggs. Tjörnin, Reykjavík, Iceland. (Jóhann Óli Hilmarsson)

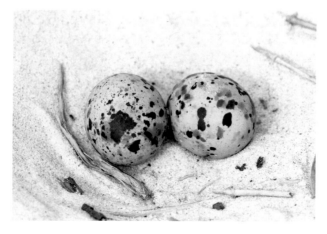

FIG 171. Grey eggs. Plymouth, USA. (Jim Fenton)

FIG 172. Arctic tern chicks also come in grey and buff colours, with few intermediates. It is not known whether grey chicks hatch from grey eggs and buff chicks hatch from buff eggs. The dark down above the bill usually distinguishes Arctic from common tern chicks. Lady's Island Lake, Co. Wexford. (Dave Daly)

Hatching success of Arctic terns is often quite low, ranging from 39 per cent to 88 per cent in the studies cited above for clutch-sizes. However, perhaps because many pairs had only one egg that hatched, chick survival was usually high, ranging from 66 per cent to 86 per cent in most of the studies (Fig. 173). Consequently, average productivity measured in those studies was often high, between 0.96 and 1.35 fledged chicks per pair (Fig. 174). However, Arctic terns are very vulnerable to fluctuations in the availability of their prey. At the Farne Islands in 1968, reduction in food availability attributed to a 'red tide' reduced productivity to about 0.23 fledged chicks per pair.[28] In the period 1984–90, as described earlier, Arctic terns suffered complete reproductive failure in their main strongholds in Orkney and Shetland, attributed to severe reduction in stocks of sandeels. During this period, clutch-sizes were abnormally small, eggs were abandoned during incubation and chicks starved within days of hatching. Sandeel stocks recovered in 1991, but Arctic tern productivity remained low through the 1990s, averaging 0.33 fledged chicks per pair (range 0–0.72) in Shetland and 0.27 (0.02–0.79) in Orkney (see Table 29 in Chapter 11).[29] Arctic terns were also severely affected by mink predation at breeding sites on islands near the western Scottish mainland in the 1980s and 1990s, reducing productivity to zero in many cases (see Chapter 11).

Thus, Arctic terns can be almost as productive as common terns in good years, but suffer many bad years, so that average productivity is much lower than that of common terns. Table 25 summarises measurements of productivity

FIG 173. Arctic tern chick, about 17 days old. When feathered, Arctic tern chicks and juveniles are greyer than common terns, and the short legs are already evident. Iceland. (John N. Murphy)

FIG 174. Arctic tern fledgling. This is distinguishable from a common tern fledgling by its short legs and bill, domed head and distinctive head pattern with black extending through the eye. Arctic terns usually take their fledglings to sea within a few days after they first fly and probably continue to feed them there. Lady's Island Lake, Co. Wexford. (Dave Daly)

TABLE 25. Numbers and productivity of Arctic terns at 17 index sites in the *Seabird Monitoring Programme*, 1986–2010.

Region	Colony site	Average number of pairs 1986–2010 (range)	Average productivity 1986–2010 (range)	Number of years
NW Scotland	The Reef, Tiree	92 (44–127)	0.01 (0.00–0.16)	7
	Isle of Eigg	76 (10–190)	0.09 (0.00–0.42)	10
Shetland	Foula	650 (50–1,500)	0.26 (0.00–0.73)	17
	Fair Isle	733 (11–2,836)	0.34 (0.00–1.15)	22
	Fetlar	422 (2–1,110)	0.18 (0.00–1.00)	15
Orkney	Papa Westray	1,422 (3–4,800)	0.15 (0.00–1.05)	17
N Scotland	Ardullie	55 (12–91)	0.60 (0.00–1.52)	8
NE Scotland	Sands of Forvie	104 (6–397)	0.38 (0.00–1.02)	17
	Kinloss	153 (20–550)	0.30 (0.00–1.13)	19
	St Fergus	315 (120–533)	0.10 (0.00–0.38)	22
SE Scotland	Isle of May	344 (34–630)	0.31 (0.00–0.74)	13
NE England	Farne Islands	986 (341–3,066)	0.64 (0.26–1.11)	15
	Coquet Island	735 (439–1,247)	0.84 (0.27–1.30)	21
	Long Nanny	753 (10–1,723)	0.69 (0.10–2.00)	22
Wales	Skerries	1,255 (33–2,912)	0.99 (0.47–1.70)	23
NW England	Foulney	44 (22–74)	0.35 (0.05–0.90)	25
SE Ireland	Rockabill	160 (20–359)	0.43 (0.05–1.39)	11
Total, 17 sites		8,279 [a]	0.43 [b]	
Scotland, 11 sites		4,366	0.22 [b]	
England, Wales and Ireland, 6 sites		3,933	0.79 [b]	

Source: Mavor *et al.*, 2008, updated to 2010 from the JNCC database.

[a] About 15 per cent of total numbers breeding in Britain and Ireland.

[b] Overall average is weighted by the average number of pairs in each colony.

(average number of chicks raised to fledging per pair) at 17 sites that were selected as 'index' sites for Arctic terns in the *Seabird Monitoring Programme* over a 25-year period, 1986–2010.[30] The list of sites includes four of the largest colonies in Britain and Ireland during that period, but also includes a representative selection of smaller colonies and locations all around Britain and Ireland. The data in Table 25 display the enormous variability in breeding success referred to earlier. Fourteen of the 17 sites had occasional bad years when productivity was reduced to zero or near zero, but all except three of the smaller colonies had several good years in which productivity exceeded one chick per pair. The large colony at the Skerries (Anglesey) had average productivity of almost one chick per pair over 23 years, and Coquet Island was not far behind. The six most southerly colonies (those in England, Wales and Ireland) had consistently higher productivity (average 0.79 chicks per pair) than those in the species' main stronghold in the Northern and Western Isles (average 0.22), which is the opposite of what might be expected under global warming. Averaging over all sites and years in the sample, the average productivity was 0.43 chicks per pair (Table 25). However, this is probably too high to be representative of Britain and Ireland as a whole, because of the heavy weighting in this average towards the southern colonies with their relatively high productivity.

MIGRATIONS

The Arctic tern is famous for its extraordinary long migrations, the greatest journeys of any bird (see Chapter 4) or indeed any animal. Arctic terns breed at higher latitudes in the Arctic than any other tern, and after the breeding season they set off on their long journeys southwards to the food-rich Antarctic seas. During its 'bipolar' life this small seabird (weighing less than 120 g) experiences more daylight than any other living creature. It is perhaps this extensive daylight allowing exceptional feeding time that provides the extra energy to fuel their immense migrations. Even those nesting in Britain and Ireland, at the southern edge of their breeding range, undertake these extraordinary movements. A return journey was formerly thought to extend some 40,000 km from the Arctic to Antarctic and back, based on recoveries of ringed birds and direct observations at sea. However, new research using geolocator technology has yielded remarkable new facts about this almost pole-to-pole migrant and has shown that the distance travelled is actually more than 60,000 km, involving repeated crossings of the North and South Atlantic (see Fig. 51 in Chapter 4).

Up to the end of 2009 a total of 201,317 Arctic terns had been ringed in Britain and Ireland, mostly as chicks, with more than 90 per cent of the 1,601 recoveries being of birds ringed as chicks.[31] Detailed analysis has been carried out for the first 1,098 recoveries reported by the end of 1997.[32] Because Arctic terns spend much of their lives at sea and almost all of the ring recoveries are on land, it is unlikely that the pattern of recoveries truly reflects the distribution and movements of the birds. Especially for birds recovered as juveniles or in their first winter, it is likely that some or most of the recoveries resulted from birds in poor condition coming to shore to die, or being driven ashore by bad weather (see Chapter 4).

After fledging some juveniles appear to disperse, with scattered recoveries during August–September in Norway, Sweden, the Netherlands and Britain, as well as several at sea. Many of these recoveries were at inland locations in unexpected places, or on boats or oil rigs in the North Sea, whereas the few recoveries of adults at this season were almost all along the coast near breeding colonies. Because juveniles normally stay with their parents and are fed by their parents during this period, it is likely that these recoveries of juveniles do not represent normal post-breeding dispersal. Other juveniles and adults appear to migrate south very early, with recoveries in August–September distributed along the west coasts of France, Iberia and West Africa, extending south as far as Angola (Fig. 175).

The only site in Britain and Ireland where large numbers of Arctic terns have been reported staging after the breeding season and prior to autumn migration is at Sandymount Strand in Dublin Bay. Arctic terns are usually in the minority among the large numbers of common terns roosting there (see Chapter 8), but extraordinarily large flocks of 20,000–30,000 terns, thought to have been mostly Arctic terns, were recorded on 31 August 1996.[33] As the number roosting exceeded the combined numbers of Arctic terns breeding in the Irish Sea, the additional terns must have originated elsewhere. Ring-reading at Rockabill, Co. Dublin, late in the season indicated that the additional birds had travelled to the Irish Sea area from colonies around the North Sea and in the Baltic states.[34]

By October, most of the recoveries of both adults and first-winter birds have been south of 15° N, ranging from Senegal south to the southern tip of Africa and east into the Indian Ocean as far as Natal (Fig. 175). While some adults and immatures are caught or trapped by small boys along the West African coastline, mortality from this cause is not as high as for other British and Irish breeding terns, because the Arctic tern only passes through this area, probably rather quickly, and is not normally a winter resident there.[35]

During the winter months (December–February), almost all adult Arctic terns are thought to be in their winter quarters in Antarctic waters, and only

FIG 175. Recovery locations of Arctic terns ringed as chicks in Britain and Ireland. During the post-breeding period in August–September, juveniles are often recorded to the east of the breeding range, occasionally inland (orange shading). In December–March, most recoveries have been in West or South Africa (blue shading, with two single recoveries marked with arrows); two birds have been recovered in South Africa in their first summers. In September–October, birds have been recovered all along the coast from Ireland to South Africa (green lines). Very few ringed Arctic terns have been recovered after their first summers, except as adults in the breeding area (orange shading). (Source: Monaghan, 2002)

four British-ringed birds have been recovered in Africa as adults during these months. This compares with 22 recoveries of first-winter birds, again distributed all along the west coast of Africa from Senegal to Natal. It is not known whether this indicates that most first-winter birds winter along the coast of Africa, or whether most Arctic terns actually migrate to the Antarctic with the adults,

FIG 176. First-winter Arctic tern. This bird was photographed in November, an unusually late date for one to be found in Britain or Ireland. It is identifiable as an Arctic tern by its very short red legs, fine bill and masked appearance, with black extending below the eye and black eyelids. Seaforth, Merseyside. (Steve Young)

and the recoveries in Africa represent stragglers or laggards that are in poor condition and unable to migrate so far (Fig. 176).

Much has been written about the distribution and movements of Arctic terns in the winter quarters, but most of this has been speculative.[36] They are thought to moult most of their body feathers twice during the short Antarctic summer, and they moult their flight feathers extremely rapidly in January–February, so they are said to be almost flightless at that time. Hence it is improbable that they perform extensive movements or circumnavigate the Antarctic continent, as has been suggested.[37] The geolocator studies of the birds from Greenland indicated that they were sedentary on the edge of the pack ice at that time (see Chapter 4). It is likely that other Atlantic birds, including those from Britain and Ireland, are similarly sedentary then. The greatest concentration of birds along the edge of the pack ice is to the south of the Indian Ocean, from 30° to 150° E,[38] but it is not known whether birds from the Atlantic Ocean travel as far east as this. Adults start to migrate north in March, but there are only two or three recoveries in Africa in March–April and it is likely that most travel in mid-Atlantic (see Chapter 4). A radar study showed large numbers of Arctic terns migrating north on the west

FIG 177. First-summer Arctic tern. The first-summer plumage resembles the adult winter plumage. It was once described as a separate species, *Sterna portlandica*, and is still sometimes referred to as the 'portlandica' plumage. Terns of all species generally remain in the winter quarters until they are two years old. One-year-olds are scarce to rare in the breeding areas, but Arctics are somewhat more likely to be seen than other terns. This bird can be identified as an Arctic tern by its short legs and fine bill. Seaforth, Merseyside. (Steve Young)

side of the Antarctic Peninsula in early March: it was thought that these were birds from the Atlantic population and that they would cross the Antarctic Peninsula to the Weddell Sea before continuing north into the South Atlantic Ocean.[39]

Little is known about the whereabouts or movements of Arctic terns in their first and second years. Birds in first-summer or 'portlandica' plumage are rarely seen at breeding colonies (Fig. 177), although they are more frequent at breeding sites in the USA and Canada. There have been two recoveries of British-ringed birds in South Africa in April–June of their first summers, and several in tropical West Africa in August–October,[40] suggesting that some migrate part-way north. In their second summers, some – perhaps most – birds migrate north and 'prospect' at breeding colonies, but they rarely breed until age three and often not until age four.[41] There have been so few recoveries of Arctic terns between the ages of 16 and 36 months that it seems likely they remain at sea like the adults.

Ringing has shown that Arctic terns ringed as chicks frequently settle to breed at other sites. Approximately one-third of the birds recovered during the breeding season were more than 20 km from their natal site, with movements showing interchange among colonies in Orkney and Shetland and among colonies in England, mainland Scotland, Ireland and Wales (although infrequently between the Northern Isles and other parts of Britain or Ireland). Several birds were recovered in breeding areas in other parts of northwest Europe, and there have been many recoveries of birds ringed as chicks in Scandinavia or the Baltic area during the breeding season in Britain.[42] Little is known about movements of adult Arctic terns among colonies in Britain and Ireland, because few breeding adults have been ringed or retrapped, but the ephemeral nature of some colonies indicates that such movements must be fairly frequent, at least over short distances.

Arctic terns from Greenland (Fig. 178) and North America migrate across the North Atlantic Ocean to waters west of Iberia and thence along the West African coast before continuing south.[43] One bird ringed in Canada and three

FIG 178. Arctic tern. Lithograph by Gitz-Johansen from *Grønlands Fugle/Birds of Greenland.* (Salomonsen & Gitz-Johansen, 1950).

ringed in Greenland have been recovered in Britain and Ireland in autumn,[44] but it appears that the main migration routes of Nearctic birds lie further to the southwest (see Fig. 51 in Chapter 4).

Finally, there is one bizarre record of a bird that was ringed as a chick in Shetland and recovered in June 14 years later in an upland area of Minnesota, USA, near the geographical centre of the North American continent. This record defies rational explanation, but there can be no doubt about the location of the recovery, the species or the ring number, because the specimen is now in one of the leading North American museums with the ring still on its leg.[45]

CHAPTER 11

Conservation

URING THE NINETEENTH AND EARLY twentieth centuries, the primary
threat to terns in Britain and Ireland was human persecution – egg-
harvesting, egg-collecting, and shooting for scientific specimens or
the plume trade. Although a series of laws protecting birds were enacted in the UK
between 1869 and 1902, wild birds were not effectively protected until passage of
the Protection of Birds Act in the UK in 1954 and the Wildlife Act in Ireland in 1976.
The most effective measures protecting terns during that period were initiated
by landowners, with notable success stories at the Farne Islands, Ravenglass and
Blakeney Point (see Chapter 5). However, during the first half of the twentieth
century public attitudes to nature gradually changed and the Royal Society for
Protection of Birds (RSPB) became an important force for conservation. By 1954
the protection of birds rather than their persecution had become the norm and
the number of protected sites was steadily increasing. However, active conservation
of seabirds still consisted primarily of establishing sanctuaries and employing
wardens to prevent human persecution and control human disturbance.

Since the 1950s, conservation of seabirds, including terns, has become a much
more complicated business. As the threats posed by egg-collectors have subsided,
threats posed by human disturbance, development of coastal sites, predation,
pollution and habitat degradation have become more important. Management
of tern colonies now requires management of habitats, control of predators and
resolution of conflicts with other activities such as recreation and agriculture.
Because terns frequently move from one breeding site to another, site-based
conservation has gradually given way to regional management of populations.
A larger shift is resulting from the current interest in conserving ecosystems
and biodiversity, which means that management of single species or groups

such as terns has to be integrated with management of many other species. Conservation has gradually shifted from being a local affair run mainly by amateurs to a professional activity involving teams of trained biologists working for government agencies or non-governmental organisations.

One important aspect of the professionalisation of conservation is the way in which it is incorporating knowledge of population dynamics and demography. Conservation is about managing changes in populations, and this requires knowledge of the factors that influence survival, breeding productivity and dispersal (see Appendix 1). Although most conservation programmes for terns in Britain and Ireland are focused on maintaining high productivity, it may be equally or more important to maintain high survival and favourable distribution of the population among breeding sites. Funding for conservation is always limiting, so it is necessary to allocate what funds are available to the measures that are most effective towards increasing populations. Consequently, planning of conservation programmes is increasingly based on mathematical population models. In Britain and Ireland, this approach has been pursued most vigorously by biologists at the RSPB under the direction of Norman Ratcliffe, who has developed population models of various kinds for little terns, Arctic and common terns, and roseate terns.[1]

A less happy aspect of the professionalisation of conservation is that it is becoming increasingly bureaucratic. Modern conservation programmes are governed by overlapping laws, regulations and directives, are based on multiple types of protected area, follow strategies, projects and plans drawn up by partnerships, alliances or committees, and are administered by overlapping government agencies and multiple non-governmental organisations. Anyone who tries to understand why, how or by whom tern populations are managed is quickly submerged in an alphabet soup of acronyms.

Given this complexity, we have not attempted a complete review of all the conservation programmes for terns in Britain and Ireland. We estimate the proportions of the total British and Irish populations that are now breeding at sites under active management as roughly 50 per cent for Arctic terns, 70 per cent for common terns, 80 per cent for little terns, 90 per cent for Sandwich terns and 100 per cent for roseate terns. However, there is no comprehensive summary or database from which these estimates can be checked or verified. In the next section of this chapter, we present four case studies which illustrate the variety of conservation issues faced by terns in Britain and Ireland, and the variety of ways in which these issues are tackled at the local and regional level. We follow this with a list of the main types of threat and how each is currently managed, and conclude with a discussion of two major threats that are not being addressed effectively: adverse factors acting in the winter quarters and climate change.

FOUR CASE STUDIES

Case study 1: little terns at Great Yarmouth, Norfolk

The greatest concentration of little terns in Britain and Ireland is in East Anglia, with a combined total of just over 1,000 pairs tallied during *Seabird 2000*, almost half the total number in Britain and Ireland.[2] For some time, the largest single colony was at Great Yarmouth, Norfolk, with 180–350 pairs in most years. At its peak in 2006, this colony held 369 pairs of little terns, about 15 per cent of the total in Britain and Ireland and about 1 per cent of the entire European population. Like most other little tern colonies in Britain and Ireland, the Great Yarmouth colony was located on a barrier beach that is attached to the mainland, accessible by terrestrial predators such as foxes and heavily used for human recreation. The tern colony was at North Denes, where the shoreline extends somewhat east of the main north–south line of the coast and the beach is bordered by a wide stretch of sand with irregular lines of dunes. Although the nesting site was located about 3 km north of the town centre, there is a high-density residential area and a caravan park only a few hundred metres to the west, and many footpaths cross to the beach (Fig. 179).

FIG 179. North Denes, Great Yarmouth, Norfolk, viewed from the north. The little tern nesting site is located behind the beach near the easternmost (left-hand) extremity of the shoreline. This was for many years the largest colony of little terns in Britain or Ireland, but was deserted in 2010 after persistent predation by hobbies and merlins. (Mike Page)

The first records of little terns nesting at the site were during World War II when human access to the beach was restricted, but breeding was sporadic thereafter until 1985, when a colony settled close to a caravan park. With local protection from human disturbance, the colony increased rapidly from 55 pairs in 1986 to 180 pairs in 1989 and fluctuated between 168 and 369 pairs from then until 2009. The only interruption was in the period 2002–04: the colony was destroyed in 2002 by vandals who tore up electric fences and smashed eggs, and the birds were disturbed at the time of egg-laying in 2003 by a low-flying helicopter searching for a missing child. Most of the birds moved to another nesting site at Winterton, 12 km north, returning to North Denes in 2005–06. A study of food and foraging in 2002–03 suggested that the food supply was better at North Denes than at Winterton, so that North Denes was a more favourable site for little terns in spite of the higher levels of disturbance there.[3] The terns again deserted the North Denes site in 2010, probably because of deterioration in the nesting habitat and increasing predation on the adults (see below). As is typical of little terns, the birds from North Denes seem to be shifting among several alternative sites, with 150 pairs at Winterton and 100 pairs at Eccles-on-Sea in 2012.[4]

Little terns at Great Yarmouth are managed under a thicket of interlocking acronyms. Great Yarmouth North Denes and Winterton–Horsey Dunes are designated under UK legislation as SSSIs (Sites of Special Scientific Interest) and Winterton is an NNR (National Nature Reserve). An area of 149 ha including the North Denes SSSI and part of Winterton SSSI is designated as an SPA (Special Protection Area) under the EU (European Union) Birds Directive, and Winterton–Horsey Dunes are designated as an SAC (Special Area of Conservation) under the EU Habitats Directive.[5] SPAs and SACs are part of a network of protected sites across the EU known as *Natura 2000*. The North Denes/Winterton SPA is threatened by continued residential development of the area, and under the East of England RSS (Regional Spatial Strategy) and the GYCS (Great Yarmouth Core Strategy), GYBC (Great Yarmouth Borough Council) conducted an AA (Appropriate Assessment) as part of an HRA (Habitats Regulations Appraisal) to evaluate whether the Great Yarmouth Waterfront AAP (Area Action Plan) would affect the SPA.[6] [An HRA should not, of course, be confused with an EIA or an SEA.]

Fortunately, management on the ground is simpler than this. The tern colony has been protected since 1986 by the RSPB with support from Great Yarmouth Borough Council and with funding by RSPB and Natural England. Until its desertion in 2010, the nesting area was fenced each year with up to 700 m of electric fence and was kept under 24-hour surveillance by RSPB wardens with the help of many volunteers. Access was carefully controlled, and the RSPB encouraged visitors to use vantage points from which they could watch the terns without disturbing them. Although losses of eggs and chicks to high tides occurred periodically, predation was the most important factor limiting breeding success, with foxes and kestrels as the most important predators. Foxes were successfully kept out of the colony with the electric fence, and the 24-hour patrols allowed wardens to detect and deter foxes, cats and hedgehogs. However, kestrels were more difficult to manage and took large numbers of chicks in several years. An early study to test whether supplying the local kestrels with supplementary food (mice and poultry chicks) at the nest could relieve predation on tern chicks was inconclusive, although a more recent and extensive study has suggested that this technique can be effective. Provision of chick shelters did not prevent predation by kestrels, but was effective in protecting the chicks from bad weather. In the end, predation on adult terns by hobbies and merlins increased in the late 2000s. As with other terns, predation on adult little terns is much more disruptive than predation on eggs or chicks, and this was probably an important factor contributing to the abandonment of the site in 2010.[7]

A wind-power facility with 30 two-megawatt turbines was built in 2003–04 on Scroby Sands, an area of sandbars a few kilometres offshore from Great Yarmouth and extending to within 2 km of the tern colony at North Denes. This is closer to shore than any other offshore wind installation currently operating or planned in the UK, and because of its proximity to the internationally important tern colony was subjected to detailed monitoring before, during and after construction. Scroby Sands had been an important tern breeding site during the 1940s and 1950s when they were permanently exposed, but had been submerged since 1965. Surveys conducted in 1995 and 1999 revealed that large numbers of little terns occasionally used the southern part of Scroby Sands for foraging, and this caused the turbines to be moved further north than originally planned, even though this brought them closer to the tern breeding site at North Denes.

A study of fish populations and tern foraging conducted in 2003 and 2004 – ironically, two of the years when the terns did not breed in large numbers at the North Denes site – indicated that the terns fed on a wide variety of fish and invertebrates (46 different taxa), but that more than 70 per cent of the diet consisted of young Atlantic herrings and sprats, 30–70 mm long. A radiotelemetry study conducted in the same years (see Chapter 6) indicated that most little terns foraged within 300 m of the shore and that very few of the foraging trips of the North Denes birds took them as far offshore as the wind turbines.[8] Even if terns were to forage among the turbines, it is unlikely that they would be killed by collisions with the turbine blades, because the lowest point of the blades' trajectory is 20 m above the sea surface and little terns rarely fly higher than 12 m while foraging. However, the array of turbines might be perceived as an obstacle by the terns and make them avoid the area – which is perhaps why fewer terns were found feeding over Scroby Sands in 2003 and 2004 than in 1995 and 1999.

In an interesting twist, the southern part of Scroby Sands re-emerged as an island in 2011, and 100 pairs of little terns nested there. It is thought that the presence of the turbines may have changed the currents and patterns of sand deposition, making Scroby Sands once again suitable for nesting terns and perhaps improving the area as a fish nursery also.[9]

The history of the colony at Great Yarmouth illustrates well why it is so difficult to manage and conserve species such as little terns, whose natural behaviour is to shift frequently among sites as the terrain and vegetation change and predators come and go. Despite occasional losses to predation and flooding, this colony achieved higher average productivity than that for little terns recorded at other sites in the nationwide *Seabird Monitoring Programme* (see Table 12 in Chapter 6). Excluding the three years when most of the birds were displaced to other sites (see above), productivity fell below 0.4 chicks per pair in only five of 21 years between 1986 and 2009 and reached a high of 1.82 chicks per pair in 2006.[10] This was a noteworthy success story for a tern colony on a heavily used beach in a largely urban area. However, the run of 24 years' occupation was unusually long for a major little tern colony. The habitat at North Denes deteriorated for little terns as marram grass spread into their nesting area, and it was not permissible to remove the grass because the sand dunes themselves were a valued feature of the SSSI. The arrival of new predators that preyed on adult terns finally made the location unsustainable.

In response to the breakup of the North Denes colony in 2010, RSPB has adopted a more regional and flexible strategy for managing little terns in eastern Norfolk. RSPB staff and volunteers throughout the county have been organised into the Norfolk Little Tern Working Group, based on a similar group set up earlier in Suffolk. This enables rapid communication so that personnel can be mobilised to protect individual colony sites in different parts of the county. The RSPB maintains a team of staff and dedicated volunteers who can locate the areas where the terns settle early in each breeding season. The RSPB supplies fencing materials which can be moved to these sites and installed quickly, and then provides support and expertise to the local groups so that they can protect the colonies themselves, with the RSPB itself targeting the site of the largest colony. Resources can thus be focused in each year on the sites with the largest numbers of terns and with the best prospects for successful breeding. This adaptable, multi-site strategy seems to be working as the birds have moved from site to site in 2010–12, and is likely to be adopted in other parts of the UK to meet the need for management of little terns nationwide.[11]

Case study 2: four species of terns at Coquet Island, Northumberland

Coquet Island is an island of about 6 ha located 1.2 km off the coast of Northumberland, near Amble (Fig. 180). It was the site of a monastery from the seventh until the sixteenth centuries and the remains of the monastery buildings were incorporated into the lighthouse when it was constructed in 1841. The lighthouse was manned until 1990 and the lighthouse keepers grew crops and raised livestock, but the light has been automated and has been solar-powered since 2007. The island is now uninhabited except for seasonal wardens protecting the nesting seabirds. It is owned by the Duke of Northumberland but has been managed by the RSPB as a reserve since 1970.

The early history of terns and other seabirds on Coquet Island is sketchy. In 1747, Bowen wrote that 'Vast flocks of wild fowl continually harbour and lay their eggs on this island, by the sale of which the fishermen make great advantages,' but this statement was not specific to terns.[12] Sandwich, common, roseate and Arctic terns were all recorded breeding in the first half of the nineteenth century, with 'a few pairs' of roseates in 1831 and 'large numbers' of Arctics in 1843 (see Chapter 5). However, Sandwich terns were exterminated by egg-collectors in the 1870s and the other species were said to have been driven away by the activities of the lighthouse keepers. The island was recolonised by two pairs of common terns

FIG 180. Coquet Island, 1.2 km off the coast of Northumberland, viewed from the southwest (looking out to sea). This island had few seabirds between the 1870s and 1958, but is now a major seabird breeding site, with the largest colony of roseate terns in the UK. It is managed as a reserve by the RSPB. This photograph was taken in winter; the island is densely vegetated in summer and terns nest mainly in areas kept open by herbicide treatment. (Paul G. Morrison, RSPB)

in 1958, and numbers increased to 1,500 pairs of common terns, with a few Arctics and roseates, in 1960. Several roseates caught in mist nets had been ringed on islands in the Firth of Forth.[13] By 1967 the island was occupied by about 1,800 pairs of Sandwich terns, 102 pairs of roseates (there had been at least 230 pairs in 1965), 1,200 pairs of commons and 560 pairs of Arctics.[14] There is no information on the reasons for the recolonisation and the rapid increase in numbers.

Numbers of roseate terns crashed on Coquet Island at the same time as at other sites in Britain, Ireland and France, falling from at least 230 pairs in 1965, 179 pairs in 1966, 102 pairs in 1967 and 80 pairs in 1975 to 16 pairs in 1977; they then fluctuated between 18 and 36 pairs until 2000, but increased rapidly to 94 pairs in 2006 in response to active management (see below). Numbers of common terns also fell to less than 500 pairs in 1984 but have since increased steadily to a peak of 1,358 pairs in 2010; numbers of Arctic terns also increased to a peak of 1,247 pairs in 2007, while numbers of Sandwich terns have fluctuated between 1,000 and 1,700 pairs without ever regaining the peak of 1,800 pairs attained in 1967. Besides terns, Atlantic puffins colonised the island in the 1960s and have increased to around 18,000 pairs today; common eiders increased to a peak of around 500 nests in the 1980s and black-headed gulls have increased to around 3,000 nesting pairs. Numbers of herring and lesser black-backed gulls were stable at around 10–20 pairs each until 1996, but suddenly increased to about 250 pairs in total in 2002 before control measures were introduced (see below). Other breeding seabirds include northern fulmars and black-legged kittiwakes. The vegetation on the island was formerly maintained as grassy sward by rabbits, but the rabbits died out about 2006 and the island is now mainly covered by nettles and rank grasses.

Coquet Island is designated as an SSSI and an SPA. It has been managed by the RSPB since 1970 as a reserve for seabirds. Resident wardens live on the island throughout the breeding season and maintain 24-hour surveillance. Landing on the island is prohibited during the seabird breeding season except as part of management or research, but boat trips run regularly from Amble to and around the island and give many visitors the opportunity to see roseate terns and other seabirds. Despite the presence of wardens, an egg-thief landed from a boat at night in June 2006 and took one clutch of roseate tern eggs.[15] The roseate terns are now under 24-hour security-camera surveillance.

The RSPB has conducted active habitat management since the 1980s. Herbicides are used periodically to control nettles and to establish and maintain open grassy areas suitable for terns. Sandwich, common and Arctic terns nest mainly within these managed plots.[16] A tiered terrace was constructed in 2000 and 2001 at the south end of the island to attract more roseate terns (Fig. 181). The terrace was faced with dry-stone walls to prevent puffins from burrowing

FIG 181. Roseate terns on nesting boxes, Coquet Island, Northumberland. The tiered terrace was constructed specifically for roseate terns in 2000 and 2001, and on Coquet Island the species now nests almost exclusively in nesting boxes. (Paul G. Morrison, RSPB)

into it and the horizontal shelves were covered with shingle. Twenty-five nesting boxes were installed in 2000, increasing to 200 by 2006. Since 2003, all roseate terns nesting on the island have used these boxes as nest sites and/ or as chick shelters. Numbers increased rapidly from 34 pairs in 2000 to 94 pairs in 2006,[17] but stabilised at about that level despite the availability of more boxes. Productivity has remained high, although not as high as that at Rockabill (see Table 22 in Chapter 9). There is little evidence that provision of the boxes increased breeding success (Fig. 182), although they do protect the chicks from predation by gulls. Prior to the deployment of nest boxes, the roseate terns nested in clumps of vegetation or in disused burrows of rabbits or puffins.

Numbers of herring and lesser black-backed gulls breeding on the island had been maintained at a low level by selective egg removal, but they suddenly increased in the late 1990s (see above). A programme of targeted disturbance was added to the egg removal operation in 2000. This was quickly successful, and the number of gull pairs declined from nearly 250 pairs in 2002 to less than 20 pairs in 2009.[18] The large gulls had affected terns primarily by displacing them from nesting space rather than by taking their eggs and chicks. The small number of breeding gulls remaining on the island is now confined to the end of the island furthest from the terns; this can be maintained with a relatively low level of effort.[19]

Coquet Island is one of the most research-tolerant of the many sites managed for breeding terns in Britain and Ireland. Many PhDs have been

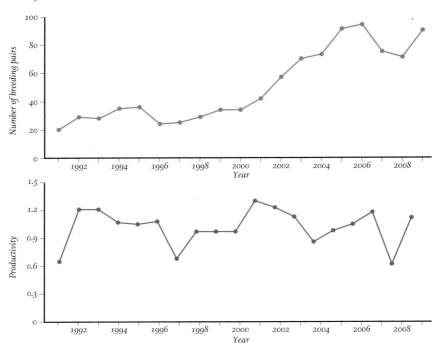

FIG 182. Numbers and productivity of roseate terns at Coquet Island, Northumberland, 1991–2009. Construction of a terrace and provision of nesting boxes in 2000–01 led to an increase in numbers, but little change in productivity. (Source: P. G. Morrison, RSPB)

based on field research carried out there, and we know of more than 30 papers published in scientific journals resulting from this research. Many tern chicks are ringed each year, and observers at Coquet Island have taken part in the intensive programme for resighting ringed roseate terns conducted at the three major breeding colonies in Britain and Ireland since 1995, with up to 135 different birds identified at Coquet Island each year.[20] This cooperative programme has generated important knowledge about the demography and population dynamics of the species (see Appendix 1). Besides terns, John Coulson of Durham University conducted a remarkable 50-year study of the common eiders nesting on the island, which demonstrated unexpectedly wide year-to-year variation in the numbers and elucidated many aspects of the breeding biology of the species.[21] The RSPB's support for scientific research is commendable, although their primary mission of protection and management sometimes limits the types of research that can be carried out there.

Case study 3: Arctic terns, common terns and American mink in the Western Isles

The *Seabird* 2000 surveys located 4,146 pairs of Arctic terns in the Western Isles (the Outer Hebrides), 7.4 per cent of the total British and Irish population. There were also about 500 pairs of common terns.[22] The Western Isles comprise five main islands extending 195 km from north to south and separated by about 25 km from the nearest point in the Inner Hebrides (Fig. 183). Both Arctic and common terns breeding in the Western Isles have been subjected to serious depredation by American mink. Mink not only cause breeding failures by direct predation of tern chicks and breeding adults, but frequent visits by mink cause colony desertions, with the terns sometimes regrouping and forming larger colonies at more secure locations.

Mink (Fig. 184) were inadvertently introduced to Lewis when they escaped during the 1950s and 1960s from two fur farms in operation there. The fur farms were closed in 1962 but by then the mink were already established in the wild, with the first feral animals reported from Lewis in 1969. Since then their range has extended southwards throughout the islands of Lewis and Harris. By the late

FIG 183. Map of the Western Isles (Outer Hebrides). A programme to eradicate American mink from the entire archipelago has been in progress since 2001 and is nearing success. Mink were known to have colonised areas marked red by 1999.

FIG 184. The American mink has become widespread in Britain and Ireland. After becoming established in the Western Isles in the 1960s this invasive predator had severe effects on Arctic and common terns nesting there, but a large-scale eradication project has almost succeeded in removing it from the entire archipelago. (John N. Murphy)

1990s they had spread south to North Uist and Benbecula, crossing the Sound of Harris (8–10 km wide) despite trapping efforts on the southernmost coastline of Harris and on nearby islands.[23]

While depredation of tern colonies by mink is well known, few studies have evaluated their specific impacts. One study was carried out by Clive Craik during 1992 and 1993 on the west coast of the Scottish mainland where there had been breeding colonies of seabirds, including Arctic and common terns, on nearshore islands. American mink had been present in increasing numbers in the area since 1965. After ten years of expansion, the density of mink in southwest Scotland was high – one or two animals per kilometre of rocky coast. Craik found that mink had depredated most colonies of terns and other seabirds within a few kilometres of the mainland and that all colonies so affected produced no or very few fledged young unless mink were intensively trapped on neighbouring parts of the mainland.[24] Productivity of common and Arctic terns ranged from 0.3 to 0.8 fledged chicks per pair on islands without mink predation, but was nearly zero at islands with mink (Table 26).

By the late 1990s the results of this and other studies had provided sufficient evidence to demonstrate detrimental impacts of mink on nesting seabirds, including terns, as well as important populations of several species of waders. By then mink were known to have colonised Lewis, Harris and North Uist, but they had not yet reached South Uist. A project to eradicate mink from the entire Western Isles was launched in 2001. While many tern conservation projects are site-specific, as in the other three case studies discussed in this chapter, this one covers a very large geographic area: about 3,050 km² in total, with 3,297 km of coastline, 4,721 km of loch edge and 1,821 km of riparian habitat.[25]

The main objective of the Hebridean Mink Project was to eradicate mink totally from the Western Isles, thus preventing further significant disturbance and losses to the internationally important populations of ground-nesting birds including terns and breeding waders, particularly those regularly found within SPAs. It was the largest eradication programme ever undertaken in the United Kingdom since the successful eradication of the coypu in the 1980s.[26] Phase I of the project, led by Scottish Natural Heritage, commenced in 2001 and aimed to trap and remove all mink from the Uists and South Harris. The project was successful in eradicating mink from the islands of North Uist, Benbecula and South Uist and reduced their numbers significantly in South Harris by the time

TABLE 26. Breeding success of common and Arctic terns on islands off western Scotland in 1992 and 1993, showing effects of predation by mink on tern productivity.

	Number of colonies	Number of pairs	Total number of chicks fledged	Productivity (chicks per pair)
Common tern				
1992 Mink predation	8	222	0	0.00
1992 No mink predation detected	8	1182	600–880	0.51–0.74
1993 Mink predation	10	321	0–7	< 0.02
1993 No mink predation detected	4	629	290–370	0.46–0.59
Arctic tern				
1992 Mink predation	6	148	2	0.01
1992 No mink predation detected	7	80	54–64	0.68–0.80
1993 Mink predation	5	298	3–7	0.01–0.02
1993 No mink predation detected	2	23	7	0.30

Source: Craik, 1995.

phase I was completed in March 2006. However, mink still posed a serious threat in Lewis: the Arctic terns there had merged into one colony of 400 pairs and at least 200 adults were killed by mink in 2005.[27]

Phase II, which started immediately after the successful programme in the Uists ended, extended active management northwards into Lewis and Harris, aiming first to establish a buffer zone for the Uists by means of a concentrated trapping effort on South Harris. Targeted trapping was conducted around established tern colonies, but the majority of trapping was, and continues to be, carried out in a methodical manner, beginning in South Harris before gradually moving north and west through Lewis. This cycle takes approximately seven months to complete, and the whole process then begins all over again. The programme included using mink scent as a lure and trained dogs to locate locations where mink were active. Around 7,500 traps are permanently in place in Lewis and Harris and are operated on a rotational basis. Phase II was completed in 2011, and by September that year some 1,675 mink had been trapped on the Western Isles.[28] The programme was then extended for a further three years to 2014.

In September 2010 Scottish Natural Heritage reported that for the first time in many years the trend towards fewer but larger colonies of terns in Lewis and Harris had been reversed. Historical colony sites had been used for the first time in 15 years in some instances, and the productivity of both Arctic and common terns was greatly improved.[29]

If no action had been taken to eradicate mink from the Western Isles, what would have been the consequences? Norman Ratcliffe and his colleagues set out to answer this question by developing a GIS model to determine the mink's potential range based on their dispersal abilities and habitat use. Calculations based on the model indicated that if the eradication programme had been abandoned in 2007, mink could have expanded to occupy all accessible areas of the Western Isles within about 38 years. The proportion of Arctic terns at risk to predation would have increased rapidly as mink spread through the Harris Sound islands between 2013 and 2019. Statistical analysis of long-term data on the productivity of both Arctic and common terns showed that unprotected sites within the range of mink had an average productivity of 0.33 chicks per pair whereas at sites where mink were trapped, average productivity was 0.84. As most of the common terns nested within the mink control area, the benefits to them were greater than those for Arctic terns, of which a larger proportion nested outside the control areas, with many of their sites isolated from or unsuitable for mink.[30]

Simulations of tern populations, assuming mink were eradicated from all the Western Isles, showed that the increased productivity would be sufficient to allow tern numbers to grow. If the mink eradication programme had been abandoned in 2007 and if mink had then recolonised the Western Isles as predicted, the model indicated that common and Arctic terns would progressively decline to equilibrium numbers of only 12 and 46 per cent, respectively, of those predicted to occur if mink were eradicated.[31] This calculation retrospectively justifies the implementation of the project and supports its continuation until eradication is fully achieved.

The Hebridean Mink Project has so far been successful, but it has had to be extended for three additional years and it remains to be seen whether its central objective – complete eradication of mink from the entire island chain – can be achieved. It has already cost more than £1.6 million and costs continue to increase. Even if mink are fully eradicated from the Western Isles, they will remain numerous in western Scotland, including the Inner Hebrides, only 25 km away at the closest point. Constant surveillance will be required to prevent mink from reaching and re-establishing themselves in the Outer Isles.

Case study 4: four species of terns at Lady's Island Lake, Co. Wexford

Lady's Island Lake is situated in the extreme southeast of Ireland. It is a shallow, brackish coastal lagoon separated from the sea by a 200 m wide sand and shingle barrier. The lake covers 324 ha and is 3.7 km in length and 1.3 km at its widest, southerly point. Water levels in the lagoon rise each winter, sometimes almost submerging the islands on which the terns nest in summer. A peninsula known as Lady's Island is situated at the north end of the lake and is a place of pilgrimage associated with the Blessed Virgin Mary: pilgrims travel here from all over Ireland in August and September. The lake is also popular with anglers and windsurfers, and the surrounding area is intensively farmed.

The lake is designated as an SPA and is part of an IBA (Important Bird Area) covering 466 ha, as well as an SAC. The two islands in the lake – Inish and Sgarbheen – hold internationally important numbers of breeding terns (Fig. 185; see also Fig. 134 in Chapter 9).

The EU Birds and Habitat Directives oblige all governments to maintain 'favourable conservation status' at sites designated as SACs and SPAs. Governments are responsible for the enforcement of regulations that will ensure the ecological integrity of these sites. The Special Conservation Interests defined for Lady's Island Lake SPA include Sandwich, roseate, common and Arctic terns. The Irish government has set out broad objectives for the SPA, including maintaining the tern populations and overall biodiversity, and maintaining liaison and cooperation with the landowners and users of the site. However, no specific targets have been set for numbers or productivity of the terns.

FIG 185. Map of Lady's Island Lake, Co. Wexford, showing the two tern nesting islands of Inish and Sgarbheen in relation to the sand and shingle barrier beach separating the lake from the sea. Terns nesting on the islands fly to the sea and feed in shallow waters to the east and west. (Source: Daly *et al.*, 2011)

The early history of terns, especially the roseate, at Lady's Island Lake is not well known, because ornithologists concealed the locations of roseate tern breeding sites to protect them from egg-collectors. Following the recovery of roseate terns from near-extinction in Britain and Ireland, they would probably have bred at Lady's Island Lake from the early twentieth century onwards. But the first known estimates of breeding numbers were not made until 1960, when some 1,000 breeding pairs were found on 2 July, together with small numbers of common terns. The following year there were only about 300 pairs of roseates, the displaced birds having moved to Tern Island in Wexford Harbour, some 13 km north, where about 2,000 pairs were nesting in the late 1960s. These seem to the only recorded cases in Britain and Ireland where roseate terns greatly outnumbered other terns breeding at the same sites. There were also some 100 breeding pairs of common and three pairs of Sandwich terns at Lady's Island Lake in 1961. Thereafter about 25 pairs of roseates bred at the lake until 1970, when predation by brown rats devastated the colony. Mortality rates of both breeding adults and chicks were extremely high, and the islands were littered with dead adults and chicks. There was a resurgence of numbers in 1978 (220 pairs), and the colony continued with fluctuating fortunes until 1981 when it was again deserted due to predation, almost certainly by brown rats.[32]

The Lady's Island Lake Tern Conservation Project is now managed and funded by the National Parks and Wildlife Service (NP&WS). NP&WS, in collaboration with BirdWatch Ireland, started wardening the tern colony from about 1993 onwards. Annual reports have been issued since 2004. Early wardening focused on ensuring that boating and other water-based recreational activities were confined to the southern parts of the Lake, well away from the breeding colony. Initially the colony was not protected throughout the day. Egg-collecting or interference has only been recorded once in the period 1993–2009, but may have occurred unobserved. There have been no prosecutions, but roseate tern eggs taken from Inish have been confiscated from collectors in Britain.

In recent years the colony has become one of the best managed in Ireland, reflected by increasing numbers of all four species of terns and their consistently high productivity (Fig. 186). The key elements in the management strategy are:

1. **Control of lake water levels.** This is a contentious issue, as local farmers would like low water levels in summer, while for successful management of the terns they must be maintained above a certain minimum level. Water levels are regulated by digging a channel through the sand–shingle bank separating the lake from the sea, and are measured on a staff gauge at the northern end of the lake. The ideal water level to protect the islands is 4.0–4.5 MOD (metres above ordnance datum), high enough to prevent predators from crossing approximately 250 m from the mainland to the islands but not so high as to swamp the southern end of Inish Island where the roseate terns nest. A Lake Committee, consisting of representatives of all interests in the lake, makes decisions about desired water levels. In general, landowners comply with the obligations arising from the SPA designation.

2. **Public access and availability of annual reports.** Visits to the islands are forbidden unless permission is granted by NP&WS. Recreational activity is confined to the southern end of the lake, and signs requesting lake users to remain at that end are erected on the southeast and southwest corners of the lake. 'Do not disturb' signs are placed along the shores of Inish and Sgarbheen islands. Annual reports explaining the conservation programme and results are made available to scientists and interested members of the public.

3. **Vegetation control.** Dense thickets of brambles and gorse that were encroaching on breeding areas of black-headed gulls and Sandwich terns on Inish were cleared in 2010. Some cleared areas were then colonised by the gulls and Sandwich terns. Walkways between the rows of wooden nest boxes

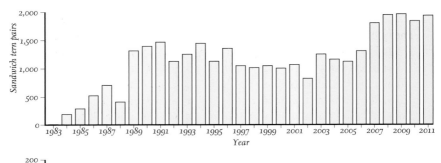

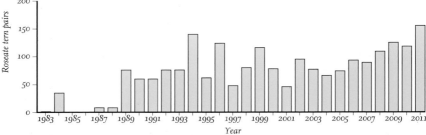

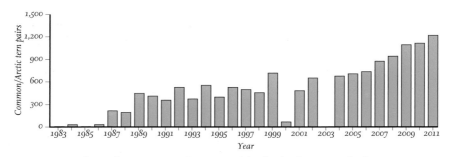

FIG 186. Numbers of nesting pairs of terns at Lady's Island Lake, Co. Wexford, 1983–2011. Top panel, Sandwich terns. Middle panel, common/Arctic terns (mainly commons). Bottom panel, roseate terns. Numbers of all four species increased after management efforts were intensified in 2003. (Source: Daly *et al.*, 2011)

laid out for nesting roseate terns were sprayed with 'Roundup' herbicide. This facilitated safer access to nest boxes for monitoring, while reducing the risk of stepping on chicks sheltering in dense vegetation.

4. **Provision of nest boxes and rubber tyres.** During 2011 some 303 wooden nest boxes (see Fig. 144 in Chapter 9) and six rubber tyres were placed in roseate nesting areas. Of the 155 nesting pairs of roseate terns that year, 141 (91 per cent)

nested in the boxes while the remaining 14 pairs nested in open vegetation. The tyres were not used as nest sites in 2011 but had been in previous years.[33]

5. **Control of mammalian predators.** Historically, brown rats have been the principal predators of tern eggs, chicks and adults at the lake. Rat bait is placed in permanent clay pipes on the island during February–March each year and topped up as needed; 12 kg of 'Klear' were used in 2011. The rat eradication programme has to be completed before early April, prior to the return of the terns and growth of vegetation that would provide shelter for rats. If water levels remain high, isolating the island from the mainland, rats cannot gain access and the terns are safe. Conversely, low water levels allow rats access to both islands. Should red foxes, badgers or American mink reach Inish, they are prevented from gaining access to the nesting area of roseate terns at the southern end of the island by a one-inch (25 mm) mesh electric fence separating the island into two parts. Otters are present in the lake but have not yet been recorded as predators, and their presence is thought to deter American mink, which have not yet been recorded as a problem. Other fencing, such as a 60 cm high half-inch (13 mm) chicken-wire fence has been used to keep out mammalian predators. A 1.2 m chicken-wire fence, topped by a single strand of electrified bull wire, has also been employed. Up to nine wire enclosures were erected around roseate colonies in some years. An unidentified predator, almost certainly a hedgehog, ate all the eggs from a colony of 150 pairs of Sandwich terns on Sgarbheen in mid-May 2011. Traps were laid but no predator was caught. It is thought that low lake water in the spring of 2011 had allowed the predator to reach the island.

6. **Avian predators.** Short-eared owls have been a problem in some years. Kestrels formerly nested in an abandoned building near the lake and visited the colony daily, taking common and Arctic tern chicks (but not roseates, which were better concealed). The building where the kestrels nested has been renovated recently and this may have solved the predation issue. A pair of hooded crows attempted to nest in the only tree on Inish. A Larsen trap was set to capture the crows and their nest was removed. However, other crows invariably arrive to replace those displaced. A peregrine falcon appears in the colony several times each season and removes a few adult terns (see Fig. 115 in Chapter 8). Both lesser and great black-backed gulls occur near the colony and have tried to nest on the islands, but have not been observed taking terns or their eggs.

7. **Other management issues.** There is a flock of feral greylag geese on the lake (100 pairs in 2011, reduced from about 150 pairs in previous years). They attempt to breed and also roost on the islands, posing a threat to the terns. Their nests and eggs are removed under licence. Nutrients in agricultural

discharges sometime make the lake water eutrophic, leading to fish kills. However, as the terns fly out over the sand–shingle barrier to feed at sea they are not affected by fish kills.

Overall, despite occasional setbacks, the Lady's Island Lake Tern Conservation Project has been very successful. During the period of enhanced management from 2004 to 2011, numbers of breeding terns of all species have been on an upward trend (Fig. 186) with generally good productivity. Rates of mortality attributable to rats and other predators have declined and are now thought to be at an all-time low. The main factor limiting tern breeding success now seems to be adverse weather conditions, with heavy rains and low temperatures occasionally causing heavy chick mortality.

The project's success in enhancing tern populations has resulted from the use of many different management techniques, modifying each as needed when new problems have arisen. The lake is now successfully managed for multiple uses, with only minor conflicts between neighbouring farmers, recreational users of the lake and the tern management programme. The key elements that have led to the project's success are: clear objectives; a single agency in charge; a full-time resident and dedicated manager; support and cooperation of many people, including the owner of Inish; and adequate funding.

CURRENT THREATS TO TERNS IN BRITAIN AND IRELAND

Egg-collecting

One would like to think that egg-collecting is a thing of the past, but unfortunately a few die-hard or obsessive collectors are still active in Britain and Ireland. One collector was prosecuted in Cleveland in 2000 for possessing little tern eggs apparently taken from a colony at Crimdon Dene, near Hartlepool.[34] Another collector was convicted and jailed in Scotland in 2002 for taking eggs of many rare birds, including little terns.[35] Thousands of gull and tern eggs, including an unspecified number of Arctic tern eggs, were stolen from the Copeland Islands, Co. Down, in 2003, apparently for consumption as food (Fig. 187).[36] One clutch of roseate tern eggs was taken from Coquet Island on 10 June 2006 by an egg-thief who landed from a boat at night.[37] Another collector was convicted in Lincolnshire in 2008 and jailed for possessing thousands of wild bird eggs, including little tern eggs.[38] More than 100 common tern eggs were stolen from the Ecréhous islands off Jersey in 2008.[39] Despite intensive investigations by the RSPB and others, the

FIG 187. The Copeland Islands (including Mew Island: see Fig. 55 in Chapter 5) have been important breeding sites for terns since at least the early nineteenth century. Big Copeland, shown here, supports an internationally important colony of Arctic terns and was the site of a major egg theft in 2003. (Robert Thompson)

cases that are detected and prosecuted are likely to be only a fraction of those that occur. Tern eggs are still attractive to the few remaining collectors, and the pervasive threat of egg theft requires continuous, round-the-clock surveillance of all managed colonies, which consumes a substantial fraction of the time and money that could be devoted to positive management.

Human disturbance

Human disturbance is primarily a threat to little terns because of their preference for nesting on mainland beaches that are used for human recreation. Many little tern colonies are now actively protected. According to a paper presented at a symposium on little terns convened by the RSPB in 2003, about 19 per cent of the little tern colonies in the UK in 1967 had part-time wardens with low-intensity management efforts, including some perimeter fencing, the erection of information signs and attempts to inform and educate the public. In 1979, almost a third of colonies had wardens, and by 2001, 15 per cent of the colonies had 24-hour protection throughout the breeding season, with a further 20 per cent wardened during daylight hours. Because management activities were focused on the larger, more stable colonies, the proportion of little tern pairs subject to active management was much larger than the 35 per cent of colonies, probably closer to 80 per cent. Most of the larger colonies were fenced and signed, and this had generally proved a successful deterrent to human disturbance.[40] However, providing wardens for 24 hours a day or even throughout daylight hours consumes much of the time and effort available for management. Although little terns can become very tolerant of human activity close to their colonies, a single incident in which humans or dogs enter the nesting areas can be very damaging, especially at night. Deliberate acts of vandalism are rare, but are also very damaging when they occur.

Where other terns nest at mainland sites on or near to beaches, they are vulnerable to human disturbance in the same way as little terns, and are protected by the same measures. Sandwich, common, roseate and Arctic terns generally nest on islands, however, and are easier to protect. A large fraction of the Sandwich and roseate terns that breed in Britain and Ireland, and a substantial fraction of the common and Arctic terns, nest at sites that are protected in one way or another. In most cases human visitation (other than by resident wardens or biologists conducting research) is prohibited or strictly controlled. However, some sites are successfully managed for multiple uses – for example, visitors to the Farne Islands are allowed to land on two islands and to pass through the tern nesting areas on boardwalks. The terns have become habituated to the constant presence of visitors and allow extremely close approach. This provides a wonderful opportunity for public education, and it is regrettable that other tern colonies are not managed in the same way, especially those where terns are already habituated to the presence of wardens and biologists. Close control of visitors would be required, but at many sites wardens spend much of the day doing very little – and this time could easily be spent with visitors.

Freshwater sites such as gravel pits and reservoirs where common terns nest pose a different type of problem, because these sites are often used by fishermen or for boating. However, many of these sites are successfully managed for multiple uses, with the terns nesting on rafts in one part of the lake and fishermen or boats using other areas.

Predation

Predation is the most pervasive threat to breeding terns in Britain and Ireland, but the extent to which it occurs, the identity of the predators, and the way in which they take terns is so variable among tern species, from site to site, and from year to year that it is very difficult to make generalisations. Nevertheless, it seems to be true that little terns are more affected by predators than the other four British and Irish terns, because of their predilection to nest on mainland beaches rather than on islands. The most important predators on little terns are foxes (Fig. 188), crows and kestrels; other predators reported include hedgehogs, weasels, gulls, other birds of prey, dogs and feral cats. In a systematic survey of beaches in East Anglia, evidence of fox presence was found on 62 per cent of beaches in April, prior to the arrival of little terns. When the terns arrived, they showed no tendency to avoid settling on beaches where foxes had been present in April, probably because they would not have been able to detect the presence of foxes until after they had laid eggs.[41]

Management of predation has to be tailored to the specific predator that is active and the manner and timing of the predation events. Typically, predation on little terns is carried out by one or a few individual specialist predators, and control measures need to be adapted to the way in which these individuals operate. Lethal control measures, such as shooting or poisoning, can be effective but are likely to provoke vigorous public opposition. Feral cats and hedgehogs can be trapped and removed. Wire fences with 10 × 20 cm mesh can be effective in excluding mammalian predators such as foxes, but electric fences are more widely used, although they require skilful deployment and frequent maintenance. To overcome problems in establishing an earth connection when the fence is set in shingle, the current practice is to use fences with alternate horizontal live and earth wires. In recent years, the widespread use of electric fencing and 24-hour on-site wardening has reduced the extent of ground predation and has led to greatly increased productivity at some little tern breeding sites. High tides, windblown sand and vegetation can all cause the charge to short out, and equipment failures or vandalism are also potential problems.[42]

FIG 188. The red fox is generally the most serious predator on little terns in Britain and Ireland. It is widespread on the mainland beaches where little terns prefer to breed and has probably become more numerous in recent years. The Burren, Co. Galway. (John N. Murphy)

Of course, fencing is ineffective against avian predators, and at some little tern breeding sites there is heavy predation by crows or kestrels. Crows are removed by shooting at some sites. Measures that have been used against kestrels include destroying nests, boarding up nesting sites, trapping the individual kestrel that is causing the problem and holding it in captivity for the duration of the season, or providing mice as alternative food near the kestrel's nest site (see case study 1, above). Where predation is by scarcer species that are conserved themselves, such as harriers, short-eared owls or falcons, the policy has generally been to do nothing and watch it happening (Tables 27 and 28). Chick shelters such as inverted V-shaped boards or camouflaged plastic piping are used at many

TABLE 27. Numbers and breeding performance of common terns in relation to predation at Scolt Head, Norfolk, 1951–69. Numbers of terns were maintained during the period 1951–57 by a programme to control numbers of black-headed gulls, but declined during the period 1960–66 when predation by short-eared owls was not controlled.

Year	Number of pairs	Number of eggs	Productivity (chicks per pair)	Predators reported
1951	1,000	1,600	0.25	Black-headed gulls
1952	1,000	1,580	0.20	Black-headed gulls
1953	1,000	1,170	0.30	Black-headed gulls [a]
1954	1,000	1,120	0.28	Black-headed gulls [a]
1955	900	1,200	0.44	Black-headed gulls [a]
1956	900	1.200	0.78	Black-headed gulls [a]
1957	1,000	1,200	1.60	None
1958	1,000	1,200	0.35	Rats, stoats
1959	400	1,100	0.04	Rats, stoats
1960	500	900	0.22	Short-eared owls
1961	550	750	0.22	Short-eared owls
1962	600	800	0.83	Short-eared owls
1963	550	700	0.55	Short-eared owls
1964	550	650	0.22	Short-eared owls
1965	400	650	0.38	Short-eared owls
1966	300	650	0.20	Short-eared owls
1967	500	1,350	0.46	Rats, stoats, weasels
1968	580	620	0.86	Weasels
1969	500	600	0.60	Short-eared owl

Source: Chestney, 1970.

[a] A programme to control black-headed gulls was instituted in 1953 and completed in 1958.

sites and protect chicks in bad weather, but critical studies have shown that they do not protect them against predation by harriers or kestrels. Individual nests can be protected with cages or exclosures, but these measures sometimes backfire and are only recommended where the cages can be closely monitored.[43] Predation by falcons (peregrines, hobbies and merlins) on adult little terns is especially disruptive and can cause temporary evacuations and permanent displacements, but is impossible to control unless the individual predator can be trapped and either held in captivity or translocated (see case study 1).

Where Sandwich or common terns nest on sites attached to the mainland, foxes can be important predators of these species as well. Numbers of foxes have increased in Britain and Ireland in recent years and they have extended their geographic range because of a decline in gamekeeping and the abandonment

TABLE 28. Numbers and breeding performance of Sandwich terns in relation to predation at Scolt Head, Norfolk, 1953–69. In contrast to the decline in numbers of common terns (Table 27), Sandwich terns increased steadily during the period 1960–66 while predation by short-eared owls was not controlled and declined only transitorily in 1967 when there was predation by rats, stoats and weasels.

Year	Number of pairs	Productivity (chicks per pair)	Adverse factors
1953	11	0.91	
1954	101	0.46	
1955	123	0.80	
1956	44	0.68	
1957	342	1.35	
1958	350	0.71	
1959	10	0.00	Predation by rats and black-headed gulls
1960	25	0.00	Disturbance by dog at time of settlement
1961	700	0.79	Flooding, bad weather, predation by short-eared owls
1962	610	0.93	Predation by short-eared owls
1963	657	0.96	Predation by short-eared owls
1964	1,050	0.76	Predation by short-eared owls
1965	2,000	1.10	Predation by short-eared owls
1966	2,400	0.88	Predation by short-eared owls
1967	1,550	1.23	Predation by rats, stoats, weasels
1968	2,900	0.69	Storm in July destroyed 100 clutches, 700 chicks
1969	3,850	0.88	Predation by rats

Source: Chestney, 1970.

of government bounty schemes, so that they have become a greater threat to our tern colonies. Terns nesting on inshore islands in shallow waters, on sand spits or beaches are all vulnerable. Fox predation at the mainland Sandwich tern colony at the Sands of Forvie National Nature Reserve, Aberdeenshire, was directly responsible for the decline of the colony from 1,500 pairs in 1983 to only 315 pairs in 1984. During the late 1980s and 1990s Sandwich tern colonies at Scolt Head in Norfolk, Havergate in Suffolk, Foulness in Essex, and Hodbarrow and Foulney in Cumbria first declined and then were abandoned due mainly to fox predation.[44] Persistent predation by foxes and peregrines eventually caused the desertion of the roseate tern colony at Ynys Feurig, Anglesey. A single visit by a fox to a colony can cause large-scale egg and chick losses. Fox predation at some tern colonies has been successfully prevented by the use of electric fencing, or by nocturnal patrols and shooting.[45]

Generally, Sandwich, common, roseate and Arctic terns nest on islands, and by far the most serious predator there is the American mink. Mink can be devastating to terns because they can to swim to islands 2 km or more offshore and they hunt silently at night, so that they can kill adult terns at will, sometimes so stealthily that other terns in the colony do not know what is happening. They also have a habit of 'surplus killing', sometimes killing dozens of terns and only eating one or two (Fig. 189). Mink have become widespread throughout Britain and Ireland and can reach most inshore islands that are occupied by terns, so that they have destroyed many small breeding colonies and threaten major colonies such as Coquet Island and Lady's Island Lake (although it is thought

FIG 189. Mink are especially destructive predators because of their habit of 'surplus killing' – killing far more prey than they need. This photograph shows two adult common terns and about 130 mostly full-grown chicks killed by mink at a breeding site at Glas Eileanan, Sound of Mull, in late July 1989. (Clive Craik)

that otters at Lady's Island Lake may be keeping the mink away: see case study 4). The effects of mink on terns have been studied in greatest detail in western Scotland and the Western Isles (see case study 3), but they have probably had similar effects in other areas where terns once nested on inshore islands.

Control of mink requires intensive trapping and is very labour-intensive (see case study 3), but the work of Clive Craik has shown that inshore tern colonies can be protected and even restored by systematic trapping of mink along the facing shoreline, even without attempts at total eradication.[46] Craik has conducted a mink–seabird project in western Scotland (Mallaig to West Loch Tarbert, including the Sound of Mull and Loch Fyne) since 1995. This project has attempted to control mink around up to 39 seabird breeding islands and has successfully prevented predation by mink at 70–90 per cent of these sites each year, although some of the seabird colonies protected from mink suffered from depredation by other predators. The terns have tended to move to protected sites, with a notable success at South Shian in Loch Creran, where disused rafts from a former mussel farm have been converted for tern nesting and mink-proofed. In 2011, about 300 pairs of common terns nested on two rafts with total area only about 150 m² and raised about 400 young. Despite the long-term project, however, numbers of common terns in the study area decreased from 1,263 pairs in 1994 to 711 in 2011, and numbers of Arctic terns decreased from 356 pairs to 74 in the same period.[47]

Other important predators on island-nesting terns include rats, hedgehogs, large gulls, crows, merlins and peregrine falcons. Some of the islands that once supported nesting terns are now occupied by rats and the terns are long gone. It has recently become feasible to eradicate rats from quite large islands, and several former seabird colonies on islands around Scotland have been restored in this way. So far as we are aware, however, none of these islands was originally an important tern colony, and only a few terns have been reported among the returning seabirds.

Hedgehogs can become major predators on tern eggs where terns occupy islands large enough to support a year-round population of hedgehogs (Fig. 190). For example, hedgehogs took most of the eggs from an Arctic tern colony at Dalsetter, Shetland, in 1987.[48] They were also major predators on tern eggs on North Ronaldsay, Orkney, and in the Outer Hebrides, although in the latter case they were a greater threat to nesting waders because the terns nest mainly on small islands. Hedgehogs were removed from North Ronaldsay, but a project to trap and kill them in the Outer Hebrides cost more than £1.2 million (£800 per hedgehog), generating intense public opposition and a counter-project (Uist Hedgehog Rescue) that took trapped hedgehogs and translocated them to the Scottish mainland.

FIG 190. Hedgehog on a sandy beach. Hedgehogs are important predators on terns at some locations, especially little terns in England and common and Arctic terns in the Northern and Western Isles. (John N. Murphy)

Herring, lesser black-backed and great black-backed gulls primarily affect terns by occupying their preferred nesting areas and displacing them to other islands, but sometimes they are important predators on tern eggs and chicks as well. One of the largest roseate tern colonies ever recorded in Scotland was on Inchmickery in the Firth of Forth, where 450 pairs bred between 1957 and 1962. The island was occupied by herring gulls during the 1960s and the terns moved to nearby Fidra by 1971 (some birds from Inchmickery founded a new colony at Coquet Island in 1960: see case study 2). The gulls were then culled on Inichmickery and the roseate terns made a return, with up to 100 pairs nesting during the 1970s, but the population gradually declined to two pairs in 1981.[49]

At the Isle of May, Fife, about 50,000 herring gulls (as well as large numbers of lesser black-backed gulls) were culled during the 1970s, but the original colony of about 15,000 pairs of gulls was reduced only to 3,000 pairs, because many replacements were recruited from other gull colonies.[50] However, gull management programmes were continued at the Isle of May during the 1980s and 1990s and the island once again supports modest numbers of common and Arctic terns (see Table 20 in Chapter 8 and Table 25 in Chapter 10). It has become easier to control herring and great black-backed gulls now that their numbers are decreasing,[51] and there have been several successful programmes to reverse their displacement of terns (for an example, see case study 2). Numbers of roseate terns nesting at Rockabill, Co. Dublin, increased rapidly after herring gulls were removed in the mid-1980s.

Habitat availability and habitat quality

None of our five breeding terns appears to be limited in total numbers by the availability or quality of nesting habitat in Britain and Ireland: there are unoccupied areas somewhere in Britain and Ireland that appear to be suitable for each of the species. However, many parts of the coast with large areas of shallow waters suitable for tern feeding have too few islands, or too little suitable habitat within the islands that exist, to support all the terns that could hypothetically breed there. For example, there are very few islands suitable for nesting terns anywhere on the east or south coasts of England except in Northumberland, Norfolk and Hampshire, nor anywhere in southwest England, west Wales or the south coast of Ireland west of Co. Wexford. Often citing the general goal of increasing biodiversity, many regional or local organisations have sought to attract or increase numbers of nesting terns, by improving habitats at existing colony sites, by attracting terns to nest at new or restored sites, or even in a few cases by building new islands. These endeavours have not always improved the overall welfare of the species, however, because they sometimes attract birds from high-quality sites to lower-quality sites where their survival or productivity may be lower.

Measures to improve the nesting habitat on existing islands include clearance of shrubby vegetation and the use of herbicides to prevent overgrowth of thick weedy vegetation. These measures can be highly successful in maintaining or increasing numbers of breeding terns (see case studies 2 and 4). At Rockabill, non-native vegetation such as hottentot fig is cleared each year and even the native tree mallow is reduced, although roseate terns can nest successfully under it (see Fig. 137 in Chapter 9). Building an artificial terrace and deploying nest boxes appears to have increased the number of roseate terns nesting at Coquet Island, even though the terrace lacked the natural vegetation that roseates usually like around their boxes (Fig. 182). Large numbers of nest boxes have also been set out at Rockabill and Lady's Island Lake, and the roseate terns there seem to prefer them to most natural sites. However, it is not clear that, on a larger scale, the provision of nest boxes has either increased total numbers of roseate terns in Britain and Ireland faster than was occurring anyway, or increased their average productivity.

Attempts to attract roseate terns to nest at new or long-abandoned sites have met with very little success. The RSPB has been trying to attract roseate terns to islands in Belfast, Larne and Strangford loughs in Northern Ireland for many years, mainly by deploying nest boxes in suitable habitat on islands already occupied by other terns. Numbers in Larne Lough increased to a peak of 19 breeding pairs in 2003, but declined again to only one pair in 2009.[52] BirdWatch Ireland has attempted for many years to attract roseate terns to join a small colony of common and Arctic terns on Maiden Rock in the Dalkey Islands, Co. Dublin, but the site is marginal at best; although 11 pairs of roseates nested there in 2004, only one or two pairs have nested since. Attempts to attract roseate terns to the Farne Islands, Northumberland, the Skerries, Anglesey, and

Sampson Island in the Isles of Scilly were also unsuccessful.[53] In 1985–89, the Irish Wildbird Conservancy (predecessor to BirdWatch Ireland) attempted to attract terns, especially roseate terns, to breed at the historical breeding site at the Keeragh Islands, Co. Wexford, by culling gulls, deploying decoys and nest boxes, and broadcasting tern calls. However, no terns of any species settled to breed. Roseate terns seem to be particularly hard to manipulate in these ways: they appear to know which breeding sites are best for them, and obstinately refuse to move to sites that we choose for them, unless we unwittingly pick a site that they would have liked anyway. For example, only four of more than 20 tern restoration projects in the USA and Canada have been successful in establishing stable colonies of more than 20 pairs of roseate terns, and only one of these consistently supports more than 100 pairs, although most of these projects were successful in re-establishing stable colonies of common terns.[54]

Projects to create new islands involve major engineering works, but some have been very successful in attracting tern colonies. Perhaps the first example was the RSPB's creation of the 'scrape' at Minsmere, Suffolk – a shallow lagoon behind the barrier beach with islands intended to serve as breeding sites for terns and waders. Common terns first nested there in 1962 and Sandwich terns in 1965,[55] and both have been present in fluctuating numbers since. After a near-absence for 30 years, 400 pairs of Sandwich terns and 190 pairs of common terns resettled in 2009, and Arctic and roseate terns nested for the first time in 2011.

At several sites in Essex, large volumes of dredge spoil were deposited in intertidal areas adjoining existing breeding sites of little terns. Although the primary goal of these projects was coastal defence rather than habitat creation, one outcome was that numbers of little terns increased and their breeding success probably improved because of greater security against flooding. The dredge spoil banks were deposited in intertidal zones adjacent to existing islands rather than as free-standing islands, and were reshaped and shifted by tidal currents within a few years.[56]

'Blue Circle Island' is an artificial island of less than 1 ha that was built in Larne Lough, Co. Down, in the 1970s (Fig. 191). Although its primary purpose was to dispose of dredge spoil and quarry material from a cement works, it was configured to be suitable for nesting terns and was quickly colonised by Sandwich and common terns. It is now managed by the RSPB and supports up to 1,000 pairs of these two species, plus a few roseate terns in recent years.

A few small islands have been created in gravel pits, lakes and reservoirs in various parts of England to attract nesting common terns, but floating rafts have been much more widely used (Fig. 192). Rafts situated well away from shorelines provide safety from most terrestrial predators and security against fluctuations

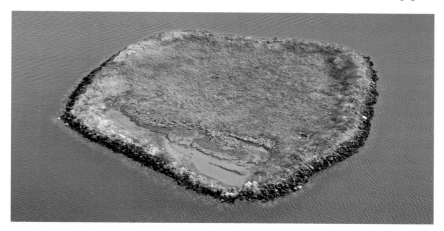

FIG 191. 'Blue Circle Island', Larne Lough, Co. Down. This artificial island of less than 1 ha was built from dredge spoil in the 1970s and was configured to be suitable for nesting terns. It now supports a flourishing colony of Sandwich and common terns, but attempts to attract roseate terns to it have had only limited success. (Robert Thompson)

FIG 192. Nesting rafts for common terns. Floating rafts are very attractive to common terns as nesting sites, especially if they can be mink-proofed. The rafts shown in this photograph have been subdivided into 49 compartments, each occupied by one pair of common terns. Rafts have been deployed on many freshwater lakes and gravel pits in Britain and Ireland and have proved very important in maintaining inland populations. Disused rafts constructed for mussel farming have been successfully modified for nesting terns on salt-water lochs in western Scotland. Breydon Water, Norfolk. (Mike Page)

in water levels; they can also be made secure from predation by mink. Well-designed nesting rafts quickly attract common terns, and the terns often have high breeding success there, although rafts sometimes turn into feeding stations for crows or herons. Methods for constructing and maintaining nesting rafts have been refined over the years, and several internet sites now have designs and specifications for building them, or offer them for sale.[57]

Food limitation and food availability

Arctic terns seem to be more sensitive to food shortages than the other four British and Irish terns, probably because they are less adaptable. Between 1985 and 1990 the abundance of sandeels, the Arctic terns' primary food, was severely reduced in waters around Shetland, and Arctic terns suffered almost complete breeding failures there for six years. The terns' breeding failures were characterised by late nesting, reduced clutch-sizes and egg-sizes, and deaths of almost all chicks from starvation; the adults were severely underweight and many apparently did not breed at all. The reduced numbers of sandeels were initially blamed on overfishing, but instead were found to be due to successive years of poor recruitment of 0-group fish (spawned in the previous year), resulting in decreases in the spawning stock and scarcity of the 1-group fish on which the terns depended (see Chapter 10). Sandeel populations recovered in 1991 (0-group) and 1992 (1-group), and breeding success of Arctic terns in Shetland improved for a few years.[58] However, it declined again in 1994 and has remained very low in every year since except 2002 (Table 29). Total numbers of Arctic terns breeding at the five sites for which data are included in Table 29 declined by more than 80 per cent during this period. This second and longer depression in breeding success was much more widespread and affected all colonies in eastern Scotland as well as those in Orkney and Shetland. Arctic tern colonies in western Scotland are generally smaller and were monitored less consistently, but productivity remained reasonably high there during the period 1988–2010 except for half a dozen bad years (Table 29). In contrast, productivity of Arctic terns remained high at colonies in northeast England and around the Irish Sea throughout this period (see Table 25 in Chapter 10). Productivity was consistently higher during this period at the Farne Islands and Coquet Island than at the Isle of May only 80–110 km away.

Common terns are somewhat less sensitive than Arctic terns to fluctuations in food availability, For example, during the shortage of sandeels in Shetland in 1988, common terns switched to feeding their chicks on saithe and were able to raise young adequately while adjacent Arctic tern chicks were starving.[59] In Britain and Ireland as a whole, there have been no clear regional patterns of

TABLE 29. Average productivity of Arctic terns in three regions of Scotland in each year from 1986 to 2010.

Year	West Scotland (7 sites)		East Scotland (4 sites)		Northern Isles (5 sites)	
	Total nests	Productivity (chicks per pair)	Total nests	Productivity (chicks per pair)	Total nests	Productivity (chicks per pair)
1986			128	0.65	665	0.01
1987			161	0.73	380	0.00
1988	20	0.50	275	0.19	408	0.00
1989	33	0.91	510	0.31	4756	0.00
1990	381	0.18	1151	0.07	5556	0.00
1991	312	0.44	765	0.14	4523	0.44
1992	327	0.74	920	0.41	3857	0.23
1993	366	0.50	859	0.07	5454	0.43
1994	539	0.22	933	0.53	4300	0.07
1995	258	0.00	734	0.74	2712	0.19
1996	120	0.03	979	0.00	2133	0.05
1997	34	0.06	1135	0.32	3755	0.03
1998	192	0.28	667	0.02	2199	0.03
1999	176	0.36	549	0.19	3298	0.09
2000	445	0.17	483	0.17	2855	0.12
2001	302	0.70	427	0.56	5097	0.00
2002	381	0.01	781	0.14	2509	0.72
2003	164	0.00	288	0.16	1038	0.02
2004	327	0.44	395	0.11	169	0.02
2005	402	0.57	1209	0.09	1472	0.05
2006	145	0.17	399	0.11	1835	0.12
2007	190	0.15	424	0.00	233	0.01
2008	92	0.80	683	0.03	148	0.01
2009	108	0.23	183	0.31	1046	0.27
2010	224	0.85	719	0.36	686	0.04
Mean	**241**	**0.35**	**423**	**0.23**	**2443**	**0.15**

Source: Mavor *et al.*, 2008, updated to 2010 from the JNCC database. Not all colonies were monitored in each year, so the changes in the numbers given for 'total nests' do not represent changes in the total population in each region.

variations in average productivity of common terns (see Table 20 in Chapter 8). Productivity at colonies in eastern Scotland remained reasonably high during the period when Arctic terns were failing, and even in Orkney and Shetland average productivities were in the range 0.3–0.4 chicks per pair when those of Arctic terns were much lower, although the common tern colonies in Shetland were all very small.[60] Nevertheless, the average productivity of 0.87 chicks per pair in Britain and Ireland (Table 20) is much lower than what common terns can achieve in good conditions, and where studies have been carried out most chick mortality is due to starvation and/or bad weather. Common terns feed closer inshore than Arctic terns and on a wider variety of prey, so that a shortage of one type of prey is often offset by availability of another. Thus, although productivity of common terns appears to be limited generally by food availability, this seems to act mainly at a local level.

For Sandwich terns, also, average productivity in Britain and Ireland is well below that achievable in good conditions (see Table 16 in Chapter 7). However, there are no marked regional patterns, and perusal of the JNCC database reveals no clear temporal patterns either. Where studies have been carried out, low productivity in Sandwich terns appears to be due mainly to predation and to food-stealing by black-headed gulls. To overcome food-stealing, Sandwich terns have to catch and bring in more food than their chicks need, and they are often not able to do this. This may be related to their dependence on distant food sources and their long commuting times.

There is little evidence that either little or roseate terns are significantly affected by variations in food availability. Average productivity of little terns in Britain and Ireland is very low (see Table 12 in Chapter 6), but this is due largely or entirely to predation, flooding or adverse weather. We are not aware of any reports of little tern chicks dying from starvation, and they can achieve very high productivity in the absence of predation (Table 12). Now that predation has been brought under control at Lady's Island Lake (see case study 4), roseate terns in Britain and Ireland rarely experience either flooding or significant predation, and their productivity is consistently very high (see Table 22 in Chapter 9)

The breeding failures of Arctic terns in the northern North Sea since 1985 seem to have resulted from profound oceanographic changes. At the Isle of May, sandeels became progressively less numerous during the 1990s and their condition declined drastically, so that the calorific value of fish of a given size measured in 2004 was barely a quarter of that measured in 1976–88 (see Chapter 2).[61] Consequently, all seabirds at the Isle of May, including Arctic and common terns, suffered reproductive failures. The change in the condition of sandeels appears to have resulted from a 'regime shift' – a term used by oceanographers for a major change in the structure of marine ecosystems – that occurred around 1988. This probably resulted from increases in sea-surface temperatures, resulting in a change in the composition of phytoplankton from dominance by diatoms to dominance by dinoflagellates. This then resulted in near-disappearance of the copepod *Calanus finmarchicus*, which had been the most important food source for fish such as sandeels.[62] Whether this 'regime shift' resulted from a cyclical change in oceanographic conditions or is a permanent change resulting from global warming remains to be seen. In any event, Arctic terns in Scotland and the Northern Isles now do not have enough food and are not producing enough young to maintain their populations, and continued long-term declines in numbers are to be expected.

As the numbers and condition of sandeels declined in the North Sea, there was a massive increase in the numbers of snake pipefish available between 2003 and 2008. These long thin fish have a stiff spine: terns find them easy to catch but difficult to swallow (Fig. 193), and they have very little nutritive value.[63] Tern chicks do not thrive when fed on them and sometimes choke to death while attempting to swallow them.

FIG 193. Common tern chick attempting to swallow a pipefish. The snake pipefish had a population 'explosion' in the North Sea in 2003–08 following a decline in the abundance and condition of sandeels. Many fish-eating birds tried to feed their young on pipefish, but these long, stiff fish proved very difficult to swallow and have very little nutritive value. Coquet Island, Northumberland. (Paul G. Morrison, RSPB)

In the southern North Sea, besides the explosion of snake pipefish, recruitment and stocks of Atlantic herrings have declined since 2002; both changes are probably due to increased sea-surface temperatures. Breeding success of common terns in northwest Germany and the Netherlands has declined sharply since 2002, and breeding numbers have declined rapidly since 2005.[64] Eric Stienen had already reported these changes for Sandwich terns in 2006, and forecast a long-term decline in numbers in the southern North Sea, the stronghold of the species.[65] Oddly, however, none of these changes has yet been manifested in the terns nesting on the British side of the southern North Sea. Numbers and productivity of Sandwich, common and Arctic terns have remained high or increased during the 1990s and 2000s in most of the major breeding sites between Northumberland and Essex (Tables 16, 20 and 25).[66]

Effects of fisheries

Against this background of drastic changes in marine ecosystems and fish populations, it is difficult to discern any clear effects of human fisheries on terns, despite the profound effects that fisheries have on fish populations. Fisheries generally target larger fish than those taken by terns, so the most likely effects would be indirect. For example, overfishing of mature fish might lead to reductions in the spawning stock, with consequent reductions in fish of the younger age-classes taken by terns. This was the explanation originally proposed for the shortage of 1-group sandeels around Shetland in the late 1980s. However, as described earlier, the sandeel crash was found to be due mainly to natural causes. Following a drastic decline in the total catch of sandeels by the international fishery in the North Sea from its peak in 1997, a management regime was introduced in 2003 and the fishery was completely closed in 2005. Atlantic herrings have been overfished in the North Sea, but – at least in eastern England – terns continue to prosper on diets of sprats and sandeels. The recent decline in recruitment and stocks of Atlantic herrings in the southern North Sea does appear to be affecting terns there, but this also appears to be attributable to natural changes (see previous paragraph).

Fisheries have also depleted stocks of many large predatory fish, and this might hypothetically have affected terns indirectly, either by allowing increases in small prey species or by reducing the numbers of prey fish driven to the surface by predators attacking them from below. There do seem to be fewer reports of terns following and feeding over predatory fish in British and Irish waters than in other parts of the world, but there is no way to make a systematic comparison. In their winter quarters in West Africa, terns might hypothetically be affected by overfishing of tuna and other predatory fish, but again there is no way to evaluate this.

A third way in which fisheries have affected terns indirectly is by promoting increases in populations of large gulls, which have displaced terns from many former breeding sites and often prey on eggs and chicks. This was important between about 1940 and 1980, when numbers of herring gulls increased enormously and several important tern colonies were overrun. However, herring gulls have declined again in recent decades[67] and there have been several successful programmes to restore tern colonies (see under *Predation*, above). Lesser black-backed gulls are still increasing, but as yet there seem to have been no reports of them encroaching on tern colonies.

Pollution

During the 1950s and 1960s, many fish-eating birds throughout Europe and North America were adversely affected by organochlorine pesticides. The worst incident was in the Netherlands in 1964 and 1965, when large numbers of terns were killed by effluents of dieldrin and telodrin from a manufacturing plant in Rotterdam. Sandwich terns breeding in the Netherlands were reduced from 40,000 breeding pairs to 650 (more than a 98 per cent reduction) and common terns from 35,000 pairs to a few thousands (about 90 per cent).[68] However, that incident involved an industrial effluent rather than agricultural use of pesticides, and terns in Britain and Ireland were not affected, except that there was net emigration of Sandwich and common terns to replenish the Dutch populations for several decades.

Unfortunately, tern populations were not well monitored in Britain or Ireland in the 1950s and 1960s, and information on levels of contamination at that period is scanty. Sporadic sampling of our five tern species in the period 1965–75 revealed very low levels of DDE and dieldrin, except for a high concentration of DDE in one little tern from Co. Wexford.[69] High residues of DDE and dieldrin were measured in other fish-eating birds at that period both in marine and freshwater environments, and levels of dieldrin in some other fish-eating birds, such as shags, grey herons and kingfishers, were high enough to have caused adverse effects.[70] A few samples of little and roseate terns from Cos. Wexford and Dublin in the period 1965–75 had high enough concentrations of polychlorinated biphenyls (PCBs) to have caused adverse effects.[71] Although it is likely that terns were adversely affected, at least locally, this remain conjectural. At the same period DDE had major adverse effects on common terns in freshwater environments in Canada.[72]

A monitoring scheme for organochlorine contaminants in common terns and other coastal birds in the Wadden Sea (Netherlands–Germany–Denmark) has been in operation since 1996, incorporating measurements made since 1981.[73]

Concentrations of organochlorine pesticides and PCBs have decreased steadily since 1981 or earlier and are now below levels of concern, although there was evidence that PCBs caused hatching failures in common terns as recently as 1993.[74] New contaminants causing current concern are the classes of brominated flame retardants known as PBDEs and HCBDs, which are occurring at increasing concentrations in aquatic ecosystems and may be approaching levels that cause adverse effects in fish-eating birds. Both PBDEs and HCBDs have been detected at potentially toxic levels in common and Arctic terns from the Netherlands and Norway.[75] However, none of these contaminants is currently being monitored in terns or other fish-eating birds in Britain and Ireland.

There is little evidence that terns in Britain or Ireland are being adversely affected by any other form of pollution. Most of the major oil spills in recent decades have occurred in winter, although the *Torrey Canyon* and *Sea Empress* spills occurred in mid-March and could have affected Sandwich terns passing through Cornwall or southwest Wales on spring migration. Terns are exposed to toxic forms of mercury via marine food chains, but much of this mercury is of natural origin and there is no evidence of adverse effects.[76]

Diseases, parasites and biological toxins

We know very little about what terns die of, except that they usually die where we do not find them. Very few adult terns are found dead during the breeding season or during the post-breeding period, and most of those that are found have been killed by predators. Hence, it appears that most adult terns die on migration or in their winter quarters. Even in the winter quarters, there have been very few mass mortality events that would suggest epidemics of diseases, outbreaks of parasites or poisonings. We know of only two cases where numbers of terns were found dead and confirmed to have died from diseases. In the first incident, large numbers of common terns were found dead in South Africa in April and May 1961, and were found to have died from a virulent form of influenza.[77] The dates and location suggest that these would have been 1-year-old birds from a northern European population (see Chapter 8). In the second incident, large numbers of common and Arctic terns died from avian cholera at a breeding colony in the USA in 1988.[78] Avian cholera is a bacterial disease usually found in wildfowl, and it is possible that the terns contracted it from common eiders breeding on the same island. These two cases seem to have been isolated, and there is nothing to suggest that there is a widespread threat to tern populations.

Two incidents have been reported in Britain in which dozens or hundreds of common and Arctic terns died from paralytic shellfish poisoning (PSP). These

FIG 194. Common tern dying from paralytic shellfish poisoning (PSP). This is caused by a toxin produced by dinoflagellate algae, whose periodic outbreaks are known as 'red tides'. The toxin accumulates in shellfish (occasionally in fish) and poisons their consumers. It causes paralysis of the skeletal muscles and, in sufficient doses, death from respiratory failure. Monomoy, USA. (Peter Trull)

occurred at the Farne Islands and Coquet Island in 1968 and 1975.[79] PSP results from ingesting a toxin that is produced by dinoflagellate algae, whose periodic outbreaks, or 'blooms', are known as 'red tides' because they sometimes become abundant enough to turn the sea surface red. The toxin is accumulated mainly by shellfish and can poison consumers of shellfish, including birds and humans. It acts by blocking propagation of nerve impulses, causing paralysis of the skeletal muscles (Fig. 194) and – in sufficient doses – death from respiratory failure. The few reported cases involving fish-eating birds resulted from accumulation of the toxin by sandeels, and it is not known why or how this occurred. Study of an incident in the USA indicated that most terns were able to detect the toxin and saved their lives by vomiting up their meals: most of the birds that died were females about to lay eggs, which for some reason were unable to vomit quickly enough.[80] 'Red tides' are thought to be promoted by organic pollution and seemed to be increasing in frequency and severity in the 1960s and 1970s, but industrial and municipal effluents are better treated nowadays and there have been no recurrences.

TWO MAJOR THREATS THAT ARE NOT BEING ADDRESSED

Mortality in the winter quarters

We remarked earlier that conservation programmes for terns are increasingly being integrated with demographic studies that can identify which parts of the life cycle are most critical for maintaining populations. It is ironic that these studies are now telling us that most of our conservation efforts are not tackling the most important threats to terns. Terns are long-lived birds, and demographic theory indicates that population trends in long-lived birds are much more strongly influenced by changes in survival rates than by changes in reproductive rates (see Appendix 1). The most important of the demographic factors that influence population changes is the survival rate of adults, and the second most important is the survival rate of young birds from fledging to recruitment. Put simply, a tern faced with something such as a predator that threatens its own life as well as that of its eggs or chicks serves its interests best if it acts to save its own life rather than defending the eggs or chicks, because it will have many opportunities to breed again in later years. Once a tern has raised a chick to the point of fledging, it is more important to nurture that chick to the point of independence than to attempt to raise another chick. The terns do not, of course, make these calculations consciously, but natural selection has taken account of these demographic relationships and has shaped the birds' behaviour in such a way as to maximise their survival rates, even when this requires sacrificing their chicks and forgoing reproduction for another year.

For these reasons, an optimal allocation of conservation efforts for terns would place high priority on measures to increase survival rates rather than on measures to improve breeding success. That is the exact opposite of what is actually done. Except for programmes to control mink, almost all of the conservation programmes for terns in Britain and Ireland are designed to maintain or increase breeding success, and virtually nothing is done to increase survival. Even when peregrine falcons are killing adult or juvenile terns, we refrain from intervening because the peregrines themselves are valued.

The dilemma is that very little is known about how to increase tern survival rates. As we remarked earlier, there is a real lack of information about where, when and how most terns die once they have fledged, though it is believed that most die during migration or in the winter quarters. That is, most die away from Britain and Ireland and outside the jurisdiction of our governments or the purview of most of our NGOs. Devoting our resources towards protecting and managing terns at the breeding sites makes good sense, in so far as we have few opportunities to conserve them in other ways. But that does not rule out doing what we can to conserve terns in their winter quarters.

British and Irish terns winter mainly in West Africa, and it has long been known from ringing recoveries that many terns are killed there by humans. The dramatic crash in numbers of roseate terns in the late 1960s and 1970s focused attention on this issue, because the crash occurred simultaneously throughout the breeding range, so a colony-specific factor could not have been responsible. About 2.5 per cent of all the roseate terns ringed in Britain and Ireland were being reported from West Africa, mainly in Ghana. Investigations on the Ghanaian coast (Fig. 195) revealed that large numbers of terns, mostly Sandwich and roseate terns and including many adult roseates, were being trapped by small boys for recreation or for food (Figs 196 and 197). The birds were caught mainly in snares laid out on beaches or on baited hooks, using dead fish as bait (Fig. 198). In October–November 1979, 20–25 terns were being caught every day at a single pierhead.[81] In response to this conservation crisis, the RSPB and the International Council for Bird Preservation approached the government of

FIG 195. Muni lagoon, near Winneba, Ghana. Large numbers of terns occur along the coast of Ghana in winter and roost on the beaches or in the lagoons. (Chris Gomersall)

FIG 196. Roseate tern trapped by boys on a beach in Ghana. Large numbers of terns were caught (mainly for recreation) in Ghana and other countries in West Africa in the 1970s and 1980s. Although most of the terns caught were Sandwich, common or black terns, this trapping seems to have been disproportionately damaging to roseate tern populations. An educational programme focused on coastal villages has raised awareness about the value of wildlife throughout Ghana and is said to have stopped the practice of trapping terns. (RSPB/Chris Gomersall)

FIG 197. Bracelet of tern rings worn by a man at Winneba, Ghana, October 1986. (Chris Gomersall)

FIG 198. Boy setting a snare for terns on a beach in Ghana, using part of a dead fish as bait. Terns do not normally take dead fish, but many terns in the winter quarters are attracted to bait such as this, perhaps because they have been unable to catch live fish close to the shore. (Chris Gomersall)

Ghana and negotiated a memorandum of agreement, establishing the *Save the Seashore Birds Project – Ghana* in 1984. This agreement was perhaps the first to be made between private conservation organisations in a developed country and the government of a developing country, and provided a model for subsequent programmes of this type.

The *Save the Seashore Birds Project* included coastal surveys, site evaluation, research, species and site protection and management, legal protection for shorebirds and seabirds, training for local personnel, and a broad-scale education programme targeted to the coastal villages. Many wildlife clubs were formed for young people, and within a few years it was thought that trapping of terns had virtually ceased. The project contributed to the formation of the now-flourishing Wildlife Society of Ghana and to raising of awareness about the value of wildlife throughout the country. It has been expanded through the Centre for African Wildlife to provide training for wildlife professionals and to develop conservation projects in other countries of West Africa, including Nigeria, Togo, Sierra Leone, Liberia, the Gambia and Senegal.[82]

The *Save the Seashore Birds Project* was thus a success in many ways. Roseate tern populations in western Europe started to increase in the early 1990s and have been increasing ever since. An international recovery plan for the roseate tern in the East Atlantic was formulated in 1995,[83] and management programmes are running in many countries.

Trapping of terns in the winter quarters was clearly a major factor in the population crash of European roseate terns, and the *Save the Seashore Birds Project* was probably an important factor in their recovery. However, there is little precise information on the extent or intensity of tern trapping before, during or after the project. Adrian del Nevo spent six winters between 1987 and 1992 searching for roseate terns and recording tern trapping in Ghana and other West African countries on behalf of the RSPB.[84] He found that terns were still being trapped at many places along the coast of Ghana as late as October–December 1989, the fifth year of the project. In a systematic survey of the coast, he found that up to five terns were being trapped per hour at 11 of 23 sites that he visited. A rough calculation suggested that about 2,000 terns were being trapped per month along the Ghana coast: most of these were black or common terns, but about 3 per cent were roseates. The population crash of roseate terns had actually occurred much earlier, between 1967 and 1980, and the highest rate of recoveries of ringed birds was between 1967 and 1974. By the time the *Save the Seashore Birds Project* started in 1985, the recovery rate had dropped below its pre-1967 level and the European population had been more or less stationary since 1980; it did not begin to increase until 1992, the eighth year of the project (see Fig. 131 in

Chapter 9).[85] Del Nevo was unable to find roseate terns anywhere along the West African coast after December in any year, and he concluded that they might have spent the latter part of the winter at sea. Apart from the fragmentary information on trapping, very little is known about the threats posed to terns in their winter quarters in Africa. Conservation of our terns there may be more complex and difficult than has been envisaged to date.

Climate change

In the medium term, climate change is probably the greatest threat posed to seabirds, including terns. Over the next 30–100 years, it is predicted that air and sea temperatures will increase by several degrees Celsius, sea levels will rise, and ocean circulation patterns, marine ecosystems and food webs may change in ways that cannot yet be predicted.

With superficial analysis, it could be posited that climate change will provide net benefits for British and Irish terns. Little, Sandwich and roseate terns are close to their northern limits here and a warmer climate might suit them better. In at least one case – little tern – there are substantial populations to the south that could move north into our area. Only the Arctic tern will be forced to retreat. Other tern species that breed a short distance to the south, such as gull-billed and whiskered terns, might extend their ranges north into Britain and Ireland. Rising sea levels will probably fragment barrier beach systems such as those of East Anglia and may form new islands.

With more thoughtful analysis, the prospects for terns seem much less favourable. Increased sea-surface temperatures in the eastern North Atlantic Ocean and North Sea have already caused profound changes in marine ecosystems, with major declines in the species of fish most important as food for terns. To date, effects on terns have only been manifested clearly in the breeding failures of Arctic terns in the Northern Isles and eastern Scotland and of common terns on the continental side of the North Sea (see under *Food limitation and food availability*, above). For unknown reasons, terns in other parts of Britain and Ireland do not seem to have been affected as yet. However, sea temperatures have risen and marine food webs have changed over a wide area of the eastern North Atlantic, not just in parts of the North Sea.[86] It seems likely that the effects of these changes will eventually spread to the parts of our coasts where the terns' food supply has not yet changed. It is uncertain whether the 'regime shift' in the North Atlantic is permanent or represents a cyclic process acting over a time-scale of decades, so that the more favourable cooler sea-surface temperatures will eventually return. Even if it is a cyclic phenomenon, however, it is to be expected that the warming climate will make the unfavourable warm periods longer and the favourable cool periods shorter. Thus, the prognosis for terns in the eastern North Atlantic, including Britain and Ireland, is not good.

The extent to which terns remaining in Britain and Ireland could adapt to a changing climate is uncertain. A study of terns at the Farne Islands – probably the only site in Britain and Ireland with records over such a long period – showed that Arctic terns advanced their arrival dates by 13 days and Sandwich and common terns by 20 days between 1971 and 2006. However, only the Arctic tern started to lay eggs significantly earlier, by about seven days over the 35-year period.[87] This suggests that terns have only limited ability to adjust their breeding seasons to the warming climate. The concern is that the fish on which the terns depend and the copepods on which the fish depend will adjust their seasonal cycles faster. Natural selection has acted over long periods to make the terns' breeding season coincide with the optimum period for raising young, including a peak in the available food supply. It is feared that climate change may shift the seasonal cycle in food availability too rapidly for the terns, with their long generation times, to adapt fast enough.

With regard to rising sea level, although this might hypothetically create more islands in some areas, it will also make many current breeding sites unsuitable. This is a particular problem for little terns, which nest at sites very close to sea level and already suffer from flooding during high tides and summer storms. Rising sea levels are likely to make many of their current nesting sites untenable, while new sites will be generated more slowly. And in any case, humans depend on the present-day barrier islands and barrier beaches as defences against the sea and value them as places of recreation. When sea levels continue to rise and the barrier beaches begin to fragment, there will be intense political pressure to use engineering measures to maintain them intact as long as possible. As human societies struggle to adapt to climate change and rising sea level, the interests of wildlife are likely to receive very low priority.

On balance, therefore, climate change is much more likely to harm tern populations than to help them. The uncertainties are very great, however, and it is impossible to forecast what may happen a few decades – or even a few years – into the future. Without firm forecasts, it is impossible to plan conservation measures that will help tern populations to adapt. Talented biologists have spent decades trying to unravel how seabird populations interact with their prey in the variable marine environment, but understanding of these relationships is still incomplete. Now that the marine environment is changing faster than our knowledge is evolving, it is unlikely that we will be able to predict the effects of climate change until they have actually occurred.

THE PROGNOSIS FOR TERN CONSERVATION

The conservation of birds, including terns, has made enormous strides in the last 60 years. In the 1950s, there were a few sanctuaries where terns were protected and the locations of many of the larger breeding colonies were known, but the total populations, their trends and the factors influencing them were largely unknown. Today, we have a network of managed sites, the populations and their breeding success are monitored annually, data are held in readily accessible databases, the population trends are known, and we have a reasonable understanding of limiting factors, at least those affecting breeding success. Most of the terns breeding in Britain and Ireland are at sites that are managed in one way or another, but we know that this kind of management will have to be continued indefinitely if tern populations are to be maintained even at their present levels. In a phrase coined by Steven Kress of the National Audubon Society about terns in the USA, terns have become 'wards of the state' and will need perpetual guardianship if they are to continue to prosper. The authors of this book have confidence that future guardians will continue to protect the interests of their charges, probably even more effectively than is being done today. However, the guardians already face problems that have never been tackled before, and future guardians will need greater knowledge, wisdom and informed judgement to protect the interests of their wards.

CHAPTER 12

Vagrants, Passage Migrants and Occasional Breeders

FIFTEEN SPECIES OR SUBSPECIES of terns have been recorded in Britain and Ireland as migrants, vagrants or occasional breeders, but do not breed here at the present day. The common names, scientific names and taxonomy used throughout this chapter are those adopted by the British Ornithologists' Union (BOU), but with little and least terns treated as separate species and with the 'crested' terns assigned to the genus *Thalasseus* (see endnote 1 in Chapter 1). For records of vagrants, we rely on the assessments of each record by the British Birds Rarities Committee (BBRC) and the Irish Rare Birds Committee (IRBC), and of first records by the British Ornithologists' Union Records Committee (BOURC),[1] updated from various sources for the most recent records to the end of 2011. We have not attempted to make independent judgements about the validity of specific records of vagrants. One additional subspecies, the Eastern common tern (*Sterna hirundo longipennis*), has been reported and photographed at Minsmere, Suffolk, on 14 May 2011, but this record has not yet been assessed by the BOURC.

For records of vagrants in Europe (outside Britain and Ireland) we have used www.tarsiger.com (English-language version) as our source, updated in a few instances with records that have been accepted by national review committees but have not yet found their way into the tarsiger.com database.

An explanation is required for including the black tern in this chapter. The black tern was a common breeding bird in eastern Britain during the eighteenth century and then experienced a large decline in numbers during the nineteenth century. It was rare by the 1850s and eventually became extinct about 1884. There was some spasmodic breeding of very small numbers during the 1960s and 1970s, but there are no recent successful breeding records apart for an adult seen with three chicks in eastern Britain in 1983 (see section on black tern below). Therefore the black tern is not in the same category as our five well-established and regular breeding terns, yet it is neither scarce nor a true vagrant in the sense of the other species listed in this chapter. The BOU has categorised the black tern as a 'former breeder, casual breeder and passage migrant', while the American subspecies (*Chlidonias niger surinamensis*) is a true vagrant to our islands.[2] So the black tern falls uneasily between being considered as one of our breeding species and assigned a chapter to itself, and being treated in this chapter. As it is not a regular and established breeder we decided to include it here.

ALEUTIAN TERN

Until recently the Aleutian tern was included in the genus *Sterna*, but it is now placed in the genus *Onychoprion* as one of the 'brown-winged' terns. This is the only member of the genus that breeds at temperate and subarctic latitudes: the other three species are tropical and oceanic (see sooty and bridled terns, below, and Chapter 1).

The Aleutian tern nests in loose colonies and has a wide breeding range around the northern Pacific Ocean, from southeast Siberia to western Alaska, including the Aleutian Islands. It is widely scattered and difficult to count, but the most recent estimate of the world population is about 15,000 pairs.[3] Its wintering areas are largely unknown but are thought to extend from the Philippines to the Malay Peninsula and perhaps to the Indian Ocean. During migration large numbers pass off the Chinese coast at Hong Kong.[4]

The Aleutian tern closely resembles the common tern in size and proportions but its black bill is shorter and narrower. In summer plumage it is distinguished by its slate-grey underparts and mantle, white rump and tail, and white forehead (Fig. 199). Its legs are black. It flies with slower and deeper wing-beats than the common tern. Against the light only the inner primaries are translucent while a narrow dark bar is visible at the tips of the secondaries on the underwing. In winter plumage this dark bar on the secondaries is the best way to distinguish it from similar species.[5]

This is the rarest vagrant tern to Britain and Ireland, and indeed to the Western Palearctic, with only one record of an adult observed and photographed on the Farne Islands, Northumberland, on 28–29 May 1979.[6] The species has not otherwise been recorded outside the North Pacific Ocean,[7] and it is hard to

FIG 199. Aleutian tern. This species resembles the sooty and bridled terns in having a dark back and upperwings and a white forehead in all plumages, but it is distinguished by the narrow dark bar at the tips of the secondaries on the underwing. In breeding plumage it is distinguished from all similar terns by its slate-grey underparts. It has a fine black bill and a white tail. Alaska, USA. (Paul Kelly)

imagine how this particular bird might have reached European waters. However, it is not the only known Pacific breeding tern to have done this, the elegant tern being the other species.

SOOTY TERN

The sooty tern is the most abundant and one of the most widely distributed of tropical seabirds, breeding on islands around the world between about latitudes 28° N and 31° S, with a global population in the order of 60–80 million adults. Those breeding in the Caribbean and the Gulf of Mexico have been estimated at 230,000–400,000 pairs, and those breeding on the tropical South Atlantic islands number some 450,000 pairs.[8] One or two pairs have nested sporadically in the Azores since 1982, and a few on islands off Senegal and in the Gulf of Guinea.[9] Otherwise, it does not nest anywhere else in the eastern North Atlantic Ocean.

The sooty tern is slightly smaller than the Sandwich tern. It has characteristic long wings and a long tail with very dark upperparts. It is white below, and the underwing shows contrasting black coverts and black flight feathers.[10] It has a deeply forked tail, and the white forehead extends back only as far as the eye and

FIG 200. Adult sooty tern. This species is distinguished from the bridled and Aleutian terns by its near-black upperparts, including upperwings and tail. The underparts are white and the white V on the forehead does not extend behind the eye. Juveniles are sooty brown with lighter belly and underwings and white speckling on the back and upperwings. Cemlyn Bay, Anglesey. (Tony Mills)

not beyond it as in the bridled tern (Fig. 200). Juveniles are entirely sooty-brown with white spots on the back and wings.

Opinion is divided on the origin of vagrant sooty terns in northwest Europe. They are rare anywhere in the eastern North Atlantic and may not breed there regularly. They are very rare in waters off Spain and Portugal,[11] so it seems unlikely that vagrants would be drawn from the south. It seems more likely that they are of transatlantic origin, from the large population breeding on islands from the Yucatan to the Florida Gulf coast and the Bahamas.[12] Birds from this population disperse north down the Gulf Stream in late summer and are sporadically transported far to the north and east by hurricanes.[13] Sooty terns and other seabirds become trapped in the eye of a hurricane and are unable to escape because of the violent winds surrounding it. They then travel with the hurricane until the eye dissipates, which may be hundreds or thousands of kilometres from their starting point.

In Britain there were 13 records of sooty terns before the end of 1949 and a further 11 between 1950 and the end of 2011. The first bird recorded in Britain was shot at the River Dove, near Tutbury, Staffordshire, in October 1852. Most of the subsequent birds have been recorded during the period June to August, peaking in July (Fig. 201). Virtually all have been reported in southern, southeastern and eastern Britain (Fig. 202). Two have been recorded

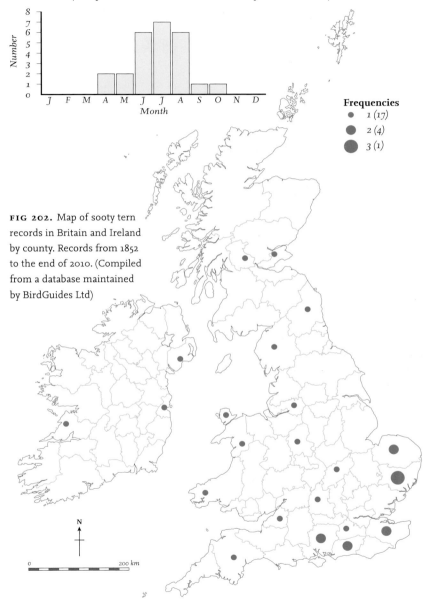

FIG 201. Histogram of sooty tern records in Britain and Ireland by month when known. (Compiled from a database maintained by BirdGuides Ltd)

Frequencies
- 1 (17)
- 2 (4)
- 3 (1)

FIG 202. Map of sooty tern records in Britain and Ireland by county. Records from 1852 to the end of 2010. (Compiled from a database maintained by BirdGuides Ltd)

from Scotland, on the upper Forth and in Fife. During the summer of 2005 a sooty tern was tracked as it moved on a remarkable journey around the Irish Sea. It was first seen, although not positively identified, at Rhosneigr, Anglesey, on 5 July and was found two days later in an Arctic tern colony on the nearby Skerries. It was later seen in the tern colony at Cemlyn Bay, also in Anglesey (Fig. 200). It then moved across the Irish Sea appearing at Rockabill, Co. Dublin, on 11 and 12 July. It went back to Cemlyn Bay and then flew out to sea on 26 July. What was probably the same bird was seen on 3–6 August off the coast of Co. Down and then on 7–15 August off the coast of Co. Dublin. The last sighting, probably of the same bird, was when it flew past Strumble Head, Pembrokeshire, in late August.[14]

There have been two records from Ireland up to the end of 2010: one adult at the Bridges of Ross, Co. Clare, on 23 July 2002, and the adult referred to above, seen at several places along the east coast in July–August 2005.[15] Other European records have been from France, Denmark, Sweden, Iceland, Spain, the Selvagens (Madeira) and the Canary Islands.[16]

BRIDLED TERN

The bridled tern is widespread in tropical oceans, but is less pelagic than the sooty tern, being absent from remote islands and feeding closer inshore. The Atlantic subspecies (*Onychoprion anaethetus melanoptera*) breeds in the eastern Caribbean and the Bahamas. It also breeds in West Africa from Mauritania to the Gulf of Guinea and (at least formerly) in Spanish Sahara.[17] There are approximately 8,400 breeding pairs in the West Indies, a significant proportion of the total Atlantic breeding populations.[18] The bridled tern is smaller than the otherwise similar sooty tern and is distinguished from it by its whitish collar around the nape, greyer back, rump and tail, and narrower white supercilium, extending behind the eye (Fig. 203).

It is most likely to be seen in Britain during the summer, from June to August, when birds from the Caribbean population disperse north along the Gulf Stream and may follow the North Atlantic Drift towards Europe (Fig. 204). Prior to 1950 there was only one record, an adult male found dead at Dungeness, Kent, on 19 November 1931. From 1950 to the end of 2011 an additional 21 records had been accepted by the BBRC. Since then one more record has been accepted to 27 July 2011. The locations of records cover most of Britain, from Orkney to Wales, the Midlands and southern England (Fig. 205). There is one record from Ireland, a corpse washed up on North Bull Island, Co. Dublin, in

FIG 203. Adult bridled tern. This species is distinguished from the otherwise similar sooty tern by lighter, greyish-brown upperparts, a white outer edge to the tail and a narrow white supercilium extending back behind the eye. North Carolina, USA. (Glen Tepke)

1953.[19] Because there was a reasonable doubt that a bird found dead on the tide line would have occurred in a natural state, this record was placed in category D (not likely to have occurred in a wild state) and consequently does not form part of the Irish list.

Elsewhere in Europe the bridled tern has been recorded, up to the end of 2010, in the Azores (14), France (3), Denmark (3), Spain (2), the Netherlands (2), Sweden (2), Belgium (1) and Norway (1). As in Britain and Ireland, most of the records have been between June and August.

FIG 204. Histogram of bridled tern records in Britain and Ireland by month of first recording. (Compiled from a database maintained by BirdGuides Ltd)

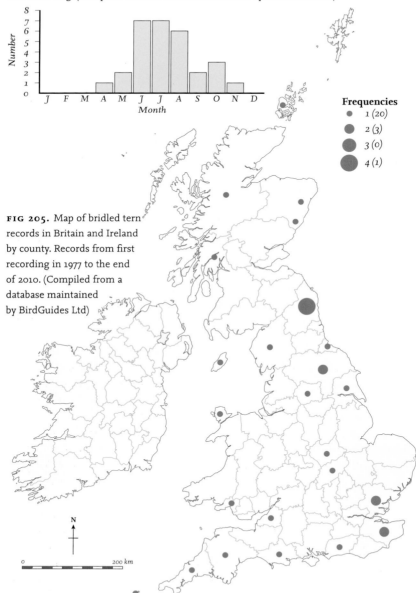

FIG 205. Map of bridled tern records in Britain and Ireland by county. Records from first recording in 1977 to the end of 2010. (Compiled from a database maintained by BirdGuides Ltd)

LEAST TERN

The least tern is very similar to our little tern and is often treated as part of the same species. It breeds widely along coastal beaches and major interior rivers of North America and winters along coasts of Central and South America (see Fig. 12 in Chapter 1). There are five subspecies, but a recent genetic study has found only minor differences among the three populations that breed in the USA, and has questioned their status as distinct subspecies.[20] The issue has important implications for conservation, because two of the 'subspecies' are currently classified as endangered and threatened in the USA, so that they are intensively managed, but the species as a whole is not threatened. The other two 'subspecies' have been described from locations in western Mexico and their validity is even more uncertain.[21]

Like little terns, least terns breed in a large number of small colonies and change sites frequently, so that they are very difficult to count. It has been estimated that there are about 30,000 pairs of all subspecies in North America and the Caribbean, of which more than 20,000 pairs breed along the Atlantic and Gulf of Mexico coasts of the USA and less than 3,000 pairs in the Caribbean.[22]

The least tern can, with some difficulty, be separated from the little tern by plumage detail. It is slightly smaller than the little tern, with shorter legs and a relatively slimmer bill, and adults usually have longer tail-streamers. The rump and tail are grey, not white, and there is no obvious contrast between the colours of the back, rump and tail (see Fig. 78 in Chapter 6). It has a much squeakier call than the little tern, which is the most diagnostic feature.

So far (to November 2011) there has been only one accepted record of the least tern in Britain and the Western Palearctic. It was discovered in the little tern colony at East Rye Harbour Local Nature Reserve, East Sussex, on 8 June 1983, and remained there until 30 June. It then returned annually until 1992, when it was last recorded on 12 July. It had a noticeably greyer rump and central tail feathers than nearby little terns. However, it was the comparison of sound recordings with those of the least and little terns that clinched its identification, a rare case where closely related species have had to be separated by voice. The record has been accepted by the BOURC as an individual of the North American *antillarum/athalassos/browni* group. The sound recordings also ruled out the possibility that the bird might have belonged to the African subspecies of the little tern (*Sternula albifrons guineae*). It was observed displaying and presenting fish to little terns, which suggested that it was a male. There was no evidence that it was breeding, however. What was assumed to be the same bird was seen in little tern colonies in West Sussex and Essex from 29 June to 1 July 1991.[23]

GULL-BILLED TERN

The gull-billed tern has a cosmopolitan but very discontinuous distribution around the world, breeding in all continents except Antarctica. The nominate subspecies (*Gelochelidon nilotica nilotica*) breeds in southern Europe and North and West Africa, and from the Middle East to Kazakhstan, Manchuria, Pakistan and perhaps even Sri Lanka. The Western Palearctic population is estimated at 9,500–12,000 pairs.[24] Only about 4,000 pairs breed in western Europe, mainly in Spain. A discrete northern population in Denmark and northwest Germany formerly included several hundred pairs, but this has declined to only one or two pairs in Denmark in 2001 and 50 pairs in Germany in 1998–99.[25] The western European population winters in coastal West Africa south to the Gulf of Guinea (Nigeria and Chad).

This is a gull-like tern, the size of a Sandwich tern but distinguished from it by a totally black and broader, almost stubby bill, a shallowly forked grey tail, a stockier build, broader wings and heavy flight. In flight the broad head and bill appear to merge into each other and it resembles a gull, lacking the up-and-down body movement of most of the smaller terns (Fig. 206). In winter and juvenile plumages its head becomes mainly white with distinctive dark ear-patches (Fig. 207). Sandwich terns always have black around the nape, but they become white on the forehead and forecrown in June–July while gull-billed terns are still largely black.[26]

FIG 206. Adult gull-billed tern. This species is superficially similar to the Sandwich tern, but is thicker-set and more gull-like, with broader wings, a shorter tail and heavier flight. Its bill is shorter, thicker and entirely black. The forehead and forecrown remain mostly black until late summer, whereas Sandwich terns have mostly white foreheads by June. (John N. Murphy)

FIG 207. Immature gull-billed tern. In immature and winter plumage, gull-billed terns have mostly white heads with dark ear-patches. Forster's terns have similar head-patterns but are much smaller. Plymouth, USA. (Jim Fenton)

In Britain, one pair of gull-billed terns bred at Abberton Reservoir, Essex, in 1950 and possibly in 1949.[27] It is otherwise a scarce vagrant, reported about six times each year. A total of 51 were recorded in Britain up to the end of 1949 and a further 289 between 1950 and the end of 2011.[28] There have been sixteen records in Ireland up to the end of 2011.[29]

Most birds in Britain have occurred in May (close to 80 records), with good numbers in June, July and August and fewer in September (Fig. 208). They have occurred with greatest frequency in southeastern and eastern Britain and north to southern Scotland (Fig. 209). Spring records have been more concentrated in southeast Britain, while there are some scattered summer records. It has been claimed that numbers of records in Britain and Ireland have decreased in recent years, possibly reflecting the decrease in the German and Danish breeding populations.[30] However, the numbers of records in Britain and Ireland during the last three decades up to 2008 have actually been 41, 31 and 43 respectively, hardly a decrease in numbers. In Ireland they have indeed become more regular in recent years, with a total of 16 records to the end of 2006, including nine individuals since 2000, although there have been no records since 2006.[31]

It is perhaps more likely that many or most birds that reach Britain and Ireland are derived from the breeding population in southwest Europe, either 'overshooting' on spring migration or dispersing north after breeding.

FIG 208. Histogram of gull-billed tern records in Britain and Ireland by month when month of first recording is known. (Compiled from a database maintained by BirdGuides Ltd)

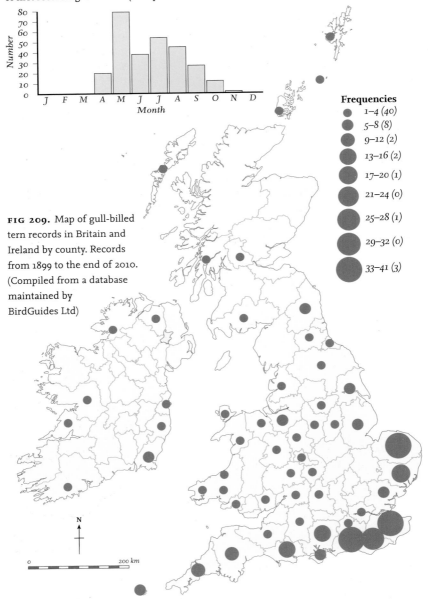

FIG 209. Map of gull-billed tern records in Britain and Ireland by county. Records from 1899 to the end of 2010. (Compiled from a database maintained by BirdGuides Ltd)

Frequencies

- 1–4 (40)
- 5–8 (8)
- 9–12 (2)
- 13–16 (2)
- 17–20 (1)
- 21–24 (0)
- 25–28 (1)
- 29–32 (0)
- 33–41 (3)

N

0   200 km

CASPIAN TERN

Like the gull-billed tern, the Caspian tern has a cosmopolitan, highly scattered breeding distribution. It occurs on every continent except South America and Antarctica. Almost all of the north European population is located in coastal habitats around the Baltic Sea with colonies varying in size from two to 100 pairs. There are also many isolated single pairs. Largest numbers breed in Finland (800–900 pairs in 2000–01), Sweden (450–470 pairs in 1999–2000) and Estonia (250–400 pairs in 2000–01).[32] The Baltic population has fluctuated greatly in recent years, declining from 2,200 pairs in 1971 to 1,500 pairs in 1999–2001. There are also about 2,500 pairs in southeast Europe and Turkey[33] and 15,000–20,000 pairs in West Africa. The European population winters in coastal West Africa, south to the Gulf of Guinea. It is often found on large bodies of fresh water as well as along the coast.

The Caspian tern is by far the largest tern, almost the size of a herring gull, and has an enormous orange-red bill (Fig. 210; see also Fig. 7 in Chapter 1). The wings are pointed with dark undersides to the primaries contrasting with the all-pale uppersides, so that the wings flash black and white as the tern flies around. In summer the crown is wholly black. In winter the crown is mottled

FIG 210. Adult Caspian tern. This is by far the largest tern, with an enormous orange-red bill and black legs. The undersides of the primaries are black, in striking contrast to the white on the rest of the underwing. See also Fig. 7 in Chapter 1. Plymouth, USA. (Jim Fenton)

FIG 211. First-winter Caspian tern. Immatures and winter adults have grey-brown or dark grey crowns with speckled foreheads. Florida, USA. (Shawn Carey)

white (Fig. 211). Juveniles have the crown and forehead mottled brownish-black, and the upperparts and wing-coverts have an intricate pattern of brownish-grey chevrons. In flight the Caspian tern has a majestic and purposeful flight with slow, shallow wing-beats.[34]

This is the third most numerous vagrant tern recorded in Britain after the gull-billed and white-winged terns, with 26 records up to the end of 1949 and then a further 266 sightings from 1950 to the end of 2011.[35] The first British record was of an immature shot at Breydon Water, Norfolk, in October 1825. Despite its frequent occurrence in Britain there have been only ten records in Ireland up to the end of 2011, half of them from Co. Cork and between 19 June and 18 August.[36]

Most occurrences in Britain have been in mid-summer, especially July, rather than in the spring or autumn (Fig. 212). Records have been concentrated in east and southeast England (Fig. 213), which suggests that most of the birds arriving in Britain have originated from the Baltic population. This is supported by three ringing recoveries. One bird, whose remains were found in a fox earth at Haddon, Cambridgeshire, in July 1972, had been ringed as a nestling in Finland in 1970. Another, found long dead on the shoreline at West Sandwick, Yell, Shetland, in early August 1976, had been ringed as a nestling near Stockholm, Sweden, in 1975. A third, also ringed in Sweden, was found in Shetland in 1976.[37]

There is one transatlantic recovery of a bird ringed as a juvenile at Beaver Island, Lake Michigan, USA, on 14 July 1927 and found dead on the tideline at Whitby, Yorkshire, in August 1939.

FIG 212. Histogram of Caspian tern records in Britain and Ireland by month. Month of first recording when known. (Compiled from a database maintained by BirdGuides Ltd)

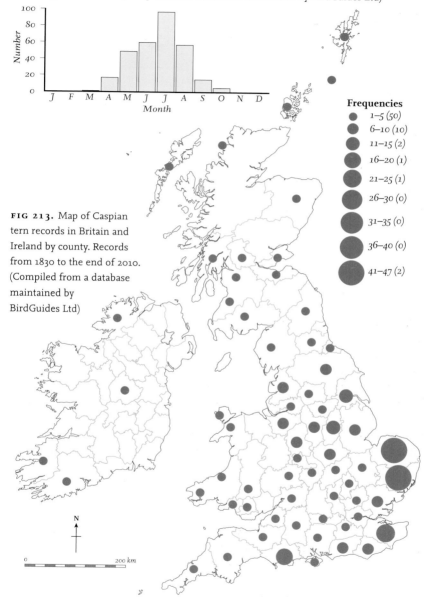

FIG 213. Map of Caspian tern records in Britain and Ireland by county. Records from 1830 to the end of 2010. (Compiled from a database maintained by BirdGuides Ltd)

Frequencies

1–5 (50)
6–10 (10)
11–15 (2)
16–20 (1)
21–25 (1)
26–30 (0)
31–35 (0)
36–40 (0)
41–47 (2)

WHISKERED TERN

The whiskered tern has a scattered breeding distribution throughout the temperate zones of Europe and Asia, from Portugal and France in the west to Kazakhstan in the east. There are other breeding populations in Africa, India, east Asia and Australia. Like other 'marsh' terns, it breeds only in freshwater marshes with emergent vegetation, where it builds floating nests. Unlike the black tern, it winters mainly on fresh waters and rarely occurs along the coast except on migration.

It is an opportunistic and erratic breeder in Europe. It has been estimated that there are 5,000–13,000 breeding pairs in western Europe and the west Mediterranean. The nearest breeding birds are within 400 km of southern England in central and western France. There were some 2,300–2,400 pairs in France in 2002. Very small numbers have bred sporadically in Belgium, the Netherlands and Germany, while there were 700–800 pairs in Poland in 2000.[38] The European population winters in tropical West and central Africa.

FIG 214. Adult whiskered tern. Adults in breeding plumage are readily distinguished from other 'marsh' terns by their dark red bills and white cheeks separating the black cap from the grey underparts. This pattern is reminiscent of Arctic tern, but the bird's shape and flight are similar to those of the black tern. Lesbos, Greece. (Dick Hoogenboom)

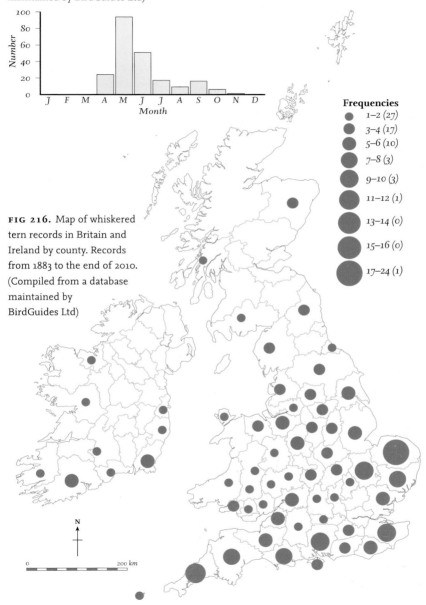

FIG 215. Histogram of whiskered tern records in Britain and Ireland by month. Records from 1883 to the end of 2010 for which month of occurrence is known. (Compiled from a database maintained by BirdGuides Ltd)

FIG 216. Map of whiskered tern records in Britain and Ireland by county. Records from 1883 to the end of 2010. (Compiled from a database maintained by BirdGuides Ltd)

Frequencies

1–2 (27)
3–4 (17)
5–6 (10)
7–8 (3)
9–10 (3)
11–12 (1)
13–14 (0)
15–16 (0)
17–24 (1)

The whiskered tern resembles the black tern, but it has longer and broader wings with a deeply forked tail, reminiscent of the *Sterna* species. The flight is similar to the black tern's, dipping towards the water surface. It is distinguished from the other 'marsh' terns by its dark red bill and the conspicuous white cheeks between its black crown and dusky underparts (Fig. 214). Outside the breeding season it lacks the black shoulder-patches of the black tern and has a grey rump and nape.

The whiskered tern is the fourth commonest of the vagrant terns to visit Britain, with 23 records up to the end of 1949 and a further 181 from 1950 to the end of 2011.[39] Virtually all records have been in the period April to October, with three-quarters in the spring, peaking in May and during the first part of June (Fig. 215). There have been notable spring influxes, for example in 1970 when nine were recorded in Britain between 19 April and 28 June, four of them in five days in May. There was also an unprecedented flock of 11 at Willington Gravel Pits, Derbyshire, on 18 May 2009. Most of the records have been from coastal areas scattered across southern England, but with some penetrating as far north as Northumberland (Fig. 216). This suggests that most of the birds are 'overshoots' from the spring migration into France and Spain. There has been only one record in Scotland, from Dumfriesshire in May 1894. There have been 21 records from Ireland to the end of 2011, mostly in the southern counties of Wexford, Waterford, Cork and Kerry.[40] It has also been recorded from many other European countries outside its breeding range, including the Azores (seven records) and Iceland (three records).

BLACK TERN

The black tern is widespread and abundant in both the Old and New Worlds. In Europe and Asia it ranges from southern Scandinavia to southern Spain, east through Europe and western Asia to central Mongolia. Individuals from this area winter predominantly on the Atlantic coast of Africa, from the Western Sahara to South Africa. A different subspecies is also found breeding across much of Canada and in northern regions of the USA (see below). Like the other 'marsh' terns, it breeds only in freshwater marshes, where it builds floating nests in emergent vegetation. Unlike other 'marsh' terns, however, it winters mainly at sea and is sometimes encountered far from land.

It is widespread in Europe, where the estimated breeding population is 83,000–170,000 pairs. Numbers in Asia and North America are less well known but are thought to be of the same order of magnitude. There were 1,000–1,250

FIG 217. Immature black tern. Juveniles and winter adults have white underparts with dark 'shoulder-patches' at the sides of the breast. They have white foreheads and solid black hoods extending down behind the eye. Lady's Island Lake, Co. Wexford. (John N. Murphy)

pairs in the Netherlands in 1998–2000, and 175–190 pairs in France in 2002.[41] Numbers in both of these countries have declined greatly since the 1950s.

The black tern is a small tern with an all-black head and body in the breeding season, contrasting with grey wings, back and tail (see Fig. 8 in Chapter 1); autumn birds have grey upperparts and wings (darker than in *Sterna* terns), white underparts, distinctive black head markings and black 'shoulder-patches' extending from the dark mantle down the sides of the breast (Fig. 217).[42] Compared with *Sterna* terns, this tern has shorter wings and a shorter tail with only a shallow fork. Its flight is erratic and buoyant over water, dipping down and almost dancing over the water while picking up insects from the water surface.

Black terns bred in large numbers in the wetlands of southern and eastern England until the eighteenth century, but in the nineteenth century the population dwindled. They became scarce after the 1840s and eventually extinct as a consequence of extensive land drainage schemes and egg-collecting. Spasmodic breeding continued until 1884, when several pairs nested at Dungeness, Kent, but their eggs were stolen. It then became extinct as a British breeding species. It was suspected of breeding in Sussex in 1940–42 but doubt has been cast on these records.[43] Breeding was again attempted successfully in the Ouse Washes on the Cambridge/Norfolk border in 1966 and 1969. There were several nests, two with eggs, and three young were reared in 1966. In 1969 there were seven nests; young hatched in five nests but probably only one young bird fledged. One pair bred in East Anglia in 1970.[44] In Ireland, there were no historic records of nesting, but a pair bred at Lough Erne, Co. Fermanagh, in 1967, raising a single chick. A pair returned to the same site in 1968 but only one bird was seen in 1969 and breeding was not repeated. In 1975 a pair attempted to breed again but the nest and eggs were abandoned.[45] In 1978 one pair bred again in the Ouse Washes, but the eggs were stolen. In 1983 one adult with three young was recorded in eastern Britain.[46] There have been no breeding attempts since 1983, perhaps reflecting the decline in numbers in adjacent countries in continental Europe.

Today the black tern is regarded as a regular visitor to Britain and Ireland, occurring during spring and autumn migrations, often in large numbers. Flocks of 20 or 30 are not unusual when spring-passage numbers peak in May. The autumn migration of European birds commences towards the end of June. The juveniles disperse widely, as with most other European tern species. There are two major European staging sites where vast numbers of these terns gather. Up to 80,000 congregate in the Ijsselmeer region of the Netherlands, where the adults undergo a partial moult of their flight feathers. Peak numbers of adults occur there between July and August, followed by large numbers of juveniles in August–September (apparently juveniles do not stay with their parents during autumn staging and migration as in other terns). Up to 10,000 gather at the Elbe estuary, Germany. Those that gather around the Ijsselmeer are probably drawn from the whole Western Palearctic population and possibly also include some birds from western Siberia. During the period from the end of August to mid-September, as the birds move south through the North Sea and the English Channel, significant numbers can be deflected by weather conditions to appear on the east coast of Britain. Small numbers of adults start to arrive on the British east coast any time from the beginning of July onwards.

Another major staging area is in Mauritania, where 100,000 black terns were reported in 1972.[47] A total of 94 black terns have been ringed in Britain and Ireland on passage, but there have been no recoveries to indicate the wintering grounds of these birds in Africa. However, there are concentrations of black terns at sea from Senegal to Namibia, with most being found in the area from the Gulf of Guinea to Namibia. Birds ringed at staging sites in Europe have been recovered from Ghana to Angola, with largest numbers in Ghana probably reflecting the intensive trapping by small boys that was discussed in Chapter 11.[48] The return spring passage through Britain and Ireland is stronger than the autumn migration, with often large numbers passing through Britain under weather conditions that divert their migration to the northwest. For example, up to 1,400 birds were observed passing through the British Midlands on one day in May 1997.[49]

AMERICAN BLACK TERN

Although the American black tern (*Chlidonias niger surinamensis*) closely resembles the European subspecies (*Chlidonias niger niger*), it differs in several minor ways and can be identified by experts in all plumages, especially juveniles. It generally has shorter wings and longer legs than *niger*. Summer adults have a deep velvety-black head and underbody contrasting more clearly with the upperparts than in *niger* and in these respects more like the white-winged tern (Fig. 218). Birds in adult winter plumage can be distinguished from *niger* by broader dark patches on the sides of the breast which merge directly into grey flanks. Juveniles are distinguished by darker, less contrastingly patterned upperparts, and they also have a darker rump (Fig. 219).[50]

The American black tern is widespread in northern North America. It breeds across Canada from British Columbia east to New Brunswick, in most of the northern states of the USA and then south to central California. Its total numbers have been estimated at 50,000–250,000 pairs,[51] the wide range reflecting

FIG 218. Adult American black tern. In breeding plumage, American black terns are blacker on the head and breast than European black terns, contrasting more with the dark grey back and wings. This bird is just starting to moult and has a few white feathers on its face. Plymouth, USA. (Jim Fenton)

FIG 219. Immature American black tern. Juveniles have darker, less contrastingly patterned upperparts and darker rumps than European black terns. Winter adults have broader and more prominent 'shoulder-patches' than the European birds. Plymouth, USA. (Craig Gibson)

its scattered distribution among thousands of small marshes that are poorly surveyed. It is a long-distance migrant, wintering mainly at sea along coasts of Central America and northern South America, both Pacific and Caribbean. It is an uncommon non-breeding migrant on the Atlantic coast.

The American black tern, after the least and Aleutian terns, is one of the rarest of the vagrant terns in Britain and Ireland. From 1950 to the end of 2011 only four British records have been accepted by the BBRC, with none recorded up to 1949.[52] The first was a juvenile seen at Weston-super-Mare, Avon, in October 1999.[53] In Ireland there have been four records to the end of 2011: a juvenile at Sandymount Strand, Co. Dublin, in September 1999, one in Co. Kerry in 2003, a first-summer bird at Lady's Island Lake and Carnsore Point, Co. Wexford, in July and August 2006, and a juvenile at Rahasane Turlough, Co. Galway, in September 2007.[54] It has probably been overlooked in Ireland in the past, since there were three records in the five years between 2003 and 2008. There are also three specimens from Iceland, in 1956, 1957 and 1970, and one record in 1996 in the Netherlands.[55]

WHITE-WINGED TERN

The white-winged tern has a large breeding range, but less so than the black tern, extending from Hungary and Bulgaria in southeast Europe eastwards through central Asia to eastern Kazakhstan. There is a discrete breeding area in eastern Asia. The total population in the western group is estimated at 800,000 to 1.2 million pairs, of which 75,000–200,000 pairs breed in Europe.[56] Closer to us, small breeding populations have been recorded in Estonia (up to ten pairs in 1998); Latvia (10–100 pairs in the 1990s) and southeast Germany (1–24 pairs in 1995–99).[57] They winter in sub-Saharan Africa, southeast Asia and Australia. Like the other 'marsh' terns, the white-winged tern breeds in freshwater marshes, where it builds floating nests among emergent vegetation. Like the whiskered tern but unlike the black tern, it winters mainly on fresh waters and does not occur much along the coast except on migration. Flocks of 10,000 or more have been recorded on migration and in winter quarters. It is a rare vagrant in North America, occurring mainly on the Atlantic coast, with a few records on the Pacific coast and inland around the Great Lakes.

This is a classic 'marsh' tern, distinguished by its black body and underwing coverts. It has a white rump, whitish tail and upperwing coverts. In winter plumage it is rather difficult to distinguish from the black tern, but it is slightly shorter and blunter-winged, with a more rounded head and delicate bill. Its flight is less 'giddy' than the black tern's with periods of gliding.[58] The summer plumage is a striking contrast of black belly, head, back and underwings with white upperwings, underbelly and tail (Fig. 220). Juveniles and adults in winter

FIG 220. Adult white-winged tern. This is a striking bird with black head and underparts contrasting with white forewing, rump and tail. Lesvos, Greece. (John N. Murphy)

FIG 221. Juvenile white-winged tern. In non-breeding plumages, white-winged terns differ from black terns in lacking dark smudges on the sides of the breast and having much less black on the sides and back of the head (compare with Figs. 217 and 219). This juvenile shows the characteristic dark 'saddle' contrasting with a white collar. Tacumshin, Co. Wexford. (Killian Mullarney)

lack the dark patches on the sides of the breast found in black terns and have less black on the sides and back of the head. Juveniles have a distinctive dark brown 'saddle' with a white collar and white rump (Fig. 221).

White-winged terns have been known to hybridise with black terns in Sweden, the Netherlands and the USA,[59] in each case at a location where white-winged terns are rare. Two juveniles thought to have been hybrids were observed at Chew Valley Lake, Somerset, in September 1978 and September 1981.[60]

The first British white-winged tern was 'collected' at Horsey Mere, Norfolk, on 17 May 1853.[61] From 1860 to 1949 at least 67 more birds occurred in 19 English and Welsh counties; 40 of those records were concentrated in May and June. Over the last 20 years, and excluding the record 49 in 1992, white-winged terns

FIG 222. Map of 892 records of white-winged tern recorded in Britain and Ireland. (Compiled from a database maintained by BirdGuides Ltd)

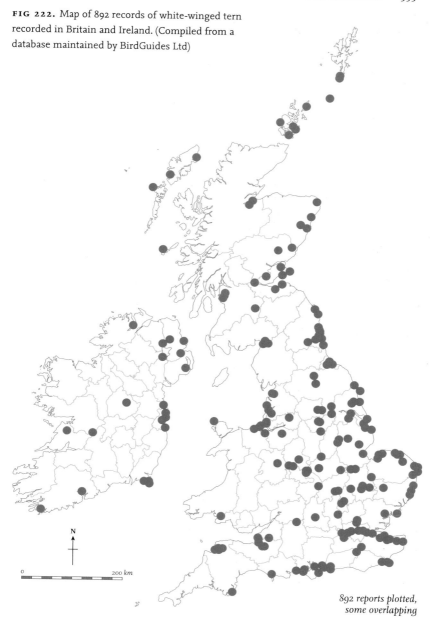

N

0   200 km

892 reports plotted,
some overlapping

have continued to occur at an average of 17 each year. As it had become such a common vagrant to Britain – in fact the commonest vagrant tern – it was taken off the BBRC's list of rare species from January 2006, with the effect that records are no longer being reviewed and compiled. In an analysis of 465 records between 1958 and 1985 there was a spring peak, mostly in May (28 per cent of all records), and a much larger autumn peak in August and September (72 per cent) (Fig. 222).[62] Autumn sightings have been concentrated in southeast and east England, but records also extend to the north of Scotland, the Midlands and Wales. In Ireland a thorough analysis showed that there were 86 records up to the end of 2011, with more autumn than spring records.[63] Most autumn records have been from the southern counties of Wexford, Cork and Kerry.

White-winged terns that breed in Europe migrate southwest in autumn and appear to cross the Mediterranean and the Sahara, because they winter as far west as Mauritania but do not migrate down the coast of northwest Africa like black terns. They pass through Italy in numbers, but occur less frequently in eastern Spain, where most records are of juveniles associated with easterly winds.[64] It is not known what causes so many birds to move west or even north of west to reach Britain and Ireland. They also appear to cross the Sahara in spring and are scarce as far west as Spain at that season. Again, it is not known what brings so many birds far to the northwest to reach Britain and Ireland.

ELEGANT TERN

The elegant tern has an extremely restricted breeding range, spanning less than 1,000 km along the Pacific coast from southern California to the Sea of Cortéz (Gulf of California) in northwest Mexico. It has a relatively small breeding population, estimated at less than 30,000 breeding pairs, of which more than 90 per cent breed in a single colony on Isla Rasa in the Sea of Cortéz. After breeding it disperses northwards along the Pacific coast as far as British Columbia. It winters on the Pacific coast from southern Mexico to southern Chile, but mainly south of the Equator.[65]

It is a medium-sized tern with a shaggy crest, similar to the lesser crested tern but with a longer, more slender and slightly drooping bill. The bill colour is orange, often with a paler yellow tip and a darker tomato-red base. It has the longest crest of any tern, forming irregular drooping tufts when closed but spiky when raised and spread (Fig. 223).[66] Its pale grey upperparts contrast with the white rump and tail, an important field character separating it from the lesser crested tern. The forehead is white during winter (Fig. 224).

FIG 223. Adult elegant terns, breeding plumage. Elegant terns resemble lesser crested terns, but have white rumps and tails contrasting with grey upperparts. The bill is longer and more slender than the lesser crested's and curves down towards the tip. It has the longest crest of any tern. California, USA. (Charles T. Collins)

FIG 224. Adult elegant tern, non-breeding plumage. In non-breeding plumages, elegant terns resemble royal or lesser crested terns and are best distinguished by the long drooping bill, white rump and white tail. California, USA. (Jørgen Kabel)

Although this tern was formerly confined to the eastern Pacific Ocean, it has been recorded with increasing frequency at locations around the North and South Atlantic in recent years. Elegant terns were suspected of interbreeding with Cabot's terns at Curaçao and Aruba in the southern Caribbean in 1960, and one interbred with a Cabot's tern in Florida in 2002.[67] In Europe, an elegant tern interbred with a Sandwich tern at the Banc d'Arguin nature reserve in southwest France from 1974 to 1985, with two mixed pairs in 1984; several hybrid young were produced. Another elegant tern, or one of the same individuals, was present from 1987 to at least 1996. Another mixed pair bred at the Ebro Delta on the Mediterranean coast of Spain in 2004 and raised a hybrid chick.[68] The presence of hybrids and backcrosses, many of which are confusingly similar to lesser crested terns and their hybrids (see under lesser crested tern, below) leads to many problems in field identification, and these and subsequent sight records have prompted much discussion and dispute in the birdwatching literature.[69] There have been subsequent sight-records of elegant terns in Spain, Belgium, Germany and Denmark, as well as in Britain and Ireland.[70]

The elegant tern has been recorded five times in Ireland to the end of 2011.[71] The first was seen from 22 June to 3 July 1982 in the Sandwich tern colony at Greencastle Point, Carlingford Lough, Co. Down. This bird was assumed to be the one seen on 1 August 1982 at Ballymacoda, Co. Cork. An adult was seen at Lady's Island Lake, Co. Wexford, from 8 to 19 July 1999. A third-year bird was seen at Mulranny, Co. Mayo, on 19 October 2001. One was observed at Dingle Harbour, Co. Kerry from 18 to 30 October 2002. Finally, one was recorded at Gormanstown Strand, Co. Meath, on 19 July 2005.

As of the end of 2011, there is no accepted record from Britain, although three records are presently being adjudicated by the BOURC: one bird was recorded at Dawlish Warren and Torbay, Devon, from 18 May to 19 July 2002; another, apparently breeding, at Stanpit Marsh, Dorset, on 10 May 2005; and a third at Porthmadog, Gwynedd, on 23 July 2002.[72]

Much remains to be learned about the movements of this tern, to enable interpretation of its European occurrences. Recent records from Argentina in the southern summer suggest that some individuals may enter the Atlantic by travelling south along the west coast of South America and then moving through the Strait of Magellan. However, it has not been recorded so far south on the Pacific coast of Chile. There is also a recent record from South Africa. These and other issues concerning the elegant tern were discussed at length in 2001.[73] Another hypothesis is that the European records of elegant tern are 'probably attributable to escapes from shipments of exotic seabirds from wintering grounds in west South America'.[74] However, this is a far-fetched explanation

Guinea-Bissau, but it is also likely to breed at undiscovered sites on isolated parts of the West African coast, notably Nigeria. Around 75,000 pairs are believed to breed in West Africa, but this estimate may be too low as 43,000 pairs were reported at one site in 1999.[84] After the breeding season in April–July, some African royal terns disperse northwards, and there have been about 20 records (not all of which have been reviewed) in southern Portugal, southern Spain, Gibraltar and the Canary Islands.[85] Two records in the Azores are more likely to have been the American subspecies.

A royal tern thought to be of the African subspecies was observed in Inchydoney Bay, Co. Cork, on 10 June 2009 (Fig. 227). Interestingly, the bird was in full breeding plumage and lacked any of the reddish-orange tones in the bill that would be typical of an American royal tern at that date; the American royal tern also has a much deeper bill base on average. Furthermore, the bird had only four dark outer primary feathers, rather than the six or seven that are typical of the American subspecies. Elegant and lesser crested terns can be ruled out on plumage characteristics. The consensus of the IRBC was that it was unsafe to ascribe the record definitely to either subspecies, and it was accepted by the IRBC as a royal tern.[86] It is thought that this bird crossed the Irish Sea to Wales, where it was observed at Abersoch, Gwynedd, on 15 June 2009. Possibly the same bird was observed at Llandudno, Conwy, five days later. Both the Welsh records were reported as royal terns without identification to subspecies.

FIG 227. Royal tern, Inchydoney Island, Co. Cork, June 2009. This bird was thought to be of the African subspecies: it had only four black primaries (American royal terns usually have six or seven) and had a black forehead and crown (usually white on American royal terns in June). (Michael O'Keeffe)

LESSER CRESTED TERN

The lesser crested tern breeds in subtropical regions from the Red Sea across the Indian Ocean to the western Pacific and Australia. There is also a significant population of the subspecies *Thalasseus bengalensis emigrata* in the southern Mediterranean, on two islands off the Libyan coast, where some 4,000 individuals were estimated in the early 1990s.[87] Breeding has been reported occasionally in Italy, Spain and France, but the European population is tiny, with one or two pairs in northeast Spain in 1998–2000 and one pair in Italy in 2000.[88] The Libyan population winters in West Africa and migrates along the North African coast, with only small numbers (up to 20 in a season) in the Strait of Gibraltar and nearby parts of the Spanish coast, mainly from August to October with much smaller numbers in March to May.[89]

Interbreeding of lesser crested terns with Sandwich terns has been recorded in Britain, France and Spain,[90] resulting in some fertile hybrids that have bred with Sandwich terns to produce backcross chicks (see below)

The lesser crested tern resembles the Sandwich tern in size and shape, but it is the smallest 'crested' tern with the brightest orange bill, similar in colouration to that of the American royal tern. It has uniform grey upperparts with grey rump and tail, plumage characteristics that separate it from the royal and elegant terns, which both have the rump and tail white. The underwing is white with a dark trailing edge to the outer wing formed by tips of the 5–7 outer primaries. It is difficult to separate from the royal tern, but the lesser crested is smaller with a slimmer bill and uniform grey upperparts (Fig. 228). The lesser crested tern has been described as an 'orange-billed Sandwich tern', whereas the royal tern is a 'Caspian in miniature' with a white rump and tail.[91] Juveniles have a yellow bill and dark bars on lesser and greater coverts.

The first lesser crested tern recorded in Britain was an adult at Cymyran Bay, Anglesey, on 13 July 1982.[92] Since then a total of nine records have been accepted by the BBRC to the end of 2011, with most sightings in July and August. There is one record from Ireland at Ballycotton, Co. Cork, on 7–8 August 1996.[93]

A female of the southern Mediterranean subspecies spent 15 summers in the Sandwich tern colony on the Farne Islands, Northumberland, from 1984 to 1998. She eventually mated with a Sandwich tern and reared in total five young to fledging, one of which went on to breed with a Sandwich tern on the Farne Islands (see detailed account below). One other nestling was colour-ringed and subsequently seen near Sables d'Olonne, Vendée, France, on 23 September 1997.[94] The history of this bird ('Elsie') is a fascinating story worthy of recounting

FIG 228. Adult lesser crested tern, non-breeding plumage. This is the smallest of the 'crested' terns with the brightest orange bill in the breeding season. It has uniform grey upperparts with grey rump and tail, which distinguish it from the royal and elegant terns. Thailand. (Paul Gale)

in detail, thanks to the careful observations by wardens on the Farne Islands. The account below has been compiled from the relevant reports of the RSPB, published in condensed form in *British Birds*.

1984 – Single lesser crested tern, 4–13 August, posturing with Sandwich terns.
1985 – Single lesser crested tern on 20 days between 16 May and 18 July. It was incubating an egg, indistinguishable from a Sandwich tern's, on 29 June, 2 and 6 July.

1986 – Single lesser crested tern on 14, 15 and 20 May, 1 June and 8 and 10 July. On the July dates, it was associating with a chick in the Sandwich tern colony.

1987 – Single lesser crested tern from 18 May to 20 June; by 25 May it was apparently paired with a Sandwich tern and incubating two eggs, but the nest was flooded and one egg was lost; the lesser crested tern sat on the other egg until 11 June.

1988 – Single lesser crested tern on 15 dates from 5 May to 5 June, and again on 13 July; no nesting attempt made.

1989 – Single lesser crested tern from 7 May to 1 July, displaying to a Sandwich tern from 7 May; single egg located 30 May, hatched 19 June; adult and chick seen regularly until 1 July. An adult lesser crested tern and a juvenile hybrid seen in Lothian in August and early September were presumed to have been these individuals.

1990 – Female lesser crested tern present from 30 April to 19 August, mated to a male Sandwich tern; one egg laid on 7 June eventually hatched, but the chick died.

1991 – Female lesser crested tern from 14 May to 18 August, mated to a Sandwich tern; probably incubating on 30 May in poor weather; nest subsequently abandoned.

1992 – Female lesser crested tern paired with a male Sandwich tern, laid a clutch of two eggs and reared one hybrid young.

1993 – Female lesser crested tern mated to a Sandwich tern, seen intermittently from 3 May to 8 August; copulating on 31 May, but no further breeding evidence. What has been assumed to be the same individual also appeared in Borders on 16 May, North Humberside during 15–20 June, Lincolnshire on 20 June and Norfolk on 8–21 July, 11 and 22 August. On each occasion, it was noted as being paired with a colour-ringed Sandwich tern, and copulation was observed in Lincolnshire.

1994 – Female lesser crested tern bred with a Sandwich tern, laid one egg which hatched on 10 July, but the chick died on 15 July. A hybrid adult, presumably one of the offspring fledged between 1989 and 1992, bred with a Sandwich tern; one chick first seen on 15 July, fledged on 28 July.

1995 – Female lesser crested tern bred with a Sandwich tern, laid one egg which was lost to unknown causes; a second clutch of one egg hatched, but the chick vanished at five days old.

1996 – Female lesser crested tern bred with a Sandwich tern, fledged one hybrid young.

1997 – Female lesser crested tern bred with a Sandwich tern, fledged one hybrid young.

1998 – Female lesser crested tern bred with a Sandwich tern, fledged one hybrid young at the usual site; the egg hatched on 18 June and the chick fledged on 18 July. The juvenile was seen in Vendée, France, on 23 September.

FORSTER'S TERN

Forster's tern is the only tern that is confined to North America, even in winter. It breeds widely in freshwater marshes in the interior of the continent, from Baja California and Alberta east to the central Great Lakes, and in saltmarshes on the southern Atlantic and Gulf coasts. Total numbers are more than 39,000 pairs, including 28,000 pairs on the Atlantic and Gulf coasts of the USA; overall trends are uncertain, but it has increased considerably in California and on the Atlantic coast.[95]

FIG 229. Adult Forster's tern. In breeding plumage, Forster's terns have red bills with black tips and can be confused with common terns, but are more thick-set, with silvery primaries and grey tail with white outer edges. Tacumshin, Co. Wexford. (Tom Shevlin)

FIG 230. Juvenile Forster's tern. In all non-breeding plumages, Forster's terns have a very distinctive head pattern: white with black 'ear-patches'. Gull-billed terns have a similar head pattern but are much larger. Plymouth, USA. (Craig Gibson)

Forster's tern is distinguished from the common tern by its larger size and relatively shorter wings. It has a heavier, longer bill, longer legs and mainly grey tail with white outer webs to the outermost feathers (common terns have dark outer webs to these feathers). The rump is white, contrasting with the grey back and tail. It also has silvery primaries (Fig. 229). Juvenile and winter plumages are very distinctive: the head is largely white except for a black patch extending behind the eye (Fig. 230).[96] Gull-billed terns have a similar head-pattern but are much larger.

Forster's terns were not recorded in Britain until 1980, when a first-winter bird was observed at Falmouth Bay, Cornwall, in February (and probably also in January) and March.[97] Since then another 19 records have been accepted by

FIG 231. Histogram of Forster's tern records in Britain and Ireland by month. (Compiled from a database maintained by BirdGuides Ltd)

FIG 232. Map of Forster's tern records in Britain and Ireland by county. Records from 1980 to the end of 2010. (Compiled from a database maintained by BirdGuides Ltd)

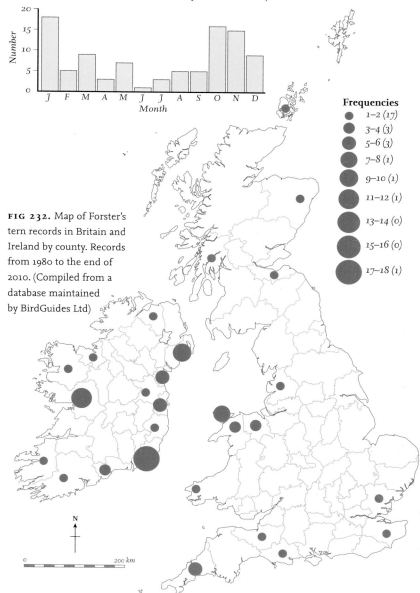

Frequencies

1–2 (17)
3–4 (3)
5–6 (3)
7–8 (1)
9–10 (1)
11–12 (1)
13–14 (0)
15–16 (0)
17–18 (1)

the BBRC to the end of 2011. The first record from Ireland was of a first-winter bird at Dublin Bay in November 1982. Since then there have been a further 34 records accepted by the IRBC to the end of 2011, based on a thorough review of all records since 1982.

The spate of recent records may have been linked with the marked increase in numbers breeding on the east coast of North America. Records have been mainly in the period October to January, with peak numbers in January (Fig. 231). They have been widely scattered throughout Britain and Ireland (Fig. 232).

Demography, Population Trends and the Basis for Conservation

DEMOGRAPHY

D EMOGRAPHY IS THE STATISTICAL STUDY of populations. It encompasses the study of the size, structure and distribution of populations, and spatial and/or temporal changes in them in relation to 'vital rates' such as births, deaths and migration. The demography of wild bird populations has become a vigorous scientific discipline in recent years as conservation programmes require more and better information on the causes of population declines and better ways to predict the future prospects of threatened populations in the face of climate change and other challenges.

Demographic theory is based on a simple equation: changes in local populations result from births, deaths, emigration and immigration. If four of the terms in the equation can be measured or estimated, the fifth can be calculated. Understanding population dynamics and predicting future prospects for a population, therefore, requires quantitative information on at least four demographic parameters. This is rarely achieved for any bird species – or indeed for any wild animal – but better data are available for some of our terns than for most other species.

Numbers and trends

Long-term data on population numbers and trends for most of the seabird species that breed in Britain and Ireland – including all five breeding terns –

were generated during the three comprehensive censuses conducted in 1969–70, 1984–88 and 1998–2002.[1] For many seabird species – again including all our five terns – there has been a continuous running record of numbers from 1986 onwards based on the *Seabird Monitoring Programme* (SMP), conducted by the Joint Nature Conservation Committee (JNCC) with input from the RSPB and many other organisations (see Appendix 3). This programme includes an annual census at 15–30 sites which were selected in 1986 as 'index' sites and which included from 25 per cent to almost 100 per cent of the total number of breeding terns in Britain and Ireland. Data from 1986 to 2006 have been summarised in a series of 18 annual reports;[2] the annual censuses have been continued, and unpublished data since 2006 are available for three tern species (but not for roseate or little terns) on the JNCC website.[3] This database provides robust information on numbers and trends of each of our five species at most of their important breeding sites, as well as at regional and national scales. Tables 10, 11, 14, 17 and 23 summarise the changes in numbers from 1970 to 2000, and we have incorporated data from the SMP up to and including 2011 into the text of Chapters 6–10.

Productivity

For terns, the birth rate, or fecundity, is best defined not as the number of chicks that hatch but as *productivity*: the average number of chicks raised to fledging per pair in a colony. The SMP also includes annual monitoring of the productivity of several seabird species. For the five tern species that breed in Britain and Ireland, productivity is estimated at most of the index sites in each year, and the results for the period 1986–2006 have been summarised in the same annual reports;[4] data since 2006 are available on the JNCC website. Again, this database provides robust information on productivity of each of our five species at most of their important breeding sites, as well as at regional and national scales. Data on productivity at the index sites from 1986 to 2011 have been summarised in Tables 12, 16, 20, 22 and 25. Data on productivity at several other sites in years prior to 1986 have been published in various sources and provide a longer-term perspective, although the coverage was sporadic in both space and time (for examples, see Tables 27 and 28 in Chapter 11).

Survival

Survival of seabirds is much harder to measure than numbers or productivity. It requires marking large numbers of birds and either tracking them individually from year to year or compiling recoveries of rings from dead birds in a systematic way. The most reliable estimates of survival rates are those derived with the former method, by systematically retrapping or resighting marked birds at breeding colonies over multiple years. There is an elaborate mathematical theory for analysing mark–recapture data which can yield unbiased estimates of survival rates, but applying this theory requires ringing hundreds or thousands of individual birds and retrapping or resighting them in a systematic way over many years (a minimum of three years' data is required to generate one estimate of survival, and many more years are required to yield estimates with tight confidence limits). Among British and Irish terns, this has been undertaken only for roseate terns,[5] although estimates of survival of common and Arctic terns derived from studies in other countries are likely to be broadly applicable to those in Britain and Ireland.

Earlier methods of estimating survival were based on constructing *life tables* from the distribution of recoveries of birds found dead, but it is now recognised that this method is biased and that the estimates of survival derived from it are almost always too low. The early estimates of survival for Sandwich and Arctic terns obtained using this method[6] were indeed much lower than more recent estimates obtained using more rigorous methodology. However, a new method of analysing data from ringing recoveries has been devised recently, and this appears to yield unbiased results (or at least less biased results: see below under Sandwich tern).[7]

Immigration and emigration: breeding dispersal and natal dispersal

The most intractable components of the demographic equation are immigration and emigration. For colonial breeders such as terns, emigration means *breeding dispersal*: movements of birds that bred at one colony site in one year to breed at another site in a subsequent year. Immigration results from the entry into a breeding colony of birds that had been raised as chicks at another site (*natal dispersal*) or had bred at another site in a previous year (*breeding dispersal*), or both. Very few terns of any species have been ringed or retrapped as adults at breeding colonies in Britain or Ireland. Consequently, the only species for which breeding dispersal has been measured directly is the roseate tern, for which there has been a systematic programme of ringing chicks with field-readable rings and resighting them in subsequent years at the three major breeding sites, so that many birds are repeatedly registered as adults even though few have been ringed or retrapped as adults. Analysis of these resighting data over multiple years has shown that roseate terns move fairly frequently from one breeding site to another.[8] Similar findings have been reported for roseate, common and Arctic terns in other countries,[9] so it is likely that breeding dispersal is fairly frequent in all terns. Although there have been no mark–recapture studies of Sandwich or little terns, entire colonies of both these species quite frequently shift from one site to another in response to predation or flooding; other terns do this from time to time.

The consequence of breeding dispersal is that estimates of survival derived from return rates of breeding birds at a single site (*local survival*) are invariably lower than true survival rates, by unknown but often large margins. Only if a species can be studied simultaneously using mark–recapture methods at all its major breeding sites – as has been done for roseate terns both in Britain and Ireland and in the USA – can true survival be estimated rigorously. For other species, the best that can be done is to estimate local survival at one or a few sites, and then make informed guesses about the net effect of dispersal. Of course, if an entire regional population is considered, internal dispersal movements among sites within the region cancel out, and reasonable estimates of average survival over the region can be obtained. This is what is done when survival rates are estimated from recoveries of dead birds based on ringing at multiple sites. That procedure was formerly unsatisfactory because of bias in the life-table method for analysing recoveries, but the new method for analysing recoveries appears promising.[10]

Age at first breeding, juvenile survival, natal dispersal and recruitment

Productivity is defined as the number of chicks raised to fledging per pair. However, young terns do not enter the breeding population as *recruits* until several years later, so deaths between fledging and recruitment need to be taken into account. This is much more difficult than estimating survival of adults from one year to the next, for two reasons. First, young birds frequently breed for the first time in colonies other than those where they were raised, so that searching for them only at the natal site will always underestimate survival. This natal dispersal is usually much more frequent than breeding dispersal of adults, and poses even greater difficulties for constructing demographic models. Second, the age at first breeding is variable: most terns breed for the first time when three or four years old, but a few (especially little terns) breed at two and some (especially Sandwich terns) do not breed until five or older. Hence, survival has to be estimated separately for birds that first breed at different ages. By the same token, estimates of the proportions of birds that breed for the first time at different ages have to take into account differences in their survival.

For these reasons, estimating juvenile survival and ages at first breeding rigorously requires systematic retrapping (or resighting) at multiple sites over multiple years. This has been attempted only for roseate terns, for which detailed studies have been carried out in the USA and in Britain and Ireland, although in the latter case only preliminary results have been reported.[11] Results reported to date for other species have been based on retrapping or resighting at the natal colony site only and are probably much too low. However, at least for common terns, there is evidence that most birds that survive to age two return to *prospect* at their natal site at that age, even if they eventually settle to breed somewhere else in a subsequent year.[12] Hence, systematic resighting of prospectors can probably yield better estimates of juvenile survival than waiting until they breed and then resighting or retrapping them as breeders at the natal site; the latter estimates are of *local survival* only. To date, systematic resighting of prospectors has been reported only for common terns at a site in Germany, although resighting data exist for roseate terns in Britain and Ireland.[13]

Closing the demographic equation: explaining population trends

The purpose of studying the demography of tern populations is to understand how population changes are related to vital rates. For example, if the population is increasing or decreasing, we may wish to relate these trends to the intrinsic population parameters such as productivity, survival and dispersal. Alternatively, given values for survival rates, we may wish to estimate how large productivity must be to maintain a stable population. These calculations can identify the most critical stages in the life cycle for maintaining population sizes, and hence provide targets for conservation.

Because of the difficulty in measuring or estimating rates of natal dispersal and breeding dispersal, it is usually possible to close the demographic equation only for large regional populations or for the entire population of a species. It is then possible to ignore dispersal among sites within the population, so that the demographic equation reduces to:

Population change = number recruited – number dying

For birds such as terns, with variable ages at first breeding, the birds recruited in any one year include some individuals that were raised as chicks over several years in the past. Then, the demographic equation can be written as follows:

Population increase from year y to year $(y + 1) =$
population in year $y \times$ (adult survival rate $-$ 1)
+ productivity in year $(y - 1) \times$ number of pairs in year $(y - 1) \times$ survival to age
2 × fraction recruited to breeding population in year $(y + 1)$
+ productivity in year $(y - 2) \times$ number of pairs in year $(y - 2) \times$ survival to age
3 × (1 – fraction recruited in year y) × fraction recruited in year $(y + 1)$
+ similar terms for birds raised in years $(y - 3)$ and $(y - 4)$ and recruited in
year $(y + 1)$

The first term on the right-hand side of this equation is the number of adults lost by death, while the remaining terms are the numbers of birds recruited at ages 2, 3, 4 and 5. If the population is approximately stable, the number of pairs in prior years will be approximately half the population in year y; otherwise, changes in numbers in each successive year need to be taken into account. If part of the adult population does not breed in one or more years, the number of pairs will be less than half the total population in those years.

Table 30 illustrates how this equation can be applied by using measured rates of productivity and survival for roseate terns to calculate the productivity required to maintain a stable population. Even this relatively simple calculation requires knowledge of three different survival rates and the proportions of birds that breed for the first time at different ages, all of which are assumed to be constant. Calculations would be much more complex if they were applied to more realistic cases in which some or all of these rates vary from year to year.

TABLE 30. Life table for roseate terns in Britain and Ireland and calculation of the productivity required to keep the population stable.

We use the estimates of annual survival measured for British and Irish roseate terns (73.5%[a] in the year after first encounter and 85.5% thereafter).[b] We assume that the values for juvenile survival (average 43% from fledging to age 2) and ages at first breeding (about 50% at age 3 and 50% at age 4) calculated for the US population[c] would be valid also for the British and Irish population. All other estimates are averages for the three British and Irish sites (Rockabill, Coquet Island and Lady's Island Lake), so movements of individuals among these sites would not affect the calculations.

We set out to calculate the productivity required to keep the population stable, given the estimated values for adult survival, juvenile survival and ages at first breeding.

Consider a stable population of 1,000 birds (500 pairs) breeding in each year. Denote the productivity required to keep the population stable by S. Then $500S$ chicks are raised to fledging in each year (this assumes all adult birds breed in each year).

Survival to age 2 is 43% and annual survival thereafter is 85.5% until first breeding, so the number of chicks surviving to age 2 is $215S$, the number surviving to age 3 is $184S$ and the number that would survive to age 4 if they did not breed at age 3 is $157S$.

In year 5, 50% of the surviving birds from year 1 and 50% of the surviving birds from year 2 enter the breeding population and breed for the first time. The total number of recruits is then: $(184S + 157S)/2 = 170.5S$

The number of breeders is assumed to be stable at 1,000 in each year, so in year 5 there are $170.5S$ first-time breeders and $(1,000 - 170.5S)$ older breeders.

Survival to year 6 is 73.5% for first-time breeders and 85.5 % for older breeders. Hence the total number of breeders from year 5 that survive to year 6 is:

$170.5S \times 0.735 + (1,000 - 170.5S) \times 0.855$, which reduces to $855 - 20.5S$.

The number of new recruits is 170.5S and the total number of breeders is 1,000, so:

1,000 = 170.5S + 855 − 20.5S, from which S = 155/150.8 = 1.03. This is the value we set out to calculate.

The observed average productivity is 1.31, so the number of recruits in year 6 is actually about 170.5 × 1.31 = 223 instead of the 170.5 × 1.03 = 176 required to keep the population stable. The breeding population is therefore expected to increase by 47 birds in year 6. This corresponds to an increase of 3.9% per year, because the total population in year 6 would have increased to 1,211 birds (1,000 × 1.039^5) and 47 is 3.9% of 1,211. This rate of increase is very close to what is observed (4.0% per year: see Fig. 131 in Chapter 9).

This calculation is optimistic, because it assumes that all adult birds breed every year, which is unlikely. Also, there is probably a low rate of net emigration from Britain and Ireland to the colonies in France, where productivity is much lower than in Britain and Ireland and survival may be lower also because of sporadic predation by mink.

If we had used the preliminary value of 0.30 for first-year survival (0.255 to age 2) for Britain and Ireland rather than the US value of 0.43 for survival to age 2, the productivity required to maintain a stable population would have been calculated as 1.79 rather than 1.03. This is much higher than the observed average for a population that is actually increasing, confirming that the preliminary estimate of first-year survival for Britain and Ireland was much too low.

---

[a] Note that survival rates can be expressed either as percentages (73.5% in this case) or as proportions (0.735 in this case); these alternative notations are interchangeable and both are used in this table.

[b] Ratcliffe *et al.*, 2008a.

[c] Lebreton *et al.*, 2003. They actually reported that some birds bred for the first time at age 2 and some did not breed until age 5, but we have pooled these birds with those aged 3 and 4, respectively, to simplify the calculation.

DEMOGRAPHIC INFORMATION ON TERNS OF BRITAIN AND IRELAND

Little tern

Less information is available about the demography of little terns than about any of our four other breeding species. The most recent monograph on the species in the Western Palearctic had no section on demography, and the only relevant information reported in it was a longevity record of 21 years 1 month, age of first breeding 'sometimes 2 years, usually older,' and breeding success 'sometimes highly variable,' with productivity varying from 0 to 2.5 young per pair at several sites.[14]

In fact, productivity has been monitored irregularly since 1969 at 110 colony sites in Britain and Ireland; these colonies included around 65 per cent of the national total during the surveys in 1985–87. Results showed wide year-to-year variations in average productivity, ranging from 0.15 to 0.85 chicks per pair between 1969 and 1998 with a long-term average of about 0.5: this increased from about 0.48 in 1969 to about 0.56 in the early 1980s and then declined to about 0.45 by 1998 (see Fig. 84 in Chapter 6).[15] The SMP recorded productivity at 19 colonies over a 25-year period from 1986 to 2010: colony averages ranged from 0.22 to 1.11 with an overall average of about 0.59[16] (see Table 12 in Chapter 6). The fact that this average was substantially higher than the average for the larger sample during the 13 years of overlap (1986–98) may have resulted from successful management of many of the colonies included in the SMP, reflected in the marked increase in the total population since 2004 (see Chapter 11).

The data on productivity were used in 2003 to construct a population model with the aim of diagnosing the cause of observed population trends in Britain and Ireland.[17] This model was quite speculative, because the only actual data available for little terns were those on productivity. It had to be assumed that the other important population parameters – annual adult survival, survival from fledging to first breeding and ages at first breeding – would be similar to those reported for other terns. The specific values assumed for use in the model were 0.89, 0.33 and three years, respectively, based on data for common terns in Germany. Net immigration into or emigration from Britain and Ireland was assumed to be negligible. Running this model in the way shown in Table 30 then led to the predictions that average productivity of 0.74 chicks per pair would be required to maintain a stable population, and that the measured average productivity of 0.59 chicks per pair would lead to a population decline at rate of about 3 per cent per year. This is close to what was observed in the period from 1969 to 1998, leading to the conclusion that average productivity would have to be increased to 0.74 to halt the decline in numbers or above 0.74 to reverse it. It should be noted, however, that the population decline was in fact reversed starting about 2005, although average productivity at index colonies in the period starting in 2002 was still lower than 0.74 (see Chapter 6). This raises questions about the validity of the model, or at least about the values assumed for the missing parameters.

Sandwich tern

Much less information is available on survival of Sandwich terns than on that of roseate or common terns. There has been no systematic programme of ringing and resighting of Sandwich terns comparable to those for roseates or commons. Young Sandwich terns frequently disperse to breed for the first time at other colonies, sometimes far from the natal colony, and adults often shift from one breeding site to another, sometimes en masse in response to predation.[18] Thus any attempt to understand or describe the demography of the species would require coordinated studies at multiple sites, which have not been attempted.

Large numbers of Sandwich terns were colour-ringed at the Sands of Forvie Nature Reserve, Aberdeenshire, in the 1960s and their behaviour and breeding success were followed for at least seven years, but no information was reported on their survival or return rates.[19] Early attempts to calculate annual survival rates of adults from ring recoveries yielded estimates in the range 0.70 to 0.84,[20] but these values were far too low to be compatible with other demographic parameters. Recently, however, a new method was devised to estimate survival rates from historical ringing and recovery data; this yielded an estimate of about 0.90 for annual survival of adult Sandwich terns ringed in Britain and Ireland.[21] This value is in the same range as those for other tern species, but the precision of the estimate is low because it was based on only 63 birds ringed as adults, and its accuracy is questionable because it relied on haphazard recoveries of dead birds and was not based on systematic resampling. The same procedure led to estimates of 0.31–0.40 survival during the first year after ringing and 0.74 during the second and third years. Combining these values yields predictions in the range 0.17–0.22 for survival from ringing to age three, which would be very low compared to that of other terns, but again the precision of the estimates is very low. The oldest Sandwich tern recorded to date was 23 years old.[22]

Sandwich terns usually breed for the first time at age three or four, rarely at age two and sometimes not until age five:[23] this is similar to the pattern for the smaller terns. Average productivity of Sandwich tern colonies is usually in the range 0.5–0.9 chicks raised to fledging per pair per year, with an average of 0.68 (see Table 16 in Chapter 7), which is much lower than regional averages for productivity of common or roseate terns. Nevertheless, Sandwich terns have maintained their numbers in Britain and Ireland in the period since 1986 (see Chapter 7) and have increased considerably and steadily since 1970 in other parts of western Europe.[24] This suggests that the estimated values for survival, productivity, or both must be too low, unless productivity has been substantially higher in other parts of western Europe and there has been substantial immigration into Britain and Ireland.

Common tern

In Britain and Ireland, the only one of the four population parameters that has been measured for common terns is productivity. Table 20 (Chapter 8) indicates an average productivity of about 0.87 chicks per pair at the index sites in the SMP during the period 1986–2006. Earlier measurements at coastal colony sites in Britain and Germany were in the same range (see Chapter 8), as were productivity estimates from seven studies at freshwater sites in France, Switzerland and Germany (0.51–1.1).[25] For North America, mean productivity

values from 21 studies at 128 sites were usually in the range 1.0–2.0 at sites on the
northern Atlantic coast, 0.5–1.0 at sites on the mid-Atlantic coast and consistently
less than 1.0 at freshwater sites in the interior.[26] Although there is enormous
variation among sites and years, broad-scale average productivities of common
terns are around 0.87 fledglings per pair both in Europe and North America.
However, more than half the studies on which this generalisation is based were
at sites that were intensively managed, with control of human disturbance and in
many cases control of predators and management of vegetation. For this reason,
these calculated averages may be higher than the true average for the species
over all types of sites.

The best information on survival comes from the long-term study of
common terns at Wilhemshaven (see Appendix 2), where virtually all birds that
return to the site (200–1,100 individuals) are detected in each year. A new mark–
recapture analysis has yielded two sets of estimates of demographic parameters:
one for the period 1992–2001 when the population was increasing and the other
for the period 2002–09 when the population was decreasing.[27] The vital rates
for these two periods were as follows: productivity 1.37 and 0.46 fledglings per
pair; annual survival rate for adults 92 per cent and 90 per cent; survival rate
for three-year-old non-breeders 87 per cent and 79 per cent; survival rate from
fledging to two years old 36 per cent and 28 per cent; average age at first breeding
3.3 and 3.9; recruitment rate (proportion of natal recruits in the breeding
population, where 'natal recruits' means birds that had been raised in the colony
that were breeding for the first time) 26 per cent and 14 per cent; annual rate of
population increase (including net immigration) 16 per cent and –2 per cent. The
change in the population trend thus resulted from deterioration in every aspect
of demography, with the greatest changes in productivity and recruitment rate.
These changes have been attributed to a decline in the abundance of Atlantic
herring.[28] Using the methods set out in Table 30, the corresponding values of the
productivity required to maintain a stable population can be calculated as 0.57 in
1992–2001 and 1.28 in 2002–09.

Unfortunately, the difference between the two demographic regimes at
Wilhelmshaven is too wide for either to be very helpful in assessing trends
in other populations. All that can be said is that the broad-scale average
productivities of about 0.87 among common terns in western Europe would lead
to rapid population increase under the Wilhelmshaven regime of 1992–2001
and rapid decline under that of 2002–09 – as in fact occurred at Wilhelmshaven.
In other parts of northwest Germany and the entire Wadden See area from
Denmark to the Netherlands, common terns have been declining in numbers
since at least 1980, and this decline accelerated after 2002.[29] The British and Irish

population appears to have been stable during this period, and there was no evidence for either increases in the 1990s or declines in the 2000s (see Chapter 8). However, within this general picture of overall stability, numbers of common terns have increased or decreased markedly at many individual sites, groups of sites and regions. Many of these changes are attributable to dispersal, because increase in one region is often matched by decrease in a neighbouring region.[30] However, it will be very difficult to disentangle the roles of dispersal, changes in productivity and changes in survival in influencing local and regional trends.

Another limitation of the Wilhelmshaven study is that it was conducted at one colony only, so the estimates of survival and recruitment rates may be too low because of emigration. It is known that the Wilhelmshaven colony includes many immigrants that were raised elsewhere, but there is virtually no information about emigration, except for one study which showed that some birds raised at the main colony 'prospected' in the year before first breeding at another colony 4 km away, although most of them returned to the main colony to nest in the next year.[31] There is otherwise no information of any kind on the extent to which European common terns emigrate to or immigrate from colony sites other than their natal site, either when first breeding (natal dispersal) or after having bred (breeding dispersal). In North America, ringing and retrapping studies have revealed both natal and breeding dispersal of common terns among breeding sites, sometimes at high rates.[32] For example, intensive trapping of adults at one coastal site where numbers of breeding pairs had been stable for many years revealed that 7 per cent of the breeders had been ringed as chicks at other sites, extending over 1,200 km of the Atlantic coast.[33] Retrapping studies at sites where colonies had been established more recently showed that almost all the breeders (82–98 per cent) were immigrants from other sites.[34] However, although more than a million common terns have been ringed in North America and tens of thousands have been retrapped as breeders at many sites, there is still no quantitative information on the importance of emigration and immigration for the local and regional dynamics and long-term stability of common tern populations.[35] Because common terns nest at hundreds of sites with tens of thousands of potential two-way exchanges, it will be virtually impossible to solve this problem.

Roseate tern

The demography of roseate terns in Britain and Ireland is better known than that of any other tern, partly because it has been studied more intensively but also because its population is concentrated into a few colony sites, all of which have been monitored for many years. Roseate terns in northwest Europe form a *metapopulation* – a term that has been defined loosely as a 'population of populations', or more precisely as a set of populations of the same species, each of which is internally homogeneous but which are connected by two-way dispersal of individuals between populations. Dispersal maintains the genetic continuity of the entire metapopulation, and increases its overall stability by smoothing out the effect of random fluctuations in numbers within populations and allowing re-establishment of populations that have gone extinct.[36] Seabirds that nest in colonies are classic examples of metapopulations, because each colony functions as a unit, but is connected with the others as individual birds move between them.

The metapopulation of roseate terns in northwest Europe is currently centred on Rockabill, which contains about 70 per cent of the total numbers, with three smaller groups at Coquet Island, Lady's Island Lake and Ile aux Dames in France (see Fig. 130 in Chapter 9). In most years, roseate terns nest at 3–6 other sites, but numbers at these sites are so small that their influence on overall dynamics is negligible (although they might theoretically become important in the future if all the large colonies should decline simultaneously, as they did in the 1880s and again in the 1970s). Detailed studies have been conducted since the 1980s at three of the four sites: there is little precise information on the site in France except for total numbers and productivity, but this site now supports less than 5 per cent of the total numbers,[37] so its omission from the detailed demographic studies is probably unimportant. The breeding population in the Azores has not been studied in nearly so much detail, but can probably be ignored in analysis of the metapopulation in northwest Europe because there is no evidence for interchange of individuals between the two areas, and any such interchanges are likely to be few and far between.

Productivity, adult survival, juvenile survival and dispersal have been well studied for roseate terns. Average productivity has been about 1.31 fledglings per pair in Britain and Ireland (see Table 22 in Chapter 9), although only about 0.6 at Ile aux Dames.[38] An early estimate of about 0.81 for adult survival[39] was based on recoveries of dead birds and was probably too low for that reason. Using the more rigorous mark–recapture methodology based on the programme of ringing and resighting between 1995 and 2007 yielded estimates of the annual survival rates of adults as 0.735 for birds in the year following first encounter (i.e. mostly young birds after their first breeding attempt), and 0.855 thereafter. It also yielded a set of estimates of the rates of dispersal of adults that had bred at one site to breed at another site in the next year: these ranged from less than 0.01 between Lady's Island Lake and Coquet Island to about 0.20 from Lady's Island Lake to Rockabill. There was net movement of breeders from Lady's Island

Lake to Rockabill during the period of study, but not to or from Coquet Island, although there was enough two-way movement of adults between Coquet Island and Rockabill to lead to turnover of about one-tenth of the population at Coquet Island every year, because the numbers at Coquet Island were relatively small.[40] This set of data on dispersal is better than any available for any other seabird except for that on roseate terns in the northeastern USA.[41]

The only part of the demographic equation that has not been worked out fully for roseate terns is Britain and Ireland is the recruitment of new birds to the breeding population – which depends on the ages at which young birds first breed and their survival to those ages. These parameters have been estimated for roseate terns in the USA, based on a large data set of recaptures and resightings of birds ringed as chicks. In the US study, survival of young birds to age two was very variable from year to year, ranging from 0.04 to 0.75 with an average over all years and sites of 0.43; about half the birds bred for the first time at age three and most of the rest at age four, although a few bred at age two and a few did not breed until age five.[42] Preliminary analysis of resighting data from colonies in Britain and Ireland in 1989–96 led to an estimate of 0.30 for first-year survival and 0.85 for survival in subsequent years, with no estimates of ages at first breeding.[43] This preliminary estimate of first-year survival is much lower than the average reported in the US study, and the analysis needs to be repeated on the larger sample of resightings from 1995 to 2007.

Given all these values for the demographic parameters, it is now possible to close the demographic equation and to compare the observed changes in population with the estimates of vital rates. Table 30 sets out a calculation of the productivity required to keep the total number of birds in the metapopulation stable, assuming that the average values for the demographic parameters are maintained in each year (and using the US value of 0.43 for survival to age two rather than the preliminary value of 0.30 for survival to age one in Britain and Ireland). The productivity required for a stable population turns out to be 1.03 fledglings per pair, although the calculation is somewhat optimistic for reasons explained in the table. The observed average productivity was considerably higher than 1.03, which is consistent with the observation that the population was increasing at about 4 per cent per year during the period for which the demographic parameters were estimated (see Fig. 131 in Chapter 9).

The average annual survival rate of 0.855 for adult roseate terns in Britain and Ireland is unusually low for a small seabird: in all other cases where the survival of terns has been calculated using rigorous mark–recapture methods, adult survival rates were in the range 0.88–0.94 (see Table 31, below). In spite of their low survival rates, roseate terns are able to maintain and increase their populations because they have consistently high productivity and relatively high survival from fledging to first breeding. A consequence of the low adult survival rate is that population turnover is rapid and that there is a high proportion of young birds in the population: the calculation presented in Table 30 indicates that, on average, 18 per cent of the population in any one year are breeding for the first time. Nevertheless, some individuals live for a long time: the colony at Rockabill, for example, has a 'core' of highly successful breeders 9–19 years old.[44] The oldest bird recorded to date in Britain and Ireland was 21 years old.[45]

There is reason to believe that the breeding population may have more females than males. This has been well documented for roseate terns in the USA, where large numbers of adults have been sexed using DNA extracted from blood. In the colony that was studied, about 11 per cent of all nests were attended by two or more females, most of them two females paired together without a male partner. The sex-ratio was therefore about 127 females to 100 males (100 nests would be attended by 89 males and 111 females). Many of the female–female pairs were easily detected because they attended 'supernormal' clutches of three or four eggs instead of the normal one or two (rare five-egg clutches were attended by three or four females without male partners). However, more than half of the female–female pairs attended clutches of two eggs (one egg laid by each female), leading to an equation:

Number of female–female pairs = 2.2 × number of supernormal clutches.[46]

In Britain and Ireland, supernormal clutches are less frequent than in the USA, so female–female pairs are probably less prevalent. Assuming that this equation would be valid here also, the occurrence of 1.75–2.0 per cent of supernormal clutches at Rockabill (see Chapter 9) suggests that about 4 per cent of the nests there are attended by female–female pairs. The overall sex-ratio would then be about 1.04/0.96, or 108 females to 100 males.

In the US study, about half of the eggs laid by females in female–female pairs were fertile and hatched (although there were no males socially attached to the females or attending their nests, neighbouring males were evidently glad to oblige). Although female–female pairs thereby succeeded in raising some chicks, their productivity was only about half that of male–female pairs (0.68 fledglings per pair versus 1.35). It was estimated that the unbalanced sex-ratio reduced overall average productivity by about 20 per cent below what would have been achieved if all females had male mates (to about 1.1 instead of 1.35).[47] The depression in productivity would probably be smaller in the British and Irish population, but if our estimate of sex-ratio derived above is valid, this would be reducing overall productivity by about 6 per cent below what would be achieved if all females had male mates (1.31 vs. 1.39).

Arctic tern

Arctic terns are long-lived, with records of marked birds as old as 29 years in Britain and 34 years in the USA.[48] Three estimates of the annual survival rates of adults based on recaptures and resightings of birds ringed at the Farne Islands all fell between 0.86 and 0.88.[49] However, these values are likely to be underestimates of true survival, because they did not incorporate corrections for incomplete resighting or for emigration to other sites. The only study of adult survival based on rigorous mark–recapture methods was conducted recently at four breeding sites in the USA and Canada: this yielded estimates of 0.90–0.94 for birds marked at three of the sites, but only around 0.80 for birds marked at the fourth.[50] The authors suggested that the last value may have been biased downwards by emigration of birds from the fourth site to sites outside the study area. The same study also yielded estimates of rates of movement from one site to another within the study area: these indicated that 1–5 per cent of the adult birds changed sites each year. This finding confirms that the survival estimates from the Farne Islands are likely to have been too low because of emigration. If the authors of the North American study were correct in discounting the low estimates from the fourth site, the values of 0.90–0.94 for the other three sites would be at the high end of the range of estimates for other terns, consistent with the longevity records.

In Britain and Ireland, interchanges among breeding colonies are common. Among 458 breeding-season recoveries of birds ringed as chicks, 38 per cent were further than 20 km from the natal site, ranging up to 1,000 km with individual birds recovered in Norway, Sweden, Denmark, Germany and the Faeroe Islands.[51] However, it is not known how many of these were breeding at the sites of recovery. It is evident from the ephemeral nature of breeding colonies that birds move about even after having bred at a site for several years, but there is little precise information about when and why individual birds change sites. Based on changes in numbers and population modelling, about 10,000 Arctic terns appear to have emigrated from Orkney to Shetland in the early 1990s, presumably in response to greater food availability in Shetland. However, it is also likely that many Arctic terns did not breed at all during the years with lowest food availability.[52]

Like other terns, Arctic terns usually breed for the first time at ages three or four, with about 5 per cent breeding at two and about 5 per cent not breeding until five years old. At the Farne Islands, only about 30 per cent of three-year-olds bred in normal years and virtually none in a year of poor food supply.[53] There is no direct information on survival between fledging and recruitment into the breeding population.

Partly because of this lack of information on survival from fledging to recruitment, no attempts have been made to model the dynamics of Arctic

tern populations. If adult survival is truly in the range 0.90–0.94 as suggested
in the North American study cited earlier, then average productivity would not
need to be as high to maintain a stable population as the values of 0.87 and 1.03
suggested earlier for common and roseate terns, respectively. Available data
for productivity of Arctic terns in Britain and Ireland yielded values higher
than these in the 1960s, but much lower in the 1980s and 1990s. The average
productivity at the 17 sites in the SMP between 1986 and 2010 was only 0.43,
and was much lower (0.22) at sites in Scotland and the Northern Isles than in
northern England, Wales and southeast Ireland (0.79) (see Table 25 in Chapter 10).
This is consistent with the observation that numbers of breeders in the main
range in the Northern Isles appear to have declined between 1980 and 2010,[54]
whereas those in Wales and Ireland have increased considerably (see Chapter
10). However, much more information on dispersal and survival will be required
before the changes in the size and distribution of the breeding population can
be fully understood.

OVERVIEW

Table 31 summarises the estimates of population parameters discussed in this
appendix and compares estimates of the productivities required to maintain a
stable population with the observed average productivities and with the observed
population trends. For roseate and common terns, the population models
explain the observed trends reasonably well. For the little tern, the population
model explained the decline from 1969 to 1998, but is inconsistent with the
observed increase since 2005. For the Sandwich tern, there is insufficient
information for numerical comparisons, but the data on productivity and trends
suggest that the estimated survival rates are probably too low. For the Arctic tern,
there is again insufficient information for numerical comparisons, but average
productivity has been much lower than those of the other terns in the species'
main range in Scotland and the Northern Isles, and the population appears to
have been decreasing there. In contrast, average productivity in the well-studied
colonies to the south of the main range has been comparable to that of common
terns, and the population has been increasing there in recent years. However,
there is no information on the extent to which these changes are influenced
by dispersal; dispersal rates appear to be relatively high in Arctic terns. In
spite of intensive studies of our tern populations over many decades, complete
understanding of their demography and population dynamics is still elusive.
This will make it difficult to set well-founded goals for their conservation.

TABLE 31. Results of population modelling for terns of Great Britain and Ireland.

Species	Adult survival rate	Ages at first breeding	Survival from fledging to age 3	Productivity required for stable population	Observed average productivity	Population trend 1986–2010
Little tern	0.89 (common tern, Germany before 1998)	2–4	0.33 (common tern, Germany before 1998)	0.74	0.59	+0.3% per year
Sandwich tern	0.90	3–5	0.17–0.22	not estimated	0.68	–0.7% per year
Common tern (Germany)						
1992–2001	0.87 to age 3, 0.92 adults	Mean 3.3	0.31	0.57		
2002–2009	0.79 to age 3, 0.90 adults	Mean 3.9	0.22	1.28		
Britain & Ireland					0.87	Stable
Roseate tern	0.735 (first year) 0.855 (subsequent years)	3–4 (2–5)	0.37 (USA)	1.03	1.31	+4.0% per year
Arctic tern	0.90–0.94 (USA/Canada)					
Britain & Ireland		3–4 (2–5)	not estimated	not estimated	0.43	–0.8 to –1.0% per year
Scotland					0.22	Decreasing
England, Wales & Ireland					0.79	Increasing

All data are for British and/or Irish populations except where stated. Population trend is for total numbers in Britain and Ireland (see Chapters 6–10). Ages at first breeding in parentheses indicate extreme values reported for less than 10 per cent of the population.

Research on Terns

INFORMATION ON THE TERNS OF BRITAIN and Ireland is scattered through a vast array of sources, including books, papers in scientific and other journals, unpublished reports, electronic databases and unpublished information derived from the experience of an army of field observers. Some of the studies reported in these sources can be characterised as descriptive natural history, some as primarily addressed to ringing, some as long-term monitoring and some as scientific research. The distinctions between these categories are ill-defined and many studies have elements of two or more of them. Especially in recent decades, most of the studies have had conservation among their goals and many have been integrated into programmes of conservation and management.

The body of information available on each of our five species of terns has been distilled into a series of major monographs in *Handbooks*, including those on the birds of Britain and Ireland, Central Europe, the Western Palearctic, the former Soviet Union, Australasia and the Antarctic, North America and the World.[1] *The Birds of the Western Palearctic* (BWP) is available as an interactive DVD (BWPi), and updates for three of our species have been published in the journal *BWP Update*.[2] Several books have been published on the natural history of terns, and two books have been published on the common tern.[3]

This appendix summarises some of the more important scientific research that has been carried out on our five breeding species. As stated above, there are no clear distinctions between descriptive natural history, monitoring and scientific research, but our focus here is on long-term studies that have produced multiple papers in scientific journals. However, we have included some of the best among older studies that provided basic information on the biology of each species, and which served as the foundation for the more detailed scientific studies in recent decades. The species are treated here in descending order from the best-studied to the least-studied, rather than in taxonomic order as in the rest of the book.

COMMON TERN

The common tern is the most thoroughly studied among our terns and is becoming one of the best-studied of all birds. It is often selected as a study species by research biologists, for several reasons. It is valued by conservationists and is vulnerable enough to justify protective management and predator control at many of its colonies, yet it is numerous enough for intensive studies to be acceptable and permitted. It nests in colonies, so that large sample sizes can be obtained with a minimum of time and travel. It nests in the open, so that all its breeding behaviour can be watched easily, and (like other terns) it brings food to the nest in its bill, one fish at a time, so that each item can be identified to species and approximate size. It usually feeds close to shore, so that its foraging can often be studied from land without the need to follow it to its feeding grounds by boat. It is a generalist feeder and very adaptable in the way it utilises food resources and breeding areas, making it practicable to study varying adaptations to local environmental conditions. It readily colonises artificial breeding sites, allowing manipulative experiments to study its use of habitats and substrates. It is extremely tolerant of research activity and quickly becomes accustomed to the constant presence of biologists, losing almost all fear and allowing very close approach (Figs. 233 and 234); it can often be studied in the field without the need to use hides or other precautions to minimise disturbance. It is easily caught at the nest and is very tolerant of repeated trapping and handling, including intrusive work such as drawing blood, pulling feathers or attaching devices such as data loggers and radio transmitters. For all these reasons, it is an almost ideal study species even for inexperienced biologists, and many PhD degrees have resulted from studies of various aspects of its behaviour, breeding performance or physiology. The 'down side' of selecting it as a study subject is that it is extremely aggressive, especially at sites when it has lost its fear of human intruders: it constantly attacks them, pecking their heads and defecating on them.

The first substantial body of research on common terns was conducted at Blakeney Point, Norfolk, by William Rowan. Rowan emigrated to Canada in 1920 and became one of the leading ornithologists of his time, but as a student in 1913–14 he worked at a field station established at Blakeney Point by Francis

FIG 233. Common terns quickly become accustomed to the activities of biologists and allow very close approach. Bird Island, USA. (Ian Nisbet)

Oliver, a botanist who was instrumental in the acquisition of the Point by the National Trust (see Chapter 5). Rowan measured thousands of common tern eggs and recorded their colours and patterns in a systematic way. Although egg-collecting had been a pastime of scientifically inclined gentlemen since the mid-nineteenth century, this was probably the first scientific study of eggs of wild birds, and certainly the first to use formal statistics. The data set was analysed by Rowan and Karl Pearson in a series of monumental papers in the statistical journal *Biometrika*.[4] Pearson was one of the fathers of statistical theory, and he explored correlations between different characters of the eggs, using the correlation coefficient that still bears his name. He interpreted the data according to his concept of *homotyposis*, which he defined as 'forming after a type' or 'the correlation between meristically repeated parts'. Although oology has fallen out of fashion as a scientific discipline and the concept of homotyposis did not develop much traction in biology, the collaboration between Rowan and Pearson, two of the giants in their fields, was an auspicious start for the use of common terns in research.

FIG 234. Some common terns become so indifferent to the presence of biologists that they will stand on the head of one person to watch the activities of others. Bird Island, USA. (Carolyn Mostello)

A second major study of common terns was also conducted at Blakeney Point, by George and Anne Marples in 1932 and 1933, and was reported in their book *Sea Terns or Sea Swallows: Their Habits, Language, Arrival and Departure*.[5] Although this book would be characterised nowadays as descriptive natural history rather than analytical science, it was well ahead of its time. It formed the basis for knowledge of all five of our breeding terns for several decades and is still a useful reference today. The Marples were 'at pains to spend many consecutive hours, days and even weeks in hide and hut in various terneries closely watching and immediately recording, feeling that only by doing so could a complete picture be obtained of the life of the terns.' They made detailed descriptions of the terns' behaviour and many aspects of their breeding biology. They conducted some of the first field experiments on terns, reporting the responses of terns to modifications or displacements of their eggs and nests. Their book also included a thorough review of the history and distribution of terns in Britain and Ireland, covering the same material as our Chapter 5 but giving more detail.

A decade earlier, in 1922, Christian Floyd started a ringing study of common and other terns in colonies around Cape Cod, USA, and this was greatly expanded and continued by Oliver Austin from 1929 to 1957. Austin was a distinguished country physician and amateur bird-ringer and was able to hire many seasonal field assistants. He ringed more than 350,000 common terns, including 80,000 adults trapped on nests, and obtained more than 250,000 retraps of breeding adults, many of known age. Austin's many publications, mostly in the journal *Bird-Banding*, documented winter quarters and migration routes, site fidelity, dispersal and 'group adherence' (a phenomenon that he discovered in which large groups of terns moved from one site to another and re-nested in close proximity to each other). His last published paper presented the first estimates of adult survival for any tern and the first evidence for ageing (decreasing survival among the oldest birds),[6] although it was discovered later that the actual numbers were invalid because of high rates of ring loss.[7] A similar ringing study has been conducted at Great Gull Island, USA, since 1968 by personnel of the American Museum of Natural History, and has also resulted in ringing and retrapping of hundreds of thousands of common terns.[8]

Another long-term study of common terns in the USA was conducted by Joanna Burger and Michael Gochfeld from 1976 to 1989 and was reported in many papers in scientific journals and in a book *The Common Tern: Its Breeding Biology and Social Behavior*.[9] This was a much more scientific investigation and was focused on 'social behaviour': the authors' stated aim was 'to examine the evolution of components of breeding behavior and coloniality'. Their research included comparisons of breeding biology among more than 60 different colonies, combined with intensive studies of behaviour and a number of field experiments. Burger and Gochfeld later incorporated their knowledge of common and other terns into what is still the standard treatise on the terns of the world, a chapter in the *Handbook of the Birds of The World*.[10]

The foregoing and many other local studies established a firm knowledge base which has served as the foundation for recent intensive research on the biology of common terns. Much of our most detailed knowledge of the species has been obtained from two recent long-term studies that were based on data from individually marked birds. Although these were conducted in Germany and the USA, common terns have been sufficiently studied in Britain, Ireland and other locations to allow confidence that the results of these studies are applicable to the species as a whole. One of the two studies has been conducted at Wilhelmshaven, Germany, by Peter Becker and his many students and colleagues since 1980.[11] This is one of the most innovative and technically ingenious studies of any seabird. The terns nest on six artificial islands in the Banter See, a body of water adjoining Wilhelmshaven harbour. The islands (originally built for other purposes) are made of concrete and each measures 6 × 11 m. They were made suitable for nesting terns by covering them with a layer of gravel and enclosing them with low perimeter walls to prevent the chicks from falling into the water. Ingeniously, the researchers installed 44 platforms at intervals along the walls, and prevented the terns from landing anywhere else on the periphery of the nesting area by stringing wires above the walls between the platforms (Fig. 235). Each platform is mounted on an electronic balance, so that the terns weigh themselves as they arrive and as they depart (Fig. 236). The birds are individually marked with transponders implanted under the skin, rather than with leg-rings as in most studies. These transponders (known as 'PIT-tags') are widely used for identification of individual animals, e.g. in laboratory studies or for location and retrieval of lost or stolen pets. The transponder responds to 'interrogation' from a nearby antenna by transmitting at a unique frequency, thereby identifying the individual bird and its location. The information on the identity and weight of

FIG 235. Common tern breeding site at the Banter See, Wilhelmshaven, Germany. The colony site consists of six artificial islands, which have been engineered so that terns flying in and out can land only on 44 platforms, each one of which is mounted on an electronic balance and is surrounded by an antenna to identify each individual tern that lands on it. The data are transmitted in real time by cable to a laboratory overlooking the colony on the nearby mainland. The baffle serves to exclude rats. (Peter Becker)

FIGS 236–238. Three approaches to weighing terns in the field without catching them. Changes in a tern's body weight reflect the amount of food available to it and the proportion of resources it allocates to maintaining its body condition. Some individual terns consistently weigh more than others, and the heavier terns tend to raise more young and to live longer. Measuring body weights is an important element in several research programmes, and these automated techniques allow repeated measurements of individual birds without disruptive trapping.

ABOVE: **FIG 236.** Common terns on a weighing platform. Each bird in this colony is marked with a transponder implanted under the skin, which responds to 'interrogation' from a nearby antenna by returning a signal with a unique frequency. Each bird in the colony is identified individually and weighed every time it lands on a platform. Wilhelmshaven, Germany. (Peter Becker)

LEFT: **FIG 237.** Common tern nest on a weighing platform. The platform rests on an electronic balance and is surrounded by an antenna to identify which member of the pair is on the nest. Wilhelmshaven, Germany. (Peter Becker)

FIG 238. Roseate tern nest on a weighing platform. This bird laid eggs inside the nest box. The box was then raised to place the nest on a platform resting on an electronic balance. Bird Island, USA. (Jeremy Hatch)

each bird is transmitted in real time by cable to a laboratory building on the shore overlooking the colony. Individual birds are matched to nests by moving additional antennas from nest to nest throughout the breeding area (Fig. 237). Thus, each adult tern is tracked and repeatedly weighed each year from its first arrival at the colony site through the pre-breeding period, identified with its mate at the nest, registered regularly through the breeding cycle, and tracked after its chicks fledge until it leaves the area in late summer.[12] The nests are marked, many of the chicks are weighed regularly to measure growth rates, and all surviving chicks are marked with transponders and monitored after fledging until they leave the area. The chicks are sexed using DNA extracted from red blood cells collected at the time of marking. Although the nesting area is entered repeatedly to mark nests and weigh chicks, the breeding adults are identified automatically without ever being trapped and handled. Where necessary for behaviour studies, the adults are marked without trapping by spraying dyes on them. In another ingenious twist, it has proved possible to draw blood for physiology studies from the adults without catching them, using a blood-sucking bug hidden in a dummy egg placed in the nest: the bug sucks blood from the incubating bird through a hole in the egg; the dummy egg is retrieved after an hour or two and the blood extracted.[13]

This highly automated system has made possible a number of unique studies. More than 90 papers have been published in scientific journals, covering almost every aspect of the biology of common terns, including behaviour, reproductive performance, food and foraging, physiology and senescence. Many papers have also been published on common terns in other parts of Germany. The ability to monitor and weigh birds that attend the colony but do not yet breed there has led to a series of unique studies on recruitment. Several papers have analysed data on demography and population dynamics, as well as food and foraging behaviour.[14] Maintenance of favourable conditions for nesting has drawn in both local recruits and immigrants from elsewhere, and numbers increased to more than 600 pairs in a total area of less than 400 m², but have decreased again since 2002 as a result of deteriorating food supply (see Appendix 1).[15] As in all long-term ecological studies, the value of the data increases with each year of additional study, and there are endless opportunities for more types of study that would be difficult or impossible anywhere else.

The other major long-term study on common terns has been conducted since 1970 by Ian Nisbet and his students and colleagues at breeding colonies in Buzzards Bay in Massachusetts, USA. This has been a more conventional type of study, in that the birds are marked with leg-rings and are resampled by trapping adults at the nest. It is integrated with a conservation programme, which includes management and restoration of habitat and control of predators, particularly addressed to conservation of the large numbers of roseate terns that nest on the same islands. This population of common terns also has increased enormously during 40 years of study and now includes more than 7,000 pairs on three islands. More than 100,000 chicks have been ringed and the breeding population now includes large numbers of birds of known age, ranging from first-time breeders two or three years old to a handful over 24. Research has focused on several topics, including the relation of breeding performance to the age of the parents; attempts to detect effects and mechanisms of ageing; testing predictions of life-history theory concerning trade-offs between reproductive effort and survival; the phenomenon in which birds founding new colonies initially have high breeding success, declining as the colony 'matures' and 'ages' in spite of increasing age and experience of the breeding adults; and physiological studies, including the relationships of endocrine and immune functions to age and breeding performance. The most recent research has involved using geolocators to track individual birds on their migrations and

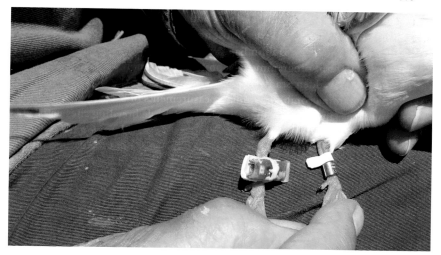

FIG 239. Common tern with a geolocator. Geolocators are tracking devices that record location by measuring changes in light intensity, which are used to determine the times of sunrise and sunset, from which latitude and longitude can be calculated. The data are stored on a chip which can retain data for up to two years. This device was mounted on a plastic leg-flag. The white flag was placed on the other leg so that the bird could be recognised if it returned without the geolocator. Bird Island, USA. (Carolyn Mostello)

in winter quarters (Fig. 239).[16] Detailed studies have also been conducted at the same sites on roseate terns, a species classified as endangered in the USA (Fig. 238). More than 100 papers on terns have been published in scientific journals. Common terns have been monitored and ringed at many other locations in the North America, including freshwater sites on the Great Lakes, but the full potential of this work to elucidate dispersal movements between colony sites has not yet been realised.

In Britain and Ireland, the most important location for research studies on the biology of common terns has been Coquet Island, Northumberland, where several students have earned their PhD degrees since 1968. Monitoring studies have been conducted at several other sites, including Scolt Head, Norfolk, in 1931–69.[17] The *Seabird Monitoring Programme* (SMP) has maintained records of numbers and productivity at more than 100 sites around Britain and Ireland each year since 1986 (see Appendix 3).[18] More than 190,000 common terns have been ringed in Britain and Ireland, mostly as chicks, and almost 5,000 have been recovered, allowing for detailed analysis of migration patterns, migration dates and winter quarters.[19] Studies of post-breeding dispersal and staging, including mist-netting, reading of rings by telescope and documentation of moult, have been conducted at several sites, most notably at Seaforth (Merseyside), Teesmouth (Cleveland) and Dublin Bay.[20]

Another long-term programme of monitoring common terns has been carried out in the Wadden Sea in northwest Germany and the Netherlands since 1981. This programme combines annual measurements of breeding success of common terns (and several other species) at multiple breeding sites with measurements of persistent contaminants in their eggs.[21] Common terns have also been used for monitoring contaminants in the USA and Canada, and have been used in experimental toxicology studies in Canada and the Netherlands. [22]

ROSEATE TERN

The roseate tern was the subject of the first monograph on any species of tern, presented by Louis Bureau at the Fourth International Ornithological Congress in London in 1905 and published in its *Proceedings*.[23] Bureau was a professor of medicine and director of the Natural History Museum of Nantes in France, but he was also a field biologist in an era of collectors. Between 1869 and 1901, he visited many islands around the coasts of northwestern France and found roseate terns nesting on at least ten of them. At that time, roseate terns were extinct or almost extinct in Britain and Ireland (see Chapter 5), and it is likely that he recorded the tenuous thread by which the European population survived through the depredations of the nineteenth century. By studying the birds in life rather than shooting them as other naturalists would have done, he may have single-handedly saved the European population from extinction. Besides descriptions of plumage and delineation of the roseate tern's world distribution, the monograph included the first accounts of its breeding biology.

In Ireland, David Cabot conducted a series of studies of roseate terns at Lady's Island Lake, Co. Wexford (1960), at Tern Island, Co. Wexford (1961–76, until the island was washed away in 1977) and at Rockabill, Co. Dublin (1988–90).[24] The studies included censusing, measuring productivity, monitoring tern eggs and fish prey for contaminants and recording prey items brought to chicks. Some 6,585 chicks and 217 adults were ringed, constituting 37 per cent of all roseate terns ringed in Britain and Ireland up to the end of 1975. Recoveries of these birds provided evidence of heightened mortality on the West African wintering grounds prior to and during the population crash. Cabot (with Karl Partridge and others) also surveyed roseate terns in Brittany, France, in 1976 and 1978, ringed chicks there and recorded food brought to nestlings.[25]

FIG 240. Intensive studies of breeding success are carried out in most of the major colonies of roseate terns in Europe and North America. Eggs are measured and weighed, and chicks are ringed and weighed at regular intervals. Common terns are studied in the same way at many sites. Growth rates of chicks provide an index of the amount of food available to the adults, and differences in growth rate among chicks of different broods provide indices of the relative performance and quality of the parents. These data are used both for monitoring productivity and in research studies. Lady's Island Lake, Co. Wexford. (Dave Daly)

The population crash in the 1970s triggered an expanded programme of conservation of the roseate tern in Britain and Ireland, combined with intensive research into the species' biology and population dynamics. Starting around 1986, nests were counted and productivity was measured at each of the major colonies in Britain and Ireland, and at several smaller ones (see Table 22 in Chapter 9). Most of the chicks were ringed in each year and many were weighed to measure growth rates (Fig 240). From 1992 onwards, all birds received field-readable rings as well as BTO rings (Fig. 241): this formed the basis for an intensive programme of resighting at the three major colony sites. By 2007, 3,205

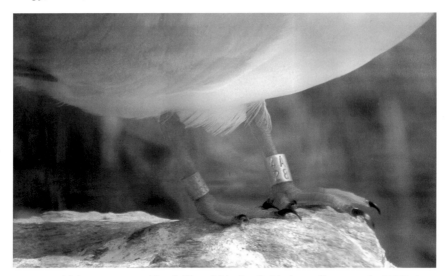

FIG 241. Adult roseate tern with a field-readable ring (left leg) as well as a standard BTO ring (right leg). The field-readable rings can be read in the field at ranges up to 25 m with a good-quality telescope. Intensive programmes of ringing and resighting roseate terns have been conducted for many years in Britain, Ireland and the USA. Lady's Island Lake, Co. Wexford. (Dave Daly)

different birds had been resighted one or more times as adults, and the mark–resighting data were used to estimate adult survival rates with high precision, as well as rates of dispersal among the three sites.[26] Studies were also carried out in the winter quarters in West Africa, identifying trapping by small boys as a major threat to the population and leading to the development of a conservation programme there (see Chapter 11). Accumulated knowledge of the European population was summarised in 2004 in the monograph in *BWP Update*.[27]

A closely parallel programme integrating conservation and research was carried out in North America (northeastern USA and southeastern Canada) at the same period. As in Britain and Ireland, roseate terns had been studied prior to a population crash in the 1970s, and that event triggered an intensive programme of conservation and research starting in 1986. This programme was more 'hands-on' than that in Britain and Ireland, involving trapping of adults as well as resighting of individuals marked as chicks.[28] In addition to estimating adult survival and dispersal among colonies, mark–recapture data were used to estimate ages at first breeding, juvenile survival and natal dispersal. Adults were sexed by genetic methods, leading to the discovery that the breeding population included many more females than males.[29] Intensive studies were conducted of chick growth and survival, factors affecting reproductive success and foraging methods. More than 50 scientific papers reporting work conducted under this programme have been published: a comprehensive review of knowledge of the species in North America was issued by the US Fish and Wildlife Service (the agency responsible for management) in 2010.[30]

Roseate terns are primarily a tropical species, and the small populations breeding in temperate North America and Europe are geographically separated and ecologically distinct from the larger populations breeding in tropical seas. A long-term study of a tropical population has been carried out at Aride Island in the Seychelles, focusing on the relationship of breeding performance to changes in oceanography and survival.[31] This formed the basis for a comparative study of the demography of tropical and temperate roseate terns.[32]

SANDWICH TERN

Two detailed studies of Sandwich terns have been carried out in the Netherlands by PhD students. Dutch students are required to publish their theses, so each of the studies is available in the form of a book. In the 1970s Jan Veen conducted a four-year study of the factors affecting the patterns of nest distribution, addressing the general question of why Sandwich terns nest in very dense groups, usually in association with black-headed gulls, and do not conceal their nests in the way that other terns do. The thesis included thorough description of the basic biology and behaviour of the species and detailed studies of predation and anti-predator adaptations.[33] Nearly 30 years later, Eric Stienen worked at the same colony site and extended Veen's studies by dissecting the relationship between Sandwich terns and black-headed gulls, showing that the terns gained net benefits from the close association despite the fact that the gulls preyed on the terns' eggs and chicks and stole food from the adults.[34] The thesis included an analysis of changes in numbers of Sandwich terns breeding in western Europe since 1900, their relationship to changing conditions and food availability in the North Sea, and an assessment of the likely future of the population under climate change. Stienen's work also included what was probably the most detailed study of the ecology of Sandwich and other terns in the winter quarters in West Africa.[35]

In Britain and Ireland, Nigel Langham studied Sandwich terns at Coquet Island for three years in the 1960s and published a paper comparing their breeding biology with that of other terns.[36] J. W. M. Smith studied Sandwich terns at the Sands of Forvie, Aberdeenshire, for at least seven years in the 1960s and 1970s. He colour-ringed large numbers of birds and studied their behaviour and breeding biology. Although he must have had good data on individually marked birds of known age, his only publication was a general account of the species in 1975.[37] Accompanied by many excellent photographs, this remains one of the best descriptions of the species' courtship and breeding behaviour. Ongoing monitoring and ringing programmes are accumulating large volumes of data on numbers, productivity, migration, dispersal and moult (see Chapter 7 and Appendix 3).

ARCTIC TERN

In 1952–55, Michael Cullen made an intensive study of the behaviour of Arctic terns at the Farne Islands, Northumberland. Cullen was a student of Niko Tinbergen at Oxford University, and he analysed the terns' behavioural repertoire using the methods developed by Tinbergen: dissecting behaviour into elements, analysing their contexts and consequences and drawing inferences about motivation and the evolution of behaviour. He also described the behaviour of common, Sandwich and roseate terns and analysed similarities and differences among the four species. Although tern display postures and actions had been described earlier by many naturalists, Cullen's analysis and interpretations explained them in a coherent way and made them instantly understandable. Cullen published only part of his findings in scientific journals, but his DPhil thesis has been widely circulated among tern biologists and is still useful reading today.[38]

Following reports of widespread breeding failures of Arctic terns in Orkney and Shetland in the 1980s, there was a flurry of research into factors responsible for the failures, which were soon found to be related to a drastic decline in availability of sandeels, their primary prey.[39] As a result of these and later studies, the relationship of breeding performance to food availability is probably better known for Arctic terns than for other tern species.

Other scientific research on Arctic terns has been sporadic and has not been based on long-term studies, except for the *Seabird Monitoring Programme* in Britain and Ireland (see Appendix 3) and the *Wadden Sea Monitoring Programme* in Germany and the Netherlands.[40] Four noteworthy papers published recently include studies of the effects of climate change, estimation of survival rates by mark–recapture methods in the USA and Canada, and tracking of the Arctic tern's global migrations using geolocators.[41]

LITTLE TERN

Comparatively little scientific research has been carried out on little terns. They are difficult to study in the field because their colonies are small and ephemeral, their nests are widely spaced, their chicks scatter over large areas and they experience high levels of predation. Many attempts to study their breeding biology have quickly turned into studies of their responses to predation. They are sensitive to disturbance and often nest on or near public beaches where scientists cannot enter the nesting areas without attracting attention and public disapproval. Much of what has been published about the breeding of little terns has been related to their conservation and management, and this often appears in agency reports, conference proceedings and the like, rather than scientific journals. We are not aware of any long-term scientific studies of little terns, other than the monitoring of colony numbers and productivity in the *Seabird Monitoring Programme*. The most recent monograph on the species cited new information reported between 1985 and 2002 on habitat selection, food, behaviour, offspring–parent recognition and moult, but none of these advances in knowledge resulted from a sustained programme of scientific research.[42] The closely related least tern of North America has been studied much more thoroughly, because two of its three regional populations are classified as endangered and are subject to intensive programmes of conservation and research.[43]

The Seabird Monitoring Programme

T HE *SEABIRD MONITORING PROGRAMME* (SMP) is a long-running programme to monitor numbers and productivity of seabirds throughout Britain and Ireland. This programme originated in 1984, when the Nature Conservancy Council and the Seabird Group started the *Seabird Colony Register* (SCR), which formed the basis for the second census of seabirds in Britain and Ireland in 1985–88.[1] In 1986, the SCR morphed into the SMP, which collects and manages data on numbers and productivity of seabird colonies throughout the UK and Ireland. The SMP is managed by the Joint Nature Conservancy Council (JNCC) and has continued each year since 1986. The JNCC issues annual reports, formerly published every two years but now online.[2]

We compiled data from the SMP as the basis for our summaries of trends and productivity in Chapters 6–10. These data were extracted from the JNCC annual reports and the SMP database at jncc.defra.gov.uk/smp. Data were provided to the SMP by its partners, other organisations and volunteers throughout Britain and Ireland. Partners to the SMP are: BirdWatch Ireland; British Trust for Ornithology; Centre for Ecology & Hydrology; Countryside Council for Wales; Department of Agriculture, Fisheries and Forestry (Isle of Man); Department of Environment, Heritage and Local Government (Republic of Ireland); Joint Nature Conservancy Council; Manx Birdlife; Manx National Heritage; the National Trust; National Trust for Scotland; Natural England; Northern Ireland Environment Agency; Royal Society for the Protection of Birds; Scottish Natural Heritage; Scottish Wildlife Trust; Seabird Group; Shetland Oil Terminal Environmental Advisory Group; States of Guernsey Government.

Scientific Names of Plants and Animals Mentioned in the Text

S CIENTIFIC AND VERNACULAR NAMES of the 39 species of terns are given in Table 1 (Chapter 1). Other species mentioned in the text are as follows:

Bootlace weed *Chorda filum*
Bracken *Pteridium aquilinum*
Frosted orache *Atriplex laciniata*
Gorse *Ulex europaeus*
Hottentot fig *Carpobrotus edulis*
Lyme grass *Leymus arenarius*
Marram grass *Ammophila arenaria*
Sand couch grass *Agropyron junceiforme*
Searocket *Cakile maritima*
Stinging nettle *Urtica dioica*
Tree mallow *Lavatera arborea*

Anchovy *Engraulis guineensis*
Atlantic cod *Gadus morhua*
Atlantic herring *Clupea harengus*
Bleak *Alburnus alburnus*
Bonito *Sarda sarda*
European sprat *Sprattus sprattus*
Fivebeard rockling *Ciliata mustela*
Flounder *Platichthys flesus*

Greater sandeel *Hyperoplus lanceolatus*
Lesser sandeel *Ammodytes marinus*
Mosquito fish *Gambusia affinis*
Perch *Perca fluviatilis*
Pipefish family Syngnathidae
Pollack *Pollachius pollachius*
Roach *Rutilus rutilus*
Ruffe *Gymnocephalus cernua*
Saithe *Pollachius virens*
Salmon *Salmo salar*
Sardine *Sardinella* spp.
Small sandeel *Ammodytes tobianus*
Smelt *Osmerus eperlanus*
Snake pipefish *Entelurus aequoreus*
Three-spined stickleback *Gasterosteus aculeatus*
Tilapia *Tilapia mariae*
Tuna *Thunnus* spp.
Whiting *Merlangius merlangus*

Amsterdam albatross *Diomedea amsterdamensis*
Arctic skua *Stercorarius parasiticus*
Atlantic puffin *Fratercula arctica*
Black guillemot *Cepphus grylle*
Black-headed gull *Chroicocephalus ridibundus*
Black-legged kittiwake *Rissa tridactyla*
Black noddy *Anous minutus*
Black skimmer *Rynchops niger*
Common eider *Somateria mollissima*
Great black-backed gull *Larus marinus*
Great skua *Stercorarius skua*
Grey heron *Ardea cinerea*
Grey phalarope *Phalaropus fulicarius*
Greylag goose *Anser anser*
Guillemot *Uria aalge*
Herring gull *Larus argentatus*
Hobby *Falco subbuteo*
Hooded crow *Corvus cornix*
Indian skimmer *Rynchops albicollis*
Kestrel *Falco tinnunculus*
Kingfisher *Alcedo atthis*
Laughing gull *Larus atricilla*
Lesser black-backed gull *Larus fuscus*
Merlin *Falco columbarius*
Noddy *Anous* spp.
Northern fulmar *Fulmarus glacialis*

Northern gannet *Morus bassanus*
Northern royal albatross *Diomedea sanfordi*
Peregrine falcon *Falco peregrinus*
Pomarine skua *Stercorarius pomarinus*
Red-necked phalarope *Phalaropus lobatus*
Ringed plover *Charadrius hiaticula*
Shag *Phalacrocorax aristotelis*
Short-eared owl *Asio flammeus*
Southern royal albatross *Diomedea epomorphora*
Wandering albatross *Diomedea exulans*
White tern *Gygis alba*

American mink *Mustela vison*
Arctic fox *Vulpes lagopus*
Badger *Meles meles*
Brown rat *Rattus norvegicus*
Coypu *Myocastor coypus*
Hedgehog *Erinaceus europaeus*
Hump-backed whale *Megaptera novaeangliae*
Otter *Lutra lutra*
Rabbit *Oryctolagus cuniculus*
Red fox *Vulpes vulpes*
Stoat *Mustela erminea*
Weasel *Mustela nivalis*

Endnotes

CHAPTER 1

1 Burger & Gochfeld, 1996. In this book, we generally follow the taxonomy and English names currently adopted by the British Ornithologists' Union (most recently updated for terns by Sangster *et al.*, 2005, 2011), but with two exceptions. We treat the little and least terns as separate species, following Burger & Gochfeld (1996), the American Ornithologists' Union (2006) and Gill & Donsker (2012), and we use the genus *Thalasseus* for the 'crested' terns, following Bridge *et al.* (2005), Efe *et al.* (2009) and Gill & Donsker (2012).
2 Schreiber *et al.*, 2002.
3 Schreiber & Burger, 2001; Hatch, 2002; Schreiber *et al.*, 2002; Becker & Ludwigs, 2004.
4 Burger & Gochfeld, 1996.
5 Baker *et al.*, 2007.
6 Baker *et al.*, 2007.
7 Bridge *et al.*, 2005.
8 Higgins & Davies, 1996; American Ornithologists' Union, 2006; Efe *et al.*, 2009; Gill & Donsker, 2012.
9 Burger & Gochfeld, 1994.
10 Bridge *et al.*, 2005.
11 Several other European languages use some variant of 'tern' or 'stern' (from the Latin *sterna*), but additional Portuguese names are *garajau* (Azores) or *trinta-réis* (Brazil).
12 Burger & Gochfeld, 1996.
13 Pyle, 2008.
14 Bridge & Nisbet, 2004; Bridge & Eaton, 2005.
15 Burger & Gochfeld, 1996; Higgins & Davies, 1996.
16 Cramp, 1985; Burger & Gochfeld, 1996.
17 Burger & Gochfeld, 1996.
18 Bridge *et al.*, 2005.

CHAPTER 2

1 Burger & Gochfeld, 1996.
2 Cramp, 1985.
3 Cramp, 1985.
4 Dunn, 1973b; Taylor, 1983.
5 Amorim *et al.*, 2009.
6 Au & Pitman, 1986; Burger & Gochfeld, 1996.
7 Schreiber *et al.*, 2002.
8 Cramp, 1985.
9 Haney, 1986.
10 Stienen *et al.*, 2001.
11 Hatch, 1970.

12 Stienen *et al.*, 2001.
13 Furness, 1978, 1987.
14 Nisbet, 1983a.
15 Au & Pitman, 1986.
16 D. Cabot, unpublished data.
17 Nisbet, 1983a.
18 Grimes, 1977.
19 Grimes, 1977.
20 Burger & Gochfeld, 1996.
21 Hays *et al.*, 1973.
22 I. Nisbet, unpublished data.
23 Taylor, 1975; Dänhardt *et al.*, 2011.
24 Nisbet, 2002.
25 Cramp, 1985; Burger & Gochfeld, 1996.
26 Nisbet, 2002.
27 Perrow *et al.*, 2011.
28 Schreiber *et al.*, 2002.
29 Burger & Gochfeld, 1996.
30 Ramos *et al.*, 1998.
31 Massias & Becker, 1990.
32 Klaassen, 1994.
33 Nisbet, 2002.
34 Hislop *et al.*, 1991.
35 Wanless *et al.*, 2005.
36 jncc.defra.gov.uk/smp.
37 Newton & Crowe, 2000.
38 Uttley *et al.*, 1989b.

CHAPTER 3

1 Burger & Gochfeld, 1996.
2 Burger & Gochfeld, 1996; Schreiber *et al.*, 2002.
3 Ramos, 1998.
4 Burger & Gochfeld, 1996.
5 Nisbet, 2002; Becker & Ludwigs, 2004.
6 Becker & Ludwigs, 2004.
7 Gochfeld *et al.*, 1998.
8 Schreiber *et al.*, 2002.
9 Burger & Gochfeld, 1996.
10 Buckley & Buckley, 2002.
11 Simmons *et al.*, 1998; Zavalaga *et al.*, 2008.
12 Nisbet, 2002; Becker & Ludwigs, 2004; Nisbet *et al.*, 2010.
13 Burger & Gochfeld, 1996.
14 Arnold *et al.*, 2004.
15 Oswald *et al.*, 2012.
16 Ashmole & Tovar 1968; Gochfeld *et al.* 1998; Barlow, 1998.
17 Burger & Gochfeld, 1996.
18 Higgins & Davies, 1996.
19 Burger & Gochfeld, 1996.
20 Burger & Gochfeld, 1996.
21 Schreiber *et al.*, 2002.
22 Burger & Gochfeld, 1996; D. Monticelli, unpublished data.
23 Nisbet, 2002.
24 Nisbet *et al.*, 2011b.
25 González-Solís *et al.*, 1999.
26 Black, 1996.
27 Black, 1996.
28 Nisbet, 2002.
29 Malling Olsen & Larsson, 1995; Higgins & Davies, 1996; Whittam, 1998; Burness *et al.*, 1999; Hatch, 2002; C. S. Mostello, unpublished data.
30 Cullen, 1956; Cramp, 1985.
31 Cullen, 1956; Cramp, 1985.
32 Bridge & Eaton, 2005.
33 Cullen, 1956; Cramp, 1985.
34 Cullen, 1956.
35 Nisbet, 1973, 1977.
36 Burger & Gochfeld, 1996.
37 Burger & Gochfeld, 1996.
38 Nisbet & Ratcliffe, 2008.
39 Nisbet, 2002; Becker & Ludwigs, 2004; Nisbet *et al.*, 2010.
40 Burness *et al.*, 1999; Gauger, 1999; Mostello *et al.*, 2000.
41 Cramp, 1985.
42 Nisbet, 2002.
43 Wendeln & Becker, 1996.
44 Nisbet, 1977.
45 Rahn *et al.*, 1979; Rahn & Paganelli, 1981.
46 Carey *et al.*, 1980.

47 Limmer & Becker, 2009.
48 Rahn *et al.*, 1976.
49 Nisbet & Welton, 1984.
50 Burger & Gochfeld, 1996.
51 Gochfeld, 1979.
52 Bollinger, 1994.
53 Lack, 1954.
54 Bollinger *et al.*, 1990.
55 Nisbet, 1983b.
56 Fasola *et al.*, 2002.
57 Nisbet, 2002.
58 Ashmole & Tovar, 1968; Barlow, 1998.
59 Burger & Gochfeld, 1994, 1996.
60 Thompson *et al.* 1997; Fasola *et al.*,
    2002.
61 Wendeln & Becker, 2000.
62 Becker & Zhang, 2011.
63 Wiggins *et al.*, 1984.
64 Hamer *et al.*, 2001; Weimerskirch, 2001.
65 Burger & Gochfeld, 1996; Schreiber &
    Burger, 2001.
66 Rubega *et al.*, 2000.
67 Nisbet & Ratcliffe, 2008.
68 Hamer *et al.*, 2001; Schreiber & Burger,
    2001; Weimerskirch, 2001.
69 Cramp, 1985; Burger & Gochfeld, 1996.
70 Thompson *et al.*, 1997; Fasola *et al.*,
    2002.
71 Burger & Gochfeld, 1996.
72 Burness *et al.*, 1999.
73 Cramp, 1985; Nisbet, 2002; Becker &
    Ludwigs, 2004; Dunn & Agro, 2009.
74 Burger & Gochfeld, 1994.
75 Coulson, 2001.
76 Hatch, 2002.
77 Hatch, 2002; Ratcliffe, 2004b.
78 Hatch, 2002.
79 Burger & Gochfeld, 1996.
80 Coulson, 2001.
81 Burger & Gochfeld, 1996.
82 Buckley & Buckley, 1980.
83 Nisbet *et al.*, 2010.
84 Cullen, 1956.
85 Coulson, 2001.

86 D. Cabot, unpublished data.
87 Ratcliffe *et al.*, 2004.
88 Nisbet, 2002.
89 Coulson, 2001.
90 Götmark, 1990.
91 Coulson, 2001.
92 Nisbet, 2002; Tims *et al.*, 2004.
93 Dittmann *et al.*, 2005.
94 Danchin & Wagner, 1997.
95 Coulson, 2001.
96 Coulson, 2001.
97 Tims *et al.*, 2004.

CHAPTER 4

1   Burger & Gochfeld, 1996.
2   Hatch, 2002.
3   Hatch, 2002.
4   Egevang *et al.*, 2010.
5   Monaghan, 2002; Hatch, 2002.
6   Monaghan, 2002.
7   Hatch, 2002.
8   Grimes, 1977; Alerstam, 1985;
    Gudmundsson *et al.*, 2002.
9   Burger & Gochfeld, 1996.
10 McNicholl *et al.*, 2001.
11 Cramp, 1985; Burger & Gochfeld, 1996.
12 Hays *et al.*, 1997; Buckley & Buckley,
    2002; Ratcliffe & Merne, 2002; Nisbet,
    2002; Becker & Ludwigs, 2004.
13 Norman, 2002; Becker & Ludwigs, 2004.
14 Hays *et al.*, 2002; Szczys *et al.*, 2012.
15 Nisbet, 2002.
16 Cramp, 1985; Noble-Rollin & Redfern,
    2002.
17 Cramp, 1985; Noble-Rollin & Redfern,
    2002.
18 Hays *et al.*, 1997.
19 Higgins & Davies, 1996; O'Neill *et al.*,
    2005.
20 Burness *et al.*, 1999.
21 Nisbet *et al.*, 2011a; I. Nisbet & C.
    Mostello, unpublished data.

22   Higgins & Davies, 1996.

23   Grimes, 1977; Cramp, 1985; Becker & Ludwigs, 2004.

24   Nisbet, 2002.

25   Cramp, 1985; Higgins & Davies, 1996.

26   Grimes, 1977; Alerstam, 1985; Hatch, 2002.

27   Burger & Gochfeld, 1996.

28   Dunlop & Johnstone, 1994.

29   Cramp, 1985.

30   Burger & Gochfeld, 1996.

31   Hays et al., 1999.

32   Schreiber et al., 2002.

33   Burger & Gochfeld, 1996.

34   Haney, 1986.

35   Burger & Gochfeld, 1996.

36   Nisbet & Ratcliffe, 2008.

CHAPTER 5

1   Tyreberg, 1998; Yalden & Albarella, 2009.

2   Fisher, 1966.

3   Marples & Marples, 1934.

4   Marples & Marples, 1934, quoting from Birds of Yorkshire.

5   Fisher, 1966.

6   Newman, 1866.

7   Thompson, 1851.

8   Gray, 1871.

9   Stoddart & Joyner, 2005.

10   National Museum of American History, Smithsonian Institution. americanhistory.si.edu/feather/ftfa.htm (accessed November 2012).

11   Witherby et al., 1942.

12   Bannerman, 1962.

13   Marples & Marples, 1934.

14   Holloway, 1996.

15   Norman & Saunders, 1969.

16   Lloyd et al., 1975.

17   Yarrell, 1843.

18   Gray, 1871.

19   Holloway, 1996.

20   Marples & Marples, 1934.

21   Parslow, 1967–68.

22   Holloway, 1996.

23   Yarrell, 1843.

24   Selby, 1826.

25   Bewick, 1804.

26   Marples & Marples, 1934.

27   Cramp et al., 1974.

28   Macpherson, 1892.

29   Lancashire & Cheshire Fauna Committee, 1934.

30   Macpherson, 1892.

31   Bickerton, 1912.

32   Gray, 1871.

33   Forrester et al., 2007.

34   Holloway, 1996.

35   Marples & Marples, 1934, quoting from Birds of Yorkshire.

36   Marples & Marples, 1934, quoting from Natural History of Birds.

37   Marples & Marples, 1934.

38   Smith, 1750.

39   Selby, 1821–34.

40   Jardine, 1843.

41   Marples & Marples, 1934.

42   Yarrell, 1843.

43   Stoddart & Joyner, 2005.

44   Watson et al., 1923; Marples & Marples, 1934.

45   Chestney, 1970.

46   Cramp et al., 1974.

47   Lovegrove et al., 1994.

48   Rodd & Harting, 1880.

49   Marples & Marples, 1934.

50   Forrester et al., 2007.

51   Marples & Marples, 1934.

52   Smith, 1750.

53   Ussher & Warren, 1900.

54   Thompson, 1851.

55   Ussher & Warren, 1900.

56   Kennedy, 1961.

57   Ussher & Warren, 1900.

58   Kennedy et al., 1954.

59 Holloway, 1996.
60 Parslow, 1967–68.
61 Thompson, 1851.
62 Marples & Marples, 1934.
63 Rodd & Harting, 1880.
64 Gray, 1871.
65 Marples & Marples, 1934.
66 Yarrell, 1843.
67 Hewitson, 1831–42.
68 Seebohm, 1896.
69 Ussher & Warren, 1900.
70 Lovegrove et al., 1994.
71 Bureau, 1907.
72 Lovegrove et al., 1994.
73 Williamson et al., 1941.
74 Cramp et al., 1974.
75 Marples & Marples, 1934.
76 Yarrell, 1843.
77 Rodd & Harting, 1880.
78 Lovegrove et al., 1994.
79 Cramp et al., 1974.
80 Forrester et al., 2007.
81 Forrester et al., 2007.
82 Cramp et al., 1974.
83 Cabot, 1962b.
84 Irish Bird Report 1955; Cabot, 1962c.
85 Cabot, 1962a.
86 Ussher & Warren, 1900.
87 Kennedy et al., 1954.
88 Lloyd et al., 1975.
89 Cramp et al., 1974.
90 Whilde, 1985.
91 Lloyd et al., 1991.
92 Hannon et al., 1997.
93 Mitchell et al., 2004.

CHAPTER 6

1 Pickerell, 2004.
2 Norman & Saunders, 1969.
3 Ratcliffe et al., 2000.
4 Joint Nature Conservation Committee, 2009, 2012.
5 Pickerell, 2004.
6 Fasola et al., 2002; a colony site marked far inland in northern England on the Seabird 2000 map (Pickerell, 2004) appears to have been an error.
7 Fasola et al., 2002.
8 Fasola et al., 2002.
9 Fasola et al., 2002.
10 Fasola & Saino, 1995.
11 Saino et al., 1994.
12 Perrow et al., 2006.
13 Fasola et al., 2002.
14 Perrow et al., 2004.
15 Collinge, 1924–27.
16 Witherby et al., 1942.
17 Cramp, 1985.
18 Fasola et al., 2002.
19 Brenninkmeijer et al., 2002.
20 Grimes, 1977.
21 Ratcliffe et al., 2000.
22 Mavor et al., 2008.
23 Clark et al., 2010.
24 Tasker & Adcock, 2002.
25 Merne, 2010.
26 Cherubini et al., 1996.

CHAPTER 7

1 Ratcliffe, 2004a.
2 Ratcliffe et al., 2000.
3 Ratcliffe, 2004a.
4 Ratcliffe et al., 2000.
5 Joint Nature Conservation Committee, 2009, 2012.
6 jncc.defra.gov.uk/smp; Lady's Island Lake Tern Report 2010.
7 Noble-Rollin & Redfern, 2002; Stienen, 2006.
8 Ratcliffe, 2004a.
9 Stienen, 2006.
10 Stienen, 2006.
11 Hannon et al., 1997.
12 jncc.defra.gov.uk/smp.

13 Whilde, 1985.
14 Ratcliffe, 2004a, citing Brown & McAvoy, 1985.
15 Cullen, 1956; Smith, 1975; Cramp, 1985.
16 Veen, 1977.
17 Shealer, 1999.
18 Stienen, 2006.
19 Veen, 1977; Stienen & Brenninkmeijer, 1999.
20 Stienen et al., 2001.
21 Cullen, 1956; Smith, 1975.
22 Stienen & Brenninkmeijer, 1999.
23 Noble-Rollin & Redfern, 2002.
24 Shealer, 1999.
25 Cramp, 1985.
26 Perrow et al., 2011.
27 Dunn, 1972.
28 Dunn, 1973b.
29 Taylor, 1983.
30 Dunn, 1972; Taylor, 1979.
31 Collinge, 1924–27.
32 Cramp, 1985.
33 Brenninkmeijer et al., 2002.
34 Quintana & Yorio, 1997; Shealer, 1999.
35 Chestney, 1970; Langham, 1974.
36 Cramp, 1985.
37 Langham, 1974.
38 Bickerton, 1912.
39 Veen, 1977.
40 Langham, 1974.
41 Clark et al., 2010.
42 Noble-Rollin & Redfern, 2002.
43 Ward, 2000.
44 Noble-Rollin & Redfern, 2002.
45 Cramp, 1985.
46 Noble-Rollin & Redfern, 2002.
47 Cramp, 1985.
48 grampianringing.blogspot.com (accessed 6 August 2011).

CHAPTER 8

1 Ratcliffe, 2004c.
2 jncc.defra.gov.uk/smp.
3 Joint Nature Conservation Committee, 2009, 2012.
4 jncc.defra.gov.uk/smp; Lady's Island Lake Tern Report 2010.
5 Ratcliffe, 2004c.
6 Becker & Ludwigs, 2004.
7 Nisbet, 2002.
8 Becker & Sudmann, 1998.
9 Greenhalgh, 1974; Bourne, 1976.
10 Forrester et al., 2007.
11 Cullen, 1956.
12 Cullen, 1956; Cramp, 1985.
13 Cullen, 1956.
14 Cullen, 1956; Cramp, 1985.
15 Nisbet, 2002; Becker & Ludwigs, 2004.
16 Nisbet, 1977.
17 Wendeln, 1997, Moore et al., 2000.
18 Nisbet, 1977, 1997.
19 Nisbet, 2002.
20 Nisbet, 2002.
21 Nisbet, 2002.
22 Burger et al., 1993.
23 Cullen, 1956.
24 Saino et al., 1994.
25 Nisbet, 2002.
26 Nisbet et al., 2011b.
27 Wendeln & Becker, 2000; Becker & Zhang, 2011.
28 Grimes, 1977.
29 Nisbet et al., 2011a.
30 Perrow et al., 2011.
31 Tims et al., 2004.
32 Nisbet, 1983a.
33 I. Nisbet, unpublished data.
34 Ludwigs, 1998.
35 García et al., 2011.
36 Oswald et al., 2012.
37 Uttley et al., 1989b.
38 Nisbet, 2002; Becker & Ludwigs, 2004.
39 Taylor, 1979.
40 Nisbet, 2002; Becker & Ludwigs, 2004.
41 Massias & Becker, 1990.
42 Massias & Becker, 1990; Chivers, 2007.

43 Cramp, 1985.
44 Greenhalgh & Greenwood, 1974.
45 Becker & Ludwigs, 2004.
46 Becker et al., 1997.
47 Becker & Ludwigs, 2004.
48 Nisbet, 2002.
49 Nisbet et al., 2002.
50 Tims et al., 2004.
51 Nisbet, 2002; Becker & Ludwigs, 2004.
52 Mavor et al., 2008; jncc.defra.gov.uk/smp.
53 Arnold et al., 2004.
54 Wendeln & Becker, 1999.
55 Tims et al., 2004.
56 Clark et al., 2010.
57 Norman, 2002.
58 Ward, 2000; Merne et al., 2008.
59 Merne et al., 2008; Merne, 2010.
60 Becker & Ludwigs, 2004.
61 Norman, 2002.
62 Dunn & Mead, 1982.
63 Urban et al., 1986.
64 Norman, 2002.
65 Cramp, 1985.
66 Cramp et al., 1974.
67 Szczys et al., 2012.
68 Nisbet & Safina, 1996.
69 Irish Bird Report, 1969.

CHAPTER 9

1 Nisbet & Ratcliffe, 2008.
2 A. Lashko, cited in Nisbet & Ratcliffe, 2008.
3 Burger & Gochfeld, 1996; Gochfeld et al., 1998.
4 Bridge et al., 2005; Efe et al., 2009.
5 Mitchell et al., 2004.
6 Cabot, 1996.
7 Quemmerais-Amice & Gager, 2010.
8 Cadiou, 2010.
9 Royal Society for Protection of Birds, unpublished data, supplied by Vivienne Booth.
10 jncc.defra.gov.uk/smp.
11 Cabot, 1996; Cadiou, 2010.
12 Cramp et al., 1974; Ewins, 1987.
13 Morrison & Gurney, 2007.
14 US Fish and Wildlife Service, 2010.
15 Ratcliffe et al., 2004.
16 Gochfeld et al., 1998.
17 Watson et al., 2011.
18 Gochfeld et al., 1998.
19 Cabot, 1996.
20 Fortin & Maheo, 2010.
21 Grimes, 1977.
22 Ratcliffe et al., 2004.
23 Newton & Crowe, 1999.
24 Langham, 1968; Dunn, 1973b.
25 Langham, 1968; Dunn, 1973a.
26 Dunn, 1973a; Shealer & Spendelow, 2002.
27 Shealer et al., 2005.
28 Cramp, 1985; Ratcliffe et al., 2004.
29 Langham, 1968; Mundy, 1997; Ratcliffe et al., 2004.
30 Ratcliffe et al., 2004.
31 Ratcliffe et al., 2004.
32 Nisbet et al., 1995.
33 Ratcliffe et al., 2004.
34 Cabot, 1996.
35 Burger et al., 1996; Ratcliffe et al., 2004.
36 Nisbet & Hatch, 1999.
37 Ratcliffe et al., 2004.
38 Nisbet & Hatch, 1999.
39 Ewins, 1987.
40 Clark et al., 2010.
41 Ratcliffe & Merne, 2002.
42 Ratcliffe et al., 2008a.
43 Ratcliffe & Merne, 2002.
44 Dunn & Mead, 1982.
45 Wallace, 1972.
46 Merne, 2010.
47 Cabot, 1996.
48 Ratcliffe & Merne, 2002.
49 Ratcliffe et al., 2008a.
50 Nisbet & Cabot, 1995; Hays et al., 2002;

Newton & Crowe, 2000; D. Hayward
and I. Nisbet, unpublished data.
51 Ratcliffe *et al.*, 2008a; Spendelow *et al.*,
2008.

CHAPTER 10

1 Malling Olsen & Larsson, 1995.
2 Ratcliffe, 2004b.
3 Hagemeijer & Blair, 1997.
4 Ratcliffe, 2004b.
5 Witherby *et al.*, 1942.
6 Ratcliffe, 2004b.
7 Ratcliffe, 2004b.
8 Joint Nature Conservation Committee,
2009; jncc.defra.gov.uk/smp.
9 Whilde, 1985.
10 Cramp, 1985.
11 Kramer, 1995.
12 Yarrell, 1843.
13 Cullen, 1956.
14 Cullen, 1956.
15 Hatch, 2002.
16 Cramp, 1985.
17 Monaghan, 2002.
18 Perrow *et al.*, 2011.
19 Cramp, 1985.
20 Cramp, 1985.
21 Horobin, 1971.
22 Cramp *et al.*, 1974; Bullock & Gomersall,
1981.
23 Monaghan *et al.*, 1989a, 1989b.
24 Uttley *et al.*, 1989b.
25 Suddaby & Ratcliffe, 1997.
26 Langham, 1974; Coulson & Horobin,
1976; Cramp, 1985; Newton & Crowe,
2000.
27 Lemmetyinen *et al.*, 1974.
28 Coulson & Horobin, 1976.
29 Ratcliffe, 2004b.
30 Mavor *et al.*, 2008; jncc.defra.gov.uk/
smp.
31 Clark *et al.*, 2010.

32 Monagahan, 2002.
33 Newton & Crowe, 1999.
34 Merne *et al.*, 2008.
35 Monagahan, 2002.
36 Higgins & Davies, 1996; Hatch, 2002.
37 Salomonsen, 1967.
38 Salomonsen, 1967.
39 Gudmundsson *et al.*, 1992.
40 Cramp, 1985; Monaghan, 2002.
41 Coulson & Horobin, 1976.
42 Monaghan, 2002.
43 Egevang *et al.*, 2010.
44 Coffait *et al.*, 2008.
45 J. J. Hatch and British Trust for
Ornithology, unpublished data.

CHAPTER 11

1 Ratcliffe, 2003; Ratcliffe *et al.*, 2008a,
2008b.
2 Pickerell, 2004.
3 Perrow *et al.*, 2004.
4 M. Smart, RSPB, personal
communication, May 2012.
5 Liley, 2008.
6 Footprint Ecology & David Tyldesley
and Associates, 2012.
7 M. & J. Smart, RSPB, personal
communications, May 2012.
8 Perrow *et al.*, 2006.
9 M. Smart, RSPB, personal
communication, May 2012.
10 jncc.defra.gov.uk/smp.
11 M. Smart, RSPB, personal
communication, May 2012.
12 E. Bowen, quoted in Northumberland
County History Committee, 1899.
13 J. Coulson, unpublished data.
14 Langham, 1974.
15 P. G. Morrison, RSPB, personal
communication, June 2012.
16 Robinson *et al.*, 2001.
17 Morrison & Gurney, 2007.

18 Booth & Morrison, 2010.
19 Morrison & Allcorn, 2006.
20 Ratcliffe *et al.*, 2008a.
21 Coulson, 2010.
22 Mitchell *et al.*, 2004.
23 Moore *et al.*, 2003; Ratcliffe *et al.*, 2008b.
24 Craik, 1995.
25 MacLeod, 2010.
26 Moore *et al.*, 2003.
27 MacLeod, 2010.
28 MacLeod, 2010.
29 MacLeod, 2010; Royal Society for the Protection of Birds, 2010.
30 Ratcliffe *et al.*, 2008b.
31 Ratcliffe *et al.*, 2008b.
32 Cabot, 1996.
33 Daly *et al.*, 2011.
34 www.hartlepoolmail.co.uk/news/local/man_accused_of_egg_theft_in_court_1_991852 (accessed November 2012).
35 www.scotsman.com/news/uk/egg_thief_jailed_for_six_months_1_619674 (accessed November 2012).
36 www.breakingnews.ie/ireland/eggs-theft-threatens-survival-of-rare-seabird-150695.html (accessed November 2012).
37 news.bbc.co.uk/2/hi/uk_news/england/tyne/5099258.stm (accessed November 2012).
38 www.telegraph.co.uk/earth/earthnews/3337929/Rare-wild-bird-egg-collector-jailed.html (accessed November 2012).
39 www.societe-jersiaise.org/ornithology/thieves-target-ecrehous-terns.html (accessed November 2012).
40 Smart, 2003.
41 Ratcliffe *et al.*, 2008c.
42 Smart, 2003.
43 Smart, 2003.
44 Ratcliffe *et al.*, 2000.
45 K. Osborn in Forrester *et al.*, 2007.

46 Craik, 1997, 1998.
47 Craik, 2011.
48 Uttley *et al.*, 1989a.
49 D. Fairlamb in Forrester *et al.*, 2007.
50 Coulson, 1991.
51 Mitchell *et al.*, 2004.
52 www.doeni.gov.uk/niea/rspb_s_work_in_and_around_larne_lough_-_rspb.pdf (accessed November 2012).
53 Colombé, 2003; Morrison, 2010.
54 US Fish and Wildlife Service, 2010.
55 Cramp *et al.*, 1974.
56 Charlton, 2003.
57 www.lincstrust.org.uk/conservation/article.php?id=21; www.filcris.co.uk/products/wildlife-products/tern-rafts (both accessed November 2012).
58 Suddaby & Ratcliffe, 1997.
59 Uttley *et al.*, 1989b.
60 jncc.defra.gov.uk/smp.
61 Wanless *et al.*, 2005.
62 Van Deurs *et al.*, 2009.
63 Harris *et al.*, 2007, 2008.
64 Dänhardt & Becker, 2011; Szostek & Becker, 2011.
65 Stienen, 2006.
66 jncc.defra.gov.uk/smp.
67 Mitchell *et al.*, 2004.
68 Koeman, 1972.
69 Bourne & Bogan, 1976; Cabot, 1996.
70 Robinson *et al.*, 1967; Potts, 1968; Coulson *et al.*, 1972; Newton *et al.*, 1993.
71 Bourne & Bogan, 1976; Cabot, 1996.
72 Nisbet, 2002.
73 Becker & Dittmann, 2010.
74 Becker *et al.*, 1993.
75 Leonards *et al.*, undated.
76 Nisbet, 1994.
77 Becker, 1967.
78 Nisbet, 2002.
79 Coulson *et al.*, 1968; Dunn, 1972; Armstrong *et al.*, 1978.
80 Nisbet, 1984.
81 Everett *et al.*, 1987.

82 Ndiaye, 2010; Owuso, 2010.

83 Avery *et al.*, 1995.

84 A. del Nevo, personal communication, 2012.

85 Cabot, 1996.

86 Beaugrand *et al.*, 2002.

87 Wanless *et al.*, 2009.

CHAPTER 12

1   British Birds Rarities Committee (www.bbrc.org.uk); Irish Rare Birds Committee (www.irbc.ie); British Ornithologists' Union Records Committee (www.bou.org.uk).

2   British Ornithologists' Union, 2006.

3   Wetlands International, 2006.

4   North, 1997.

5   Malling Olsen & Larsson, 1995.

6   Dixey *et al.*, 1981; Weir, 1983.

7   North, 1997.

8   Saliva, 2000; Schreiber *et al.*, 2002; Bradley & Norton, 2009.

9   Monteiro *et al.*, 1996; Keijl *et al.*, 2001; Schreiber *et al.*, 2002.

10 Malling Olsen & Larsson, 1995.

11 Paterson, 1997.

12 Dunn, E., in Hagemeijer & Blair, 1997.

13 Nisbet *et al.*, 2013.

14 Fraser *et al.*, 2007; Milne & McAdams, 2008.

15 Milne, 2004; Milne & McAdams, 2008.

16 Paterson, 1997.

17 Cramp, 1985.

18 Bradley & Norton, 2009.

19 Kennedy, 1960.

20 Draheim *et al.*, 2010.

21 Thompson *et al.*, 1997.

22 Thompson *et al.*, 1997; Bradley & Norton, 2009.

23 Yates & Taffs, 1990; Clifton, 1992.

24 J.-P. Biber, in Hagemeijer & Blair, 1997; Sanchez & Fasola, 2002.

25 Sanchez *et al.*, 2004.

26 Malling Olsen & Larsson, 1995.

27 Pyman & Wainwright, 1952.

28 Hudson & the Rarities Committee, 2012.

29 Fahy, 2012.

30 Dymond *et al.*, 1989.

31 Milne & McAdams, 2008; K. Fahy, personal communication, 2012.

32 BirdLife International, 2004.

33 Wetlands International, 2006.

34 Malling Olsen & Larsson, 1995.

35 Hudson & the Rarities Committee, 2012.

36 Fahy, 2012.

37 Spencer & Hudson, 1978; Dymond *et al.*, 1989.

38 BirdLife International, 2004.

39 Hudson & the Rarities Committee, 2012.

40 Irish Rare Birds Committee, 2009; Fahy, 2012.

41 BirdLife International, 2004; Wetlands International, 2006.

42 Malling Olsen & Larsson, 1995.

43 Holloway, 1996.

44 Sharrock & the Rare Birds Breeding Committee, 1977.

45 Hutchinson, 1989.

46 Sharrock & Rare Birds Breeding Panel, 1980; Spencer & Rare Birds Breeding Panel, 1986.

47 Cramp, 1985.

48 Toms, 2002.

49 Nightingale & Allsopp, 1998.

50 Malling Olsen & Larsson, 1995.

51 Kushlan *et al.*, 2002.

52 Hudson & the Rarities Committee, 2012.

53 Andrews *et al.*, 2006.

54 Adriaens, 1999; Bradshaw, 2003; Mullarney, 2003; Milne & McAdams, 2008.

55 British Ornithologists' Union

Records Committee, 2002; www.
radioactiverobins.com/terns (accessed
20 August 2011).

56 Wetlands International, 2006.
57 BirdLife International, 2004.
58 Malling Olsen & Larsson, 1995.
59 Alexandersson, 1979; van IJzendoorn,
    1980; Dunn & Agro, 2009.
60 Vinicombe, 1980.
61 British Ornithologists' Union Records
    Committee, 2005.
62 Dymond et al., 1989.
63 Fahy, 2012.
64 Cramp, 1985; Paterson, 1997.
65 Burness et al., 1999.
66 Malling Olsen & Larsson, 1995.
67 Burness et al., 1999; Paul et al., 2003.
68 Alström & Colston, 1991.
69 See, for example, listserv.arizona.edu/
    archives/birdwg01.html.
70 Alström & Colston, 1991; www.
    surfbirds.com (accessed August 2011).
71 Hutchinson, 1989; Milne & McAdams,
    2008; www.birdguides.com (accessed
    August 2011); Fahy, 2012.
72 Chappell, 2008.
73 listserv.arizona.edu/archives/birdwg01.
    html. See February 2001 week 4
    (accessed October 2011).
74 Burger & Gochfeld, 1996.
75 Efe et al., 2009; Sangster et al., 2011.
76 Shealer, 1999; Wetlands International,
    2006.
77 Scharringa, 1980; Garner et al., 2007.
78 Buckley & Buckley, 2002; Kushlan et al.,
    2002; Nisbet et al., 2013.
79 Malling Olsen & Larsson, 1995.
80 Nisbet et al., 2013.
81 Smith & the Rarities Committee, 1972;
    Rogers & the Rarities Committee, 1982,
    1992, 2000.
82 Hutchinson, 1989.
83 Paterson, 1997.
84 Keijl et al., 2001; Buckley & Buckley,

2002; J. Veen, cited in Wetlands
International, 2006.
85 Paterson, 1997.
86 K. Fahy, personal communication, 2012.
87 Meininger et al., 1994.
88 BirdLife International, 2011.
89 Paterson, 1997.
90 Dies & Dies, 1998.
91 Malling Olsen & Larsson, 1995.
92 Rogers & the Rarities Committee, 1985.
93 Milne & O'Sullivan, 1998.
94 Rogers & the Rarities Committee, 1998;
    Ogilvie & the Rare Breeding Birds
    Panel, 1999.
95 McNicholl et al., 2001; Nisbet et al., 2013.
96 Malling Olsen & Larsson, 1995.
97 British Ornithologists' Union, 2006.

APPENDIX 1

1   Mitchell et al., 2004.
2   Mavor et al., 2003, 2005, 2008.
3   jncc.defra.gov.uk/smp.
4   Mavor et al., 2008.
5   Ratcliffe et al., 2008a.
6   Coulson & Horobin, 1976; Green et al.,
    1990; Shealer, 1999.
7   Robinson, 2010.
8   Ratcliffe et al., 2008a.
9   Nisbet & Cam, 2002; Devlin et al., 2008;
    Spendelow et al., 2008.
10 Robinson, 2010.
11 Ratcliffe, 1997; Lebreton et al., 2003.
12 Wendeln & Becker, 1998.
13 Dittmann & Becker, 2003; Ratcliffe,
    1997.
14 Fasola et al., 2002.
15 Ratcliffe et al., 2000.
16 Mavor et al., 2008.
17 Ratcliffe, 2003.
18 Cramp, 1985.
19 Smith, 1975.
20 Green et al., 1990; Shealer, 1999.

21 Robinson, 2010.
22 Cramp, 1985.
23 Cramp, 1985.
24 Stienen, 2006.
25 Becker & Ludwigs, 2004.
26 Nisbet, 2002.
27 Szostek & Becker, 2011.
28 Dänhart & Becker, 2011.
29 Szostek & Becker, 2011.
30 Ratcliffe, 2004c.
31 Dittmann et al., 2005.
32 Nisbet, 2002.
33 Nisbet & Cam, 2002.
34 Tims et al., 2004.
35 Nisbet, 2002.
36 Hanski, 1998.
37 Quemmerais-Amice & Gager, 2010.
38 Cadiou, 2010.
39 Green, 1995.
40 Ratcliffe et al., 2008a.
41 Lebreton et al., 2003.
42 Lebreton et al., 2003.
43 Ratcliffe, 1997.
44 Newton & Crowe, 2000.
45 Ratcliffe et al., 2004.
46 Nisbet & Hatch, 1999.
47 Nisbet & Hatch, 1999.
48 Coulson & Horobin, 1976; Hatch, 2002.
49 Coulson & Horobin, 1976.
50 Devlin et al., 2008.
51 Monaghan, 2002.
52 Ratcliffe, 2004b.
53 Coulson & Horobin, 1976.
54 Ratcliffe, 2004b.

APPENDIX 2

1 Witherby et al., 1942; Bannerman, 1962;
  Glutz von Blotzheim & Bauer, 1982;
  Cramp, 1985; Il'icev & Zubakin, 1990;
  Burger & Gochfeld, 1996; Higgins &
  Davies, 1996; Poole & Gill, 1992–2002.
2 Fasola et al. 2002; Becker & Ludwigs,
  2004; Ratcliffe et al., 2004.
3 Bickerton, 1912; Marples & Marples,
  1934; Burger & Gochfeld, 1991; Hume,
  1993.
4 Rowan et al., 1914, 1919; Watson et al.,
  1923.
5 Marples & Marples, 1934.
6 Austin & Austin, 1956.
7 Nisbet, 1978.
8 Hays et al., 1997.
9 Burger & Gochfeld, 1991.
10 Burger & Gochfeld, 1996.
11 Wendeln & Becker, 1999.
12 Becker & Wendeln, 1997.
13 Becker et al., 2006.
14 Becker et al., 1997; Ezard et al., 2006.
15 Szostek & Becker, 2011.
16 Nisbet et al., 2011a.
17 Chestney, 1970.
18 jncc.defra.gov.uk/smp.
19 Clark et al., 2010; Norman, 2002.
20 Ward, 2000; Merne et al., 2008;
   S. White, unpublished data.
21 Becker & Dittmann, 2010; Koffijberg
   et al., 2010.
22 Nisbet, 2002.
23 Bureau, 1907.
24 Cabot, 1989–91, 1992, 1996.
25 Cabot & Partridge, 1977; Cabot et al.,
   1978.
26 Ratcliffe et al., 2008a.
27 Ratcliffe et al., 2004.
28 Nisbet & Spendelow, 1999; Lebreton
   et al., 2003; Spendelow et al., 2008.
29 Nisbet & Hatch, 1999.
30 US Fish and Wildlife Service, 2010.
31 Monticelli et al., 2007, 2008.
32 Nisbet & Ratcliffe, 2008.
33 Veen, 1977.
34 Stienen, 2006.
35 Brenninkmeijer et al., 2002.
36 Langham, 1974.
37 Smith, 1975.
38 Cullen, 1956.

39 Monaghan *et al.*, 1989a, 1989b, 1992;
    Suddaby & Ratcliffe, 1997.

40 Koffijberg *et al.*, 2010.

41 Møller *et al.*, 2006; Devlin *et al.*, 2008;
    Wanless *et al.*, 2009; Egevang *et al.*, 2010.

42 Fasola *et al.*, 2002.

43 Thompson *et al.*, 1997; Draheim *et al.*,
    2010.

APPENDIX 3

1 Lloyd *et al.*, 1991.

2 Joint Nature Conservancy Council,
   2009; jncc.defra.gov.uk/smp.

References

Adriaens, P. (1999). The American black tern in County Dublin. *Birding World* **12**, 378–9.

Alerstam, T. (1985). Strategies of migratory flight, illustrated by Arctic and common terns, *Sterna paradisaea* and *Sterna hirundo*. *Contributions in Marine Sciences Supplement* **27**, 580–603.

Alexandersson, H. (1979). En hybridisering mellan vitvingad tärna *Childonias leucopterus* och svarttärna *Childonias niger* på Öland 1978. *Calidris* **8**, 151–3.

Alström, P. & Colston, P. (1991). *A Field Guide to the Rare Birds of Britain and Europe*. HarperCollins, London.

American Ornithologists' Union (1998). *Check-List of North American Birds*, 7th edition. Allen Press, Lawrence, KS.

American Ornithologists' Union (2006). Forty-seventh supplement to the American Ornithologists' Union Check-List of North American Birds. *Auk* **123**, 926–36.

Amorim, P., Figueiredo, M., Machete, M. *et al.* (2009). Spatial variability of seabird distribution associated with environmental factors: a case study of marine important bird areas in the Azores. *ICES Journal of Marine Sciences* **66**, 29–40.

Andrews, R. M., Higgins, R. J. & Martin, J. D. (2006). American black tern at Weston-super-Mare: new to Britain. *British Birds* **99**, 450–9.

Armstrong, I. H., Coulson, J. C., Hawkey, P. & Hudson, M. J. (1978). Further mass seabird deaths from paralytic shellfish poisoning. *British Birds* **71**, 58–68.

Arnold, J. M., Hatch, J. J. & Nisbet, I. C. T. (2004). Seasonal declines in reproductive success of the common tern: timing or parental quality? *Journal of Avian Biology* **35**, 33–45.

Ashmole, N. & Tovar S, H. (1968). Prolonged parental care in royal terns and other birds. *Auk* **85**, 90–100.

Au, D. W. K. & Pitman, R. L. (1986). Seabird interactions with dolphins and tuna in the eastern tropical Pacific. *Condor* **88**, 304–17.

Austin, O. L. & Austin, O. L., Jr. (1956). Some demographic aspects of the Cape Cod population of common terns (*Sterna hirundo*). *Bird-Banding* **27**, 55–66.

Avery, M., Couthard, N., del Nevo, A. *et al.* (1995). A recovery plan for roseate terns in the east Atlantic: an international programme. *Bird Conservation International* **5**, 441–53.

Baker, A. J., Pereira, S. L. & Paton, T. A. (2007). Phylogenetic relationships and divergence times of Charadriiformes genera: multigene evidence for the Cretaceous origin of at least 14 clades of shorebirds. *Biology Letters* **3**, 205–7.

Bannerman, D. A., ed. (1962). *The Birds of the British Isles, Vol. XI.* Oliver and Boyd, Edinburgh.

Barlow, M. (1998). Movements of Caspian terns (*Sterna caspia*) from a colony near Invercargill, New Zealand, and some notes on their behaviour. *Notornis* **45**, 193–220.

Beaugrand, G., Reid, P. C., Ibañez, F., Lindley, J. A. & Edwards, M. (2002). Reorganization of North Atlantic marine copepod biodiversity and climate. *Science* **296**, 1692–4.

Becker, P. H. & Dittmann, T. (2010). Contaminants in bird eggs in the Wadden Sea: trends and perspectives. In: Marencic, H., Eskildsen, K., Farke, H. & Hedtkamp, S., eds., *Science for Nature Conservation and Management: the Wadden Sea Ecosystem and EU Directives.* Proceedings of the 12th International Scientific Wadden Sea Symposium in Wilhelmshaven, Germany, 30 March – 3 April 2009. Wadden Sea Ecosystem No. 26. Common Wadden Sea Secretariat, Wilhelmshaven, pp. 205–10.

Becker, P. H. & Ludwigs, J.-D. (2004). *Sterna hirundo* Common Tern. *BWP Update* **6**, 91–138.

Becker, P. H. & Sudmann, S. R. (1998). Quo vadis *Sterna hirundo*? Schlussfolgerungen für den Schutz der Flussseeschwalbe in Deutschland. *Vogelwelt* **119**, 293–304.

Becker, P. H. & Wendeln, H. (1997). A new application for transponders in population ecology of the Common Tern. *Condor* **99**, 534–8.

Becker, P. H. & Zhang, E. (2011). Renesting of Common terns *Sterna hirundo* in the life history perspective. *Journal of Ornithology* **123** (Supplement 1), 213–25.

Becker, P. H., Schuhmann, S. & Koepff, C. (1993). Hatching failure in Common Terns (*Sterna hirundo*) in relation to environmental chemicals. *Environmental Pollution* **79**, 207–13.

Becker, P. H., Frank, D. & Wagener, M. (1997). Luxury in fresh water and stress at sea? The foraging of the Common Tern *Sterna hirundo*. *Ibis* **139**, 264–9.

Becker, P. H., Voigt, C. C., Arnold, J. M. & Nagel, R. (2006). A non-invasive technique to bleed incubating birds without trapping: a blood-sucking bug in a hollow egg. *Journal of Ornithology* **47**, 115–18.

Becker, W. B. (1967). Experimental infection of common terns with tern virus: influenza virus A/tern/South Africa/1961. *Journal of Hygiene* **65**, 61–5.

Bewick, T. (1804). *History of British Birds, Vol. II.* Edward Walker, Newcastle.

Bickerton, W. (1912). *The Home-life of the Terns, or Sea Swallows.* Witherby, London.

BirdLife International (2004). *Birds in Europe, Population Estimates, Trends and Conservation Status. BirdLife Conservation Series No. 12.* BirdLife International, Cambridge.

BirdLife International (2011). Species factsheet: *Sterna bengalensis.* www.birdlife.org (accessed 31 July 2011).

Black, J. M., ed. (1996). *Partnerships in Birds: the Study of Monogamy.* Oxford University Press, Oxford.

Bollinger, P. B. (1994). Relative effects of hatching order, egg-size variation, and parental quality on chick survival in common terns. *Auk* **111**, 263–73.

Bollinger, P. B., Bollinger, E. K. & Malecki, R. A. (1990). Tests of three hypotheses of hatching asynchrony in the common tern. *Auk* **107**, 696–706.

Booth, V. & Morrison, P. (2010). Effectiveness of disturbance methods and egg removal to deter large gulls *Larus* spp. from competing with terns *Sterna* spp. on Coquet Island RSPB reserve, Northumberland, England. *Conservation Evidence* **7**, 39–43.

Bourne, W. R. P. (1976). Seabirds in the Wash. *Seabird Report* **5**, 18–20.

Bourne, W. R. P. & Bogan, J. A. (1976). Estimations of chlorinated hydrocarbons in marine birds. In: Johnston, R., ed., *Marine Pollution*. Academic Press, London, pp. 482–93.

Bradley, P. E. & Norton, R. L. (2009). Status of Caribbean seabirds. In: Bradley, P. E. &. Norton, R. L., eds., *An Inventory of Breeding Seabirds of the Caribbean*. University of Florida Press, Gainesville, FL, pp. 270–82.

Bradshaw, C. (2003). The American black tern in County Kerry. *Birding World* **16**, 434.

Brenninkmeijer, A., Stienen, E. M. W., Klaassen, M. & Kersten, M. (2002). Feeding ecology of wintering terns in Guinea-Bissau. *Ibis* **144**, 602–13.

Bridge, E. S. & Eaton, M. D. (2005). Does ultraviolet reflectance accentuate a sexually selected signal in terns? *Journal of Avian Biology* **36**, 18–21.

Bridge, E. S. & Nisbet, I. C. T. (2004). Wing-molt and assortative mating in common terns: a test of the molt-signaling hypothesis. *Condor* **106**, 336–43.

Bridge, E. S., Jones, A. W. & Baker, A. J. (2005). A phylogenetic framework for the terns (Sternini) inferred from mtDNA sequences: implications for taxonomy and plumage evolution. *Molecular Phylogenetics and Evolution* **35**, 459–69.

British Ornithologists' Union (2006). The British list: a checklist of Birds of Britain (7th edition). *Ibis* **148**, 526–63.

British Ornithologists' Union Records Committee (2002). 28th report (October 2001). *Ibis* **144**, 181–4.

British Ornithologists' Union Records Committee (2005). 31st report (October 2004). *Ibis* **147**, 246–50.

Brown, R. A. & McAvoy, W. (1985). Nesting terns in Strangford Lough, 1969–84: a review. *Irish Birds* **5**, 33–47.

Buckley, P. A. & Buckley, F. G. (1980). Population and colony site trends of Long Island waterbirds for five years in the mid-1970s. *Transactions of the Linnaean Society of New York* **9**, 23–56.

Buckley, P. A. & Buckley, F. G. (2002). Royal tern *Thalasseus maximus*. In: Poole, A. & Gill, F., eds., *The Birds of North America*, No. 700. The Birds of North America, Inc., Philadelphia.

Bullock, I. D. & Gomersall, C. H. (1981). The breeding populations of terns in Orkney and Shetland in 1980. *Bird Study* **28**, 187–200.

Bureau, L. (1907). Monographie de la sterne de Dougall (*Sterna dougallii*). *Proceedings of the Fourth International Ornithological Congress, London, June 1905*, 289–346.

Burger, J. & Gochfeld, M. (1991). *The Common Tern: Its Breeding Biology and Social Behavior*. Columbia University Press, New York.

Burger, J. & Gochfeld, M. (1994). Predation and effects of humans on island-nesting seabirds. In: Nettleship, D., Burger, J. & Gochfeld, M., eds., *Seabirds on Islands: Threats, Case Studies and Action Plans*. BirdLife Conservation Series No. 1. BirdLife International, Cambridge.

Burger, J. & Gochfeld, M. (1996). Family Sternidae (terns). In: del Hoyo, J.,

Elliott, A. & Sargatal, J., eds., *Handbook of the Birds of the World, Vol. 3*. Lynx Edicions, Barcelona, pp. 624–43.

Burger, J., Shealer, D. A. & Gochfeld, M. (1993). Defensive aggression in terns: discrimination and response to individual researchers. *Aggressive Behavior* **19**, 303–11.

Burger, J., Nisbet, I. C. T. & Gochfeld, M. (1996). Temporal patterns in reproductive success of the endangered roseate tern (*Sterna dougallii*) nesting at Bird Island, Massachusetts, and Cedar Beach, New York. *Auk* **113**, 131–42.

Burness, G. P., Lefevre, K. & Collins, C. T. (1999). Elegant tern *Thalasseus elegans*. In: Poole, A. & Gill, F., eds., *The Birds of North America*, No. 404. The Birds of North America, Inc., Philadelphia, PA.

Cabot, D. (1962a). Birds on Roaninish, Co. Donegal. *Irish Naturalists' Journal* **13**, 238–9.

Cabot, D. (1962b). Birds on Inishduff, Co. Donegal. *Irish Naturalists' Journal* **14**, 36–7.

Cabot, D. (1962c). An ornithological expedition to Inishmurray, Co. Sligo. *Irish Naturalists' Journal* **14**, 59–61.

Cabot, D. (1989–91). Studies on the breeding biology of the roseate tern *Sterna dougallii* at Rockabill, Co. Dublin [1988–91]. Four unpublished reports for the RSPB, Sandy, Bedfordshire and the Irish Wildbird Conservancy, Dublin.

Cabot, D. (1992). Research work on roseate terns carried out on Rockabill, Co. Dublin, and at Maiden Rock, Dalkey Sound, Co. Dublin. Unpublished report for the Irish Wildbird Conservancy, Dublin.

Cabot, D. (1996). Performance of the Roseate Tern population breeding in north-west Europe: Ireland, Britain and France, 1960–94. *Proceedings of the Royal Irish Academy* **96B**, 55–68.

Cabot, D. & Partridge, K. (1977). Report on a survey of roseate terns *Sterna dougallii* breeding in Brittany 1976. Unpublished report prepared for the Centre National de la Recherche Scientifique, Paris.

Cabot, D., Partridge, K. & Brien, Y. (1978). Survey of *Sterna dougallii* and other seabirds breeding in NW Brittany during 1976 and 1978. Unpublished report.

Cadiou, B. (2010). Status report of roseate tern populations in Europe. In: Capoulade, M., Quemmerais-Amice, G. & Cadiou, B., eds., *For Roseate Tern Conservation*. Proceedings of the LIFE seminar Roseate Tern Conservation in Brittany. *Penn-ar-Bed* **208**, 7–11.

Carey, C., Rahn, H. & Parisi, P. (1980). Calories, water, lipid and yolk in bird eggs. *Condor* **82**, 335–43.

Casey, S., Moore, N., Ryan, L. *et al.* (1995). The roseate tern conservation project on Rockabill, Co. Dublin: a six year review 1989–1994. *Irish Birds* **5**, 251–64.

Chappell, L. (2005). The Elegant Tern in Dorset. *Birding World* **18**, 211–13.

Charlton, P. (2003). Habitat creation for little terns. In: Allcorn, R. I., ed., *Proceedings of a Symposium on Little Terns* Sterna albifrons. RSPB Research Report no. 8. Royal Society for the Protection of Birds, Sandy, pp. 32–8.

Cherubini, G., Serra, L. & Baccetti, N. (1996). Primary moult, body mass and moult migration of little terns *Sterna albifrons* in NE Italy. *Ardea* **84**, 99–114.

Chestney, R. (1970). Notes on the breeding habits of common and Sandwich terns on Scolt Head Island. *Transactions of the Norfolk and Norwich Naturalists' Society* **21**, 353–63.

Chivers, L. S. (2007). Courtship feeding and food provisioning of chicks by common terns *Sterna hirundo* at Belfast Harbour Lagoon. *Irish Birds* **8**, 215–22.

Clark, J. A., Robinson, R. A., Blackburn, J. R. *et al.* (2010). Bird ringing in Britain and Ireland in 2009. *Ringing & Migration* **25**, 88–127.

Clifton, J. (1992). Least tern at Colne Point EWT Reserve 29th June to 1st July 1991. *Essex Bird Report* **120**, 121.

Coffait, L., Clark, J. A., Robinson, R. A. *et al.* (2008). Bird ringing in Britain and Ireland in 2006. *Ringing & Migration* **24**, 15–79.

Collinge, W. E. (1924–27). *The Food of Some British Wild Birds*. Privately published, York.

Colombé, S. (2003). An overview of seabird social facilitation projects in the UK, the US and elsewhere, with particular reference to the *Sterna* terns. In: Allcorn, R. I., ed., *Proceedings of a Symposium on Little Terns* Sterna albifrons. RSPB Research Report no. 8. Royal Society for the Protection of Birds, Sandy, pp. 60–5.

Coulson, J. (1991). The population dynamics of culling Herring Gulls and Lesser Black-backed Gulls. In: Perrins, C. M., Lebreton, J.-D. & Hirons, G. J. M., eds., *Bird Population Studies: Relevance to Conservation and Management*. Oxford University Press, Oxford, pp. 479–97.

Coulson, J. (2001). Colonial breeding in seabirds. In: Schreiber, E. A. & Burger, J., eds., *Biology of Marine Birds*. CRC Press, Boca Raton, FL, pp. 87–114.

Coulson, J. C. (2010). A long-term study of the population dynamics of common eiders *Somateria mollissima*: why do several parameters fluctuate markedly? *Bird Study* **57**, 1–18.

Coulson, J. C. & Horobin, J. (1976). The influence of age on the breeding biology and survival of the Arctic tern *Sterna paradisaea*. *Journal of Zoology, London* **178**, 247–60.

Coulson, J. C., Potts, G. R., Deans, I. R. & Fraser, S. M. (1968). Exceptional mortality of shags and other seabirds caused by paralytic shellfish poison *British Birds* **61**, 381–404.

Coulson, J. C., Deans, I. R., Potts, G. R., Robinson, J. & Crabtree, A. N. (1972). Changes in organochlorine contamination of the marine environment of eastern Britain monitored by shag eggs. *Nature* **236**, 454–6. doi:10.1038/236454a0.

Craik, J. C. A. (1995). Effects of North American mink on the breeding success of terns and smaller gulls in west Scotland. *Seabird* **17**, 3–11.

Craik, J. C. A. (1997). Long-term effects of North American Mink *Mustela vison* on seabirds in western Scotland, *Bird Study* **44**, 303–9.

Craik, J. C. A. (1998). Recent mink-related declines of gulls and terns in west Scotland and the beneficial effects of mink control. *Argyll Bird Report* **14**, 98–110.

Craik, J. C. A. (2011). Results of the Mink-Seabird Project in 2011. Unpublished report, Scottish Association for Marine Science, Oban.

Cramp, S., ed. (1985). *The Birds of the Western Palearctic. Vol. IV: Terns to Woodpeckers*. Oxford University Press, Oxford. Available as *BWPi. The Birds of the Western Palearctic on interactive DVD-ROM*. BirdGuides, London.

Cramp. S., Bourne, W. R. P. & Saunders, D. (1974). *The Seabirds of Britain and Ireland*. Collins, London.

Croxall, J. P., Rothery, P. & Crisp, A.

(1992). The effect of maternal age and experience on egg-size and hatching success in the Wandering Albatross (*Diomedea exulans*). *Ibis* **134**, 219–28.

Cullen, J. M. (1956). A study of the behaviour of the Arctic tern (*Sterna macrura*). DPhil thesis, University of Oxford.

Cullen, M. (1962). An introduction to the behaviour and displays of British terns, In: Bannerman, D. A., *The Birds of the British Isles, Vol. XI.* Oliver & Boyd, Edinburgh, pp. 80–6.

Daly, D. Wilson, C. J. & Murray, T. (2011). *Lady's Island Lake Tern Report 2011.* National Parks and Wildlife Service, Department of Arts, Heritage and the Gaeltacht, Dublin.

Danchin, E. & Wagner, R. H. (1997). The evolution of coloniality: the emergence of new perspectives. *Trends in Ecology and Evolution* **12**, 342–7.

Dänhardt, A. & Becker, P. H. (2011). Herring and sprat abundance indices predict chick growth and reproductive performance in common terns breeding in the Wadden Sea. *Ecosystems* **65**, 791–805. doi:10.1007/s10021-011-9445-7.

Dänhardt, A., Fresemann, T. & Becker, P. H. (2011). To eat or to feed? Prey utilization of common terns *Sterna hirundo* in the Wadden Sea. *Journal of Ornithology* **15**, 347–57.

Devlin, C. M., Diamond, A. W., Kress, S. W., Hall, C. S. & Welch, L. (2008). Breeding dispersal and survival of Arctic terns (*Sterna paradisaea*) nesting in the Gulf of Maine. *Auk* **125**, 850–8.

Dies, J. I. & Dies, B. (1998). Hybridisation between lesser crested and Sandwich terns in Valencia, Spain, and plumage of offspring. *British Birds* **91**, 165–70.

Dittmann, T. & Becker, P. H. (2003) Sex, age, experience and condition as factors of arrival date in prospecting common terns. *Animal Behaviour* **65**, 981–6.

Dittmann, T., Zinsmeister, D. & Becker, P. H. (2005). Dispersal decisions: common terns, *Sterna hirundo*, choose between colonies during prospecting. *Animal Behaviour* **70**, 13–20.

Dixey, A. E., Ferguson, A., Heywood, R. & Taylor, A. R. (1981). Aleutian tern: new to the Western Palearctic. *British Birds* **74**, 411–16.

Draheim, H. M., Miller, M. P., Baird, P. & Haig S. M. (2010). Subspecific status and population genetic structure of least terns (*Sternula antillarum*) inferred by mitochondrial DNA control-region sequences and microsatellite DNA. *Auk* **127**, 807–19.

Dunlop, J. N. & Johnstone, R. E. (1994). The migration of bridled terns *Sterna anaethetus* breeding in Western Australia. *Corella* **18**, 125–9.

Dunn, E. H. & Agro, D. J. (2009). Black tern *Chlidonias niger*. In: Poole, A. & Gill, F., eds., *The Birds of North America*, No. 147. The Birds of North America, Inc., Philadelphia, PA.

Dunn, E. K. (1972). Studies on terns with particular reference to feeding ecology. PhD thesis, University of Durham.

Dunn, E. K. (1973a). Robbing behavior of roseate terns. *Auk* **90**, 641–51.

Dunn, E. K. (1973b). Changes in fishing ability of terns associated with windspeed and sea surface conditions. *Nature* **244**, 520–1.

Dunn, E. K. & Mead, C. J. (1982). Relationship between sardine fisheries and recovery rates of ringed terns in West Africa. *Seabird* **6**, 98–104.

Dymond, J. N., Fraser, P. A. & Gantlett, S. J. M. (1989). *Rare Birds in Britain and Ireland*. Poyser, Calton.

Efe, M. A., Tavares, E. S., Baker, A. J. & Bonatto, S. L. (2009). Multigene phylogeny and DNA barcoding indicate that the Sandwich tern complex (*Thalasseus sandvicensis*, Laridae, Sternini) comprises two species. *Molecular Phylogenetics and Evolution* **52**, 263–7.

Egevang, C., Stenhouse, I. J., Phillips, R. A. et al. (2010). Tracking of Arctic terns *Sterna paradisaea* reveals longest animal migration. *Proceedings of the National Academy of Sciences of the USA* **107**, 2078–81.

Everett, M. J., Hepburn, I. R., Ntiamou-Baidu, Y, & Thomas, G. J. (1987). Roseate terns in Britain and West Africa. *RSPB Conservation Review* **1**, 56–8.

Ewins, P. J. (1987). Probable interbreeding of roseate and Arctic terns. *Scottish Birds* **14**, 215–16.

Ezard, T. H. G., Becker, P. H. & Coulson, T. (2006). The contribution of age and sex to variation in common tern growth rate. *Journal of Animal Ecology* **71**, 1379–86.

Fahy, K. (2012). Interim Irish rare bird report 2011. www.irbc.ie/reports/report2011.php (accessed November 2012).

Fasola, M. & Saino, N. (1995). Sex-biased parental care allocation in three tern species (Laridae, Aves). *Canadian Journal of Zoology* **73**, 1461–7.

Fasola, M., Guzman, J. M. S. & Roselaar, C. S. (2002). *Sterna albifrons* little tern. *BWP Update* **4**, 89–114.

Fisher, J. (1966). *The Shell Bird Book*. Ebury Press & Michael Joseph, London.

Footprint Ecology & David Tyldesley and Associates (2012). *Habitats Regulations Assessment of the Great Yarmouth Local Plan Core Strategy*. Footprint Ecology, Wareham, Dorset.

Forrester, R. W., Andrews, I. J., McInerny, C.J. et al., eds. (2007). *The Birds of Scotland. Vol. 1*. Scottish Ornithologists' Club, Aberlady.

Fortin, M. & Maheo, H. (2010). Migratory behaviour of roseate tern populations in Brittany and in the Gulf of Morbihan. In: Capoulade, M., Quemmerais-Amice, G. & Cadiou, B., eds., *For Roseate Tern Conservation*. Proceedings of the LIFE seminar Roseate Tern Conservation in Brittany. *Penn-ar-Bed* **208**, 50–8.

Fraser, P. A., Rogers, M. J. & the British Birds Rarities Committee. (2007). Report on rare birds in Great Britain in 2005. Part 1: non-passerines. *British Birds* **100**, 16–61.

Furness, R. W. (1978). Kleptoparasitism by great skuas (*Catharacta skua* Brünn.) and Arctic skuas (*Stercorarius parasiticus* L.) at a Shetland seabird colony. *Animal Behaviour* **26**, 1167–77.

Furness, R. W. (1987). *The Skuas*. Poyser, Calton, UK.

García, G. O., Becker, P. H. & Favero, M. (2011). Kleptoparasitism during courtship in *Sterna hirundo* and its relationship with female reproductive performance. *Journal of Ornithology* **152**, 103–10.

Garner, M., Lewington, I. & Crook, J. (2007). Identification of American Sandwich tern *Sterna sandvicensis acuflavida*. *Dutch Birding* **29**, 273–87.

Gauger, V. H. (1999). Black noddy *Anous minutus*. In: Poole, A. & Gill, F., eds., *The Birds of North America*, No. 412. The Birds of North America, Inc., Philadelphia, PA.

Gill, F. & Donsker, D., eds. (2012). *IOC World Bird Names* (v 3.2). Available at www.worldbirdnames.org (accessed November 2012).

Glutz von Blotzheim, U. & Bauer, K. (1982). *Handbuch der Vögel Mitteleuropas. Band 8/1.* Akademische Verlagsgesellschaft, Wiesbaden, Germany.

Gochfeld, M. (1979). Learning to eat by young Common Terns: consistency of presentation as an early cue. *Proceedings of the Conference of the Colonial Waterbird Group* **3**, 108–18.

Gochfeld, M., Burger, J. & Nisbet, I. C. T. (1998). Roseate tern *Sterna dougallii.* In: Poole, A. & Gill, F., eds., *The Birds of North America*, No. 370. The Birds of North America, Inc., Philadelphia, PA.

González-Solís, J., Becker, P. H. & Wendeln, H. (1999). Divorce and asynchronous arrival in common terns (*Sterna hirundo*). *Animal Behaviour* **58**, 1123–9.

Götmark, F. (1990). A test of the information-centre hypothesis in a colony of Sandwich terns *Sterna sandvicensis. Animal Behaviour* **39**, 487–95.

Gray, R. (1871). *The Birds of the West of Scotland.* Murray, Glasgow.

Green, R. E. (1995). Diagnosing causes of bird population declines. *Ibis* **137**, 547–55.

Green, R. E., Baillie, S. R. & Avery, M. I. (1990). Can ringing recoveries help to explain the population dynamics of British terns? *The Ring* **13**, 133–7.

Greenhalgh, M. E. (1974). Population growth and breeding success in a saltmarsh common tern colony. *Naturalist* **931**, 121–7.

Greenhalgh, M. E. & Greenwood, M. J. (1974). Foods of an estuarine common tern colony. *Naturalist* **935**, 145–6.

Grimes, L. G. (1977). A radar study of tern movements along the coast of Ghana. *Ibis* **119**, 28–36.

Gudmundsson, G. A., Alerstam, T. & Larsson, B. (1992). Radar observations of northbound migration of the Arctic tern, *Sterna paradisaea*, at the Antarctic Peninsula. *Antarctic Science* **4**, 163–70.

Gudmundsson, G. A., Alerstam, T., Green, M. & Hedenström, A. (2002). Radar observations of Arctic bird migration at the Northwest Passage, Canada. *Arctic* **55**, 21–43.

Hagemeijer, W. J. M. & Blair, M. J. (1997). *The EBBC Atlas of European Breeding Birds: Their Distribution and Abundance.* Poyser, London.

Hamer, K. C., Schreiber, E. A. & Burger, J. (2001). Breeding biology, life histories, and life history–environment interactions in seabirds. In: Schreiber, E. A. & Burger, J., eds., *Biology of Marine Birds.* CRC Press, Boca Raton, FL, pp. 217–62.

Haney, J. C. (1986). Seabird patchiness in tropical oceanic waters: the influence of *Sargassum* 'reefs'. *Auk* **103**, 141–51.

Hannon, C., Berrow, D. & Newton, S. F. (1997). The status and distribution of breeding Sandwich *Sterna sandvicensis*, roseate *S. dougallii*, common *S. hirundo*, Arctic *S. paradisaea* and little terns *S. albifrons* in Ireland in 1995. *Irish Birds* **6**, 1–22.

Hanski, I. (1998). Metapopulation dynamics. *Nature* **396**, 41–9.

Harris, M.P., Beare, D., Toresen, R., *et al.* (2007). A major increase in snake pipefish (*Entelurus aequoreus*) in northern European seas since 2003: potential implications for seabird breeding success. *Marine Biology* **151**, 973–83.

Harris, M. P., Newell, M., Daunt, F., Speakman, J. R. & Wanless, S. (2008). Snake pipefish *Entelurus aequoreus* are poor food for seabirds. *Ibis* **150**, 413–15.

Hatch, J. J. (1970). Predation and piracy by gulls at a ternery in Maine. *Auk* **87**, 244–54.

Hatch, J. J. (2002). Arctic tern *Sterna paradisaea*. In: Poole, A. & Gill, F., eds., *The Birds of North America*, No. 707. The Birds of North America, Inc., Philadelphia, PA.

Hays, H., Dunn, E. & Poole, A. (1973). Common, arctic, roseate, and Sandwich terns carrying multiple fish. *Wilson Bulletin* **85**, 233–6.

Hays, H., DiCostanzo, J., Cormons, G. *et al.* (1997). Recoveries of roseate and common terns in South America. *Journal of Field Ornithology* **68**, 79–90.

Hays, H., Lima, H., Monteiro, L. *et al.* (1999). A nonbreeding concentration of roseate and common terns in Bahia, Brazil. *Journal of Field Ornithology* **70**, 455–64.

Hays, H., Neves, V. & Lima, P. (2002). Banded roseate terns from different continents trapped in the Azores. *Journal of Field Ornithology* **73**, 180–4.

Hewitson, W. (1831–42). *British Oology*. Newcastle-on-Tyne.

Higgins, P. J. & Davies, S. J. J. F., eds. (1996). *Handbook of Australian, New Zealand and Antarctic Birds. Vol. 3: Snipe to Pigeons.* Oxford University Press, Melbourne.

Hislop, J. R. G., Harris, M. P. & Smith, J. G. M. (1991). Variation in the calorific value and total energy content of the lesser sandeel (*Ammodytes marinus*) and other fish preyed upon by seabirds. *Journal of Zoology (London)* **224**, 501–17.

Holloway, S. (1996). *The Historical Atlas of Breeding Birds in Britain and Ireland, 1875–1900.* Poyser, London.

Horobin, J. M. (1971). The effect of age on the breeding biology of the Arctic tern. PhD thesis, University of Durham.

Hudson, N. & the Rarities Committee (2012). Report on rare birds in Great Britain in 2011. *British Birds* **105**, 556–625.

Hume, R. (1993). *The Common Tern.* Hamlyn, London.

Hutchinson, C. D. (1989). *Birds in Ireland.* Poyser, London.

Il'icev, V. D., and V. A. Zubakin. (1990). *Handbuch der Vögel der Sowjetunion.* Band 6/Teil 1. A. Ziemsen Verlag, Wittenberg Lutherstadt, Germany. [German translation of Russian original.]

Irish Rare Birds Committee (2009). *Irish Rare Bird Report 2008.* BirdWatch Ireland, Dublin.

Jardine, W. (1843). *The Naturalist's Library. Ornithology. Birds of Great Britain and Ireland. Part 4: Natatores.* W. H. Lizars, Edinburgh.

Joint Nature Conservation Committee (2009). *UK Seabirds in 2008. Results from the UK Seabird Monitoring Programme.* JNCC, Peterborough.

Joint Nature Conservation Committee (2012). *Seabird Population Trends and Causes of Change: 2012 Report.* JNCC, Peterborough. http://www.jncc.gov.uk/page-3201 (accessed November 2012).

Keijl, G. O., Brenninkmeijer, A., Scheepers, F. J. *et al.* (2001). Breeding gulls and terns in Senegal in 1998, and proposals for new population estimates of gulls and terns in north-west Africa. *Atlantic Seabirds* **3**, 59–74.

Kennedy, P. G. (1960). Bridled tern in Dublin. *British Birds* **48**, 89–90.

Kennedy, P. G. (1961). *A List of the Birds of Ireland.* National Museum of Ireland, Dublin.

Kennedy, P. G., Ruttledge, R. F. & Scroope, C. F. (1954). *Birds of Ireland.* Oliver and Boyd, London.

Klaassen, M. (1994). Growth and energetics of tern chicks from temperate and polar environments. *Auk* **111**, 525–44. Erratum: *Auk* **112**, 264.

Koeman, J. H., ed. (1972). Side-effects of persistent pesticides and other chemicals on birds and mammals in the Netherlands. *TNO-Nieuws* 1972, 551–632.

Koffijberg, K., Dijksen, L., Hälterlein, B. *et al.* (2010). Trends in numbers and distribution of breeding birds in the Wadden Sea. In: Marencic, H., Eskildsen, K., Farke, H. & Hedtkamp, S., eds., *Science for Nature Conservation and Management: the Wadden Sea Ecosystem and EU Directives.* Proceedings of the 12th International Scientific Wadden Sea Symposium in Wilhelmshaven, Germany, 30 March – 3 April 2009. Wadden Sea Ecosystem No. 26. Common Wadden Sea Secretariat, Wilhelmshaven, pp. 47–52.

Kramer, D. (1995). Inland spring passage of Arctic terns in southern Britain. *British Birds* **88**, 211–17.

Kushlan, J. A., Steinkamp, M. J., Parsons, K. *et al.* (2002). *North American Waterbird Conservation Plan, version 1.* Waterbird Conservation for the Americas, Washington, DC.

Lack, D. (1954). *The Natural Regulation of Animal Numbers.* Oxford University Press, Oxford.

Lancashire and Cheshire Fauna Committee (1934). Nineteenth annual report. *Naturalist* **133**, 718–19.

Langham, N. P. E. (1968). The comparative biology of terns, *Sterna* spp. PhD thesis, University of Durham.

Langham, N. P. E. (1974). Comparative breeding biology of the Sandwich tern. *Auk* **91**, 255–77.

Lebreton, J.-D., Hines, J. E., Pradel, R., Nichols, J. D. & Spendelow, J. A. (2003). Estimation by capture–recapture of recruitment and dispersal over several sites. *Oikos* **101**, 253–64.

Lemmetyinen, R., Portin, P. & Vuolanto, S. (1974). Polymorphism in relation to the substrate in chicks of *Sterna paradisaea* Pontopp. *Annales Zoologici Fennici* **11**, 265–70.

Leonards, P., Bæk, K., Bytingsvik, J. *et al.* (undated). Spatial distribution of PBDEs and HBCD in fish, marine mammals and birds: results of the FIRE project. Unpublished report, Institute for Environmental Studies, Vrije Universiteit, Amsterdam.

Liley, D. (2008). Little terns at Great Yarmouth. Disturbance to birds and implications for strategic planning and development control. Unpublished report to Great Yarmouth Borough Council and RSPB. Footprint Ecology, Wareham, Dorset.

Limmer, B. & Becker, P. H. (2009). Improvement of chick provisioning with parental experience in a seabird. *Animal Behaviour* **77**, 1095–101.

Lloyd, C. S., Bibby, C. J. & Everett, M. J. (1975). Breeding terns in Britain and Ireland in 1969–74. *British Birds* **68**, 221–37.

Lloyd, C. S., Tasker, M. L. & Partridge, K. (1991). *The Status of Seabirds in Britain and Ireland.* Poyser, London.

Lovegrove, R., Williams, G & Williams, I. (1994). *Birds in Wales.* Poyser, London.

Ludwigs, J.-D. (1998). Kleptoparasitismus bei der Flussseeschwalbe *Sterna hirundo* als Anzeiger für Nahrungsmangel. *Vogelwelt* **119**, 193–203.

MacLeod, I. (2010). The mink threat in Scotland. In: Capoulade, M., Quemmerais-Amice, G. & Cadiou, B., eds., *For Roseate Tern Conservation.* Proceedings of the LIFE seminar

Roseate Tern Conservation in Brittany. *Penn-ar-Bed* **208**, 19–23.

Macpherson, H. A. (1892). *A Vertebrate Fauna of Lakeland*. Douglas, Edinburgh.

Malling Olsen, K. & Larsson, H. (1995). *Terns of Europe and North America*. Princeton University Press, Princeton, NJ.

Marples, G. & Marples, A. (1934). *Sea Terns or Sea Swallows: Their Habits, Language, Arrival and Departure*. Country Life, London.

Massias, A. & Becker, P. H. (1990). Nutritive value of food and growth in common tern (*Sterna hirundo*) chicks. *Ornis Scandinavica* **21**, 187–94.

Mavor, R. A., Parsons, M., Heubeck, M., Pickerell, G. & Schmitt, S. (2003). *Seabird numbers and breeding success in Britain and Ireland, 2002*. UK Nature Conservation No. 27. Joint Nature Conservation Committee, Peterborough.

Mavor, R. A., Parsons, M., Heubeck, M. & Schmitt, S. (2005). *Seabird numbers and breeding success in Britain and Ireland, 2004*. UK Nature Conservation No. 29. Joint Nature Conservation Committee, Peterborough.

Mavor, R. A., Heubeck, M. & Schmitt, S. (2008). *Seabird numbers and breeding success in Britain and Ireland, 2006*. UK Nature Conservation No. 31. Joint Nature Conservation Committee, Peterborough.

McNicholl, M. K., Lowther, P. E. & Hall, J. A. (2001). Forster's tern (*Sterna forsteri*). In: Poole, A. & Gill, F., eds., *The Birds of North America*, No. 595. The Birds of North America, Inc., Philadelphia, PA.

Meininger, P. L., Wolf, P. A., Hadoud, D. A. & Essghaier, M. F. A. (1994). Rediscovery of lesser crested terns breeding in Libya. *British Birds* **87**, 160–70.

Merne, O. J. (2010). Terns roosting in Dublin Bay, autumn 2010. *Irish Birds* **9**, 126–8.

Merne, O. J., Madden, B., Archer, E. & Porter, B. (2008). Autumn roosting by terns in South Dublin Bay. *Irish Birds* **8**, 335–40.

Milne, P. (2004). Fiftieth Irish bird report. *Irish Birds* **7**, 385–412.

Milne, P. & McAdams, D. G. (2008). Irish rare bird report 2005. *Irish Birds* **8**, 373–94.

Milne, P. & O'Sullivan, O. (1998). Forty-fourth Irish bird report. *Irish Birds* **6**, 61–90.

Mitchell, P. I., Newton, S. F., Ratcliffe, N. & Dunn, T. E., eds. (2004). *Seabird Populations of Britain and Ireland*. Poyser, London.

Møller, A. P., Flensted-Jensen, E. & Mardal, W. (2006). Dispersal and climate change: a case study of the Arctic tern *Sterna paradisaea*. *Global Change Biology* **12**, 2005–13.

Monaghan, P. (2002). Arctic tern *Sterna paradisaea*. In: Wernham, C., Toms, M., Marchant, J. et al., eds., *The Migration Atlas: Movements of the Birds of Britain and Ireland*. Poyser, London, pp. 392–4.

Monaghan, P., Uttley, J. D. & Okill, J. D. (1989a). Terns and sandeels: seabirds as indicators of changes in marine fish populations. *Journal of Fish Biology* **35**, 339–40.

Monaghan, P., Uttley, J. D., Burns, M. D., Thaine, C. & Blackwood, J. (1989b). The relationship between food supply, reproductive effort and breeding success in Arctic terns *Sterna paradisaea*. *Journal of Animal Ecology* **58**, 261–74.

Monaghan, P., Uttley, J. D. & Burns, M. D. (1992). Effects of changes in food availability on reproductive effort in Arctic terns. *Ardea* **80**, 71–81

Monteiro, L. R., Ramos, J. A. & Furness, R. W. (1996). Past and present status and conservation of the seabirds breeding in the Azores Archipelago. *Biological Conservation* **78**, 319–28.

Monticelli, D., Ramos, J. A. & Quartly, G. D. (2007). Effects of annual changes in primary productivity and ocean indices on the breeding performance of tropical roseate terns in the western Indian Ocean. *Marine Ecology Progress Series* **351**, 273–86.

Monticelli, D., Ramos, J. A., Guerreiro-Milheiras, S. A. & Doucet, J. L. (2008). Adult survival of tropical roseate terns breeding on Aride Island, Seychelles, Western Indian Ocean. *Waterbirds* **31**, 330–7.

Moore, D. J., Williams, T. D. & Morris, R. D. (2000). Mate-provisioning, nutritional requirements for egg-production, and primary reproductive effort of female common terns *Sterna hirundo*. *Journal of Avian Biology* **31**, 183–96.

Moore, N. P., Roy, S. S. & Helyar, A. (2003). Mink (*Mustela vison*) eradication to protect ground-nesting birds in the Western Isles, Scotland, United Kingdom. *New Zealand Journal of Zoology* **30**, 443–52.

Morrison, P. G. (2010). Managing roseate terns in the UK. In: Capoulade, M., Quemmerais-Amice, G. & Cadiou, B., eds., *For Roseate Tern Conservation.* Proceedings of the LIFE seminar Roseate Tern Conservation in Brittany. *Penn-ar-Bed* **208**, 83–7.

Morrison, P. & Allcorn, R. I. (2006). The effectiveness of different methods to deter large gulls *Larus* spp. from competing with terns *Sterna* spp. on Coquet Island RSPB reserve, Northumberland, England. *Conservation Evidence* **3**, 84–7.

Morrison, P. & Gurney, M. (2007). Nest boxes for roseate terns *Sterna dougallii* on Coquet Island RSPB reserve, Northumberland, England. *Conservation Evidence* **4**, 1–3.

Mostello, C. S., Palaia, N. A. & Clapp, R. B. (2000). Gray-backed tern *Onychoprion lunatus*. In: Poole, A. & Gill, F., eds., *The Birds of North America*, No. 525. The Birds of North America, Inc., Philadelphia, PA.

Mullarney, K. (2003). The American black tern in Co. Wexford. *Birding World* **19**, 279–82.

Mundy, R. (1997). Diet and chick provisioning rates of roseate terns in relation to chick age on Rockabill. In: Monteiro, L. R., ed., *Proceedings of the 7th Roseate Tern Workshop.* University of Azores, Horta, Portugal, pp. 28–30.

Ndiaye, I. (2010). Larid project and monitoring of roseate tern: new wintering sites in Senegal. In: Capoulade, M., Quemmerais-Amice, G. & Cadiou, B., eds., *For Roseate Tern Conservation.* Proceedings of the LIFE seminar Roseate Tern Conservation in Brittany. *Penn-ar-Bed* **208**, 63–4.

Newman, E. (1866). *A Dictionary of British Birds, Being a Reprint of Montagu's Ornithological Dictionary, Together with the Additional Species.* W. Swan Sonnenschein and Allen, London. Reprinted by Elibron Classics, 2005.

Newton, I., Wyllie, I. & Asher, A. (1993). Long-term trends in organochlorine and mercury residues in some predatory birds in Britain. *Environmental Pollution* **79**, 143–51.

Newton, S. F. & Crowe, O. (1999). *Kish Bank: a preliminary assessment of its ornithological importance.* BirdWatch Ireland Conservation Report No 99/8, Monkstown, Dublin.

Newton, S. F. & Crowe, O. (2000). *Roseate Terns: The Natural Connection*. Maritime Ireland/Wales INTERREG Report No. 2. Marine Institute, Dublin.

Nightingale, B. & Allsopp, K. (1998). An ornithological year 1997. *British Birds* **91,** 526–39.

Nisbet, I. C. T. (1973). Courtship-feeding, egg-size and breeding success in Common Terns. *Nature* **241,** 141–2.

Nisbet, I. C. T. (1977). Courtship-feeding and clutch size in common terns. In: Stonehouse, B. & Perrins, C., eds., *Evolutionary Ecology*. Macmillan, London, pp. 101–10.

Nisbet, I. C. T. (1978). Population models for common terns in Massachusetts. *Bird-Banding* **49:** 50–8.

Nisbet, I. C. T. (1983a). Territorial feeding by common terns. *Colonial Waterbirds* **6,** 64–70.

Nisbet, I. C. T. (1983b). Belly-soaking by incubating and brooding common terns. *Journal of Field Ornithology* **54,** 190–2.

Nisbet, I. C. T. (1984). Paralytic shellfish poisoning: effects on breeding terns. *Condor* **85,** 338–45.

Nisbet, I. C. T. (1994). Effects of pollution on marine birds. In: Nettleship, D., Burger. J. & Gochfeld, M., eds., *Seabirds on Islands: Threats, Case Studies and Action Plans*. BirdLife Conservation Series 1. BirdLife International, Cambridge, pp. 8–25.

Nisbet, I. C. T. (1997). Female common terns eating mollusc shells: evidence for calcium deficits during egg laying. *Ibis* **139,** 400–1.

Nisbet, I. C. T. (2002). Common tern *Sterna hirundo*. In: Poole, A. & Gill, F., eds., *The Birds of North America*, No. 618. The Birds of North America, Inc., Philadelphia, PA.

Nisbet, I. C. T. & Cabot, D. (1995). Transatlantic recovery of a ringed roseate tern. *Ringing & Migration* **16,** 14–15.

Nisbet, I. C. T. & Cam, E. (2002). Test for age-specificity in survival of the common tern. *Journal of Applied Statistics* **29,** 65–83.

Nisbet, I. C. T. & Hatch, J. J. (1999). Consequences of a female-biased sex ratio in a socially monogamous bird: female–female pairs in the roseate tern *Sterna dougallii*. *Ibis* **141,** 307–20.

Nisbet, I. C. T. & Ratcliffe, N. (2008). Comparative demographics of tropical and temperate roseate terns. *Waterbirds* **31,** 346–56.

Nisbet, I. C. T. & Safina, C. (1996). Transatlantic recoveries of ringed common terns *Sterna hirundo*. *Ringing & Migration* **17,** 28–30.

Nisbet, I. C. T. & Spendelow, J. A. (1999). Contribution of research to management and recovery of the roseate tern: review of a twelve-year project. *Waterbirds* **22,** 239–52.

Nisbet, I. C. T. & Welton, M. (1984). Seasonal variations in breeding success of common terns: consequences of predation. *Colonial Waterbirds* **86,** 53–60.

Nisbet, I. C. T., Spendelow, J. A. & Hatfield, J. S. (1995). Variations in growth of roseate tern (*Sterna dougallii*) chicks. *Condor* **97,** 335–44.

Nisbet, I. C. T., Apanius, V. & Friar, M. S. (2002). Breeding performance of very old common terns. *Journal of Field Ornithology* **73,** 117–24.

Nisbet, I. C. T., Wingate, D. B. & Szczys, P. (2010). Demographic consequences of a catastrophic event in the isolated population of common terns at Bermuda. *Waterbirds* **33,** 405–10.

Nisbet, I. C. T., Mostello, C. S., Veit, R. R., Fox, J. W. & Afanasyev, V. (2011a). Migrations and winter quarters of five common terns tracked using geolocators. *Waterbirds* **34**, 32–9.

Nisbet, I. C. T., Szczys, P., Mostello, C. S. & Fox, J. A. (2011b). Female common terns start autumn migration before males. *Seabird* **24**, 103–6.

Nisbet, I. C. T., Veit, R. R., Auer, S. A. & White, T. P. (2013). Marine birds of the eastern United States and the Bay of Fundy: distribution, numbers, trends, threats, and conservation. *Nuttall Ornithological Monographs* **29**, 1–188.

Noble-Rollin, D. & Redfern, C. (2002). Sandwich tern *Sterna sandvicensis*. In: Wernham, C., Toms, M., Marchant, J. *et al.*, eds., *The Migration Atlas: Movements of the Birds of Britain and Ireland*. Poyser, London, pp. 381–4.

Norman, D. (2002). Common tern *Sterna hirundo*. In: Wernham, C., Toms, M., Marchant, J. *et al.*, eds., *The Migration Atlas: Movements of the Birds of Britain and Ireland*. Poyser, London, pp. 388–91.

Norman, R. K. & Saunders, D. R. (1969). Status of little terns in Great Britain and Ireland in 1967. *British Birds* **62**, 4–13.

North, M. R. (1997). Aleutian tern *Onychoprion aleuticus*. In: Poole, A. & Gill, F., eds., *The Birds of North America*, No. 291. The Birds of North America, Inc., Philadelphia, PA.

Northumberland County History Committee (1899). *A History of Northumberland. Volume V*. Andrew Reid, Sons & Company, Newcastle-upon-Tyne.

Ogilvie, M. A. & the Rare Breeding Birds Panel (1999). Rare breeding birds in the United Kingdom in 1966. *British Birds* **92**, 120–54.

O'Neill, P., Minton, C., Ozaki, K. & White, R. (2005). Three populations of non-breeding roseate terns (*Sterna dougallii*) in the Swain Reefs, Southern Great Barrier Reef. *Emu* **105**, 57–76.

Oswald, S., Arnold, J., Hatch. J. & Nisbet, I. (2012). Piracy at the nest: factors driving kleptoparasitic behaviour by common tern *Sterna hirundo* chicks. *Acta Ornithologica* **47**, 95–100.

Owuso, E. (2010). Roseate tern in Ghana. In: Capoulade, M., Quemmerais-Amice, G. & Cadiou, B., eds., *For Roseate Tern Conservation*. Proceedings of the LIFE seminar Roseate Tern Conservation in Brittany. *Penn-ar-Bed* **208**, 77–9.

Parslow, J. L. F. (1967–68). Changes in status among breeding birds in Britain and Ireland. *British Birds* **60**, 2–47, 97–123, 177–202, 262–85; 396–404, 493–508; **61**, 49–64, 241–55.

Paterson, A. M. (1997). *Las Aves Marinas de España y Portugal*. Lynx Edicions, Barcelona.

Paul, R. T., Paul, R. F., Pranty, B., Hodgson, A. B. & Powell, D. J. (2003). Probable hybridization between elegant tern and Sandwich tern in west-central Florida: the first North American nesting record of elegant tern away from the Pacific coast. *North American Birds* **57**, 280–2.

Pearson, T. H. (1968). The feeding biology of seabird species breeding on the Farne Islands, Northumberland. *Journal of Animal Ecology* **37**, 521–52.

Perrow, M. R., Tomlinson, M. L., Lines, P. *et al.* (2004). Is food supply behind little tern *Sterna albifrons* colony location? The case of the largest colony in the UK at the North Denes/Winterton SPA in Norfolk. In: Allcorn, R. I., ed., *Proceedings of a Symposium on Little Terns* Sterna albifrons. RSPB Research Report

8. Royal Society for the Protection of Birds, Sandy, pp. 39–59.

Perrow, M. R., Skeate, E. R., Lines, P., Brown, D. & Tomlinson, M. L. (2006). Radio telemetry as a tool for impact assessment of wind farms: the case of little terns *Sterna albifrons* at Scroby Sands, Norfolk, UK. *Ibis* **148** (Supplement S1), 57–75.

Perrow, M. R., Skeate, E. R. & Gilroy, J. J. (2011). Visual tracking from a rigid-hulled inflatable boat to determine foraging movements of breeding terns. *Journal of Field Ornithology* **82**, 68–79.

Pickerell, G. (2004). Little tern *Sterna albifrons*. In: Mitchell, P. I., Newton, S. F., Ratcliffe, N. & Dunn, T. E., eds., *Seabird Populations of Britain and Ireland*. Poyser, London, pp. 339–49.

Poole, A. & Gill, F., eds. (1992–2002). *The Birds of North America*, Nos. 1–720. The Birds of North America, Inc., Philadelphia. Continued and updated as *The Birds of North America Online*. bna.birds.cornell.edu (accessed November 2012).

Potts, G. R. (1968). Success of eggs of the shag on the Farne Islands, Northumberland, in relation to their content of dieldrin and pp' DDE. *Nature* **217**, 1282–4.

Pyle, P. (2008). *Identification Guide to North American Birds, Part II. Anatidae to Alcidae*. Slate Creek Press, Point Reyes Station, CA.

Pyman, G. A. & Wainwright, C. B. (1952). The breeding of the gull-billed tern in Essex. *British Birds* **45**, 337–9.

Quemmerais-Amice, G. & Gager, L. (2010). LIFE-Nature programme 'Conservation of the roseate tern in Brittany' LIFE05NAT/F/137. In: Capoulade, M., Quemmerais-Amice, G. & Cadiou, B., eds., *For Roseate Tern Conservation*.

Proceedings of the LIFE seminar Roseate Tern Conservation in Brittany. *Penn-ar-Bed* **208**, 128–31.

Quintana, F. & Yorio, P. (1997). Breeding biology of royal and Cayenne terns at a mixed-species colony in Patagonia. *Wilson Bulletin* **109**, 650–62.

Rahn, H. & Paganelli, C. V. (1981). *Gas Exchange in Avian Eggs: Publications in Gas Exchange, Physical Properties, and Dimensions of Bird Eggs*. State University of New York, Buffalo, NY.

Rahn, H., Paganelli, C. V., Nisbet, I. C. T. & Whittow, G. C. (1976). Regulation of incubation water-loss in eggs of seven species of terns. *Physiological Zoology* **49**, 249–59.

Rahn, H., Ar, A. & Paganelli, C. V. (1979). How bird eggs breathe. *Scientific American* **240**, 46–55.

Ramos, J. A. (1998). Nest-site selection by roseate terns nesting on Aride Island, Seychelles. *Waterbirds* **21**, 438–43.

Ramos, J. A., Solá, E., Monteiro, L. R. & Ratcliffe, N. (1998). Prey delivered to roseate tern chicks in the Azores. *Journal of Field Ornithology* **69**, 419–29.

Ratcliffe, N. (1997). Estimates of roseate tern survival and natal fidelity in Britain and Ireland from ring resightings. In: Monteiro, L. R., ed., *Proceedings of the 7th Roseate Tern Workshop*. University of Azores, Horta, pp. 28–30.

Ratcliffe, N. (2003). Little terns in Britain and Ireland: estimation and diagnosis of population trends. In: Schmitt, S., ed., *Proceedings of the 2003 Little Tern Symposium*. RSPB, Sandy, pp. 4–18.

Ratcliffe, N. (2004a). Sandwich tern *Sterna sandvicensis*. In: Mitchell, P. I., Newton, S. F., Ratcliffe, N. & Dunn, T. E., eds., *Seabird Populations of Britain and Ireland*. Poyser, London, pp. 291–301.

Ratcliffe, N. (2004b). Arctic tern *Sterna paradisaea*. In: Mitchell, P. I., Newton, S. F., Ratcliffe, N. & Dunn, T. E., eds., *Seabird Populations of Britain and Ireland*. Poyser, London, pp. 302–14.

Ratcliffe, N. (2004c). Common tern *Sterna hirundo*. In: Mitchell, P. I., Newton, S. F., Ratcliffe, N. & Dunn, T. E., eds., *Seabird Populations of Britain and Ireland*. Poyser, London, pp. 315–27.

Ratcliffe, N. & Merne, O. (2002). Roseate tern *Sterna dougallii*. In: Wernham, C., Toms, M., Marchant, J. *et al.*, eds., *The Migration Atlas: Movements of the Birds of Britain and Ireland*. Poyser, London, pp. 385–7.

Ratcliffe, N., Pickerell, G. & Brindley, E. (2000). Population trends of little and Sandwich terns *Sterna albifrons* and *S. sandvicensis* in Britain and Ireland from 1969 to 1998. *Atlantic Seabirds* 2, 211–26.

Ratcliffe, N., Nisbet, I. C .T. & Newton, S. (2004). Roseate tern *Sterna dougallii*. *BWP Update* 6, 77–90.

Ratcliffe, N., Newton, S, Morrison, P. *et al.* (2008a). Adult survival and breeding dispersal of roseate terns within the northwest European metapopulation. *Waterbirds* 31, 320–9.

Ratcliffe, N., Craik, C., Helyar, A., Roy, S. & Scott, M. (2008b). Modelling the benefits of American mink *Mustela vison* management options for terns in west Scotland. *Ibis* 150 (Supplement S1), 114–21.

Ratcliffe, N., Schmitt, S., Mayo, A. & Drewitt, A. (2008c). Colony habitat selection by little terns *Sternula albifrons* in East Anglia: implications for coastal maganement. *Seabird* 21, 55–63.

Robinson, J., Richardson, A., Crabtree, A. N., Coulson, J. & Potts, G. R. (1967), Organochlorine residues in marine organisms. *Nature* 214, 1307–11. doi:10.1038/2141307a0.

Robinson, J. A., Hamer, K. C. & Chivers, L. S. (2001). Contrasting brood sizes in common and Arctic terns: the role of food provisioning rates and parental brooding. *Condor* 103, 108–17.

Robinson, R. A. (2010). Estimating age-specific survival from historical ringing data. *Ibis* 152, 651–3.

Rodd, E. H. & Harting, J. E. (1880). *The Birds of Cornwall and the Scilly Islands*. Trübner & Co., London.

Rogers, M. J. & the Rarities Committee (1978–2000). [Annual reports on rare birds in Great Britain.] *British Birds* 71, 481–532; 73, 491–534; 75, 482–533; 76, 476–529; 77, 506–62; 79, 526–88; 85, 507–54; 91, 455–517; 93, 512–67.

Rowan, W., Parker, K. M. & Bell, J. (1914). On homotyposis and allied characters in eggs of the common tern. *Biometrika* 10, 144–68.

Rowan, W., Wolff, E., Sulman, K. L. *et al.* (1919). On the nest and eggs of the common tern (*S. Fluviatilis*): a cooperative study. *Biometrika* 12, 308–54.

Royal Society for the Protection of Birds (2010). Tern monitoring on Lewis & Harris 2009. Report to Scottish Natural Heritage.

Rubega, M. A., Schamel, D. & Tracy, D. M. (2000). Red-necked phalarope *Phalaropus lobatus*. In: Poole, A. & Gill, F., eds., *The Birds of North America*, No. 538. The Birds of North America, Inc., Philadelphia, PA.

Saino, N., Fasola, M. & Crocicchia, E. (1994). Adoption behaviour in little and common terns (Aves; Sternidae): chick benefits and parents' fitness costs. *Ethology* 97, 294–309.

Saliva, J. E. (2000). Conservation priorities for sooty terns in the West Indies. In:

Schreiber, E. A. & Lee, D. S., eds., *Status and Conservation of West Indian Seabirds*. Society of Caribbean Ornithology, Special Publication 1. Society of Caribbean Ornithology, Ruston, LA, pp. 87–95.

Salomonsen, F. (1967). Migratory movements of the Arctic tern *Sterna paradisaea* Pontoppidan in the Southern Ocean. *Konglige Danske Videnskabernes Selskab Biologiske Meddelelser* **24**, 1–42.

Salomonsen, F. & Gitz-Johansen, A. (1950). *Grønlands Fugle. The Birds of Greenland*. Munksgaard, København.

Sanchez, J. M. & Fasola, M. (2002). *Gelochelidon nilotica* gull-billed tern. *BWP Update* **4**, 21–33.

Sanchez, J. M., Munoz del Viejo, A., Corbacho, C., Costillo, E. & Fuentes, C. (2004). Status and trends of gull-billed tern *Gelochelidon nilotica* in Europe and Africa. *Bird Conservation International* **14**, 335–51.

Sangster, G., Collinson, J. M., Helbig, A. J., Knox, A. G. & Svensson, L. (2005). Taxonomic recommendations for British birds: third report. *Ibis* **147**, 821–8.

Sangster, G., Collinson, J. M., Crochet, P.-A. *et al.* (2011). Taxonomic recommendations for British birds: seventh report. *Ibis* **153**, 883–92.

Scharringa, J. (1980). American Sandwich tern *Sterna sandivcensis acuflavida* in the Netherlands. *Dutch Birding* **1**, 60.

Schreiber, E. A. & Burger, J. (2001). Data on life-history characteristics, breeding range, size, and survival for seabird species. In: Schreiber, E.A. & Burger, J., eds., *Biology of Marine Birds*. CRC Press, Boca Raton, FL, Appendix 2, pp. 665–85.

Schreiber, E. A., Feare, C. J., Harrington, B. A. *et al.* (2002). Sooty tern *Sterna fuscata*. In: Poole, A. & Gill, F., eds., *The Birds of North America*, No. 665. The Birds of North America, Inc., Philadelphia, PA.

Seebohm, H. (1896). *Coloured Figures of the Eggs of British Birds with Descriptive Notices*. Pawson and Brailsford, Sheffield.

Selby, P. J. (1821–34). *Illustrations of British Ornithology*. W. H. Lizars, Edinburgh and London.

Selby, P. J. (1826). Catalogue of the various Birds which at present inhabit or resort to the Farn Islands, with observations on their habits, etc. *Zoological Journal* **2**, 454–65.

Sharrock, J. T. R. & the Rare Birds Breeding Committee (1977). Rare bird breeding report 1977. *British Birds* **70**, 2–23.

Sharrock, J. T. R. & Rare Birds Breeding Panel (1980). Report for 1978. *British Birds* **7**, 5–26.

Shealer, D. (1999). Sandwich Tern *Sterna sandvicensis*. In: Poole, A. & Gill, F., eds., *The Birds of North America*, No. 405. The Birds of North America, Inc., Philadelphia, PA.

Shealer, D. A. & Spendelow, J. A. (2002). Individual foraging strategies of kleptoparasitic roseate terns. *Waterbirds* **25**, 436–41.

Shealer, D. A., Spendelow, J. A., Hatfield, J. S. & Nisbet, I. C. T. (2005). The adaptive significance of stealing in a marine bird and its relationship to parental quality. *Behavioral Ecology* **16**, 371–6.

Simmons, R. E., Cordes, I. & Braby, R. (1998). Latitudinal trends, population size and habitat preferences of the Damara tern *Sterna balaenarum* on Namibia's desert coast. *Ibis* **140**, 439–45.

Smart, J. (2003). Managing colonies for little terns. In: Allcorn, R. I., ed.,

Proceedings of a Symposium on Little Terns Sterna albifrons. RSPB Research Report no. 8. Royal Society for the Protection of Birds, Sandy, pp. 19–28.

Smith, C. (1750). *The Ancient and Present State of the County and City of Cork*. Royal Dublin Society, Dublin.

Smith, J. W. M. (1975). Studies of breeding Sandwich terns. *British Birds* **68**, 142–56.

Smith, R. F. & the Rarities Committee (1972). Report on rare birds in Great Britain in 1971. *British Birds* **65**, 322–54.

Spencer, R. & Hudson, R. (1978). Report on bird-ringing for 1976. *Ringing & Migration* **1**, 189–252.

Spencer, R. & Rare Birds Breeding Panel (1986). Report for 1983. *British Birds* **79**, 69–92.

Spendelow, J. A., Hines, J. E., Nichols, J. D. *et al.* (2008). Temporal variation in adult survival rates of roseate terns during periods of increasing and declining populations. *Waterbirds* **31**, 309–19.

Starck, J. M. & Ricklefs, R. E. (1998). Data set of avian growth parameters. In: Starck, J. M. & Ricklefs, R. E., eds., *Avian Growth and Development*. Oxford University Press, Oxford, pp. 381–423.

Stienen, E. W. M. (2006). Living with gulls: trading off food and predation in the Sandwich tern *Sterna sandvicensis*. PhD thesis, University of Groningen, the Netherlands. *Alterra Scientific Communications* 15. Alterra, Wageningen.

Stienen, E. & Brenninkmeijer, A. (1999). Keep the chicks moving: how Sandwich terns can minimize kleptoparasitism by black-headed gulls. *Animal Behaviour* **57**, 1135–44.

Stienen, E., Brenninkmeijer, A. & Geschiere, K. E. (2001). Living with gulls: the consequences for Sandwich terns of breeding in association with black-headed gulls. *Waterbirds* **24**, 68–82.

Stoddart, A. & Joyner, S. (2005). *The Birds of Blakeney Point*. Wren Publishing, Sheringham, Norfolk.

Suddaby, D. & Ratcliffe, N. (1997). The effects of fluctuating food supply on breeding Arctic terns *Sterna paradisaea*. *Auk* **114**, 524–30.

Szczys, P., Nisbet, I. C. T. & Wingate, D. B. (2012). Conservation genetics of the common tern (*Sterna hirundo*) in the North Atlantic region: implications for the critically endangered population at Bermuda. *Conservation Genetics* **13**, 1039–43. DOI 10.1007/s10592-012-0351-0.

Szostek, K. L. & Becker, P. H. (2011). Terns in trouble: demographic consequences of low breeding success and recruitment on a common tern population in the German Wadden Sea. *Journal of Ornithology* **153**, 313–26. doi 10.1007/s10336-011-0745-7.

Tasker, M. I. & Adcock, M. (2002). Little tern *Sterna albifrons*. In: Wernham, C., Toms, M., Marchant, J. *et al.*, eds., *The Migration Atlas: Movements of the Birds of Britain and Ireland*. Poyser, London, pp. 395–6.

Taylor, I. R. (1975). The feeding behaviour and ecology of terns on the Ythan Estuary, Aberdeenshire. PhD thesis, University of Aberdeen.

Taylor, I. R. (1979). Prey selection during courtship feeding in the common tern. *Ornis Scandinavica* **10**, 142–144.

Taylor, I. R. (1983). Effect of wind on the foraging behaviour of common and Sandwich terns. *Ornis Scandinavica* **14**, 90–6.

Thompson, B. C., Jackson, J. A., Burger, J. *et al.* (1997). Least tern *Sternula antillarum*. In: Poole, A. & Gill, F., eds., *The Birds of North America*, No. 290.

The Birds of North America, Inc., Philadelphia, PA.

Thompson, W. (1851). *The Natural History of Ireland. Vol III: Birds.* Reeve and Benham, London.

Tims, J., Nisbet, I. C. T., Friar, M. S., Mostello, C. S. & Hatch, J. J. (2004). Characteristics and performance of common terns in old and newly-established colonies. *Waterbirds* **27**, 321–32.

Toms, M. (2002). Black tern *Chlidonias niger*. In: Wernham, C., Toms, M., Marchant, J. *et al.*, eds., *The Migration Atlas: Movements of the Birds of Britain and Ireland.* Poyser, London, pp. 713–14.

Tyreberg, T. (1998). *Pleistocene Birds of the Palaearctic: a Catalogue.* Nuttall Ornithological Club, Cambridge, MA.

Urban, E. K., Fry, C. H. & Keith S. K., eds. (1986). *The Birds of Africa. Vol 2.* Academic Press, London.

US Fish and Wildlife Service (2010). *Caribbean Roseate Tern and North Atlantic Roseate Tern (Sterna dougallii dougallii). 5-Year Review: Summary and Evaluation.* US Fish and Wildlife Service, Boquerón, PR, and Concord, NH.

Ussher, R. J. & Warren, R. (1900). *The Birds of Ireland.* Gurney and Jackson, London.

Uttley, J., Monaghan, P. & Blackwood, J. (1989a). Hedgehog *Erinaceus europaeus* predation on Arctic tern *Sterna paradisaea* eggs: the impact on breeding success. *Seabird* **12**, 3–6.

Uttley, J., Monaghan, P. & White, S. (1989b). Differential effects of reduced sandeel availability on two sympatrically breeding species of tern. *Ornis Scandinavica* **20**, 273–7.

van Deurs, M., van Hal, R., Maciej, T. T., Sigrún, H. J. & Dolmer, P. (2009). Recruitment of lesser sandeel *Ammodytes marinus* in relation to

density dependence and zooplankton composition. *Marine Ecology Progress Series* **381**, 249–58.

van IJzendoorn, E. J. (1980). Broedgeval van zwarte *Childonias niger* × witvleugelstern *C. leucopterus. Dutch Birding* **2**, 62–5.

Veen, J. (1977). *The Sandwich Tern: Functional and Causal Aspects of Nest Distribution.* E. J. Brill, Leiden.

Vinicombe, K. (1980). Tern showing mixed characters of black tern and white-winged black tern. *British Birds* **73**, 223–5.

Wallace, D. I. M. (1972). Seabirds at Lagos and in the Gulf of Guinea. *Ibis* **115**, 559–71.

Wanless, S., Harris, M. P., Redman, P. & Speakman, J. (2005). Low energy values of fish as a probable cause of a major seabird breeding failure in the North Sea. *Marine Ecology Progress Series* **294**, 1–8.

Wanless, S., Frederiksen, M., Walton, J. & Harris, M. P. (2009). Long-term changes in breeding phenology at two seabird colonies in the western North Sea. *Ibis* **151**, 274–85.

Ward, R. M. (2000). Migration patterns and moult of common terns *Sterna hirundo* and Sandwich terns *Sterna sandvicensis* using Teesmouth in late summer. *Ringing & Migration* **20**, 19–28.

Watson, D. M. S., Watson, K. M., Pearson, H. S. *et al.* (1923). On the nest and eggs of the common tern (*S. Fluviatilis*): a third cooperative study. *Biometrika* **15**, 294–345.

Watson, M. A., Spendelow, J. A. & Hatch, J. J. (2011). Post-fledging brood and care division in the roseate tern (*Sterna dougallii*). *Journal of Ethology* **30**, 29–34. doi 10.1007/s10164-011-0286-9.

Weimerskirch, H. (1992). Reproductive effort in long-lived birds: age-specific patterns of condition, reproduction, and survival in the wandering albatross. *Oikos* **64**, 464–73.

Weimerskirch, H. (2001). Seabird demography and its relationship with the marine environment. In: Schreiber, E. A. & Burger, J., eds., *Biology of Marine Birds*. CRC Press, Boca Raton, FL, pp. 115–36.

Weir, D. (1983). The Northumberland Aleutian tern. *British Birds* **76**, 459–60.

Wendeln, H. (1997). Body mass of female common terns (*Sterna hirundo*) during courtship: relationships to mate quality, egg mass, diet, laying date and age. *Colonial Waterbirds* **20**, 235–43.

Wendeln, H. & Becker, P. H. (1996). Body mass changes in breeding common terns *Sterna hirundo*. *Bird Study* **43**, 85–95.

Wendeln, H. & Becker, P. H. (1998). Populationsbiologische Untersuchungen an einer Kolonie der Flussseeschwalbe *Sterna hirundo*. *Vogelwelt* **119**, 209–22.

Wendeln, H., & Becker, P. H. (1999). Effects of parental quality and effort on the reproduction of common terns. *Journal of Animal Ecology* **68**, 205–14.

Wendeln, H. & Becker, P. H. (2000). Parental care of replacement clutches in common terns (*Sterna hirundo*). *Behavioral Ecology and Sociobiology* **47**, 382–92.

Wetlands International (2006). *Waterbird Population Estimates, 4th edition.* Wetlands International, Wageningen.

Whilde, T. (1985). The 1984 All Ireland Tern Survey. *Irish Birds* **3**, 1–32.

Whittam, R. M. (1998). Interbreeding of Arctic and roseate terns. *Wilson Bulletin* **110**, 65–70.

Wiggins, D. A., Morris, R. D., Nisbet, I. C. T. & Custer, T. W. (1984). Occurrence and timing of second clutches in common terns. *Auk* **101**, 281–7.

Williamson, K., Rankin, D. N., Rankin, N. M. & Jones, H. C. (1941). Survey of Copeland Islands, 1941. Unpublished report.

Witherby, H. F., Jourdain, F. C. R., Ticehurst, N. F. & Tucker, B. W. (1942). *The Handbook of British Birds, Vol. V.* Witherby, London.

Yalden, D. W., & Albarella, U. (2009). *The History of British Birds.* Oxford University Press, Oxford.

Yarrell, W. (1843). *A History of British Birds. Vol. III.* Van Voorst, London.

Yates, B. & Taffs, H. (1990). Least tern in East Sussex: a new Western Palearctic bird. *Birding World* **3**, 197–9.

Zavalaga, C. B., Plenge, M. A. & Bertolero, A. (2008). The breeding biology of the Peruvian tern (*Sterna lorata*) in Perú. *Waterbirds* **31**, 550–60.

Indexes

SPECIES INDEX

Page numbers in **bold** include
illustrations.

The New Naturalist Library